W9-BZM-424

Shojo Beat

ORESAMA TEACHER

Vol. 17

Story & Art by
Izumi Tsubaki

ORESAMA TEACHER

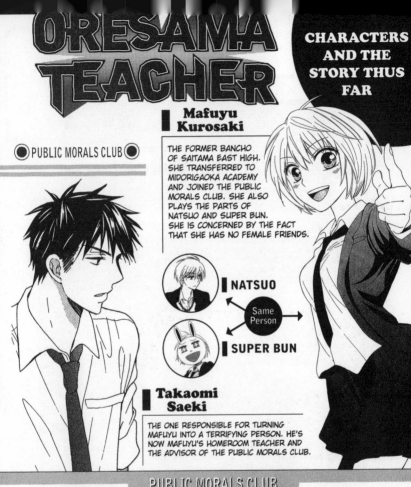

CHARACTERS AND THE STORY THUS FAR

PUBLIC MORALS CLUB

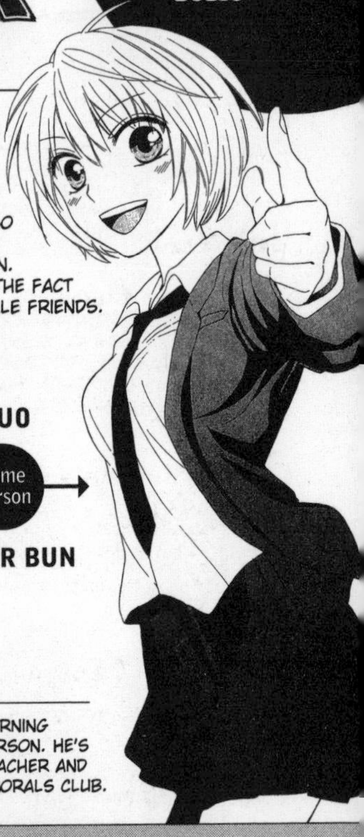

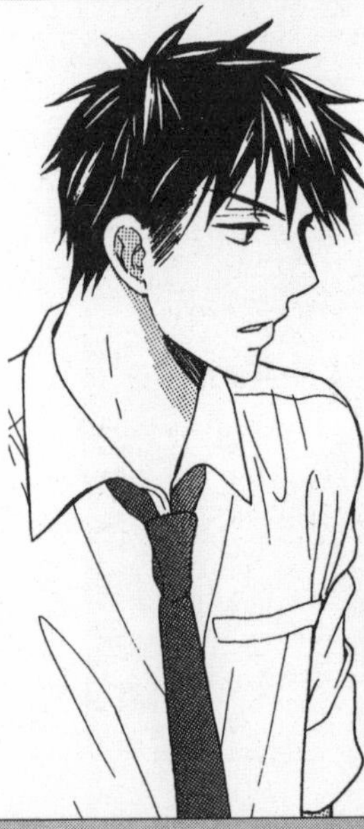

Mafuyu Kurosaki

THE FORMER BANCHO OF SAITAMA EAST HIGH. SHE TRANSFERRED TO MIDORIGAOKA ACADEMY AND JOINED THE PUBLIC MORALS CLUB. SHE ALSO PLAYS THE PARTS OF NATSUO AND SUPER BUN. SHE IS CONCERNED BY THE FACT THAT SHE HAS NO FEMALE FRIENDS.

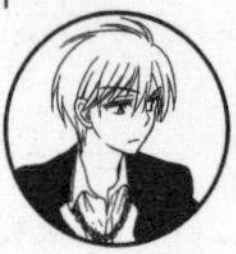

NATSUO

Same Person

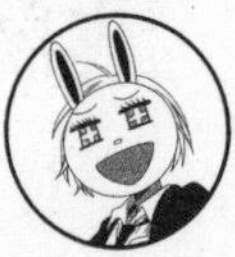

SUPER BUN

Takaomi Saeki

THE ONE RESPONSIBLE FOR TURNING MAFUYU INTO A TERRIFYING PERSON. HE'S NOW MAFUYU'S HOMEROOM TEACHER AND THE ADVISOR OF THE PUBLIC MORALS CLUB.

PUBLIC MORALS CLUB MEMBERS

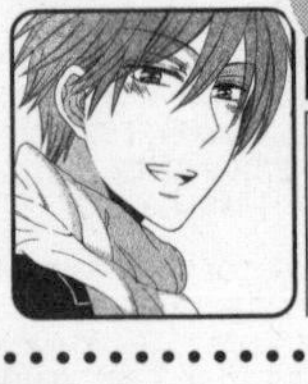

Hayasaka

MAFUYU'S CLASSMATE. HE ADMIRES SUPER BUN. HE IS A PLAIN AND SIMPLE DELINQUENT. HE IS ONE OF THE FOUNDING MEMBERS OF THE PUBLIC MORALS CLUB, BUT MAFUYU DOESN'T KNOW MUCH ABOUT HIS PRIVATE LIFE.

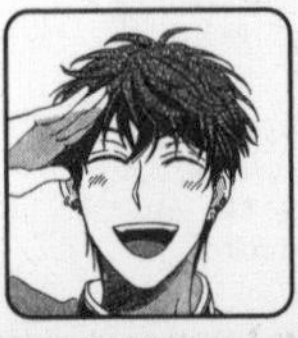

Aki Shibuya

A TALKATIVE AND WOMANIZING UNDERCLASSMAN. HIS NICKNAME IS AKKI. HE'S NOT GOOD AT FIGHTING. HE QUIT THE PUBLIC MORALS CLUB TO PROTECT SOME GIRLS.

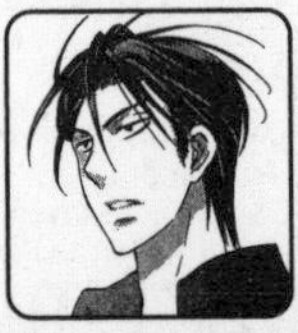

Kyotaro Okegawa

THE BANCHO OF MIDORIGAOKA. HE FLUNKED A YEAR, SO HE'S A SUPER SENIOR THIS YEAR. HE JOINED THE PUBLIC MORALS CLUB, BUT RECENTLY HAD TO QUIT.

STUDENT COUNCIL

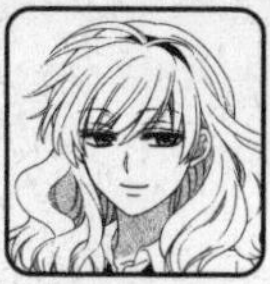

Runa Momochi

THIRD YEAR, CLASS THREE. HANABUSA'S CLASSMATE.

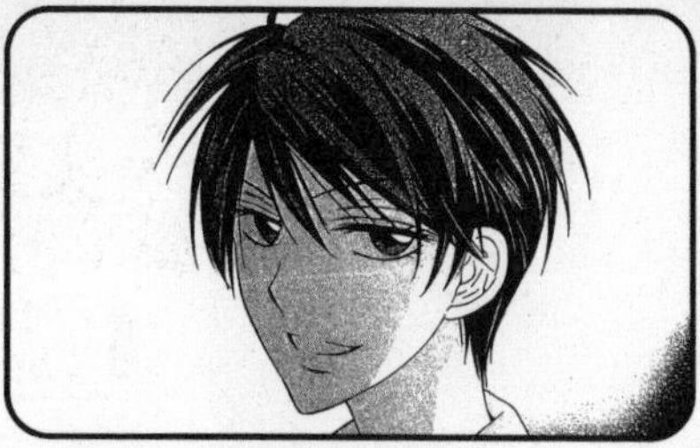

Miyabi Hanabusa

THE SCHOOL DIRECTOR'S SON AND THE PRESIDENT OF THE STUDENT COUNCIL. HE HAS THE POWER TO ENCHANT ANY WHO MEET HIS GAZE.

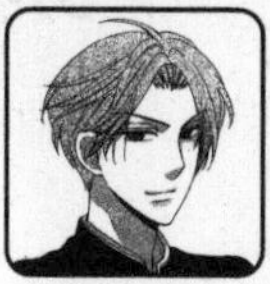

Shuntaro Kosaka

HE'S OBSESSED WITH MANUALS. HE DOES NOT HANDLE UNEXPECTED EVENTS WELL.

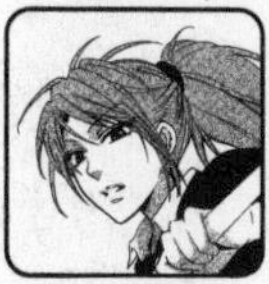

Wakana Hojo

SHE HAS A STOIC ATTITUDE AND WATCHES OVER HANABUSA. SHE HAS FEELINGS FOR YUI.

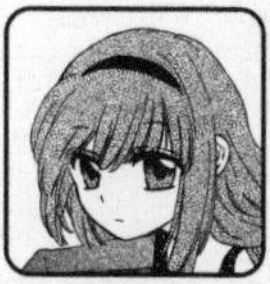

Komari Yukioka

USING HER CUTE LOOKS, SHE CONTROLS PEOPLE AROUND HER WITHOUT SAYING A WORD. INSIDE, SHE'S LIKE A DIRTY OLD MAN.

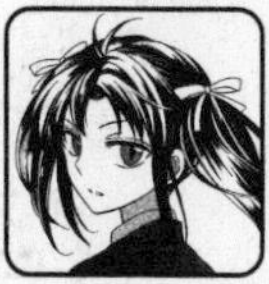

Kanon Nonoguchi

SHE HATES MEN. HER FAMILY RUNS A DOJO, SO SHE'S STRONG. SHE PLANS TO DESTROY THE PUBLIC MORALS CLUB OUT OF GRATITUDE TOWARDS MIYABI.

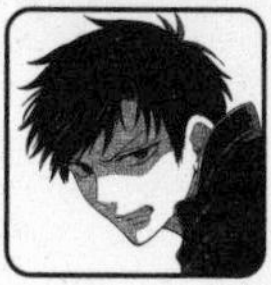

Reito Ayabe

HE LOVES CLEANING. HE GETS STRONGER IN DIRTY PLACES. HE IS A STUDENT COUNCIL OFFICER, BUT HE'S ALSO FRIENDS WITH MAFUYU.

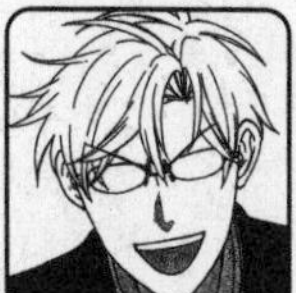

Shinobu Yui

A FORMER MEMBER OF THE STUDENT COUNCIL AND A SELF-PROCLAIMED NINJA. HE JOINED THE PUBLIC MORALS CLUB AND PRETENDED TO BE THEIR ALLY IN ORDER TO DESTROY THEM FROM WITHIN BY USING THE ART OF THE ECHO. HE RETURNED TO THE STUDENT COUNCIL WHEN HANABUSA ORDERED HIM TO. HE ALSO MOVED FROM DORM 2 BACK TO DORM 1.

story

★ MAFUYU KUROSAKI WAS ONCE THE BANCHO WHO CONTROLLED ALL OF SAITAMA, BUT WHEN SHE WAS TRANSFERRED TO MIDORIGAOKA ACADEMY, SHE CHANGED COMPLETELY AND BECAME A NORMAL (BUT SPIRITED) HIGH SCHOOL GIRL...OR AT LEAST SHE WAS SUPPOSED TO! TAKAOMI SAEKI, MAFUYU'S CHILDHOOD FRIEND AND HOMEROOM TEACHER, FORCED HER TO JOIN THE PUBLIC MORALS CLUB, THUS MAKING SURE HER LIFE CONTINUED TO BE FAR FROM AVERAGE.

★ THE PUBLIC MORALS CLUB IS FIGHTING THE STUDENT COUNCIL FOR CONTROL OF MIDORIGAOKA ACADEMY, AND HAS ALREADY BESTED STUDENT COUNCIL MEMBERS KOSAKA AND AYABE. AND NOW THE PUBLIC MORALS CLUB HAS A NEW MEMBER NAMED SHIBUYA. THEIR CLASH WITH KANON NONOGUCHI, THE NEXT STUDENT COUNCIL MEMBER TO OPPOSE THEM, TURNED INTO A HUGE RIOT INVOLVING THE INFAMOUS KIYAMA HIGH SCHOOL. BUT BANCHO OKEGAWA JOINED THE PUBLIC MORALS CLUB AND THEY WERE ABLE TO OVERCOME THE THREAT.

★ MAFUYU AND THE OTHER SECOND-YEAR STUDENTS WENT ON A SCHOOL TRIP! EVEN THOUGH THEY RAN INTO WEST HIGH STUDENTS, THEY MANAGED TO HAVE A FUN TIME. MEANWHILE, WITH MAFUYU AND HER FRIENDS GONE, SHIBUYA WAS TARGETED BY KOMARI YUKIOKA OF THE STUDENT COUNCIL! KOMARI DECEIVES EVERYONE AROUND HER WITH HER TERRIFYING CUTENESS, BUT SHIBUYA SENSED HER TRUE NATURE!

Chapter 94

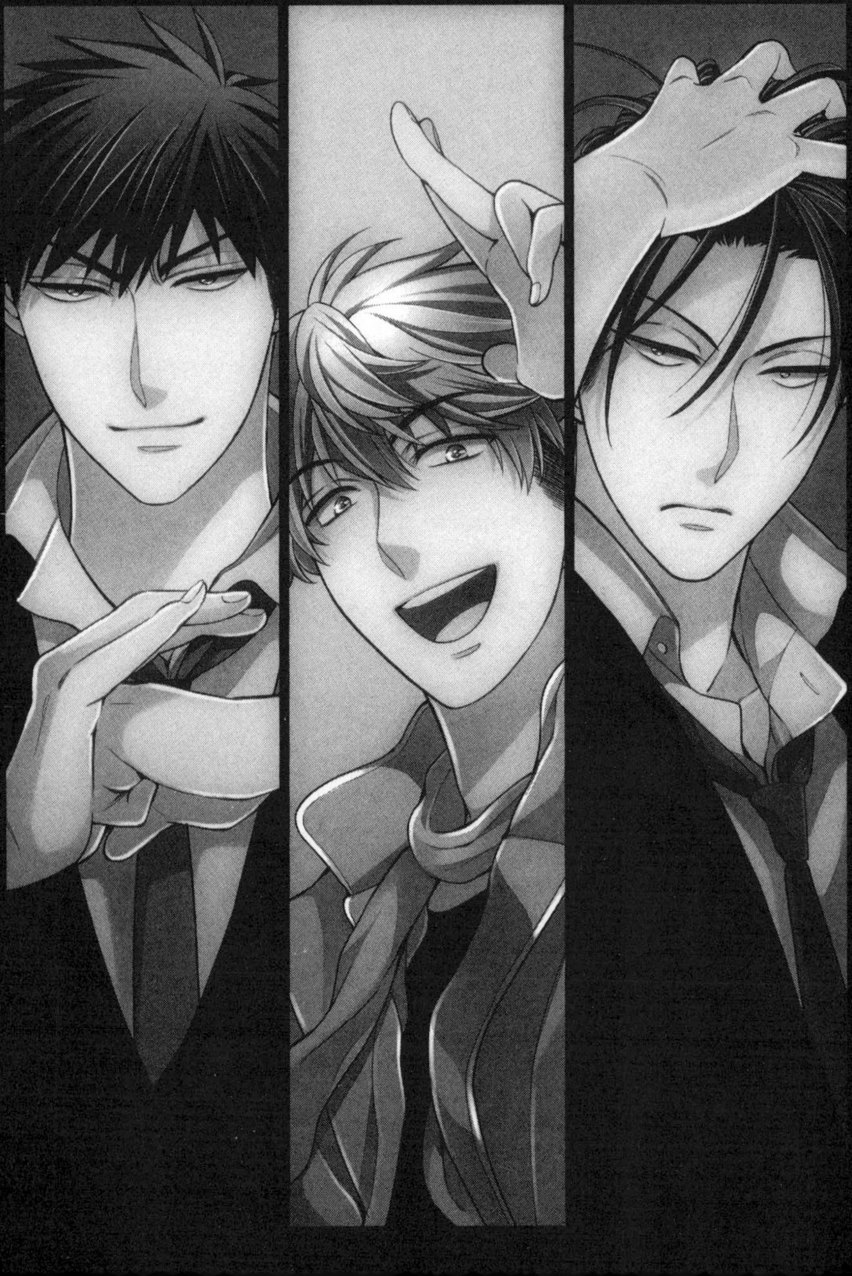

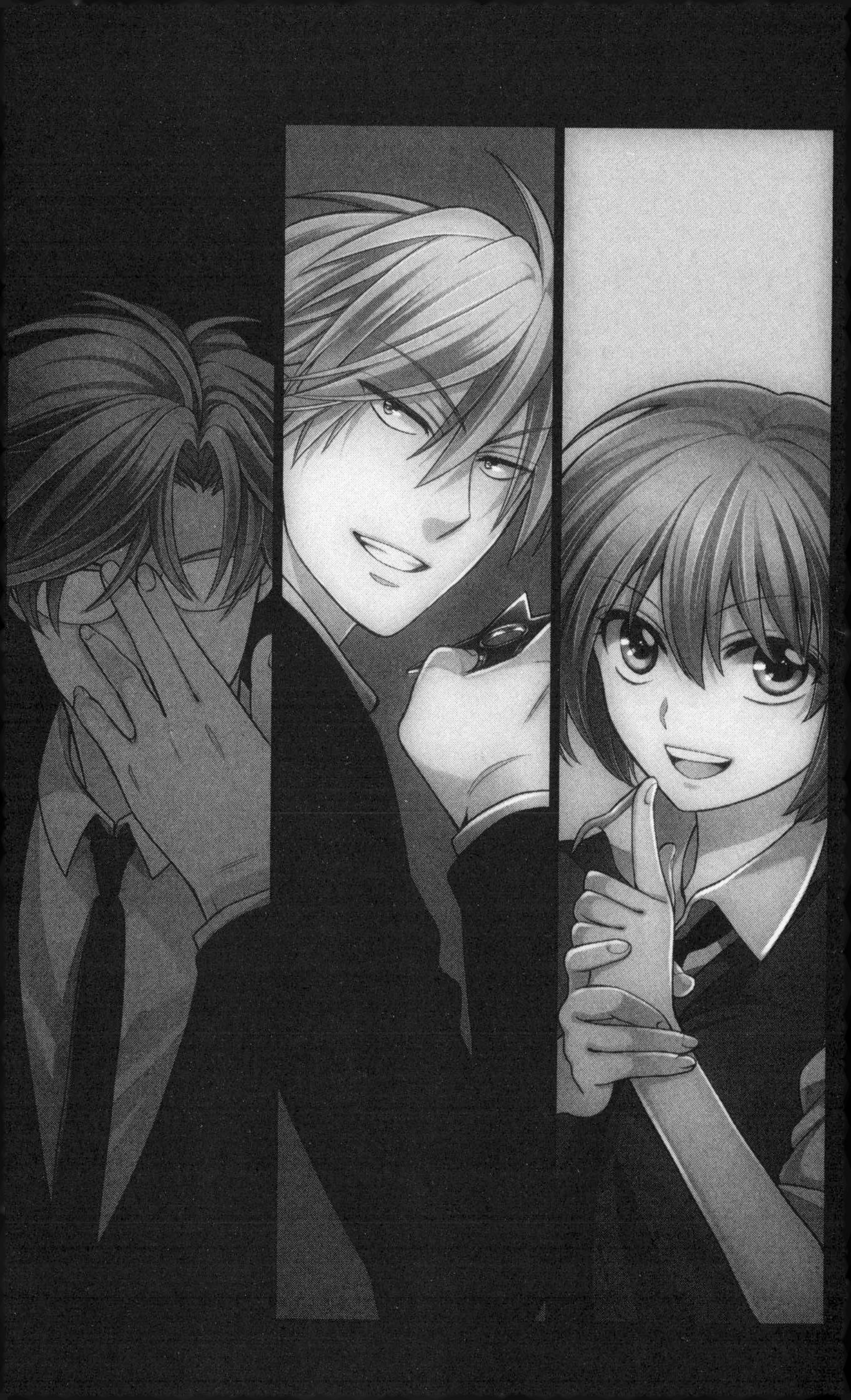

ORESAMA TEACHER

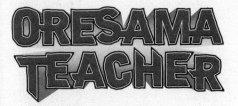

Volume 17
CONTENTS

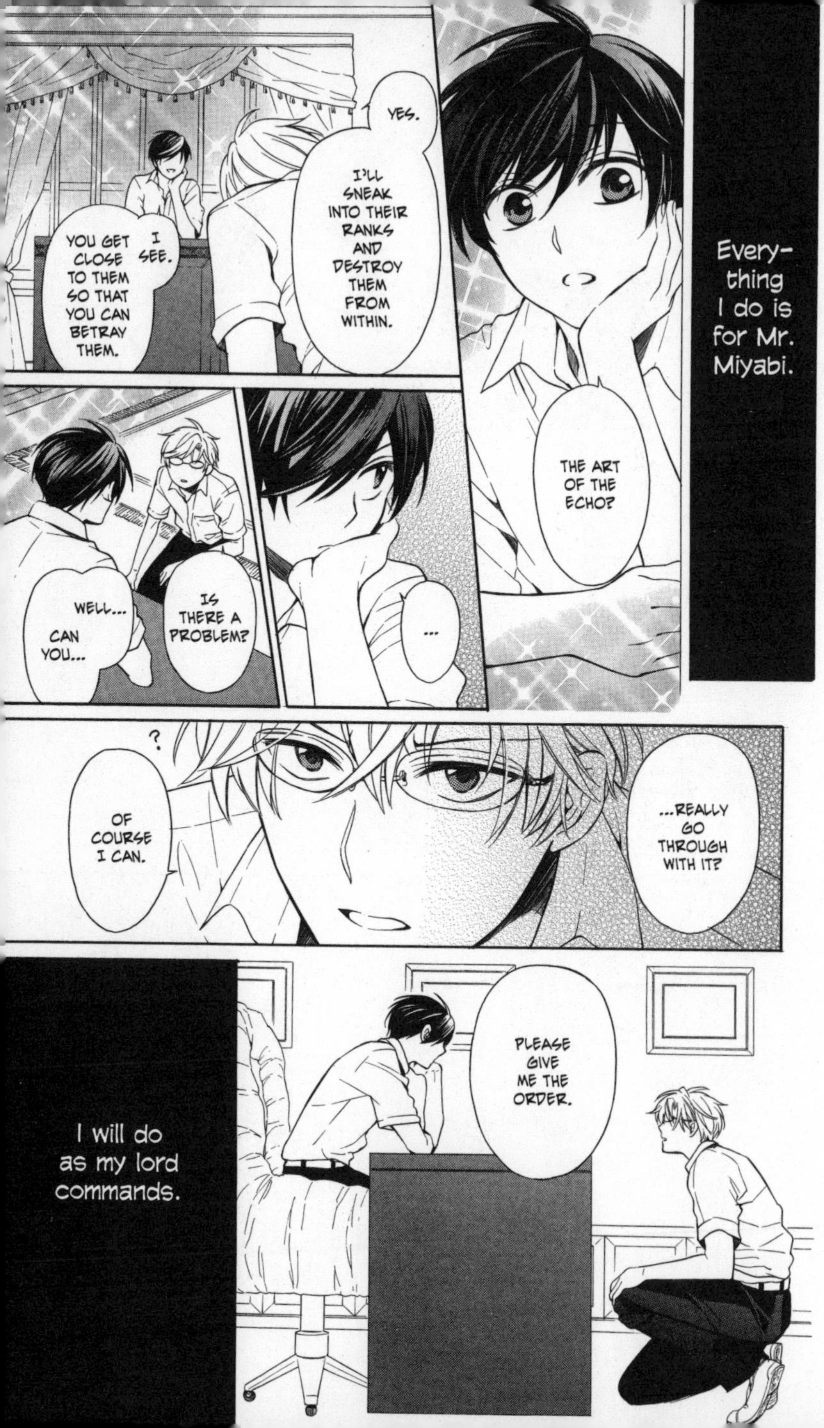
Every-thing I do is for Mr. Miyabi.
THE ART OF THE ECHO?
YES.
I'LL SNEAK INTO THEIR RANKS AND DESTROY THEM FROM WITHIN.
I SEE.
YOU GET CLOSE TO THEM SO THAT YOU CAN BETRAY THEM.
...
IS THERE A PROBLEM?
WELL...
CAN YOU...
...REALLY GO THROUGH WITH IT?
?
OF COURSE I CAN.
PLEASE GIVE ME THE ORDER.
I will do as my lord commands.

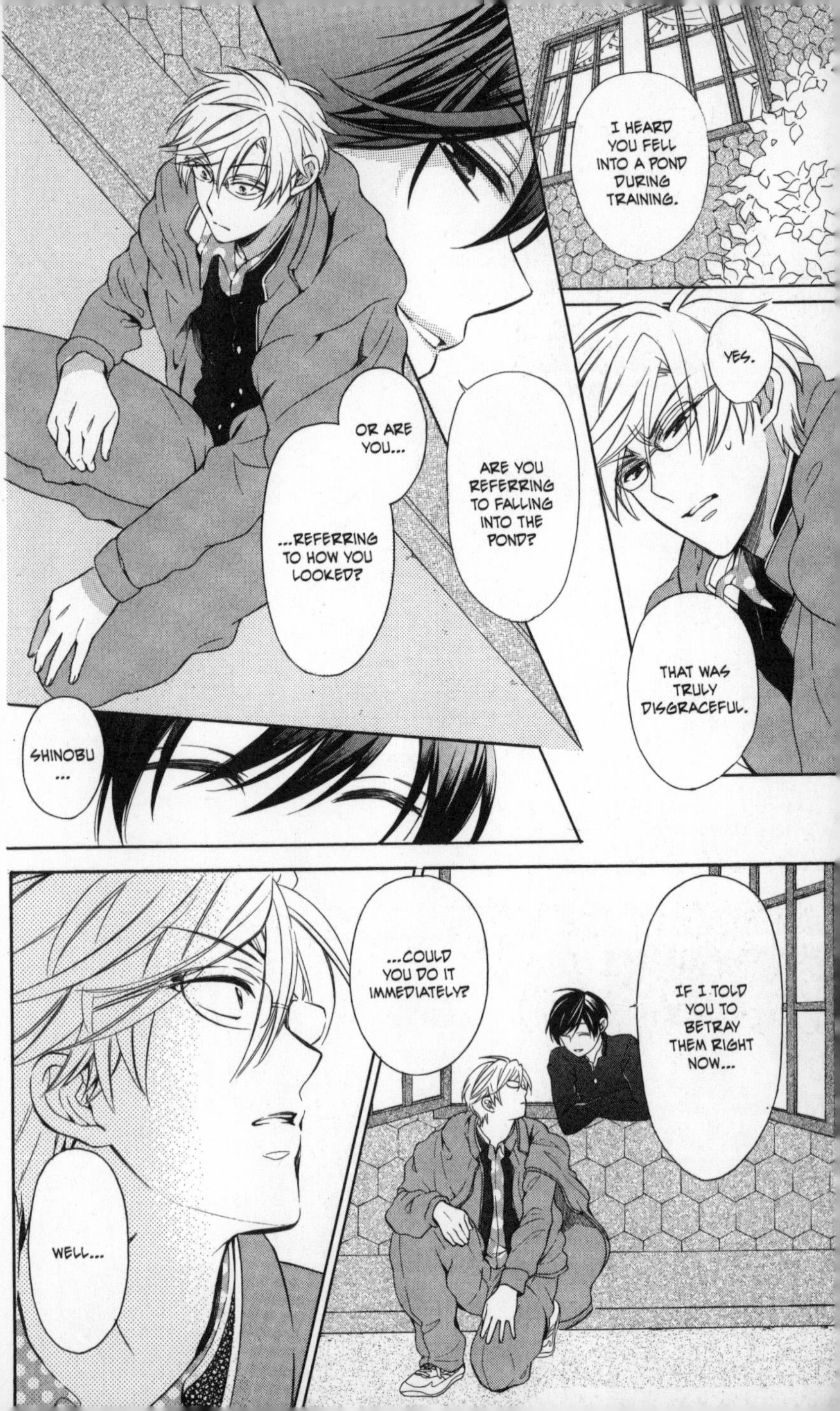
I HEARD YOU FELL INTO A POND DURING TRAINING.
YES.
THAT WAS TRULY DISGRACEFUL.
ARE YOU REFERRING TO FALLING INTO THE POND?
OR ARE YOU...
...REFERRING TO HOW YOU LOOKED?
SHINOBU...
IF I TOLD YOU TO BETRAY THEM RIGHT NOW...
...COULD YOU DO IT IMMEDIATELY?
WELL...

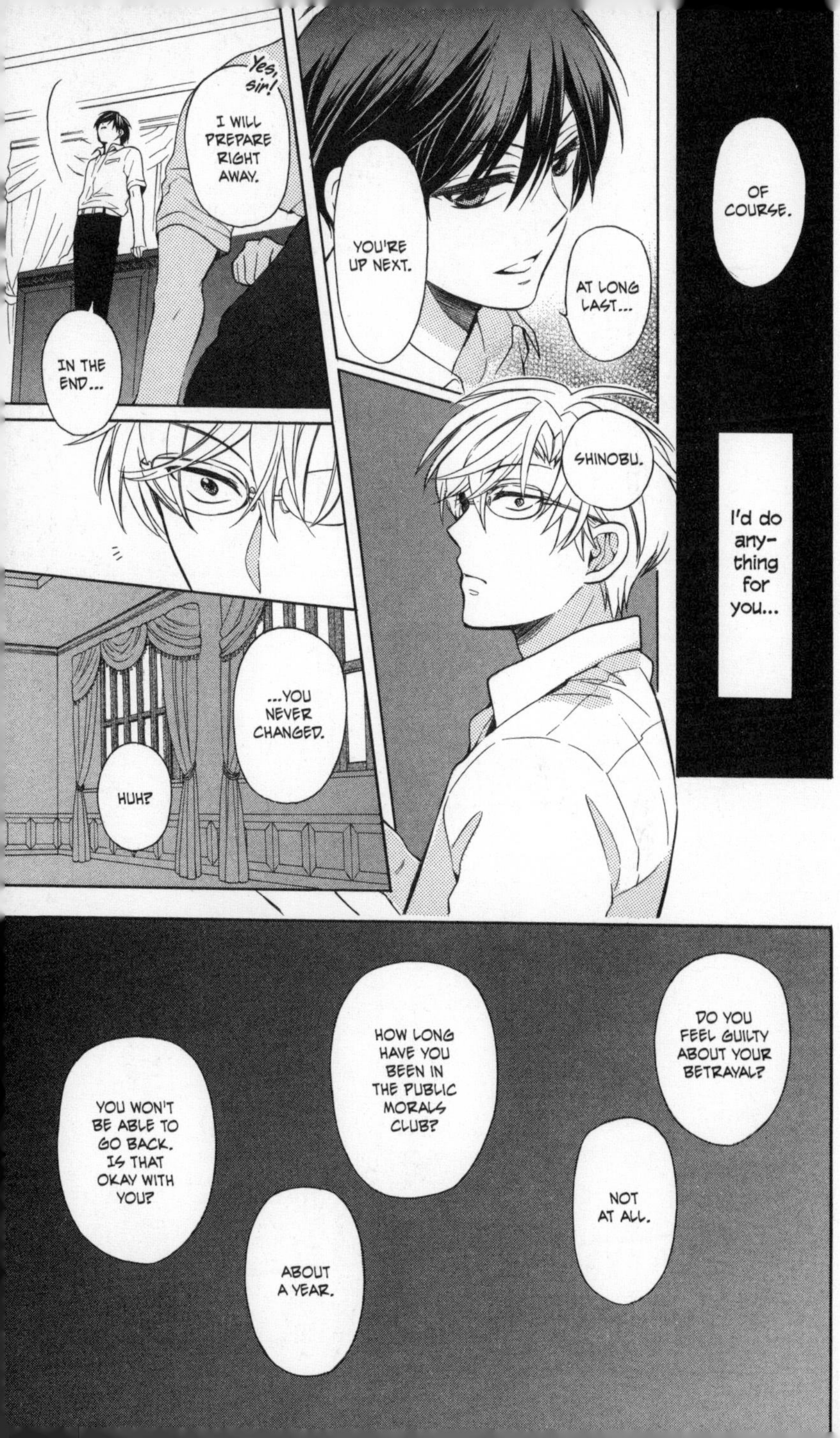
OF COURSE.
I'd do anything for you...
AT LONG LAST...
YOU'RE UP NEXT.
Yes, sir!
I WILL PREPARE RIGHT AWAY.
IN THE END...
SHINOBU.
...YOU NEVER CHANGED.
HUH?
DO YOU FEEL GUILTY ABOUT YOUR BETRAYAL?
NOT AT ALL.
HOW LONG HAVE YOU BEEN IN THE PUBLIC MORALS CLUB?
ABOUT A YEAR.
YOU WON'T BE ABLE TO GO BACK. IS THAT OKAY WITH YOU?

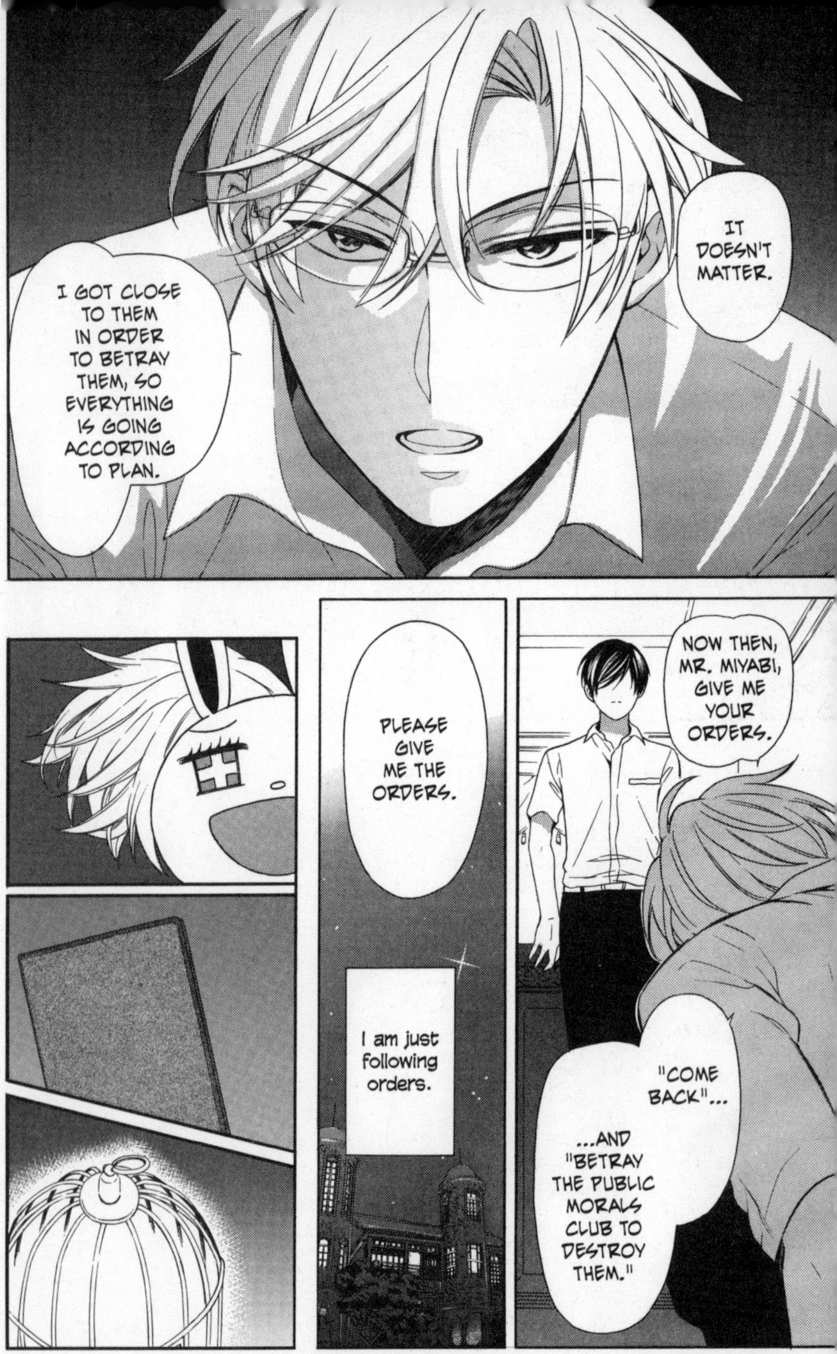
IT DOESN'T MATTER.
I GOT CLOSE TO THEM IN ORDER TO BETRAY THEM, SO EVERYTHING IS GOING ACCORDING TO PLAN.
NOW THEN, MR. MIYABI, GIVE ME YOUR ORDERS.
"COME BACK"...
...AND "BETRAY THE PUBLIC MORALS CLUB TO DESTROY THEM."
PLEASE GIVE ME THE ORDERS.
I am just following orders.

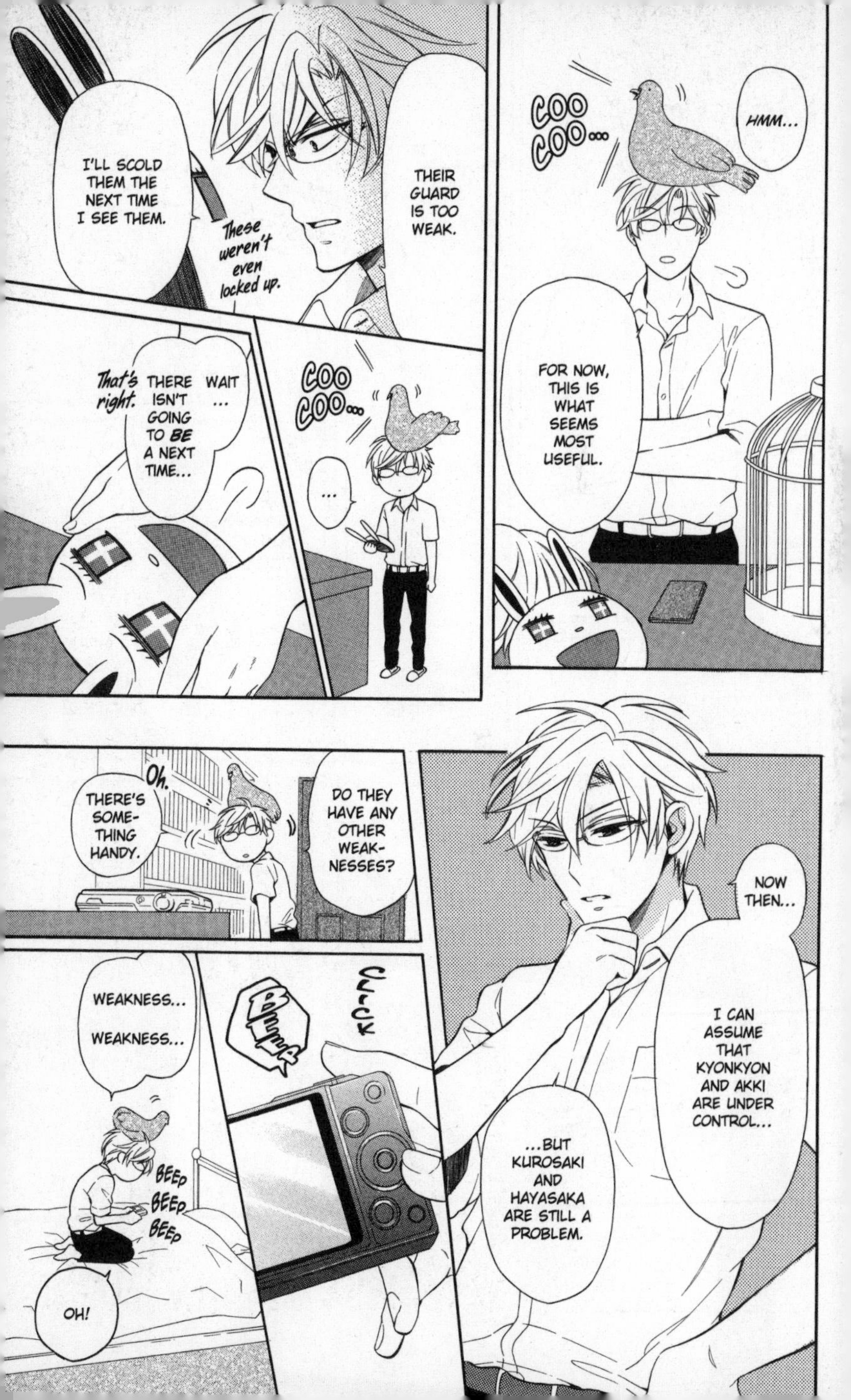
HMM...
COO COO...
FOR NOW, THIS IS WHAT SEEMS MOST USEFUL.
THEIR GUARD IS TOO WEAK.
These weren't even locked up.
I'LL SCOLD THEM THE NEXT TIME I SEE THEM.
COO COO...
...
WAIT...
THERE ISN'T GOING TO BE A NEXT TIME...
That's right.
NOW THEN...
I CAN ASSUME THAT KYONKYON AND AKKI ARE UNDER CONTROL...
...BUT KUROSAKI AND HAYASAKA ARE STILL A PROBLEM.
DO THEY HAVE ANY OTHER WEAKNESSES?
Oh.
THERE'S SOME-THING HANDY.
CLICK
WEAKNESS...
WEAKNESS...
BEEP
BEEP
BEEP
OH!

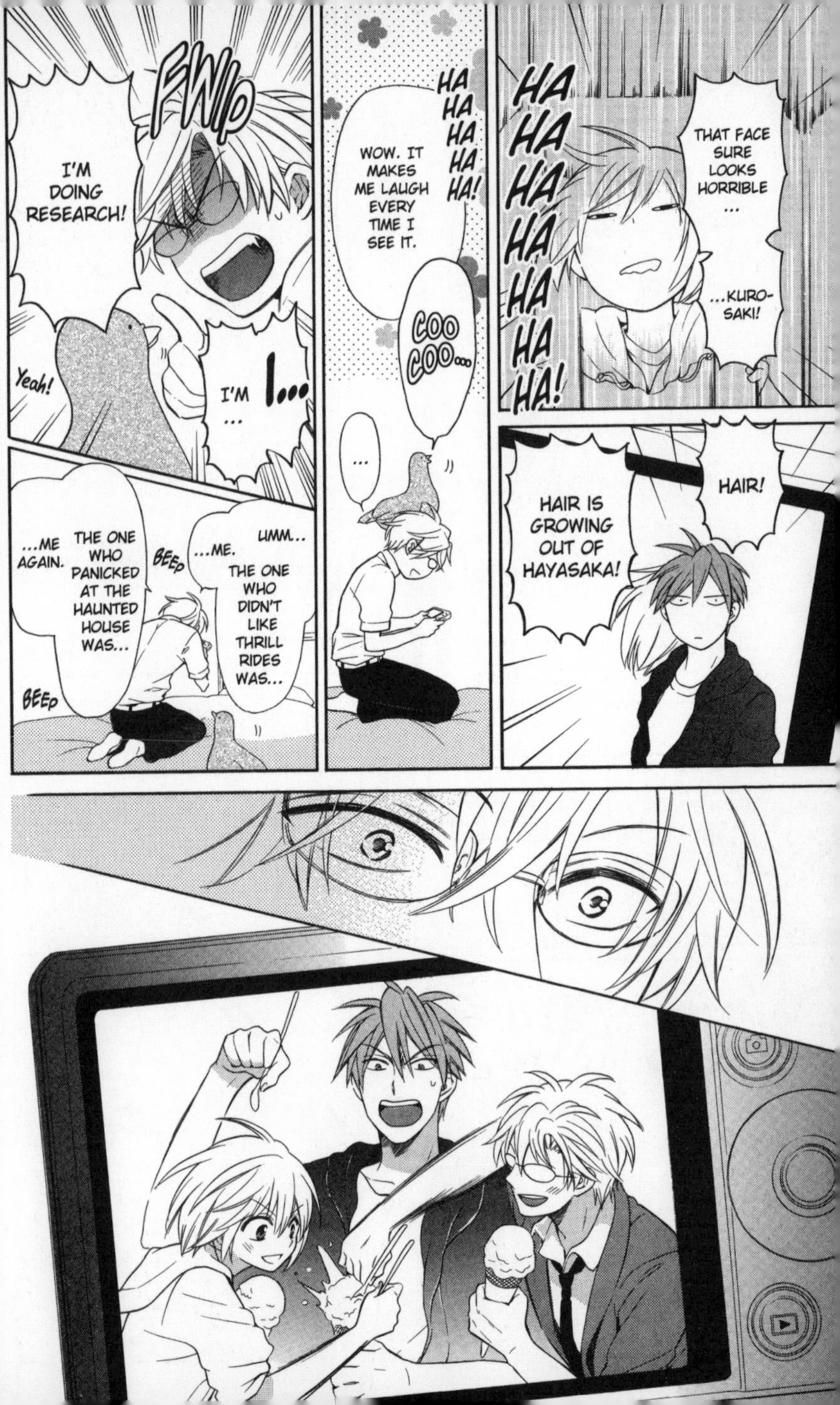
THAT FACE SURE LOOKS HORRIBLE ...
...KURO-SAKI!
HA HA HA HA HA HA HA HA!
HAIR!
HAIR IS GROWING OUT OF HAYASAKA!
HA HA HA HA HA!
WOW. IT MAKES ME LAUGH EVERY TIME I SEE IT.
COO COO...
...
FWIP
I'M DOING RESEARCH!
I'M ... I...
Yeah!
UMM... THE ONE WHO DIDN'T LIKE THRILL RIDES WAS...
...ME.
BEEP
THE ONE WHO PANICKED AT THE HAUNTED HOUSE WAS...
...ME AGAIN.
BEEP

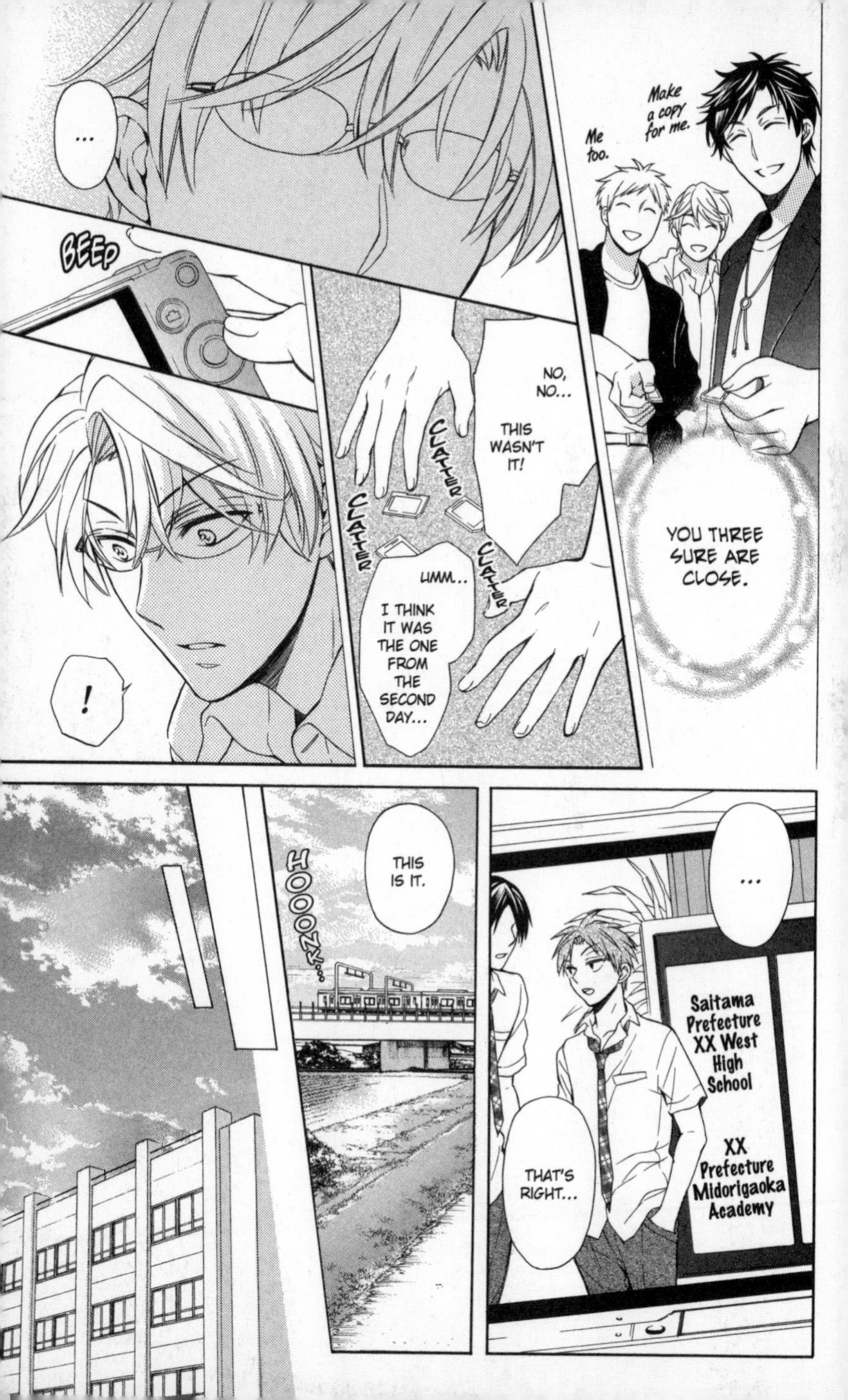
Make a copy for me.
Me too.
YOU THREE SURE ARE CLOSE.
NO, NO...
THIS WASN'T IT!
CLATTER
CLATTER
CLATTER
CLATTER
UMM...
I THINK IT WAS THE ONE FROM THE SECOND DAY...
...
BEEP
!
...
Saitama Prefecture XX West High School
XX Prefecture Midorigaoka Academy
THAT'S RIGHT...
THIS IS IT.
HOOONK...

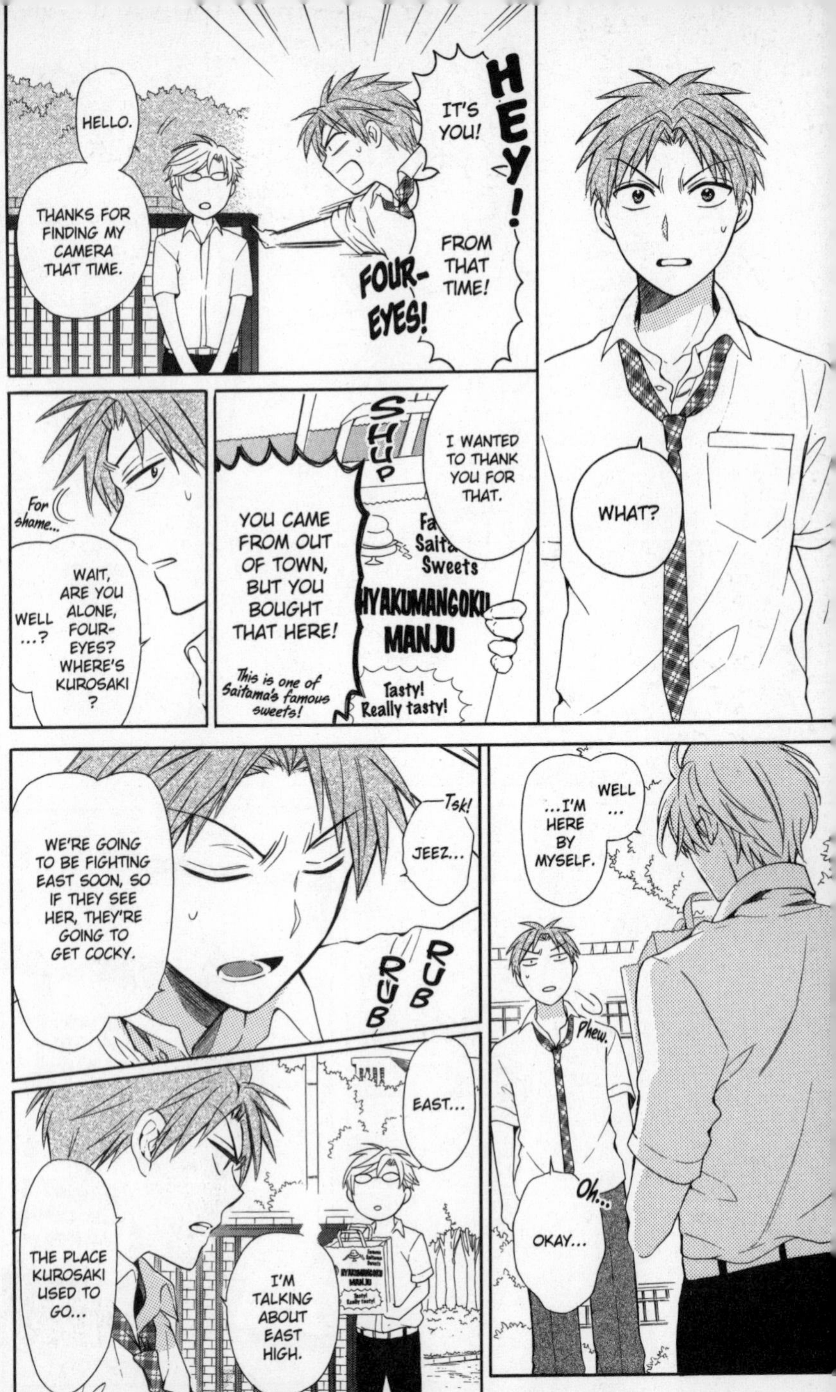
WHAT?
HEY!
IT'S YOU!
FROM THAT TIME!
FOUR-EYES!
HELLO.
THANKS FOR FINDING MY CAMERA THAT TIME.
SHUP
I WANTED TO THANK YOU FOR THAT.
Sweets
HYAKUMANGOKU MANJU
YOU CAME FROM OUT OF TOWN, BUT YOU BOUGHT THAT HERE!
This is one of Saitama's famous sweets!
Tasty! Really tasty!
For shame...
WAIT, ARE YOU ALONE, FOUR-EYES? WHERE'S KUROSAKI?
WELL...?
WELL...
...I'M HERE BY MYSELF.
Phew.
Oh...
OKAY...
Tsk!
JEEZ...
WE'RE GOING TO BE FIGHTING EAST SOON, SO IF THEY SEE HER, THEY'RE GOING TO GET COCKY.
RUB RUB
EAST...
I'M TALKING ABOUT EAST HIGH.
THE PLACE KUROSAKI USED TO GO...

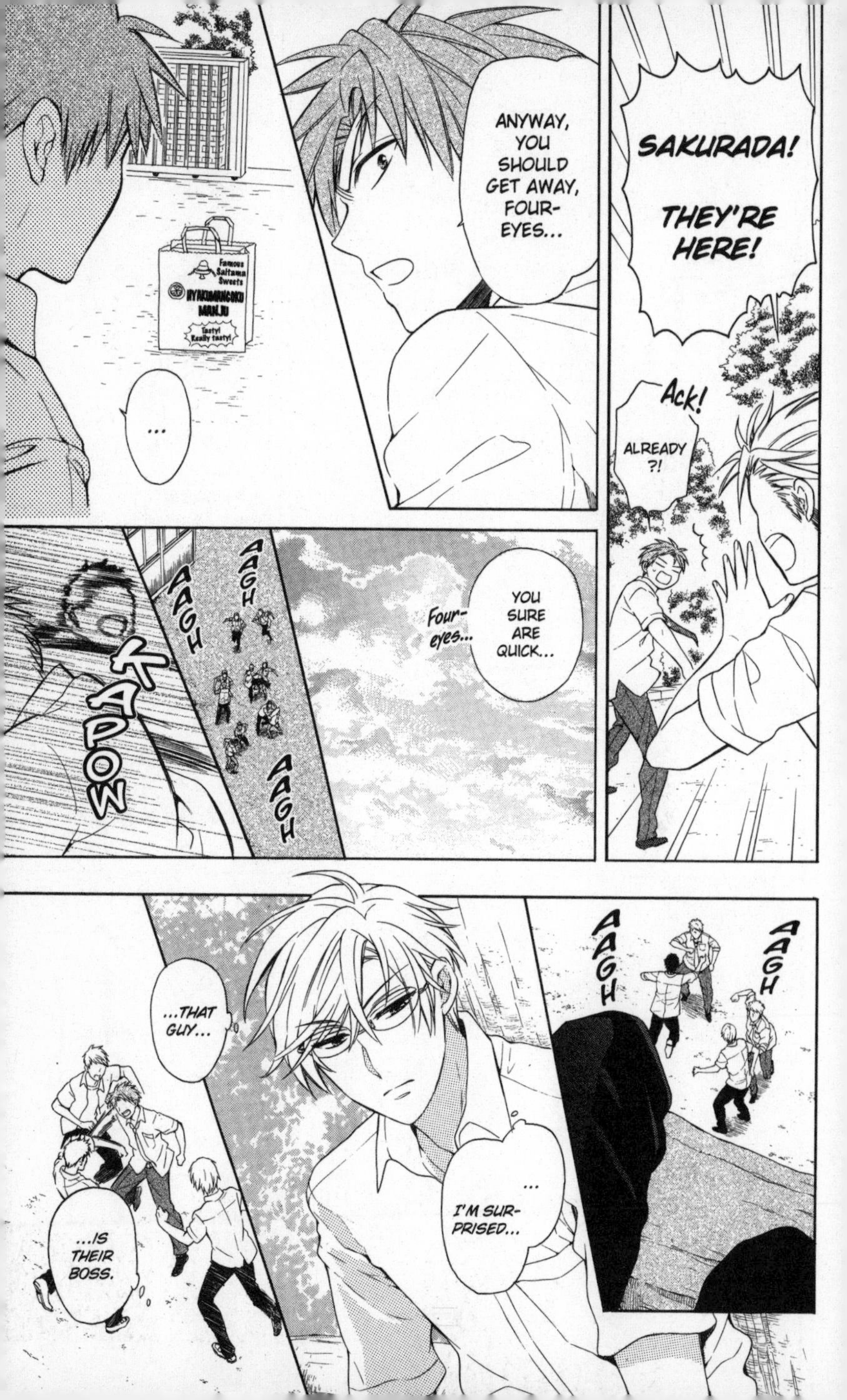
SAKURADA! THEY'RE HERE!
Ack!
ALREADY ?!
ANYWAY, YOU SHOULD GET AWAY, FOUR-EYES...
Famous Saitama Sweets
HYAKUMANGOKU MANJU
Tasty! Really tasty!
...
Four-eyes...
YOU SURE ARE QUICK...
AAGH
AAGH
AAGH
AAGH
KAPOW
AAGH
AAGH
...
I'M SUR-PRISED...
...THAT GUY...
...IS THEIR BOSS.

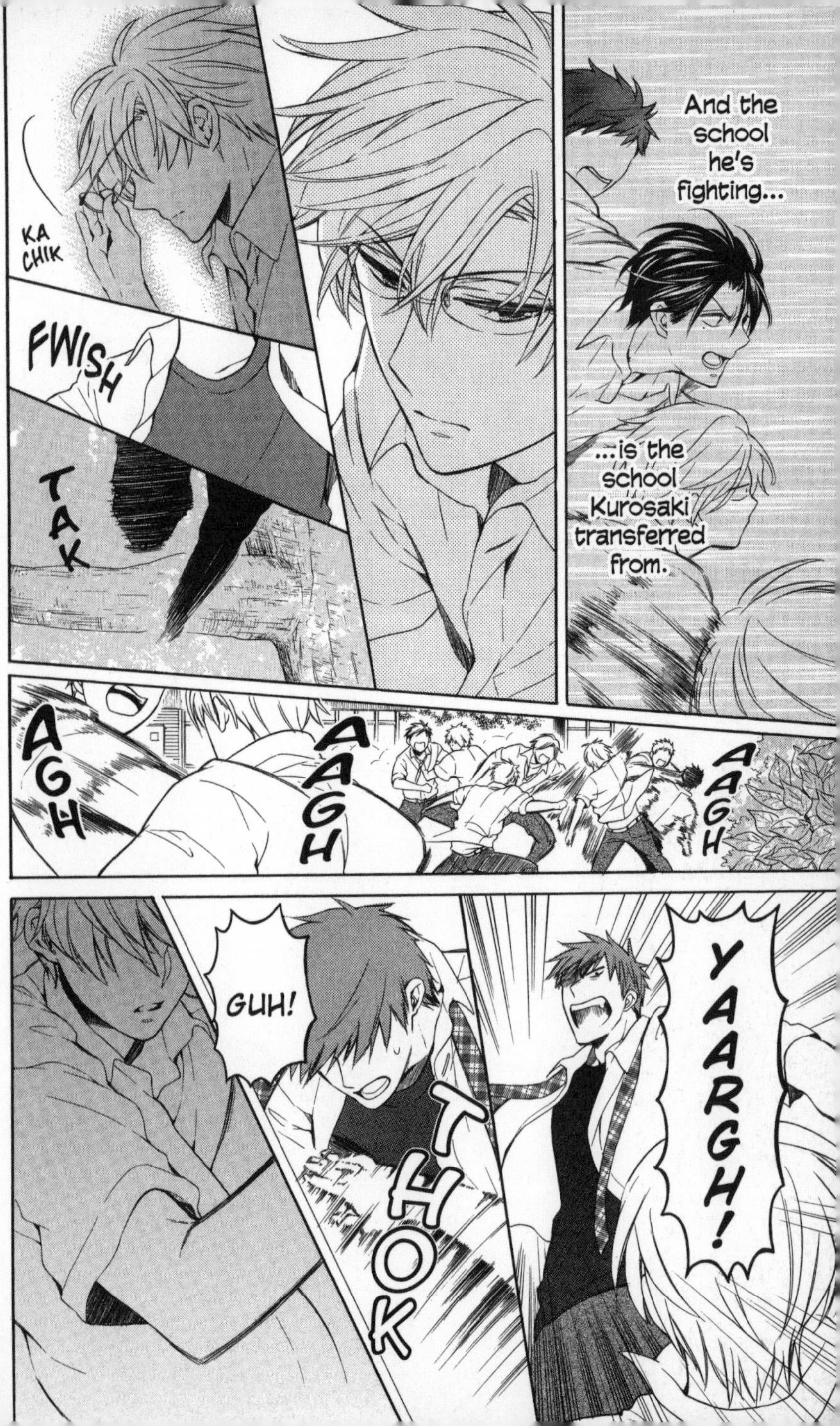
And the school he's fighting...
...is the school Kurosaki transferred from.
KA CHIK
FWISH
TAK
AAGH
AAGH
AGH
YAARGH!
THOK
GUH!

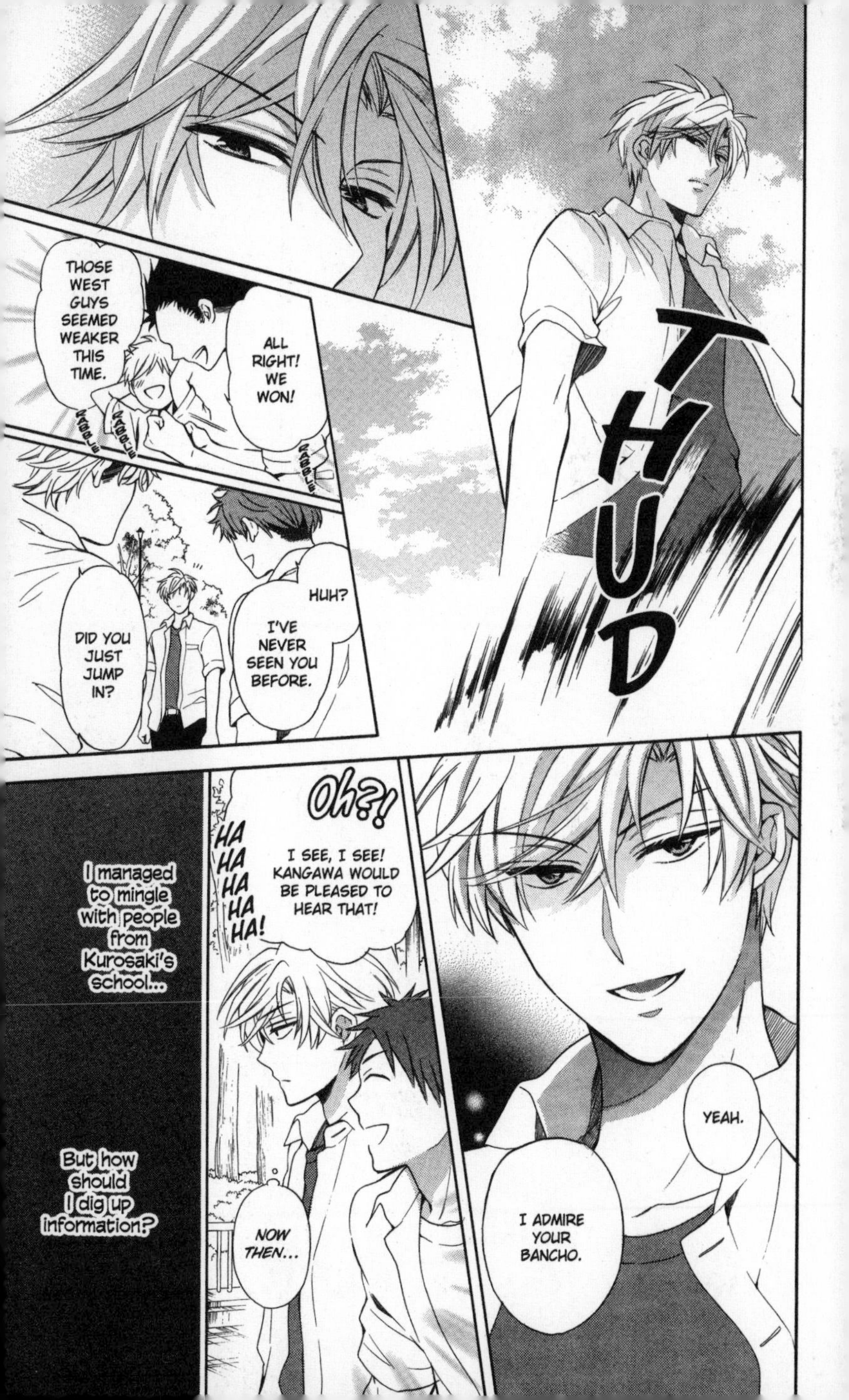
THUD
ALL RIGHT! WE WON!
THOSE WEST GUYS SEEMED WEAKER THIS TIME.
RABBLE RABBLE
RABBLE
HUH?
I'VE NEVER SEEN YOU BEFORE.
DID YOU JUST JUMP IN?
YEAH.
I ADMIRE YOUR BANCHO.
Oh?!
I SEE, I SEE! KANGAWA WOULD BE PLEASED TO HEAR THAT!
HA HA HA HA HA!
NOW THEN...
I managed to mingle with people from Kurosaki's school...
But how should I dig up information?

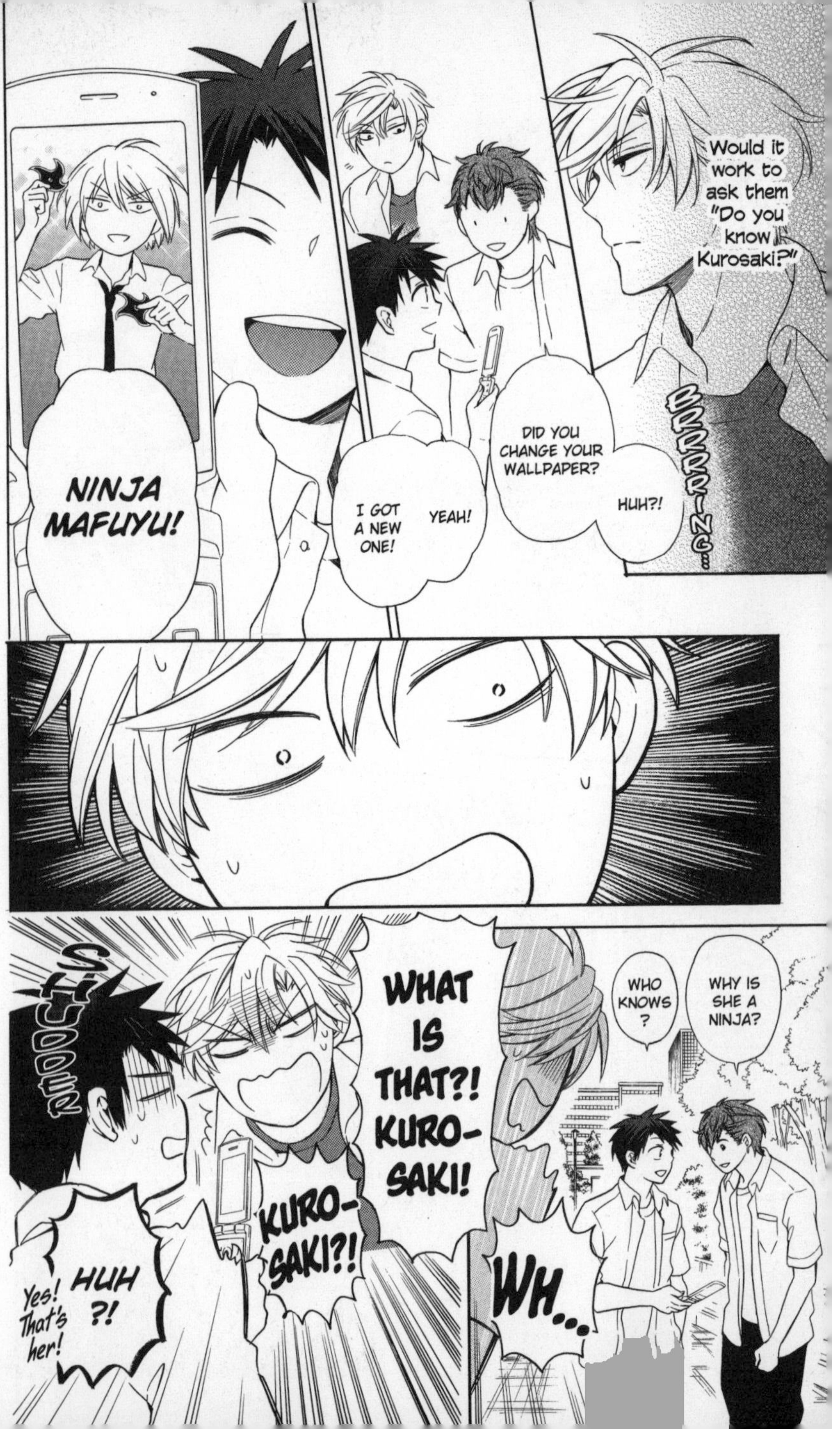
Would it work to ask them "Do you know Kurosaki?"
BRRRRING...
DID YOU CHANGE YOUR WALLPAPER?
HUH?!
YEAH!
I GOT A NEW ONE!
NINJA MAFUYU!
WHY IS SHE A NINJA?
WHO KNOWS?
WH...
WHAT IS THAT?! KURO-SAKI!
KURO-SAKI?!
SHUDDER
HUH?!
Yes! That's her!

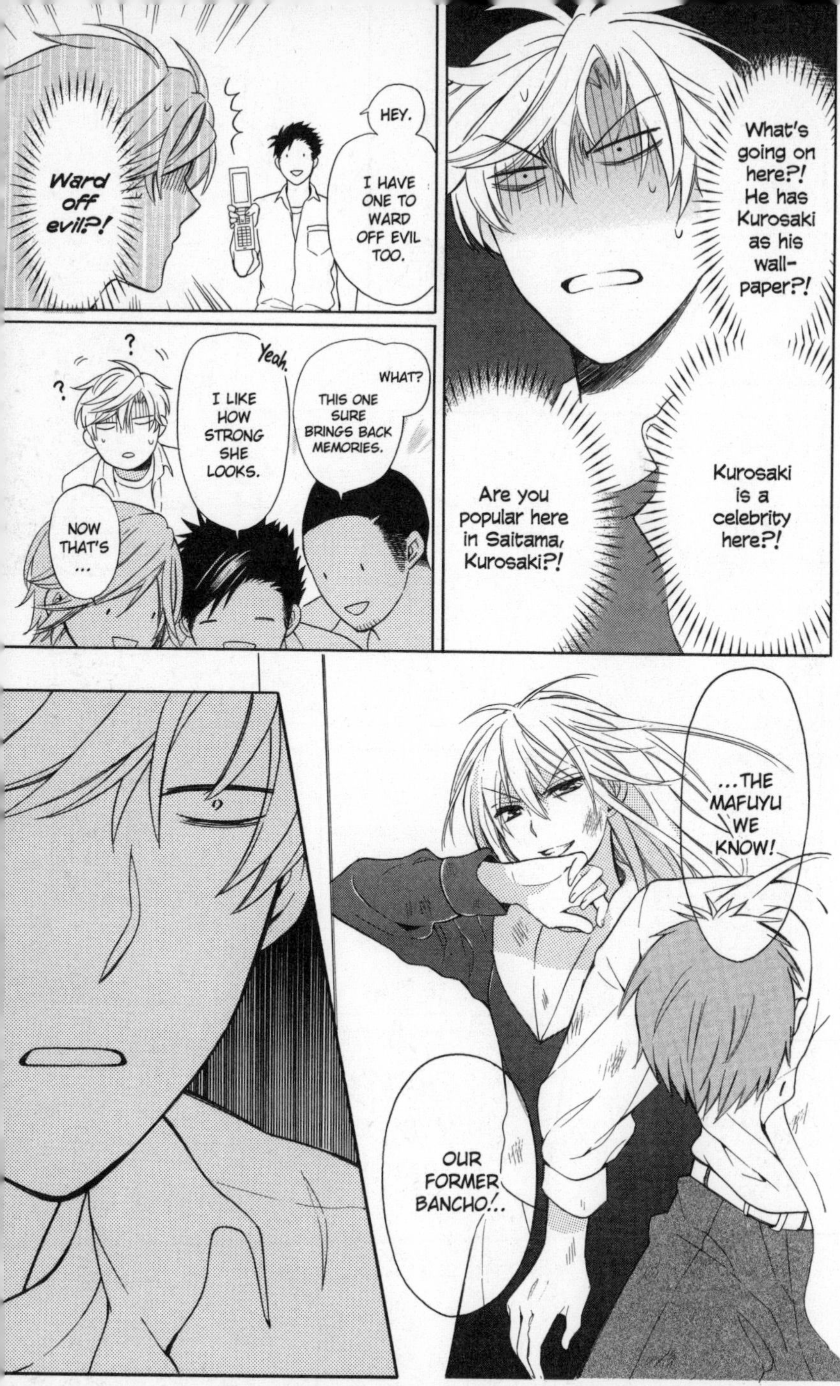

What's going on here?! He has Kurosaki as his wall-paper?!
Kurosaki is a celebrity here?!
Are you popular here in Saitama, Kurosaki?!
HEY.
I HAVE ONE TO WARD OFF EVIL TOO.
Ward off evil?!
WHAT?
THIS ONE SURE BRINGS BACK MEMORIES.
Yeah.
I LIKE HOW STRONG SHE LOOKS.
?
?
NOW THAT'S ...
...THE MAFUYU WE KNOW!
OUR FORMER BANCHO!..

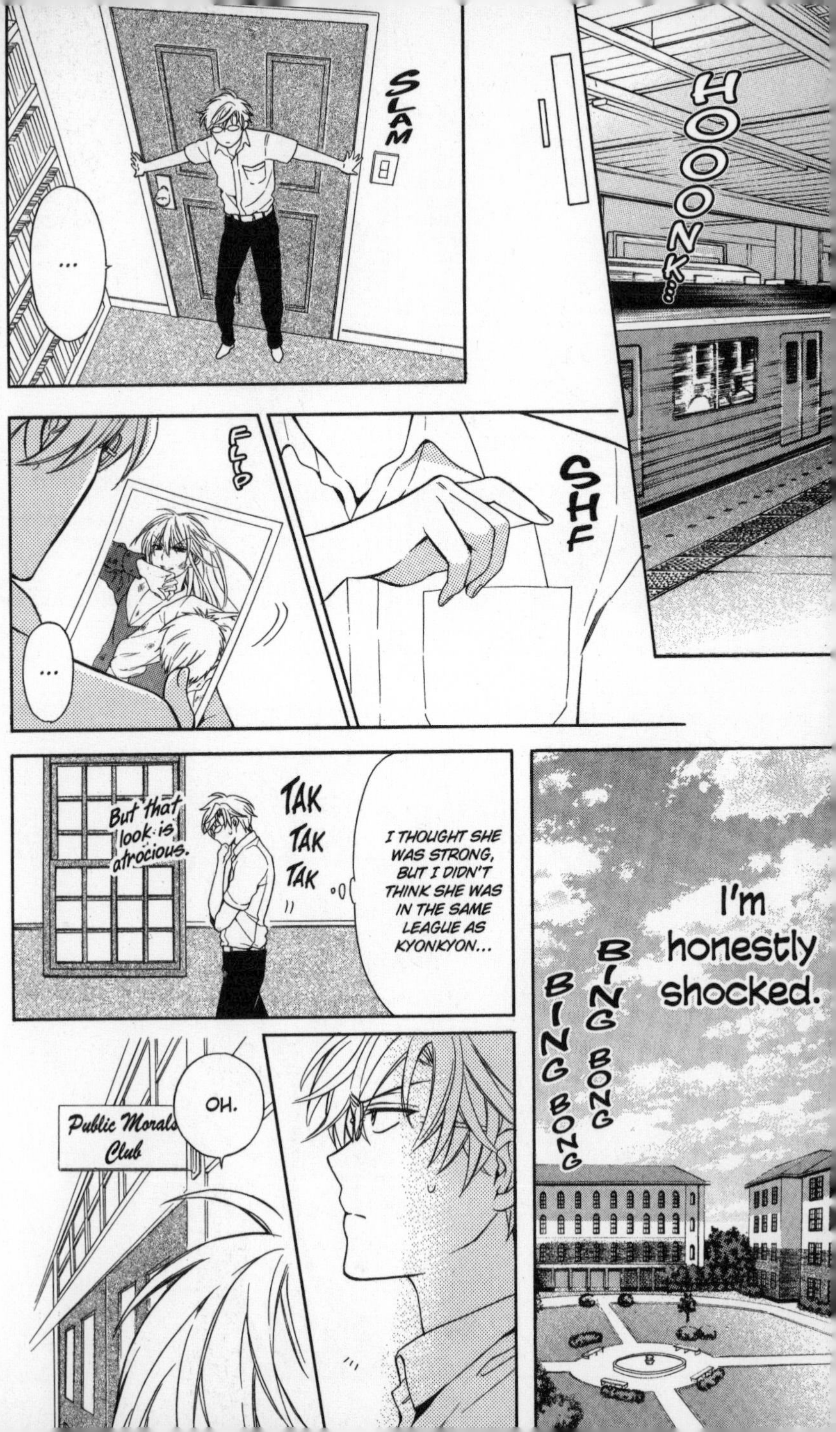
HOOOONK...
SLAM
...
SHF
FLIP
...
I'm honestly shocked.
BING BONG
BING BONG
TAK TAK TAK
I THOUGHT SHE WAS STRONG, BUT I DIDN'T THINK SHE WAS IN THE SAME LEAGUE AS KYONKYON...
But that look is atrocious.
OH.
Public Morals Club

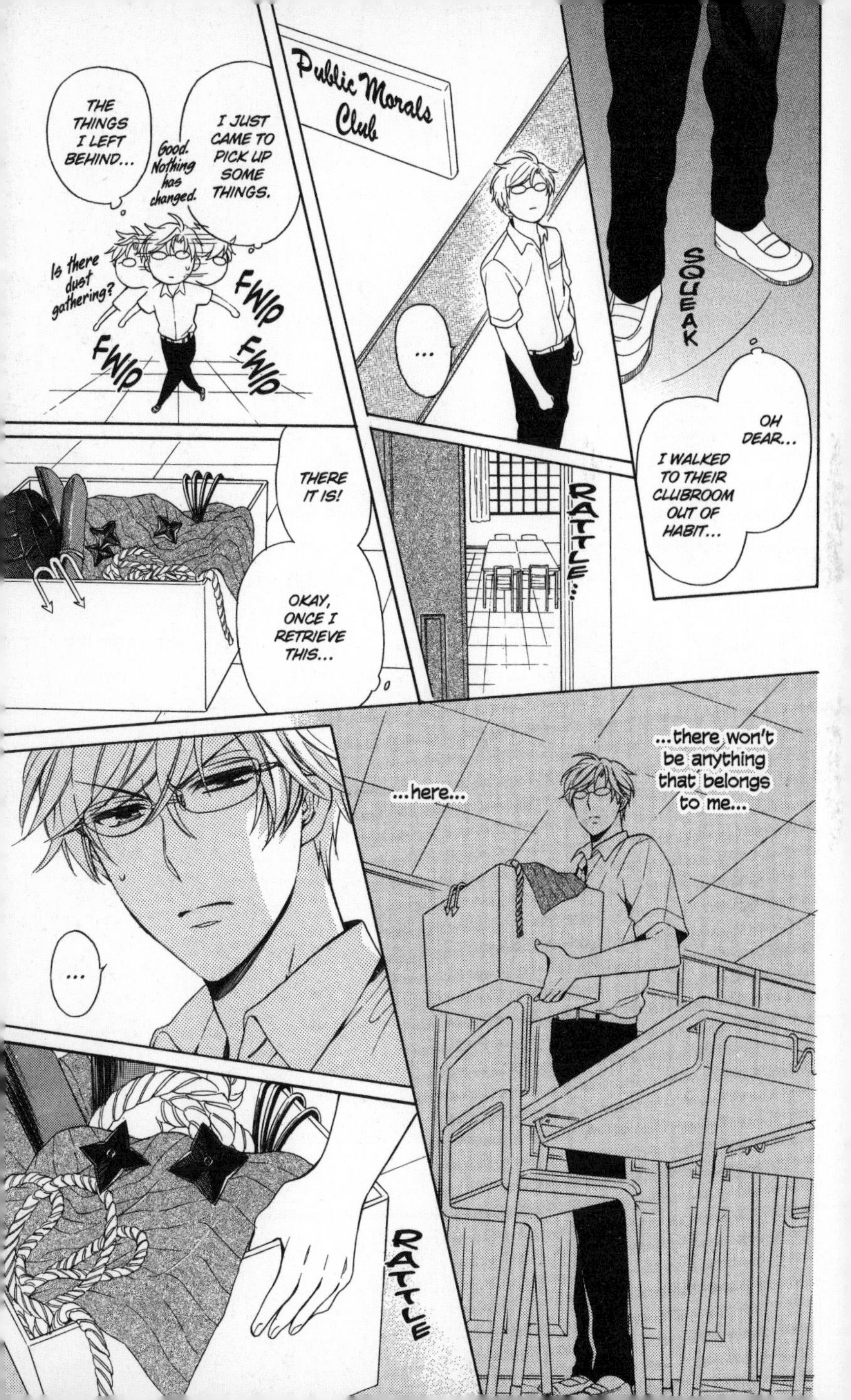
SQUEAK
OH DEAR...
I WALKED TO THEIR CLUBROOM OUT OF HABIT...
Public Morals Club
...
I JUST CAME TO PICK UP SOME THINGS.
Good. Nothing has changed.
THE THINGS I LEFT BEHIND...
Is there dust gathering?
FWIP
FWIP
FWIP
RATTLE...
THERE IT IS!
OKAY, ONCE I RETRIEVE THIS...
...there won't be anything that belongs to me...
...here...
...
RATTLE

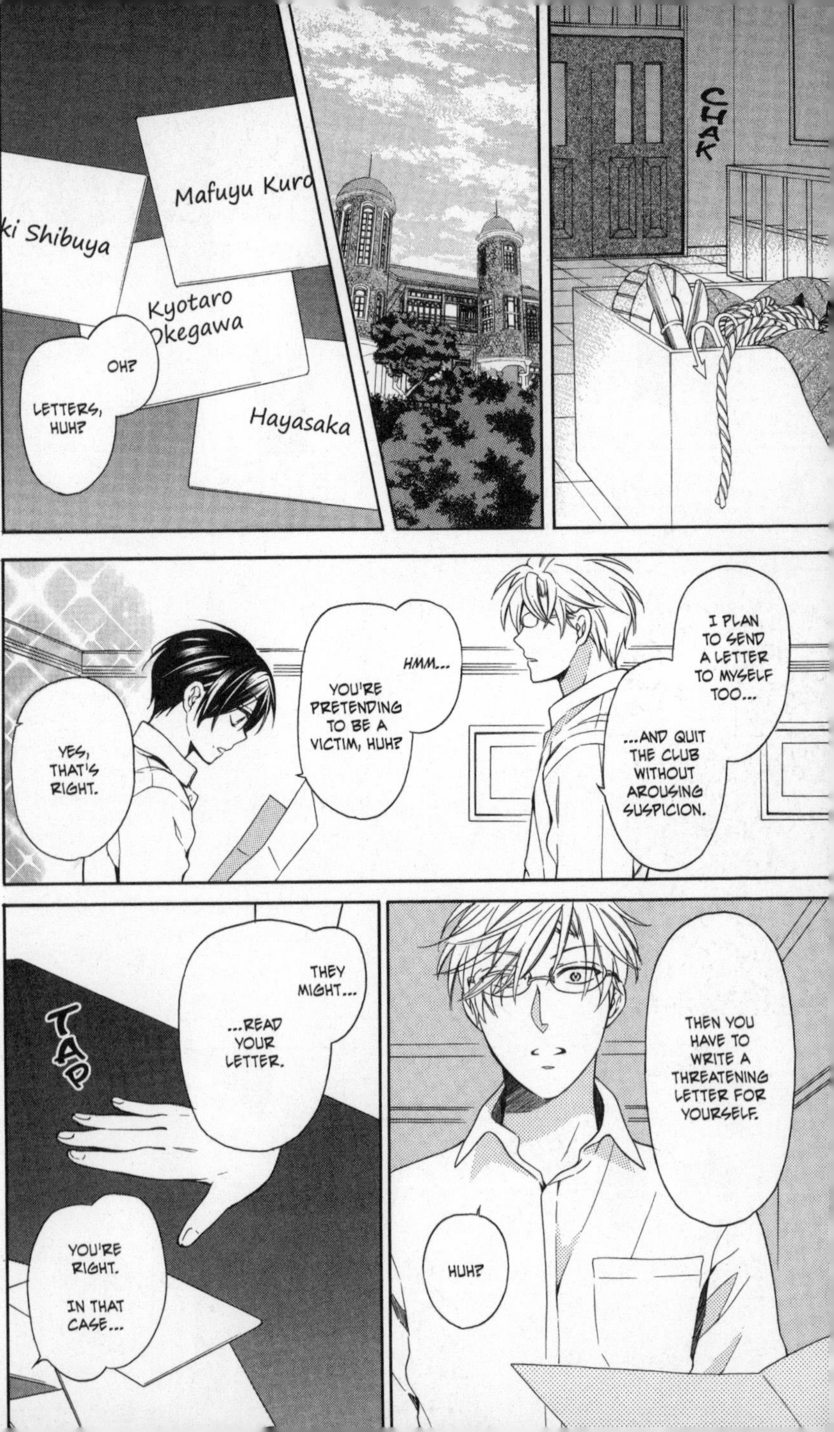

CHAK
Mafuyu Kuro
ki Shibuya
Kyotaro Okegawa
Hayasaka
OH?
LETTERS, HUH?
I PLAN TO SEND A LETTER TO MYSELF TOO...
...AND QUIT THE CLUB WITHOUT AROUSING SUSPICION.
HMM...
YOU'RE PRETENDING TO BE A VICTIM, HUH?
YES, THAT'S RIGHT.
THEN YOU HAVE TO WRITE A THREATENING LETTER FOR YOURSELF.
HUH?
THEY MIGHT...
...READ YOUR LETTER.
TAP
YOU'RE RIGHT.
IN THAT CASE...

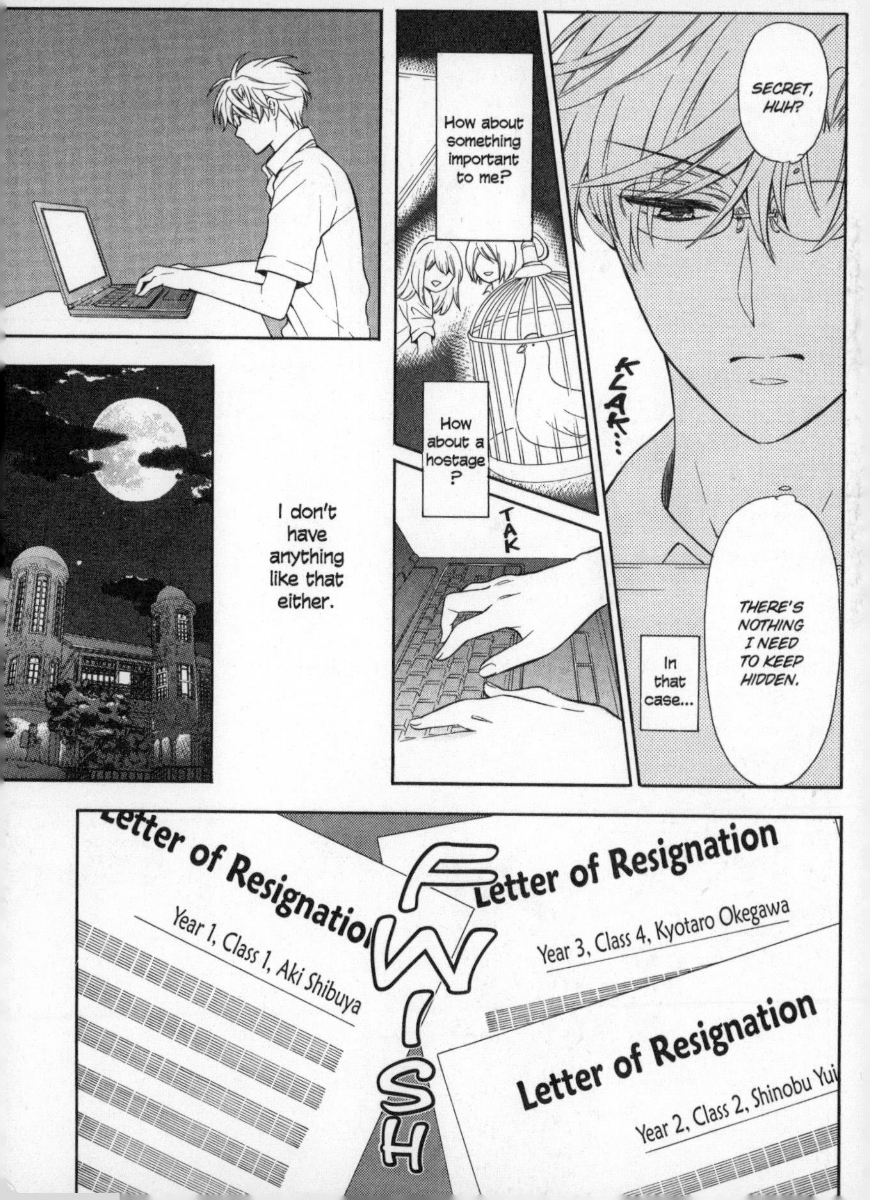
SECRET, HUH?
KLAK...
THERE'S NOTHING I NEED TO KEEP HIDDEN.
In that case...
How about something important to me?
How about a hostage?
TAK
I don't have anything like that either.
Letter of Resignation
Year 1, Class 1, Aki Shibuya
FWISH
Letter of Resignation
Year 3, Class 4, Kyotaro Okegawa
Letter of Resignation
Year 2, Class 2, Shinobu Yui

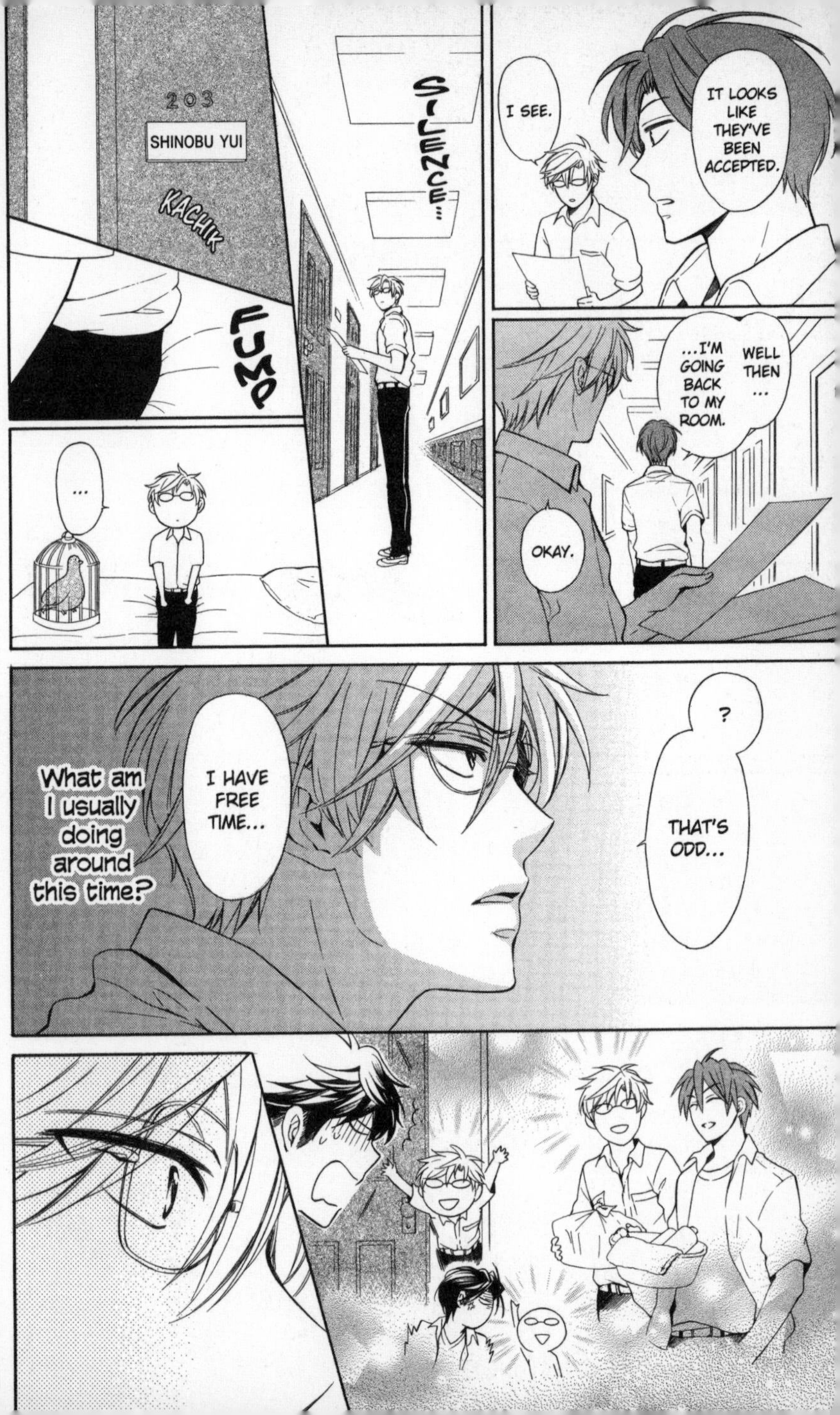
IT LOOKS LIKE THEY'VE BEEN ACCEPTED.
I SEE.
WELL THEN...
...I'M GOING BACK TO MY ROOM.
OKAY.
SILENCE...
203
SHINOBU YUI
KACHIK
FUMP
...
?
THAT'S ODD...
I HAVE FREE TIME...
What am I usually doing around this time?

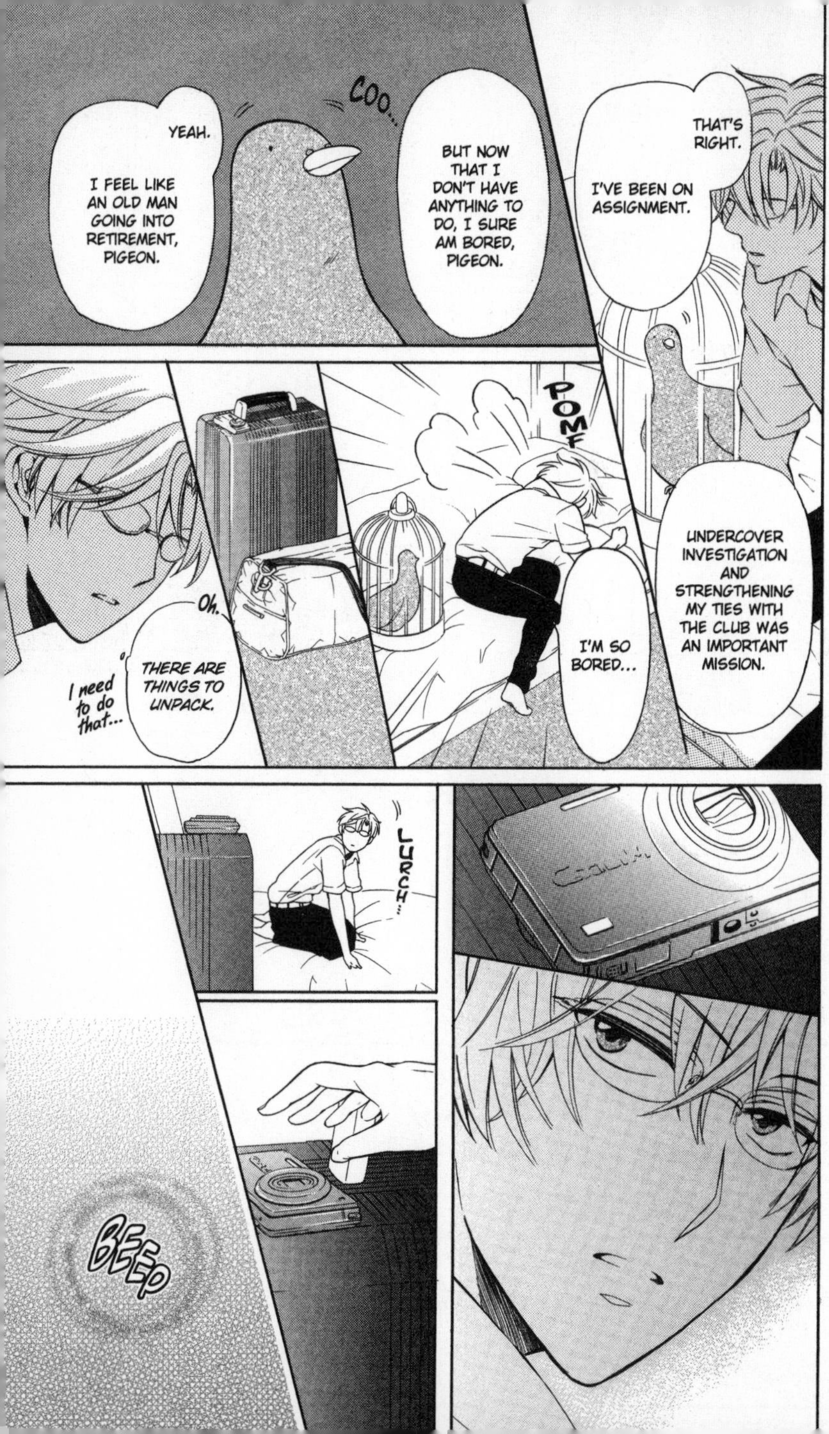
THAT'S RIGHT.
I'VE BEEN ON ASSIGNMENT.
UNDERCOVER INVESTIGATION AND STRENGTHENING MY TIES WITH THE CLUB WAS AN IMPORTANT MISSION.
COO...
BUT NOW THAT I DON'T HAVE ANYTHING TO DO, I SURE AM BORED, PIGEON.
YEAH.
I FEEL LIKE AN OLD MAN GOING INTO RETIREMENT, PIGEON.
POMF
I'M SO BORED...
Oh.
THERE ARE THINGS TO UNPACK.
I need to do that...
LURCH...
BEEP

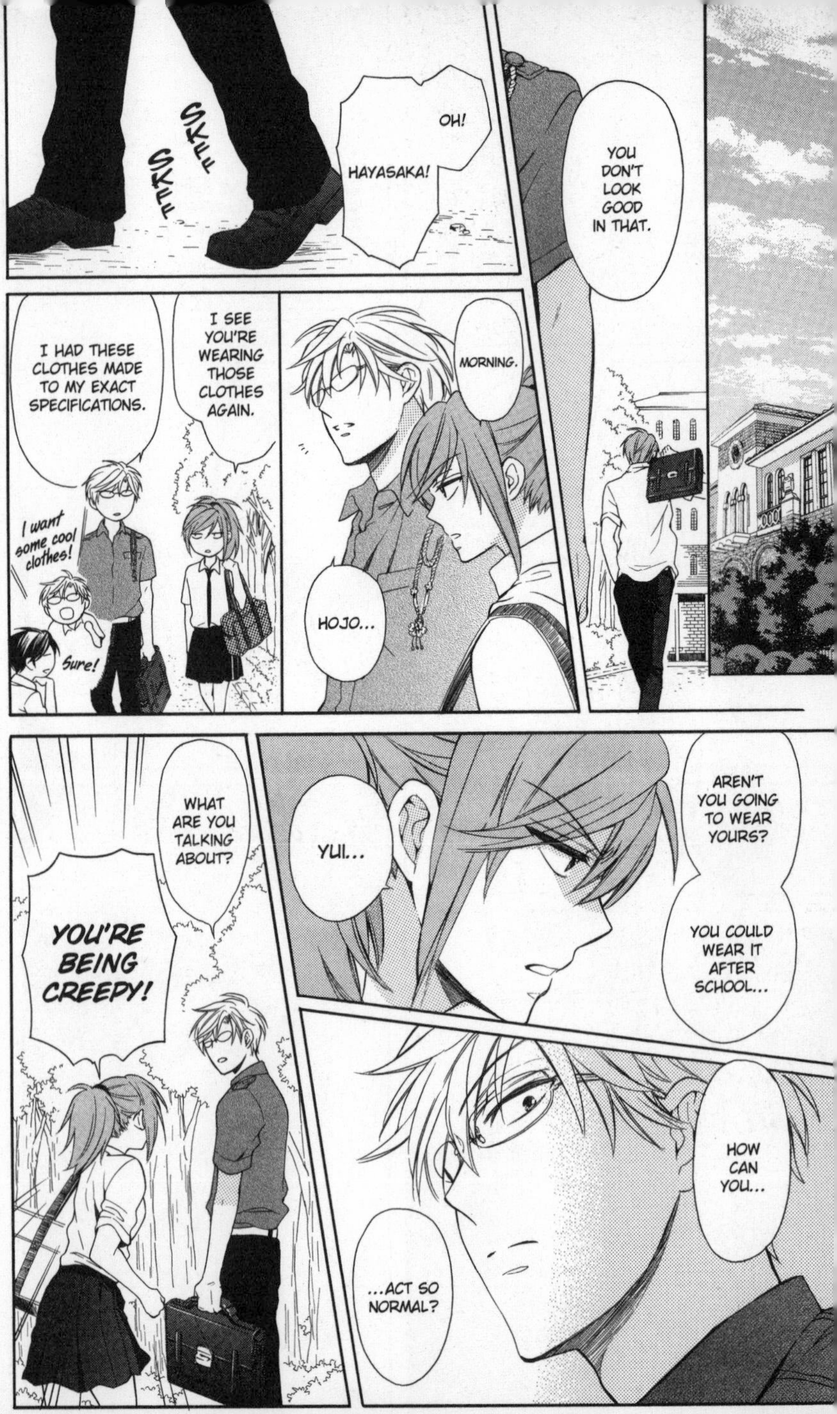
YOU DON'T LOOK GOOD IN THAT.
OH!
HAYASAKA!
SKFF
SKFF
MORNING.
HOJO...
I SEE YOU'RE WEARING THOSE CLOTHES AGAIN.
I HAD THESE CLOTHES MADE TO MY EXACT SPECIFICATIONS.
I want some cool clothes!
Sure!
AREN'T YOU GOING TO WEAR YOURS?
YOU COULD WEAR IT AFTER SCHOOL...
YUI...
HOW CAN YOU...
...ACT SO NORMAL?
WHAT ARE YOU TALKING ABOUT?
YOU'RE BEING CREEPY!

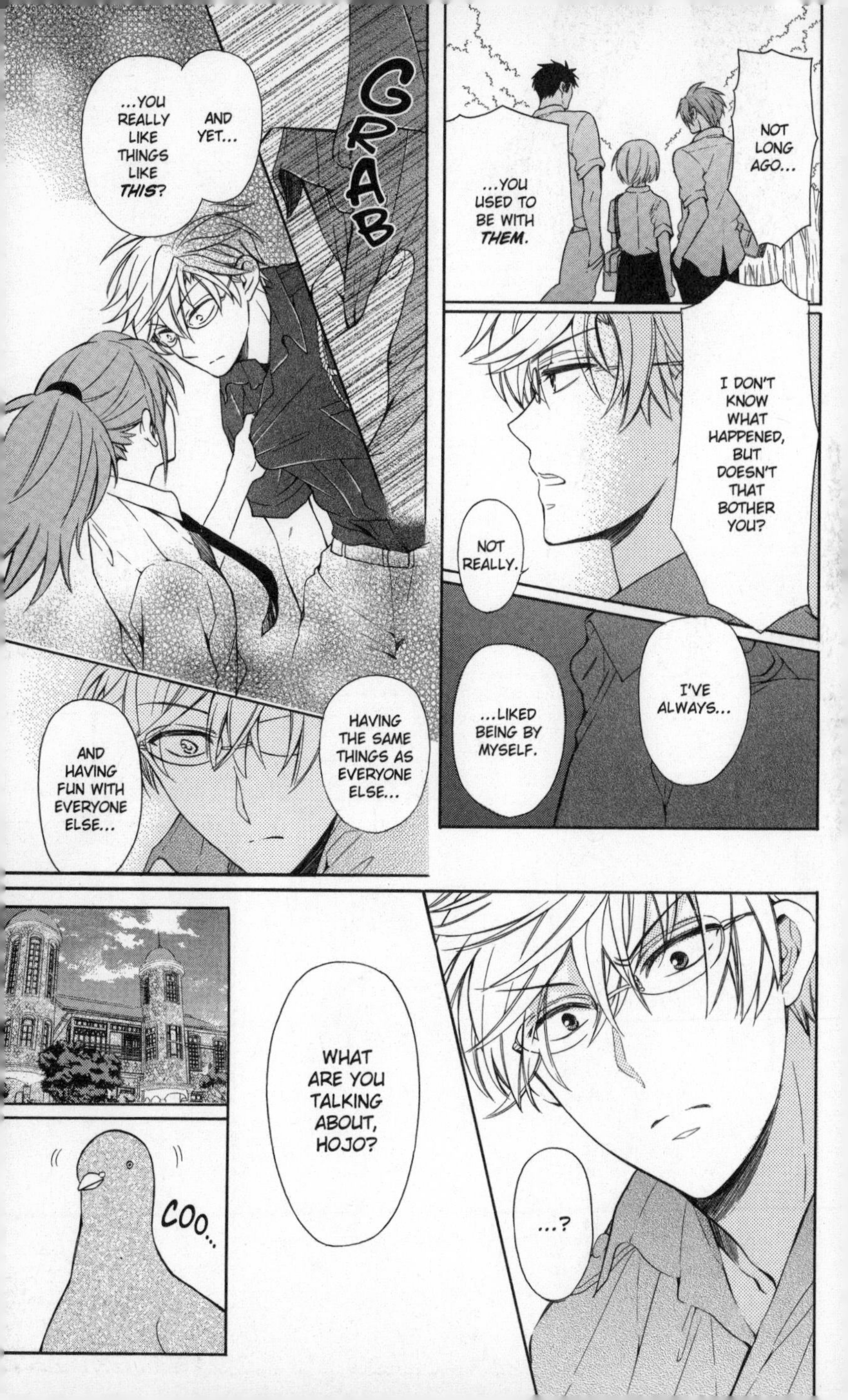
NOT LONG AGO...
...YOU USED TO BE WITH THEM.
I DON'T KNOW WHAT HAPPENED, BUT DOESN'T THAT BOTHER YOU?
NOT REALLY.
I'VE ALWAYS...
...LIKED BEING BY MYSELF.
GRAB
AND YET...
...YOU REALLY LIKE THINGS LIKE THIS?
HAVING THE SAME THINGS AS EVERYONE ELSE...
AND HAVING FUN WITH EVERYONE ELSE...
WHAT ARE YOU TALKING ABOUT, HOJO?
...?
COO...

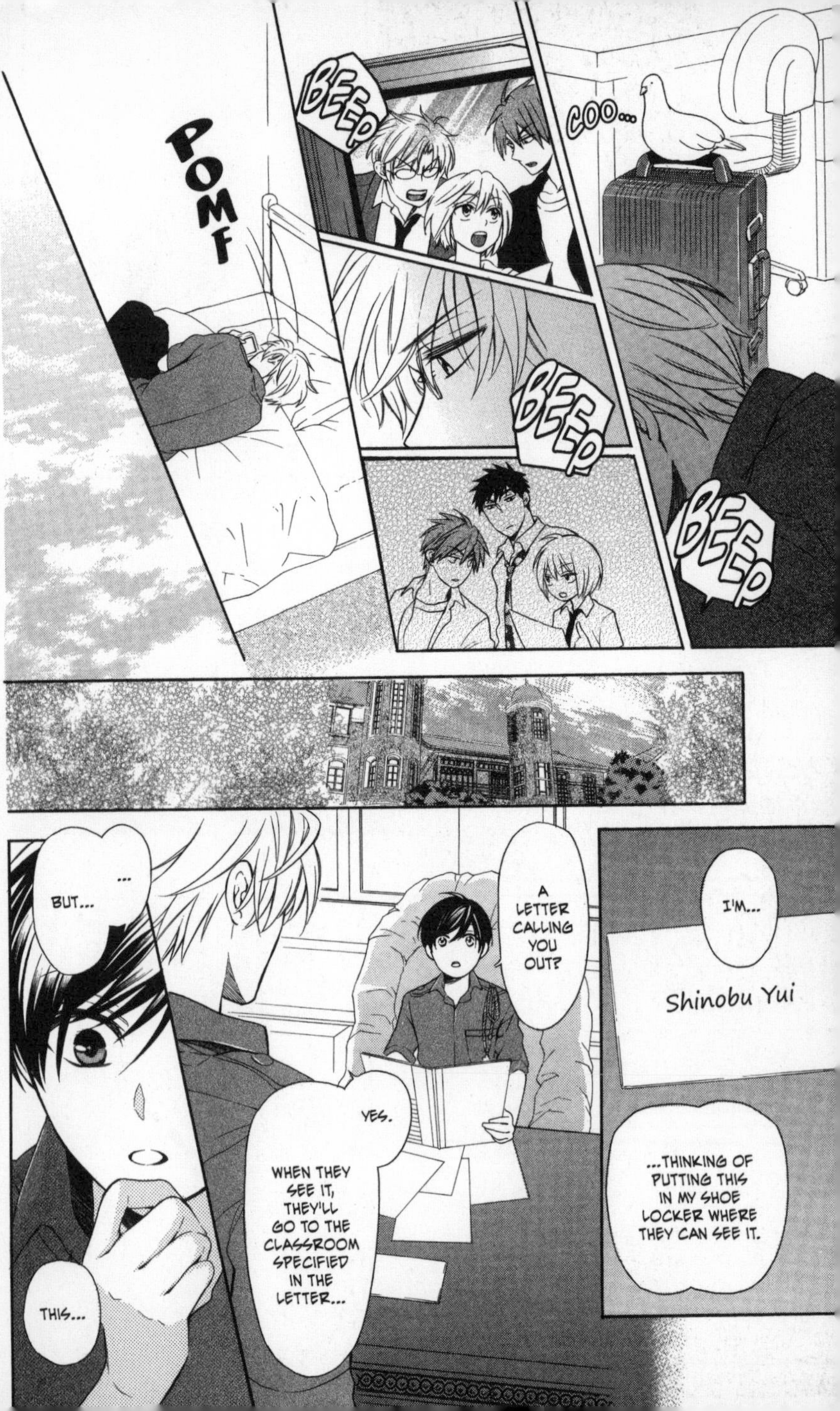
COO...
BEEP
BEEP
BEEP
POMF
I'M...
Shinobu Yui
...THINKING OF PUTTING THIS IN MY SHOE LOCKER WHERE THEY CAN SEE IT.
A LETTER CALLING YOU OUT?
YES.
WHEN THEY SEE IT, THEY'LL GO TO THE CLASSROOM SPECIFIED IN THE LETTER...
... BUT...
THIS...

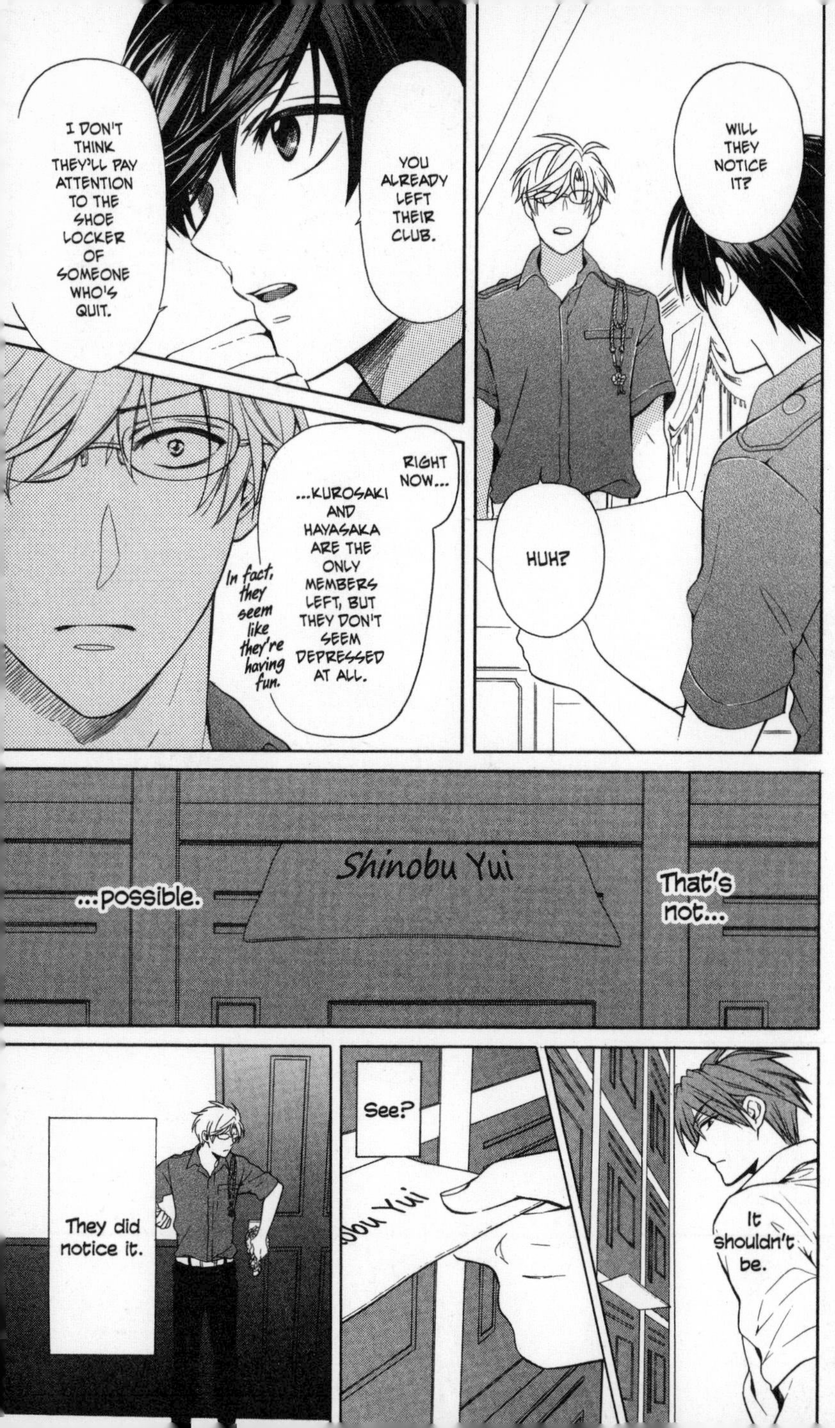
WILL THEY NOTICE IT?
HUH?
YOU ALREADY LEFT THEIR CLUB.
I DON'T THINK THEY'LL PAY ATTENTION TO THE SHOE LOCKER OF SOMEONE WHO'S QUIT.
RIGHT NOW...
...KUROSAKI AND HAYASAKA ARE THE ONLY MEMBERS LEFT, BUT THEY DON'T SEEM DEPRESSED AT ALL.
In fact, they seem like they're having fun.
That's not...
Shinobu Yui
...possible.
It shouldn't be.
See?
They did notice it.

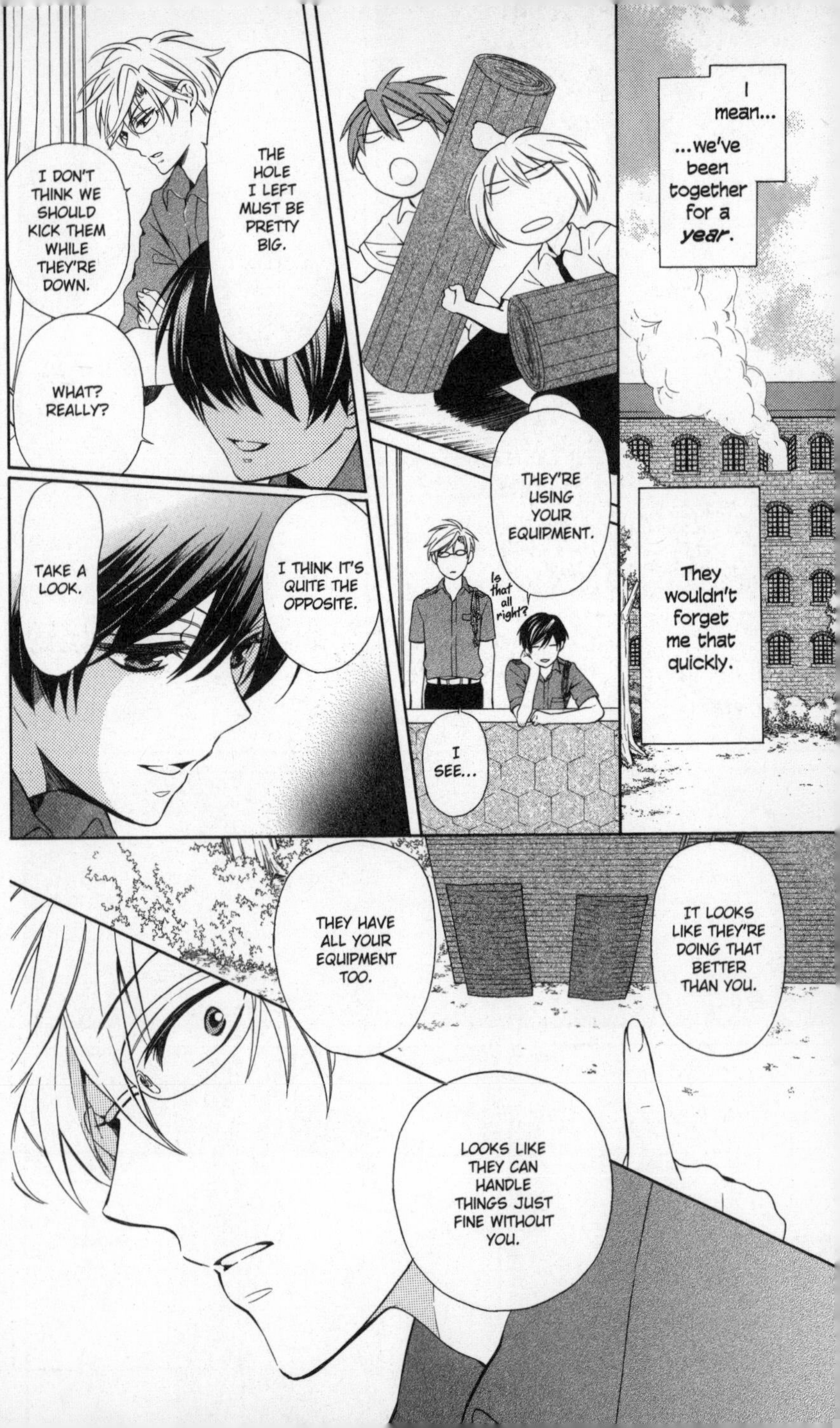

I mean...
...we've been together for a *year*.
They wouldn't forget me that quickly.
THEY'RE USING YOUR EQUIPMENT.
Is that all right?
I SEE...
THE HOLE I LEFT MUST BE PRETTY BIG.
I DON'T THINK WE SHOULD KICK THEM WHILE THEY'RE DOWN.
WHAT? REALLY?
I THINK IT'S QUITE THE OPPOSITE.
TAKE A LOOK.
IT LOOKS LIKE THEY'RE DOING THAT BETTER THAN YOU.
THEY HAVE ALL YOUR EQUIPMENT TOO.
LOOKS LIKE THEY CAN HANDLE THINGS JUST FINE WITHOUT YOU.

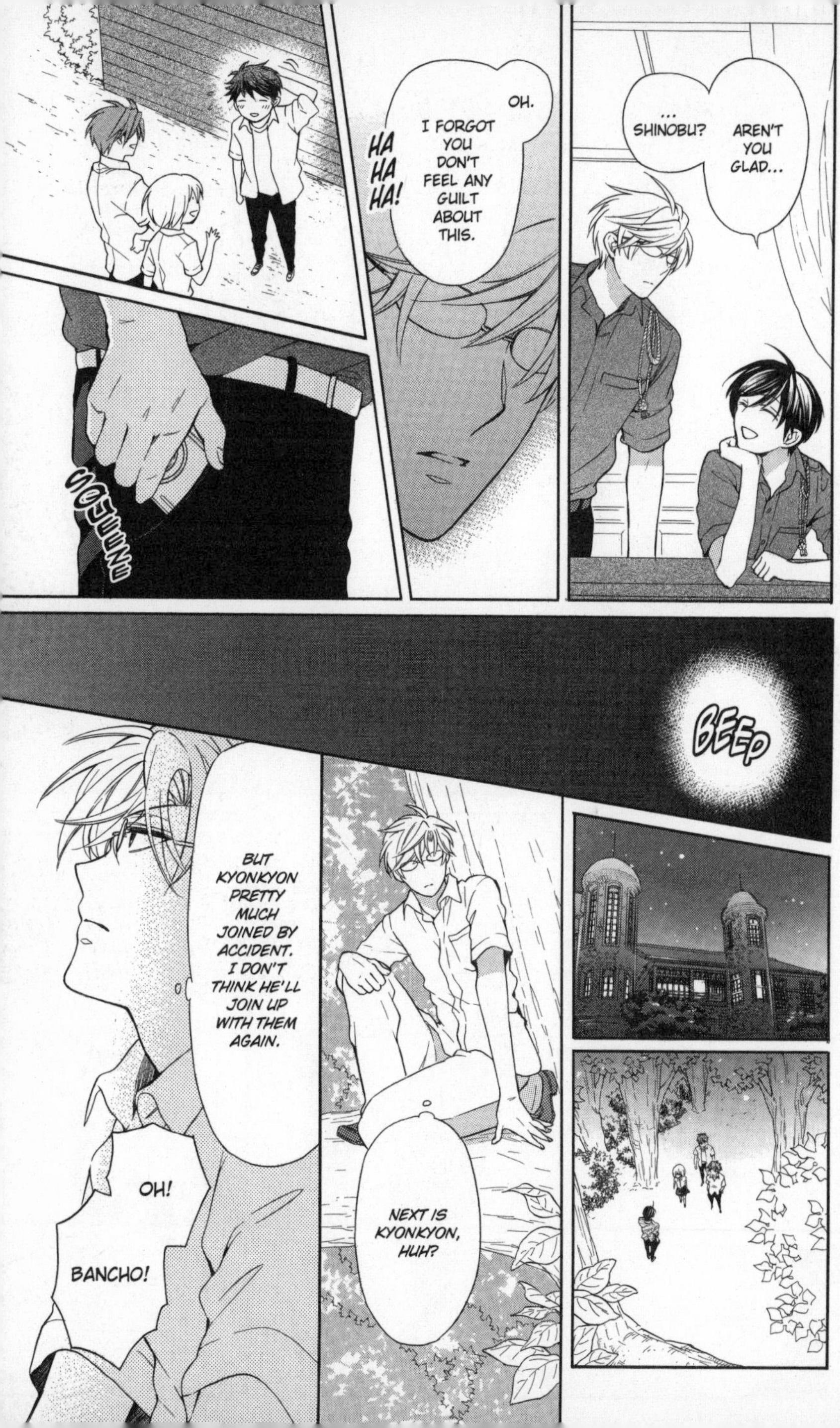
AREN'T YOU GLAD...
...SHINOBU?
OH. I FORGOT YOU DON'T FEEL ANY GUILT ABOUT THIS.
HA HA HA!
SQUEEEZE
BEEP
NEXT IS KYONKYON, HUH?
BUT KYONKYON PRETTY MUCH JOINED BY ACCIDENT. I DON'T THINK HE'LL JOIN UP WITH THEM AGAIN.
OH!
BANCHO!

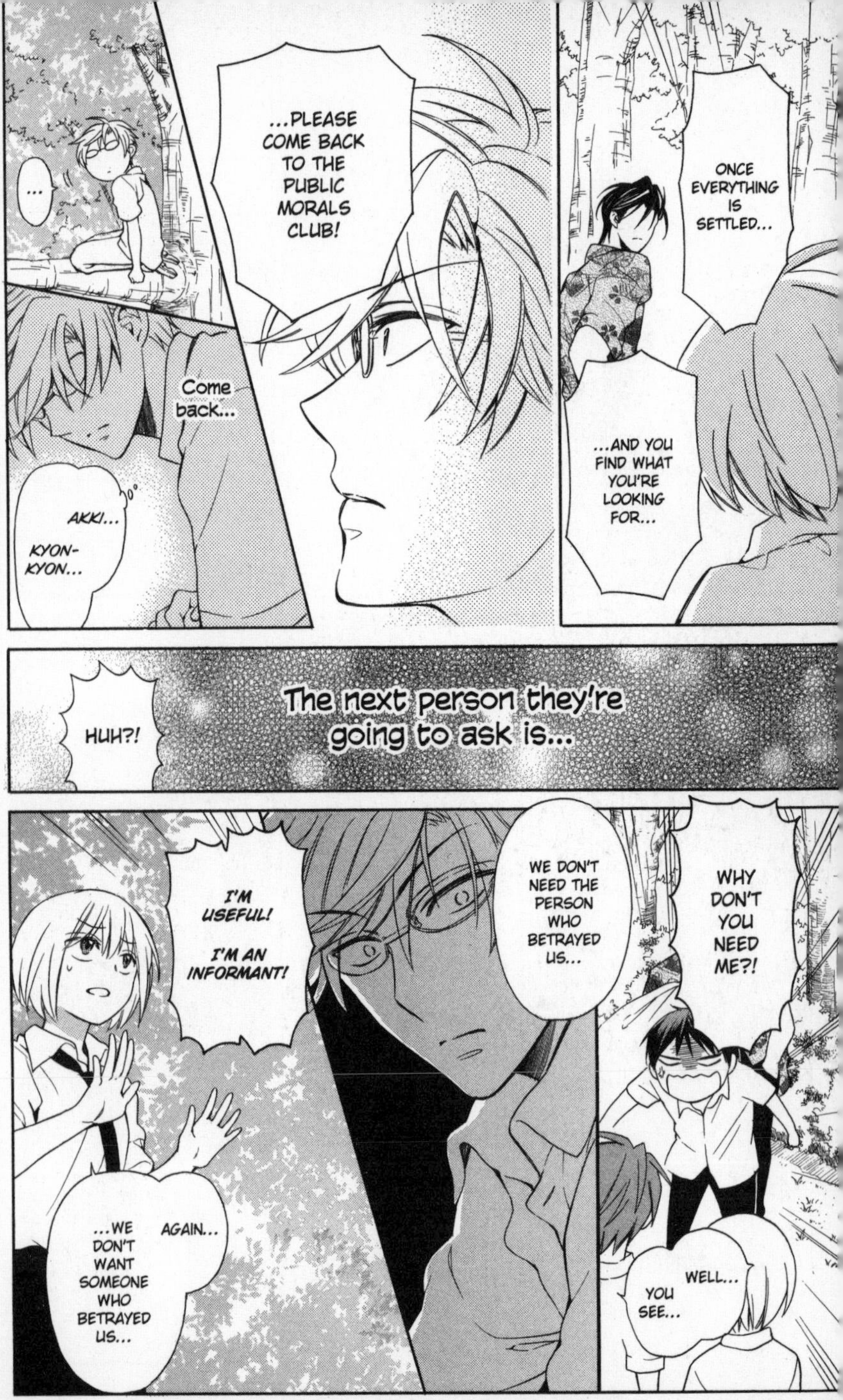
ONCE EVERYTHING IS SETTLED...
...AND YOU FIND WHAT YOU'RE LOOKING FOR...
...PLEASE COME BACK TO THE PUBLIC MORALS CLUB!
...
Come back...
AKKI... KYON-KYON...
The next person they're going to ask is...
HUH?!
WHY DON'T YOU NEED ME?!
WELL... YOU SEE...
WE DON'T NEED THE PERSON WHO BETRAYED US...
I'M USEFUL! I'M AN INFORMANT!
...WE DON'T WANT SOMEONE WHO BETRAYED US... AGAIN...

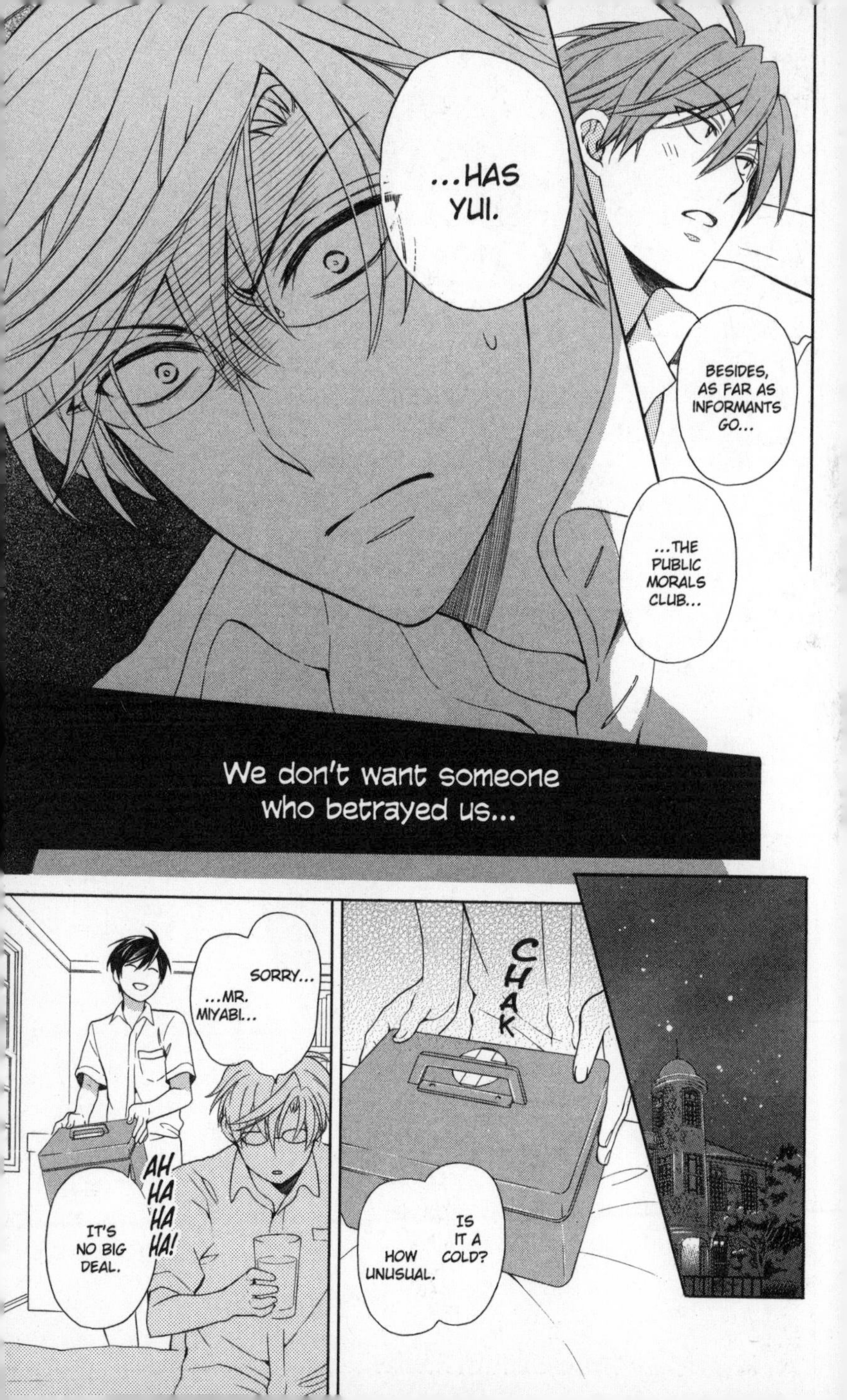
BESIDES, AS FAR AS INFORMANTS GO...
...THE PUBLIC MORALS CLUB...
...HAS YUI.
We don't want someone who betrayed us...
CHAK
IS IT A COLD?
HOW UNUSUAL.
SORRY...
...MR. MIYABI...
AH HA HA HA!
IT'S NO BIG DEAL.

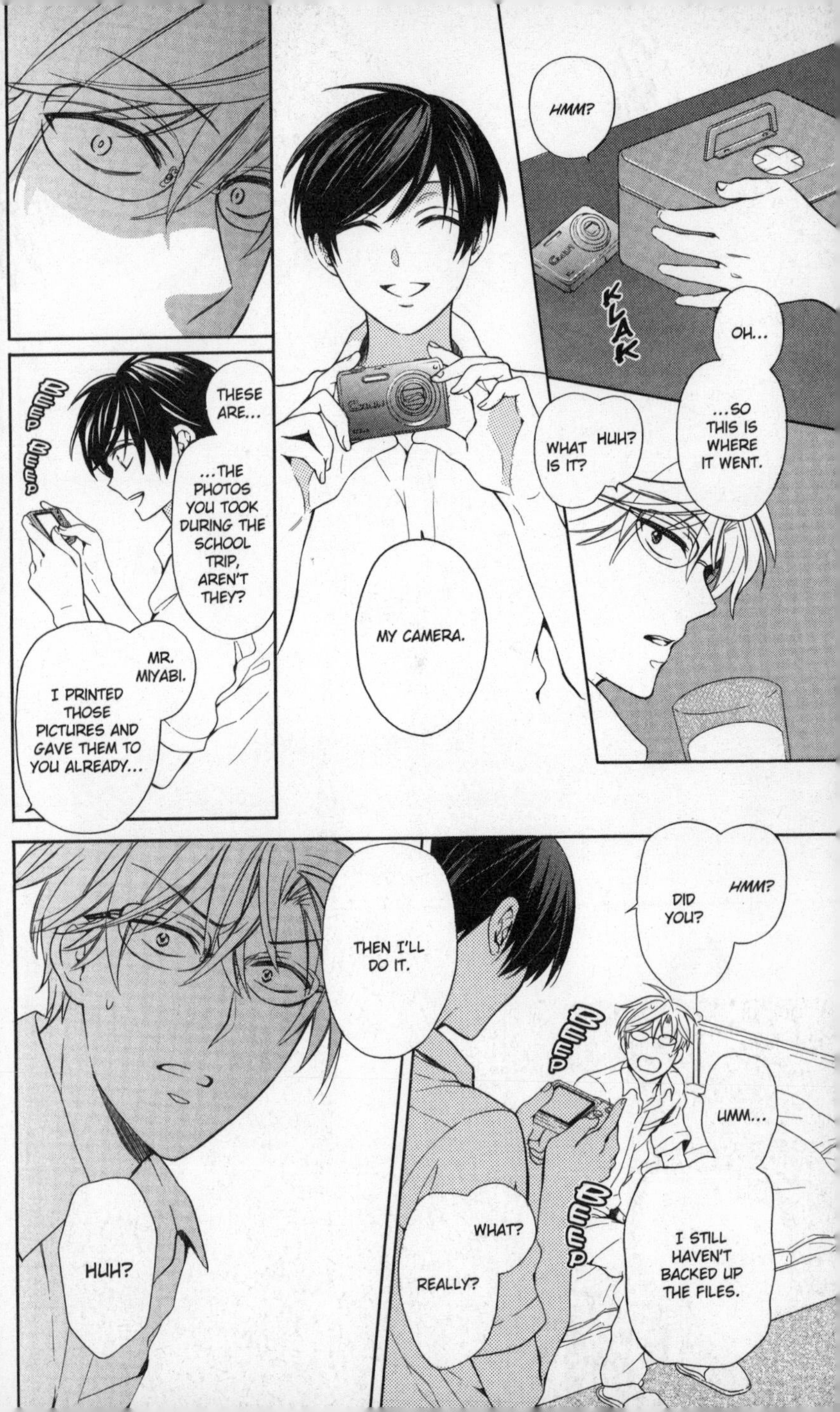
HMM?
KLAK
OH...
...SO THIS IS WHERE IT WENT.
HUH? WHAT IS IT?
MY CAMERA.
THESE ARE...
...THE PHOTOS YOU TOOK DURING THE SCHOOL TRIP, AREN'T THEY?
MR. MIYABI. I PRINTED THOSE PICTURES AND GAVE THEM TO YOU ALREADY...
HMM? DID YOU?
UMM...
I STILL HAVEN'T BACKED UP THE FILES.
WHAT? REALLY?
THEN I'LL DO IT.
HUH?

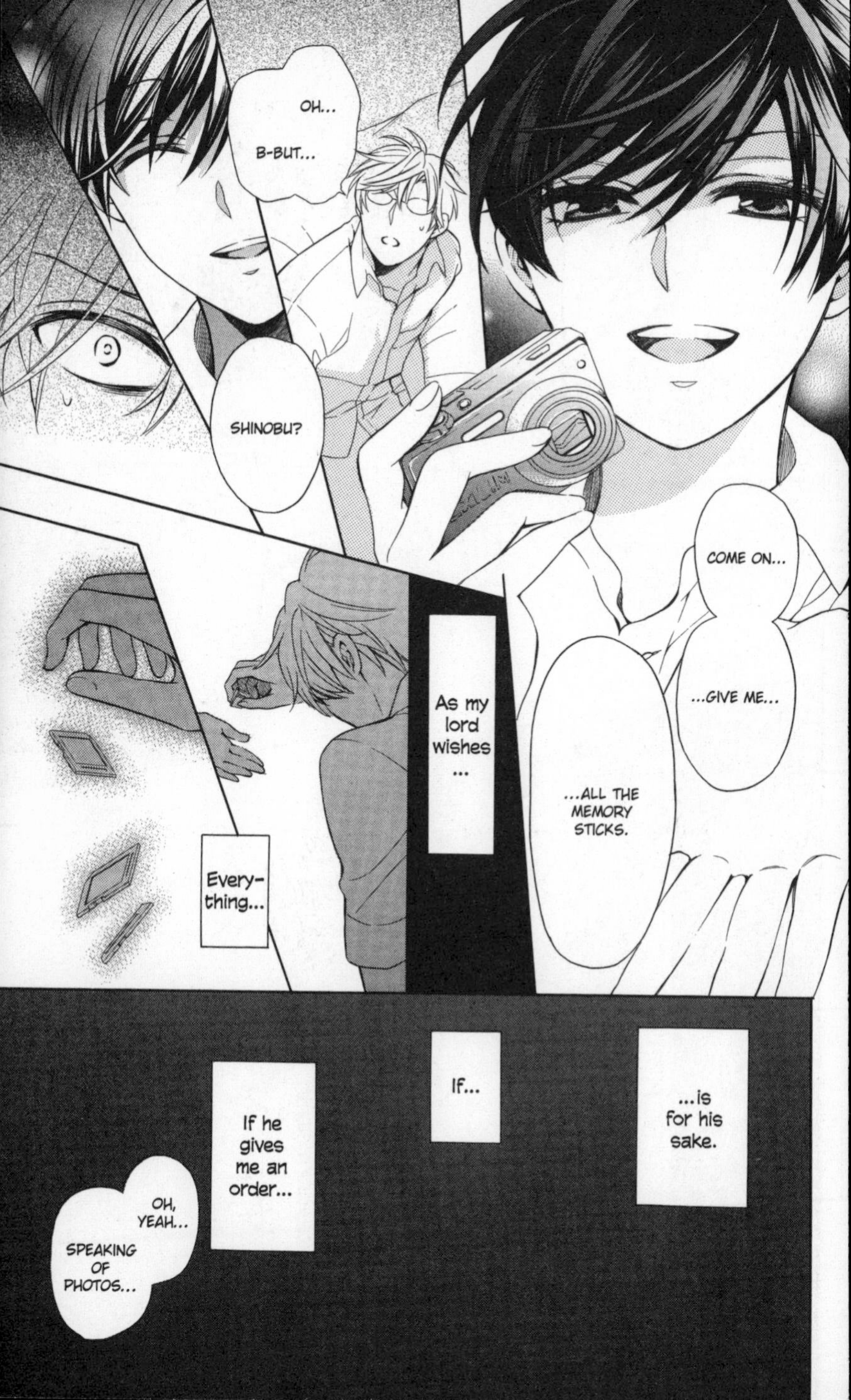
COME ON...
...GIVE ME...
...ALL THE MEMORY STICKS.
OH...
B-BUT...
SHINOBU?
As my lord wishes...
Every-thing...
...is for his sake.
If...
If he gives me an order...
OH, YEAH...
SPEAKING OF PHOTOS...

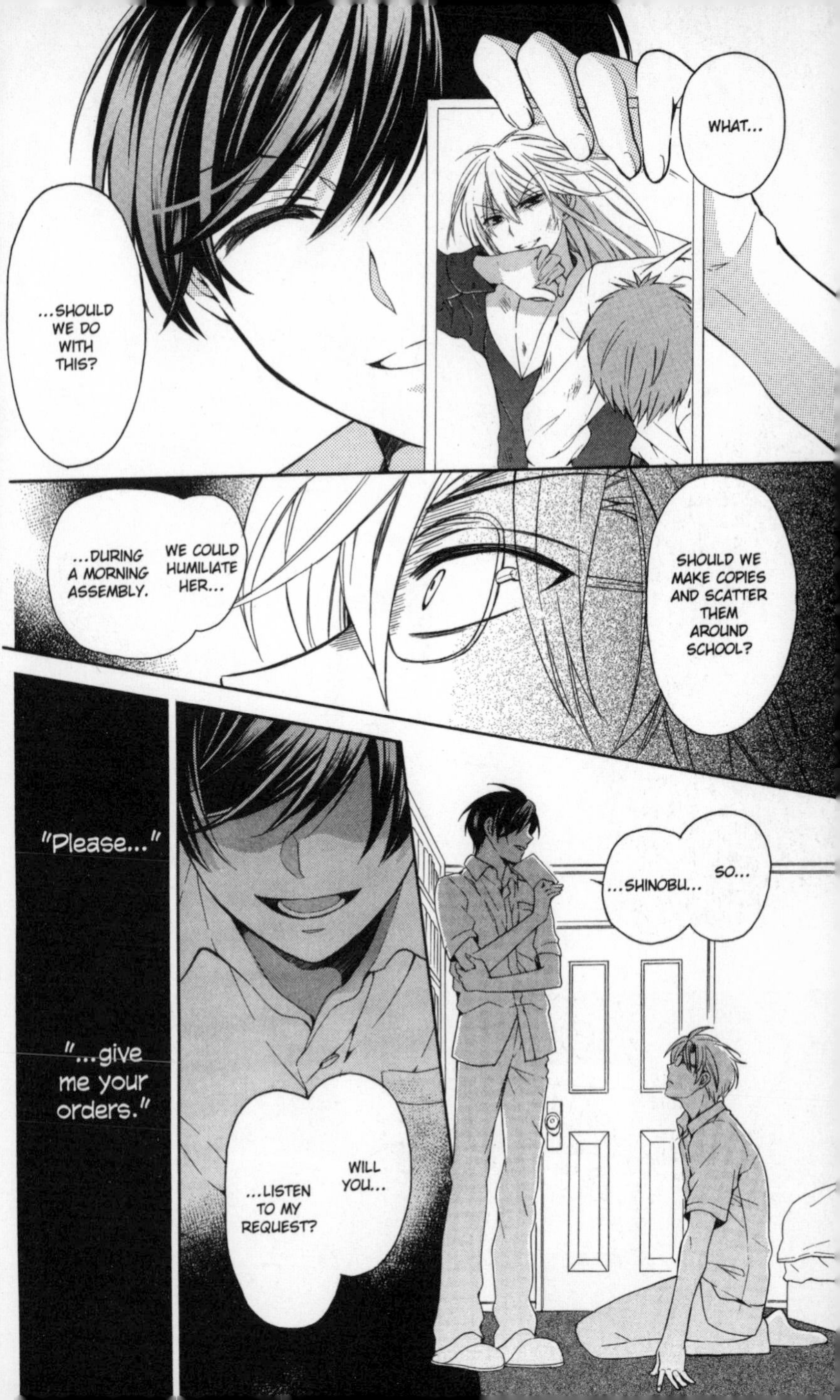
WHAT...
...SHOULD WE DO WITH THIS?
SHOULD WE MAKE COPIES AND SCATTER THEM AROUND SCHOOL?
WE COULD HUMILIATE HER...
...DURING A MORNING ASSEMBLY.
SO...
...SHINOBU...
WILL YOU...
...LISTEN TO MY REQUEST?
"Please..."
"...give me your orders."

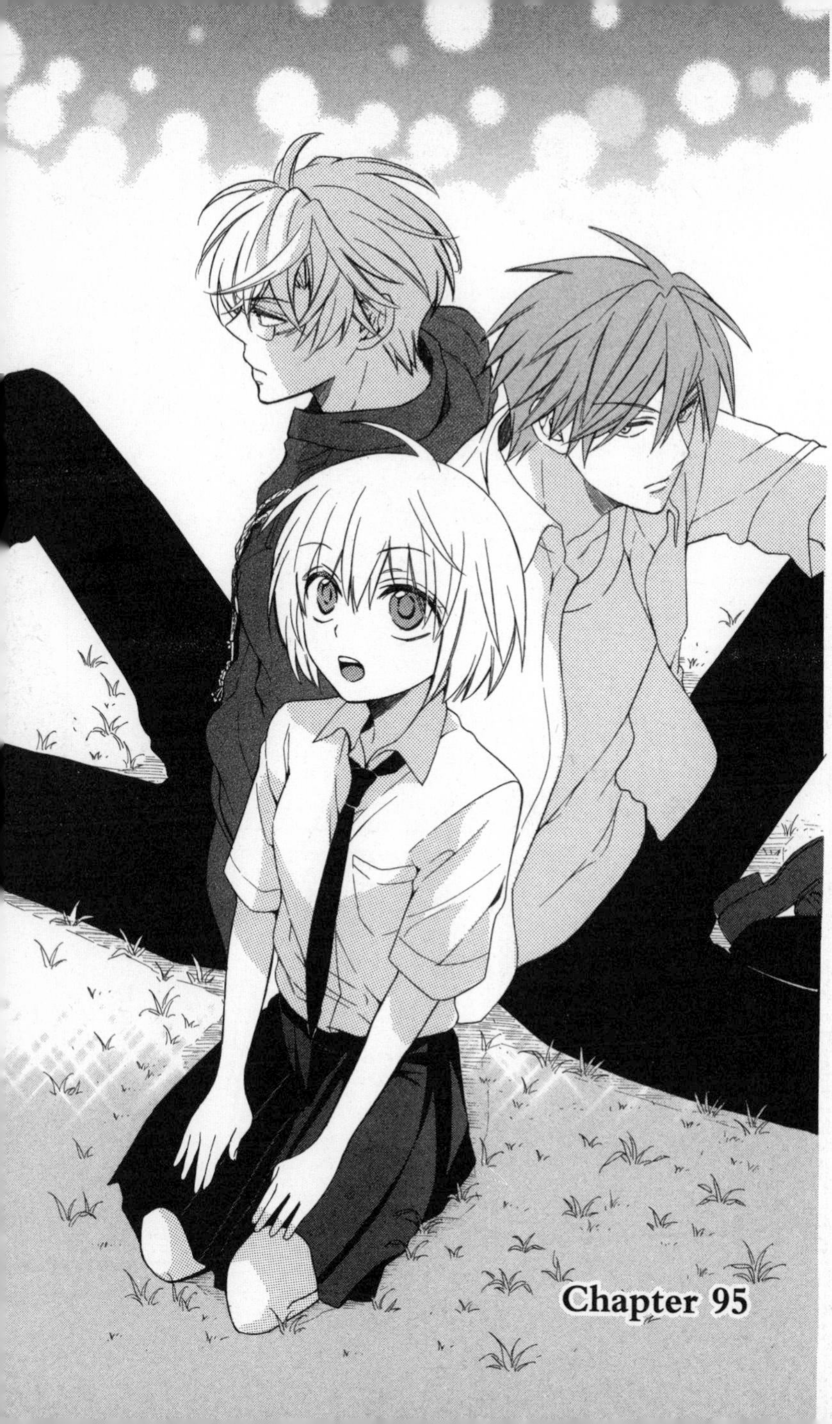

Chapter 95

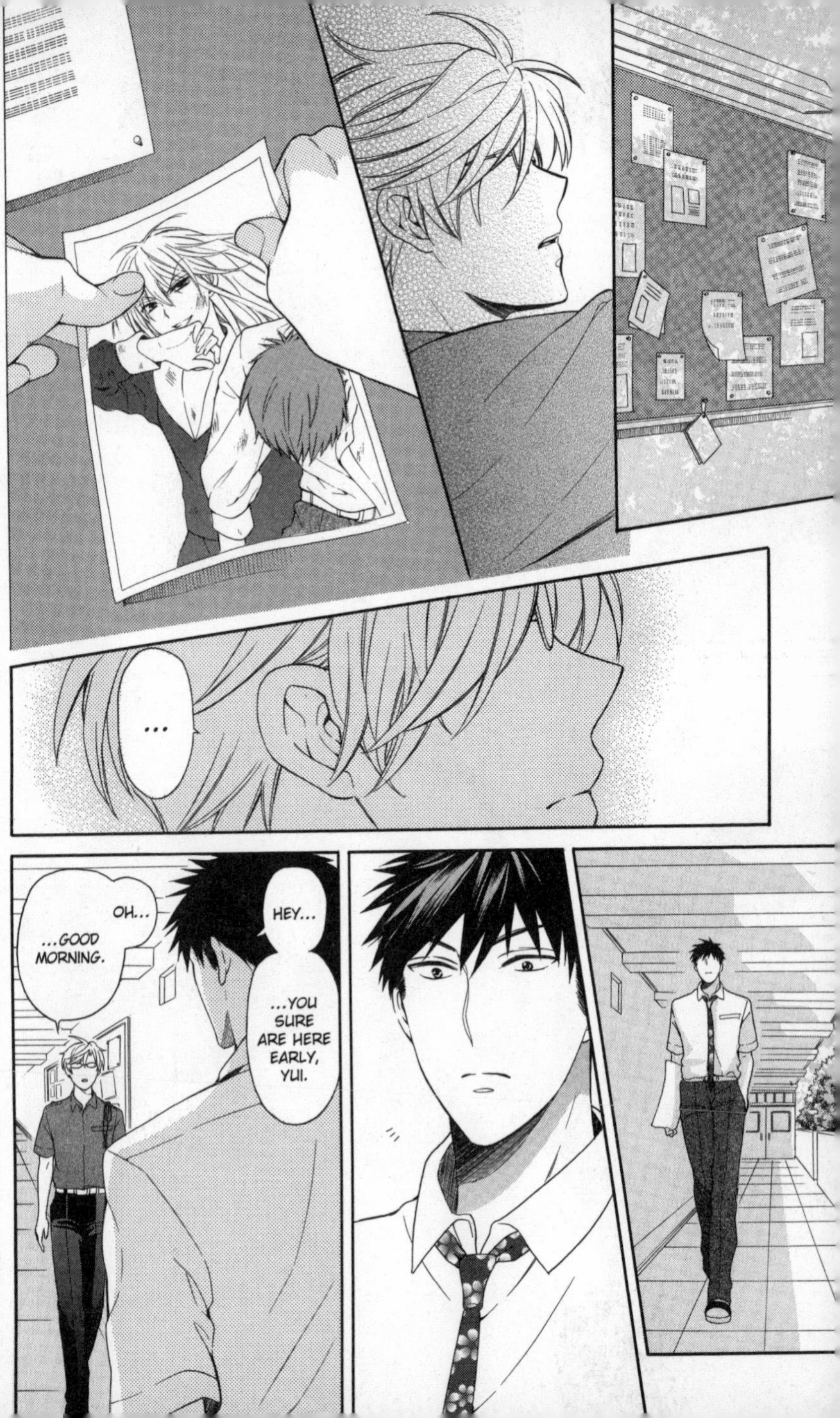
...
HEY...
...YOU SURE ARE HERE EARLY, YUI.
OH...
...GOOD MORNING.

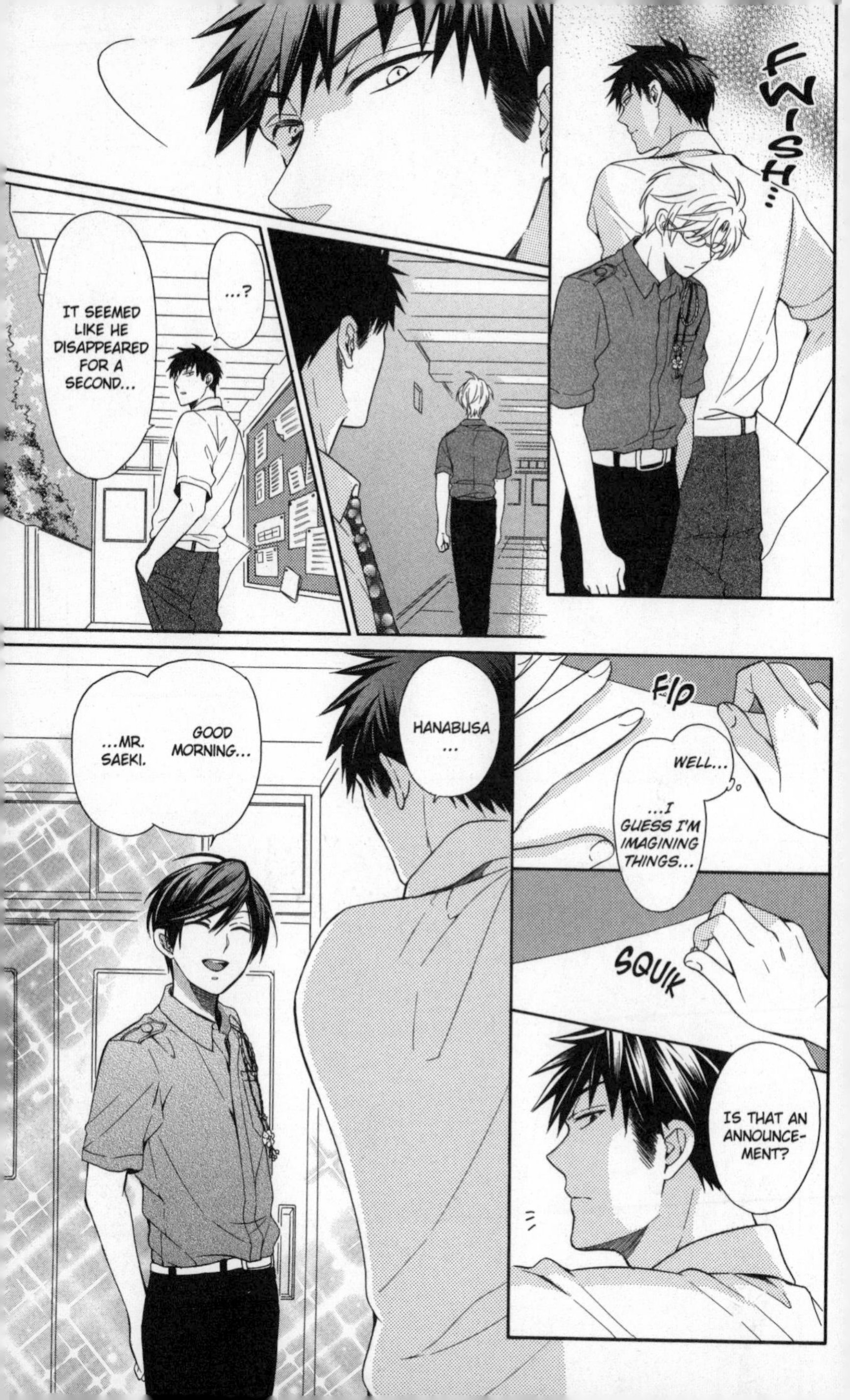
FWISH...
...?
IT SEEMED LIKE HE DISAPPEARED FOR A SECOND...
Flip
WELL...
...I GUESS I'M IMAGINING THINGS...
SQUIK
IS THAT AN ANNOUNCEMENT?
HANABUSA...
GOOD MORNING...
...MR. SAEKI.

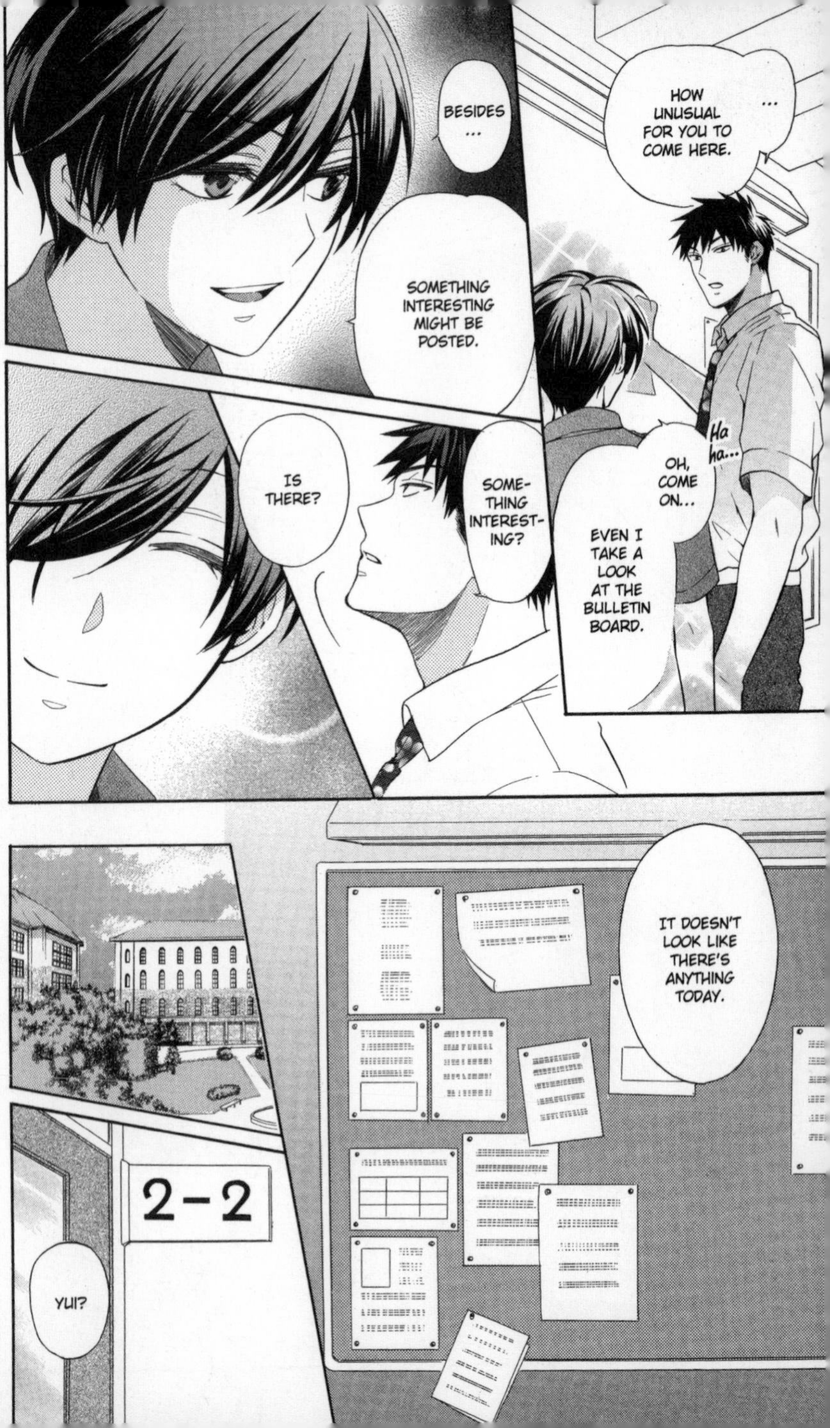

HOW UNUSUAL FOR YOU TO COME HERE.
...
Ha ha...
OH, COME ON...
EVEN I TAKE A LOOK AT THE BULLETIN BOARD.
BESIDES...
SOMETHING INTERESTING MIGHT BE POSTED.
SOME-THING INTEREST-ING?
IS THERE?
IT DOESN'T LOOK LIKE THERE'S ANYTHING TODAY.
2-2
YUI?

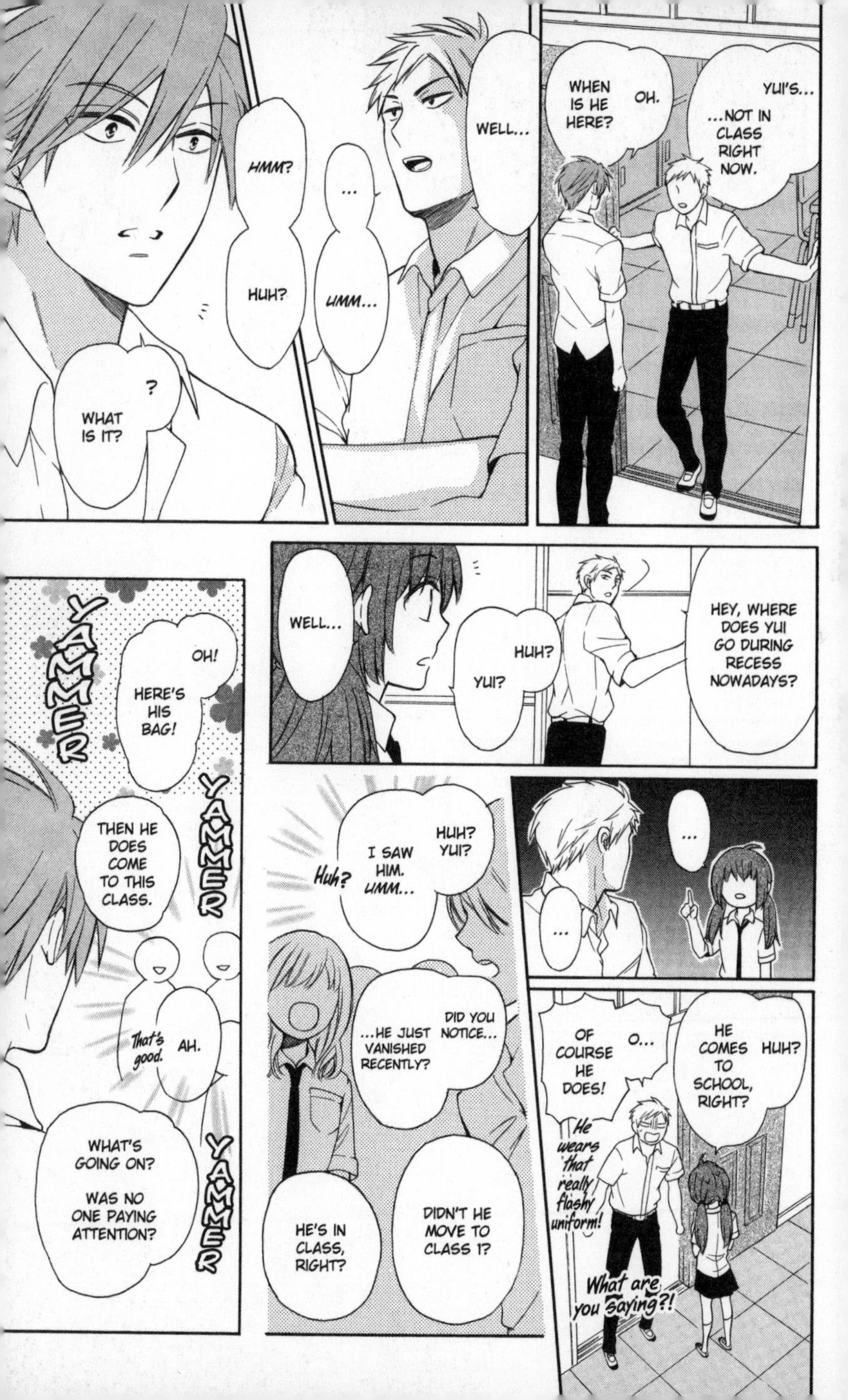
YUI'S... ...NOT IN CLASS RIGHT NOW.
OH.
WHEN IS HE HERE?
WELL...
...
UMM...
HMM?
HUH?
?
WHAT IS IT?
HEY, WHERE DOES YUI GO DURING RECESS NOWADAYS?
HUH?
YUI?
WELL...
...
...
HE COMES TO SCHOOL, RIGHT?
HUH?
O...
OF COURSE HE DOES!
He wears that really flashy uniform!
What are you saying?!
HUH? YUI?
I SAW HIM. UMM...
Huh?
DID YOU NOTICE...
...HE JUST VANISHED RECENTLY?
DIDN'T HE MOVE TO CLASS 1?
HE'S IN CLASS, RIGHT?
YAMMER
OH!
HERE'S HIS BAG!
YAMMER
THEN HE DOES COME TO THIS CLASS.
AH.
That's good.
YAMMER
WHAT'S GOING ON?
WAS NO ONE PAYING ATTENTION?

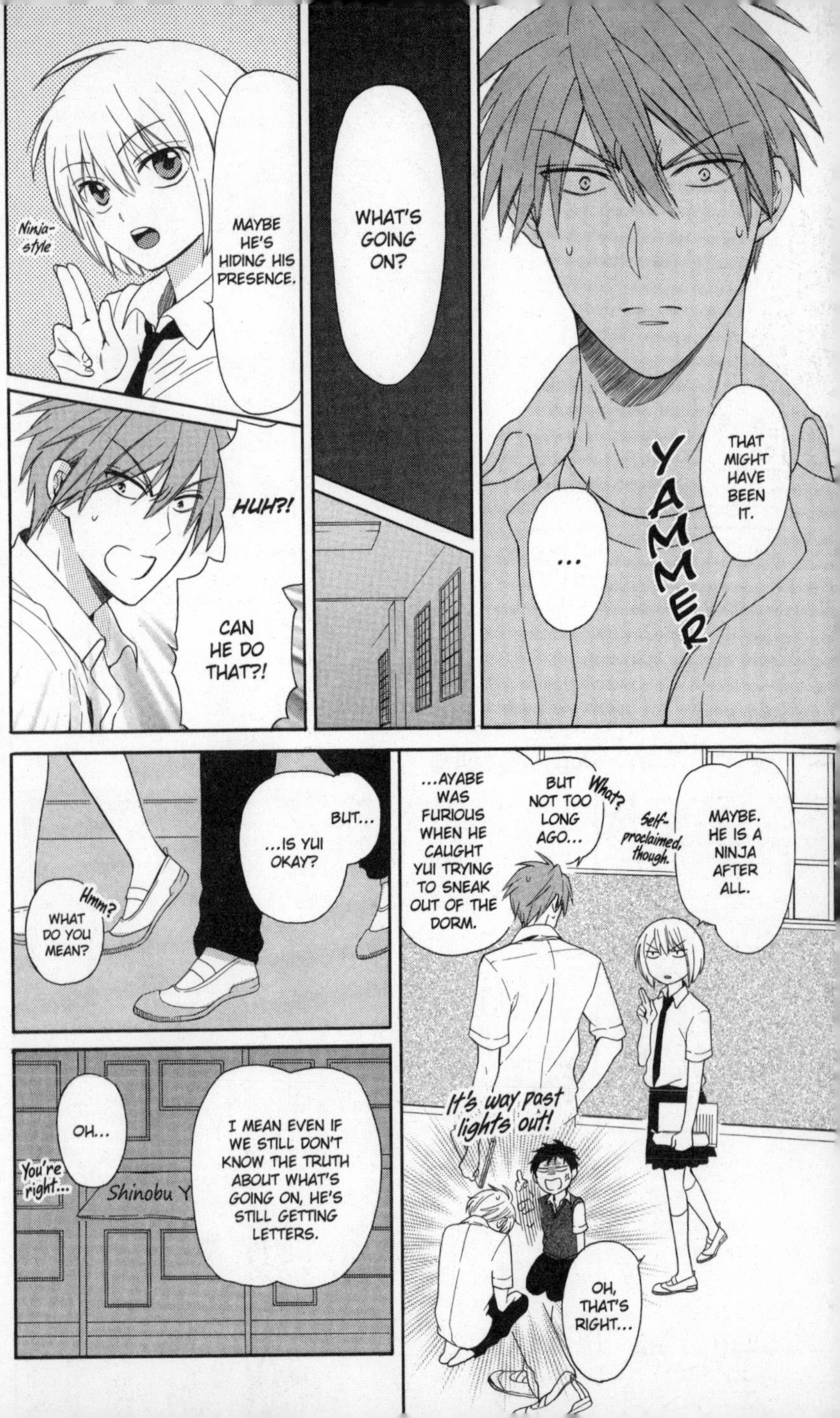
THAT MIGHT HAVE BEEN IT.
YAMMER
...
WHAT'S GOING ON?
Ninja-style
MAYBE HE'S HIDING HIS PRESENCE.
HUH?!
CAN HE DO THAT?!
MAYBE. HE IS A NINJA AFTER ALL.
Self-proclaimed, though.
What?
BUT NOT TOO LONG AGO...
...AYABE WAS FURIOUS WHEN HE CAUGHT YUI TRYING TO SNEAK OUT OF THE DORM.
It's way past lights out!
OH, THAT'S RIGHT...
BUT...
...IS YUI OKAY?
Hmm?
WHAT DO YOU MEAN?
I MEAN EVEN IF WE STILL DON'T KNOW THE TRUTH ABOUT WHAT'S GOING ON, HE'S STILL GETTING LETTERS.
Shinobu Y
OH...
You're right...

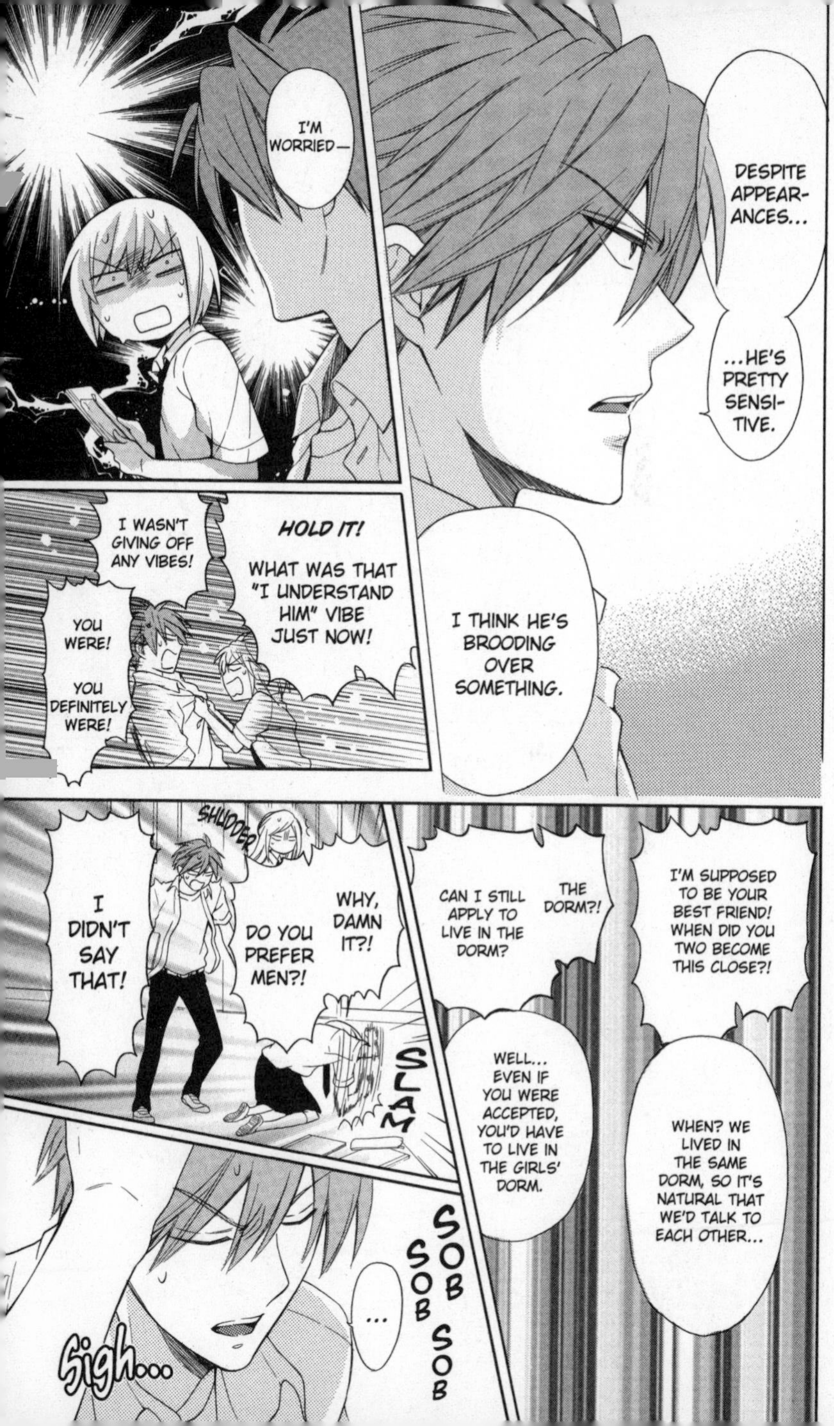
DESPITE APPEARANCES...
...HE'S PRETTY SENSITIVE.
I'M WORRIED—
I THINK HE'S BROODING OVER SOMETHING.
HOLD IT!
WHAT WAS THAT "I UNDERSTAND HIM" VIBE JUST NOW!
I WASN'T GIVING OFF ANY VIBES!
YOU WERE!
YOU DEFINITELY WERE!
I'M SUPPOSED TO BE YOUR BEST FRIEND! WHEN DID YOU TWO BECOME THIS CLOSE?!
WHEN? WE LIVED IN THE SAME DORM, SO IT'S NATURAL THAT WE'D TALK TO EACH OTHER...
CAN I STILL APPLY TO LIVE IN THE DORM?
THE DORM?!
WELL... EVEN IF YOU WERE ACCEPTED, YOU'D HAVE TO LIVE IN THE GIRLS' DORM.
SHUDDER
WHY, DAMN IT?!
DO YOU PREFER MEN?!
I DIDN'T SAY THAT!
SLAM
SOB SOB
SOB SOB
...
Sigh...

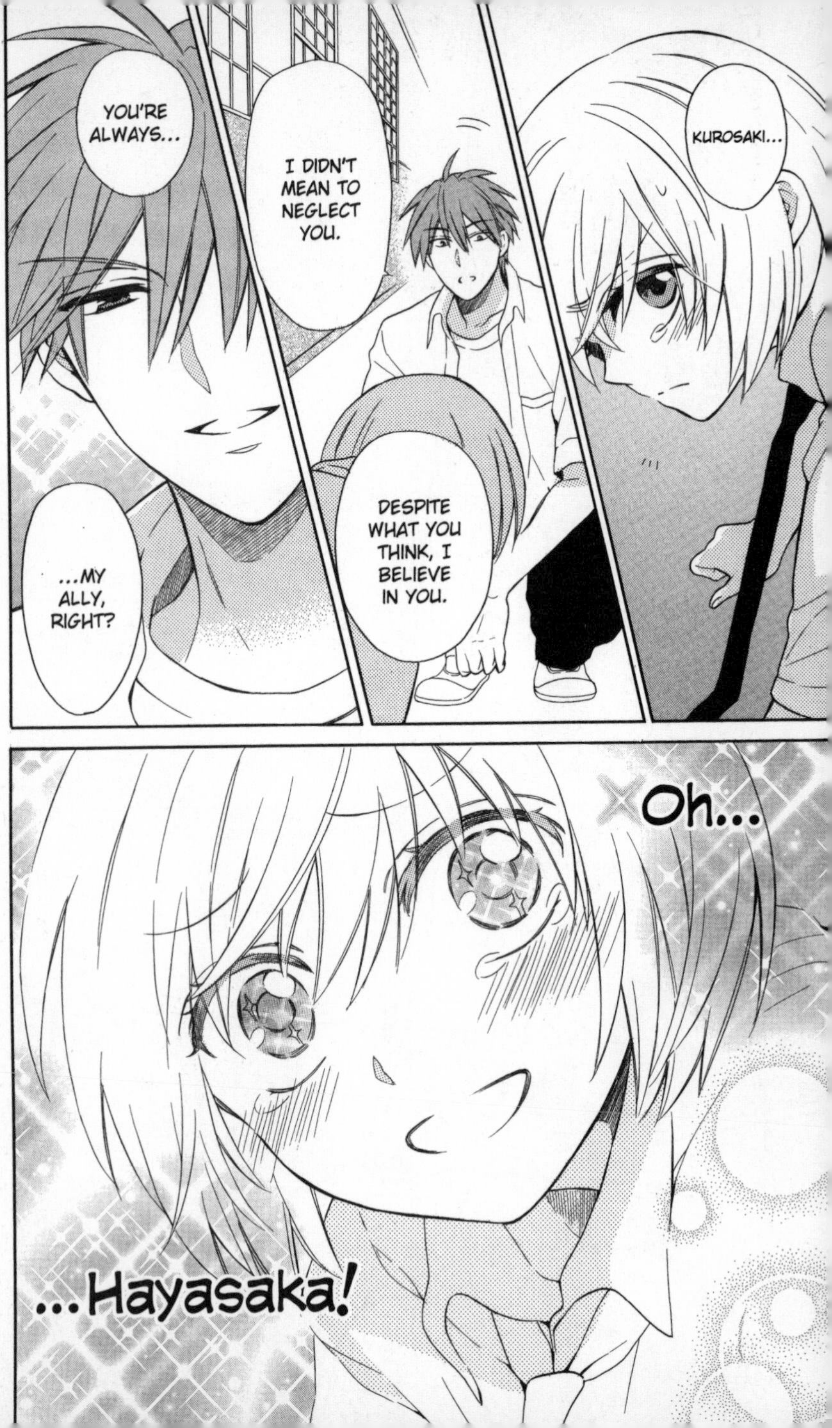
KUROSAKI...
I DIDN'T MEAN TO NEGLECT YOU.
DESPITE WHAT YOU THINK, I BELIEVE IN YOU.
YOU'RE ALWAYS...
...MY ALLY, RIGHT?
Oh...
...Hayasaka!

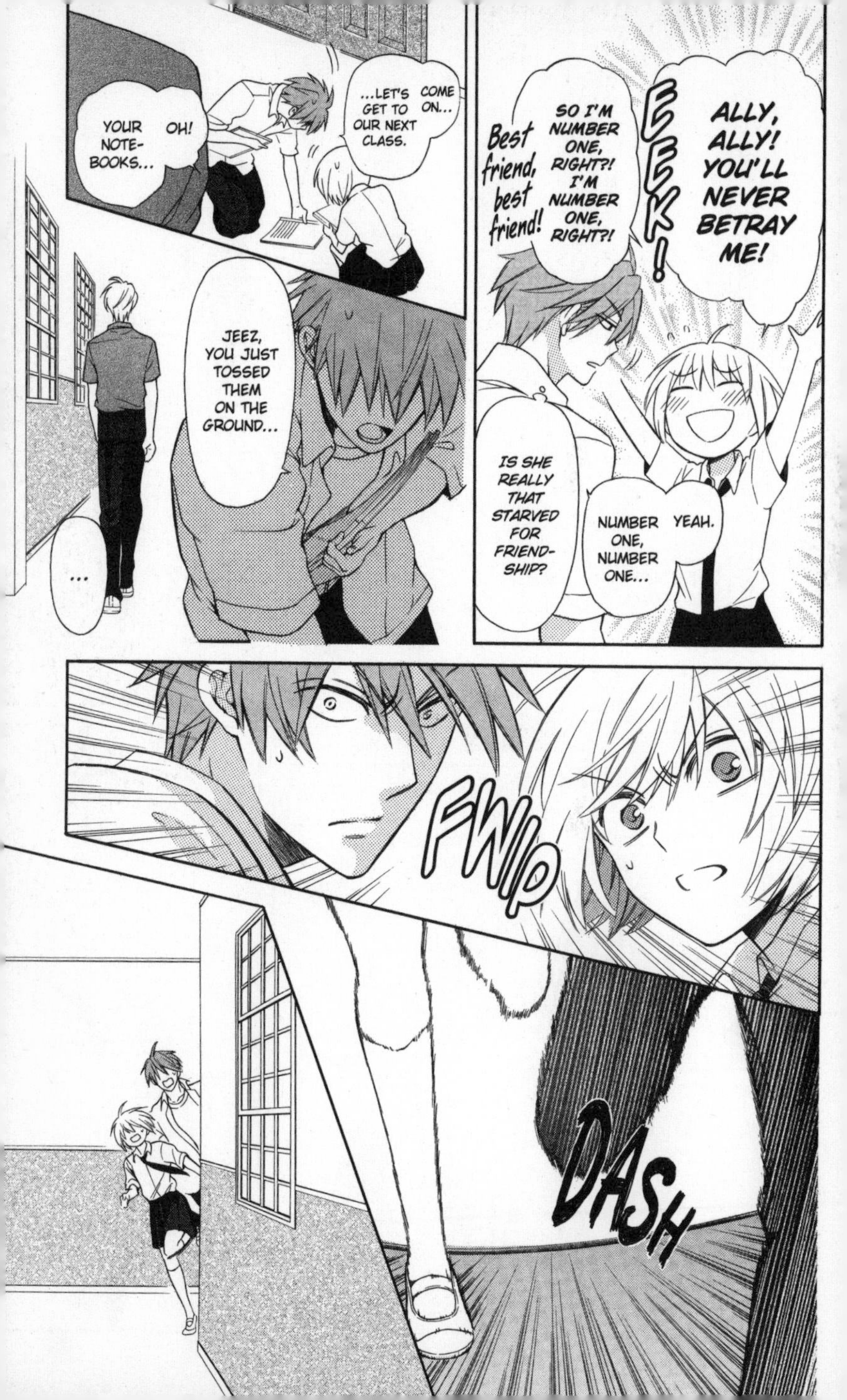
ALLY, ALLY! YOU'LL NEVER BETRAY ME!
EEEK!
SO I'M NUMBER ONE, RIGHT?! I'M NUMBER ONE, RIGHT?!
Best friend, best friend!
YEAH.
NUMBER ONE, NUMBER ONE...
IS SHE REALLY THAT STARVED FOR FRIEND-SHIP?
COME ON... ...LET'S GET TO OUR NEXT CLASS.
OH! YOUR NOTE-BOOKS...
JEEZ, YOU JUST TOSSED THEM ON THE GROUND...
...
FWIP
DASH

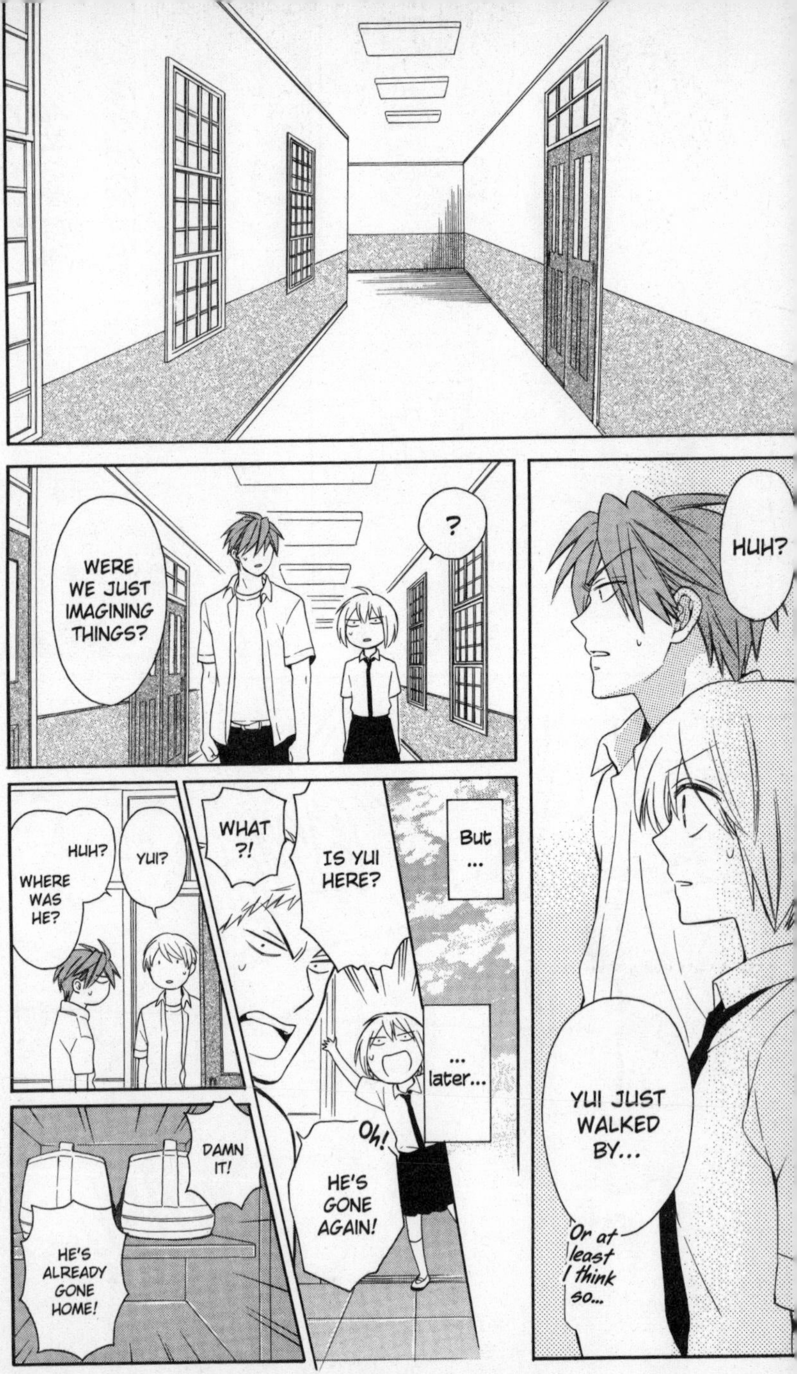
HUH?
YUI JUST WALKED BY...
Or at least I think so...
?
WERE WE JUST IMAGINING THINGS?
But ...
... later...
WHAT ?!
IS YUI HERE?
Oh!
HE'S GONE AGAIN!
YUI?
HUH? WHERE WAS HE?
DAMN IT!
HE'S ALREADY GONE HOME!

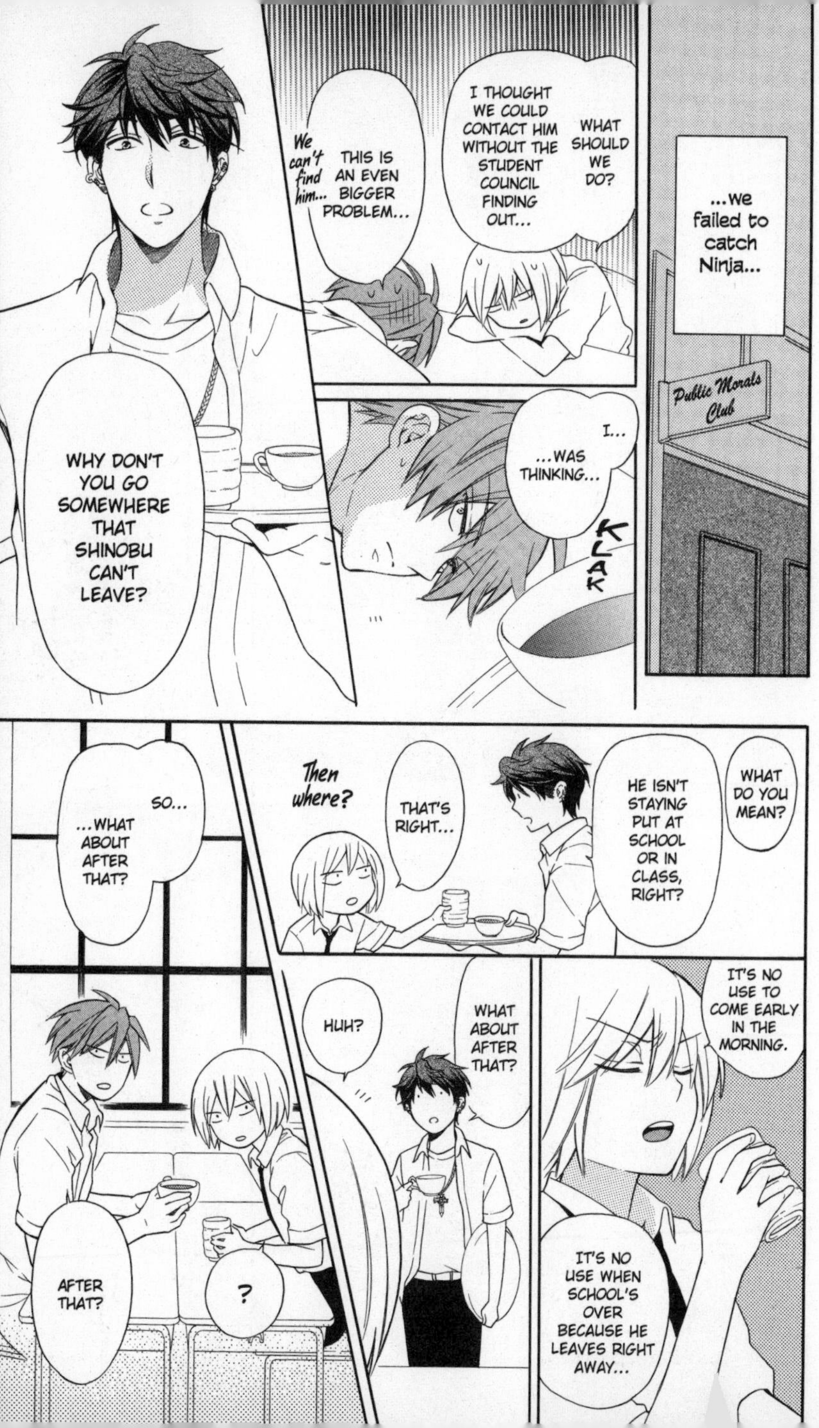
...we failed to catch Ninja...
Public Morals Club
WHAT SHOULD WE DO?
I THOUGHT WE COULD CONTACT HIM WITHOUT THE STUDENT COUNCIL FINDING OUT...
THIS IS AN EVEN BIGGER PROBLEM...
We can't find him...
I...
...WAS THINKING...
KLAK
WHY DON'T YOU GO SOMEWHERE THAT SHINOBU CAN'T LEAVE?
WHAT DO YOU MEAN?
HE ISN'T STAYING PUT AT SCHOOL OR IN CLASS, RIGHT?
THAT'S RIGHT...
Then where?
IT'S NO USE TO COME EARLY IN THE MORNING.
IT'S NO USE WHEN SCHOOL'S OVER BECAUSE HE LEAVES RIGHT AWAY...
WHAT ABOUT AFTER THAT?
HUH?
SO...
...WHAT ABOUT AFTER THAT?
AFTER THAT?
?

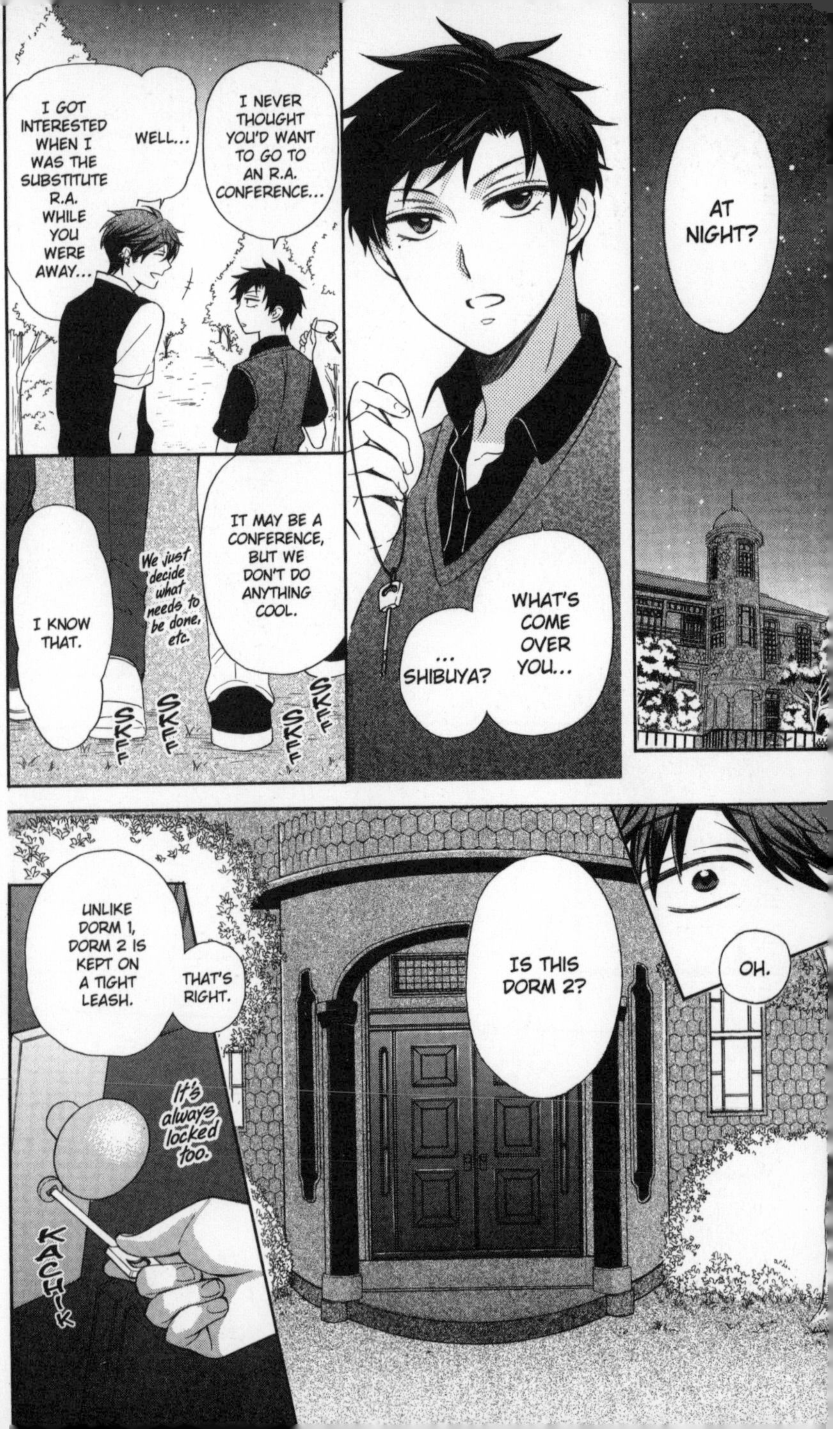
AT NIGHT?
WHAT'S COME OVER YOU...
... SHIBUYA?
I NEVER THOUGHT YOU'D WANT TO GO TO AN R.A. CONFERENCE...
WELL...
I GOT INTERESTED WHEN I WAS THE SUBSTITUTE R.A. WHILE YOU WERE AWAY...
IT MAY BE A CONFERENCE, BUT WE DON'T DO ANYTHING COOL.
SKFF SKFF
We just decide what needs to be done, etc.
SKFF
I KNOW THAT.
SKFF
OH.
IS THIS DORM 2?
THAT'S RIGHT.
UNLIKE DORM 1, DORM 2 IS KEPT ON A TIGHT LEASH.
It's always locked too.
KACHIK

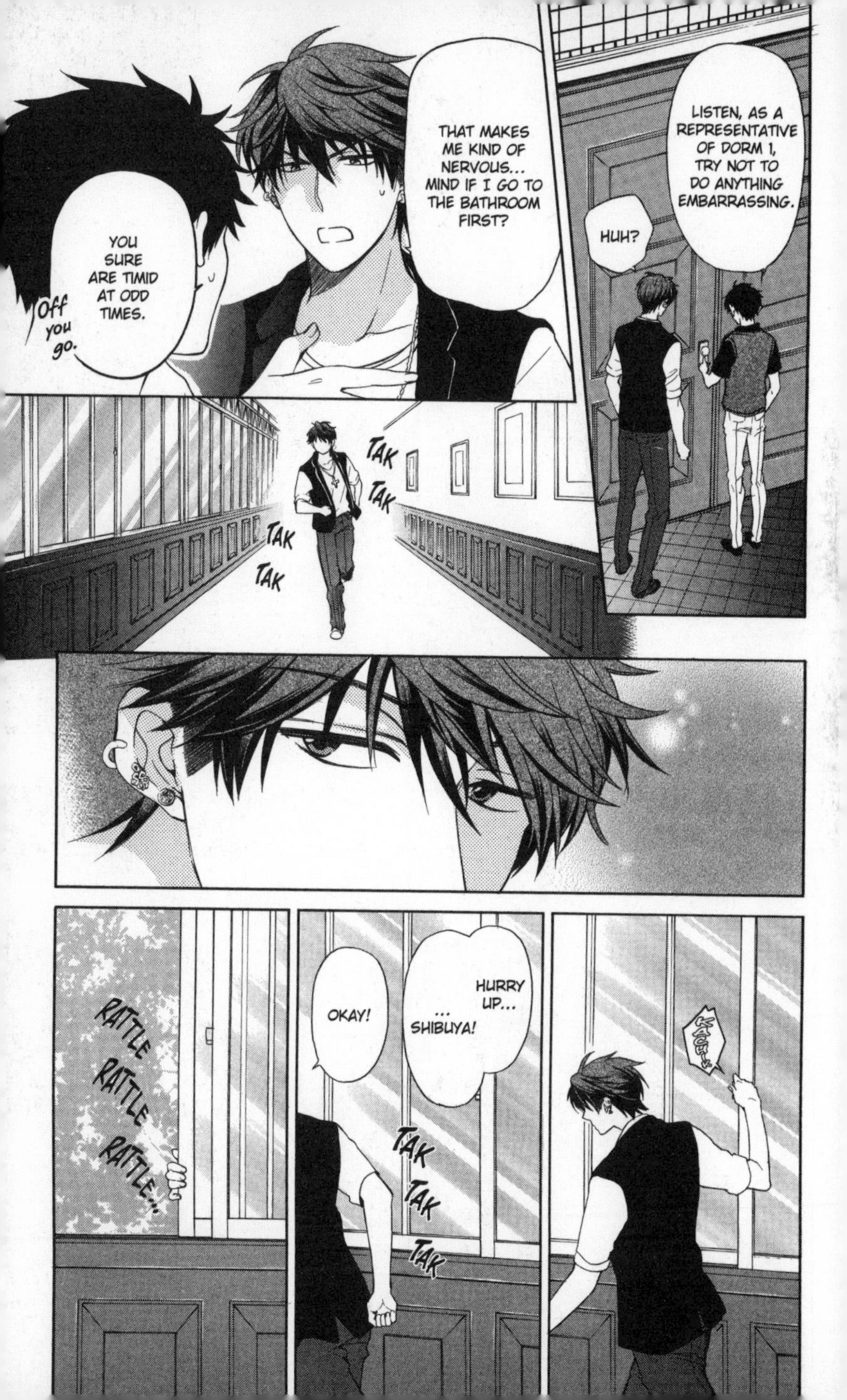
LISTEN, AS A REPRESENTATIVE OF DORM 1, TRY NOT TO DO ANYTHING EMBARRASSING.
HUH?
THAT MAKES ME KIND OF NERVOUS... MIND IF I GO TO THE BATHROOM FIRST?
YOU SURE ARE TIMID AT ODD TIMES.
Off you go.
TAK
TAK
TAK
TAK
KACHI-K
HURRY UP... ...SHIBUYA!
OKAY!
TAK
TAK
TAK
RATTLE
RATTLE
RATTLE...

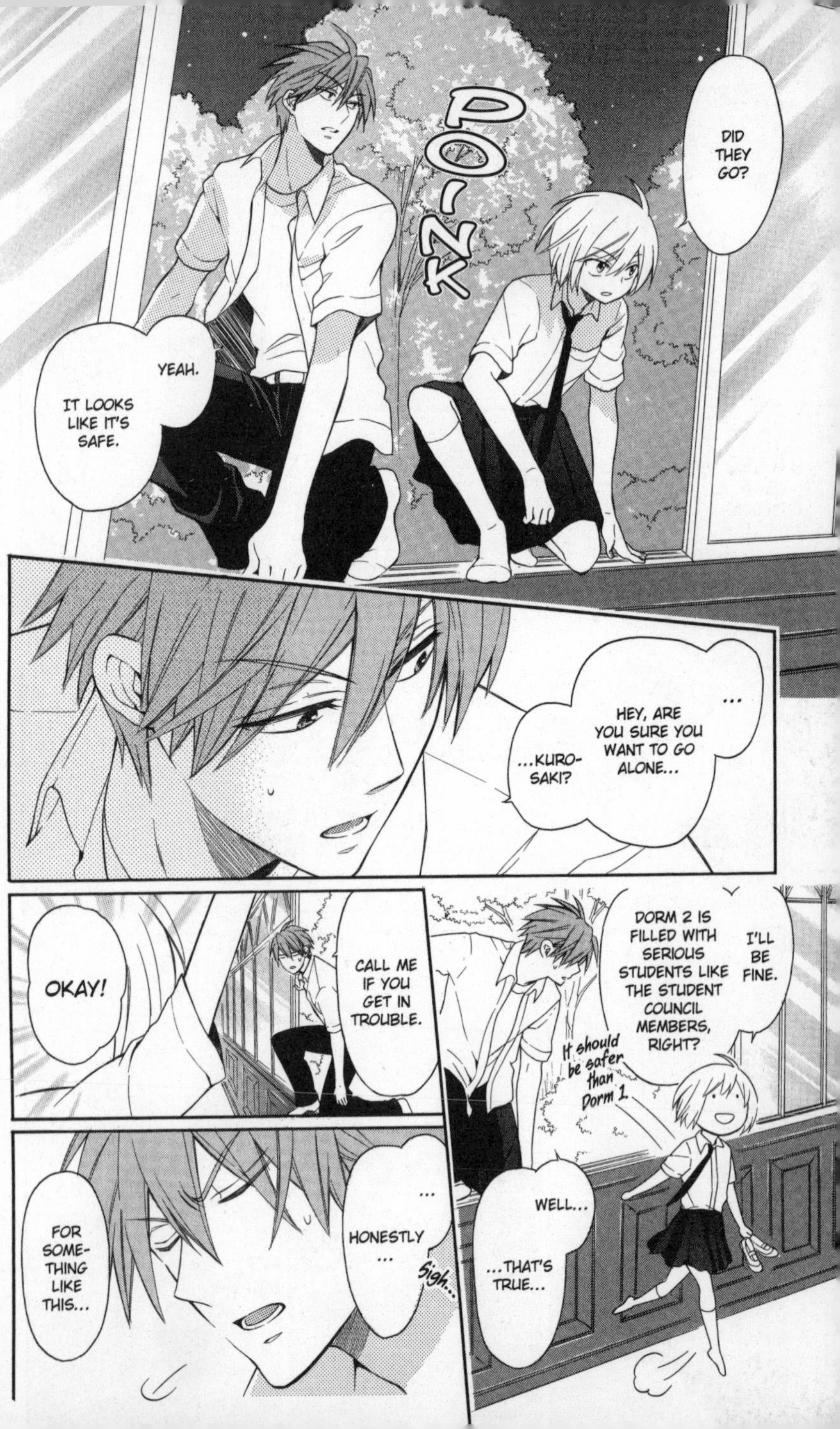
DID THEY GO?
POINK
YEAH.
IT LOOKS LIKE IT'S SAFE.
...
HEY, ARE YOU SURE YOU WANT TO GO ALONE...
...KURO-SAKI?
I'LL BE FINE.
DORM 2 IS FILLED WITH SERIOUS STUDENTS LIKE THE STUDENT COUNCIL MEMBERS, RIGHT?
It should be safer than Dorm 1.
WELL...
...THAT'S TRUE...
CALL ME IF YOU GET IN TROUBLE.
OKAY!
...
HONESTLY...
Sigh...
FOR SOMETHING LIKE THIS...

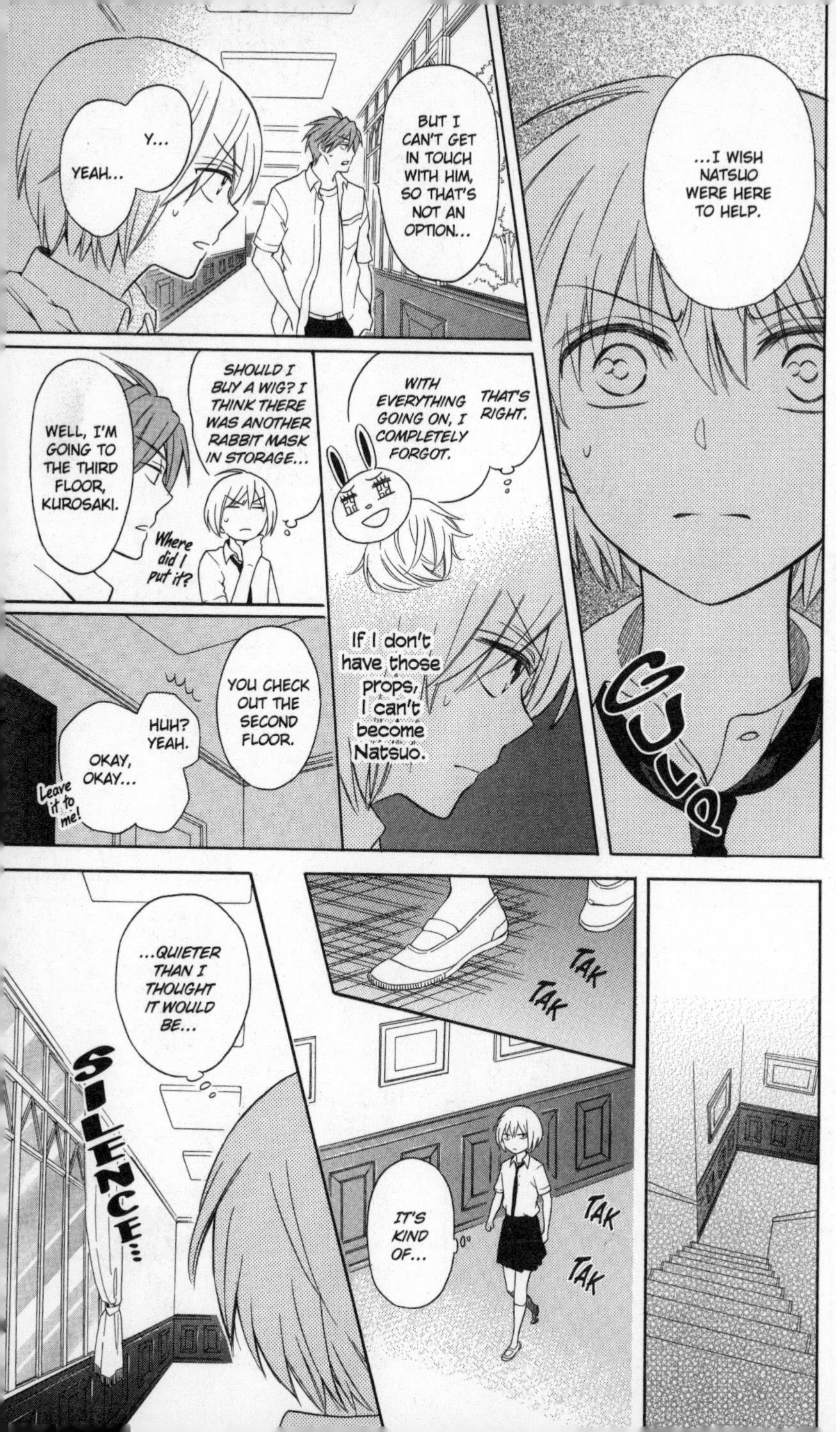
...I WISH NATSUO WERE HERE TO HELP.
GYUP
BUT I CAN'T GET IN TOUCH WITH HIM, SO THAT'S NOT AN OPTION...
Y... YEAH...
THAT'S RIGHT.
WITH EVERYTHING GOING ON, I COMPLETELY FORGOT.
If I don't have those props, I can't become Natsuo.
SHOULD I BUY A WIG? I THINK THERE WAS ANOTHER RABBIT MASK IN STORAGE...
WELL, I'M GOING TO THE THIRD FLOOR, KUROSAKI.
Where did I put it?
YOU CHECK OUT THE SECOND FLOOR.
HUH? YEAH.
OKAY, OKAY...
Leave it to me!
TAK
TAK
TAK
TAK
...QUIETER THAN I THOUGHT IT WOULD BE...
SILENCE...
IT'S KIND OF...

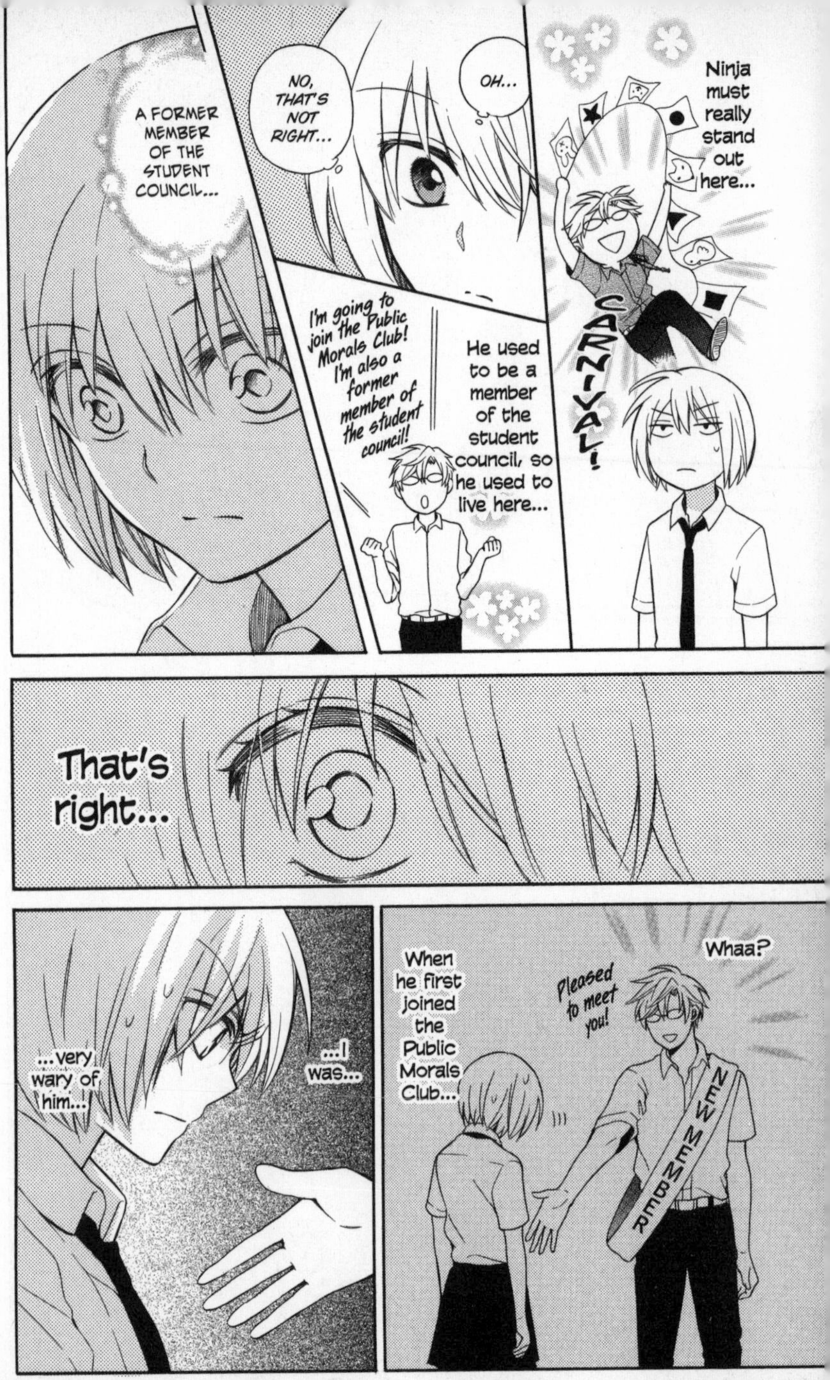
Ninja must really stand out here...
CARNIVAL!
OH...
NO, THAT'S NOT RIGHT...
He used to be a member of the student council, so he used to live here...
I'm going to join the Public Morals Club! I'm also a former member of the student council!
A FORMER MEMBER OF THE STUDENT COUNCIL...
That's right...
Whaa?
Pleased to meet you!
When he first joined the Public Morals Club...
NEW MEMBER
...I was...
...very wary of him...

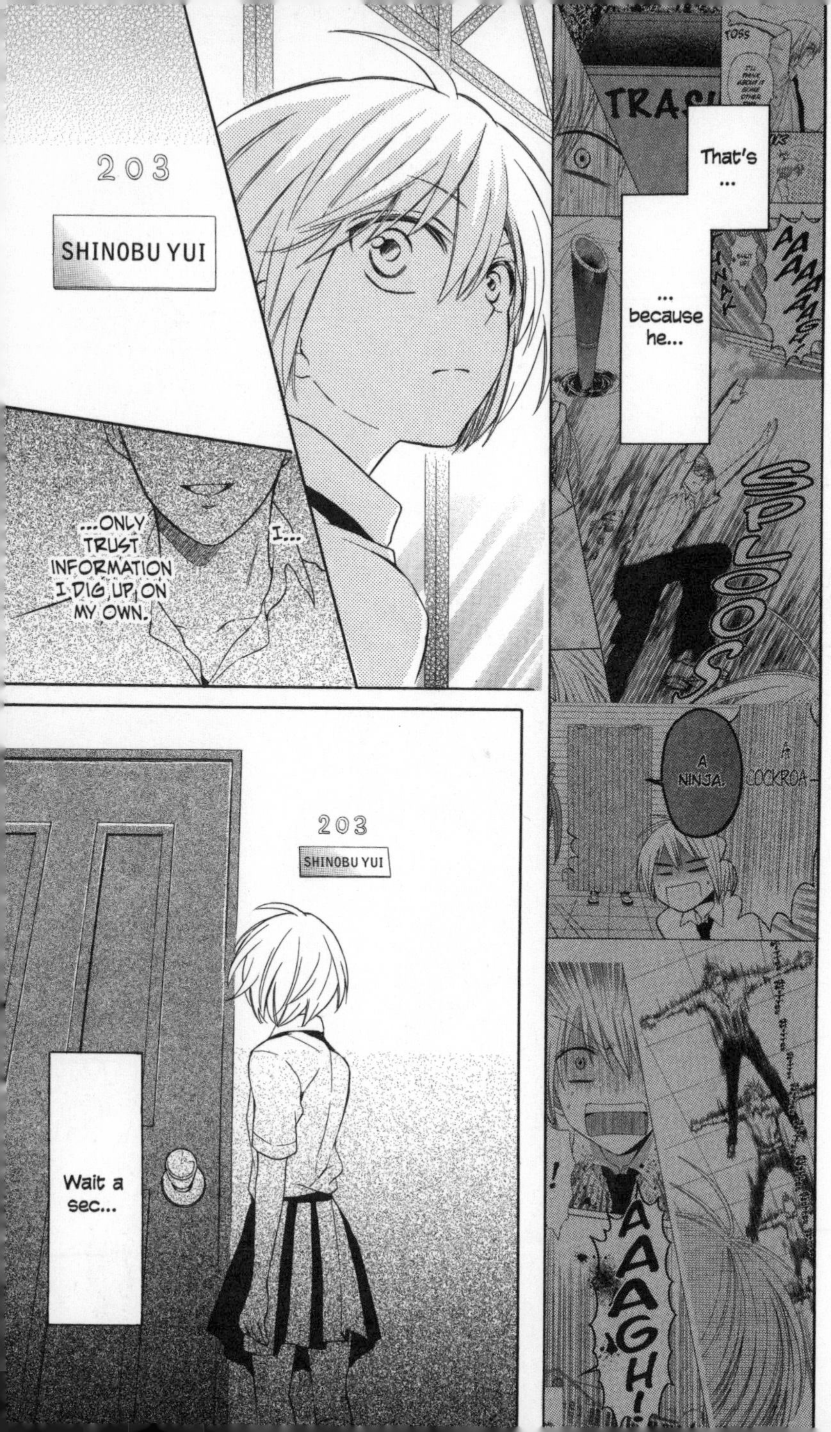

TOSS
TRAS
That's ...
... because he...
AAAAAAAGH!
SPLOOOOSH
A NINJA.
A COCKROA-
AAAGH!
203
SHINOBU YUI
I...
...ONLY TRUST INFORMATION I DIG UP ON MY OWN.
203
SHINOBU YUI
Wait a sec...

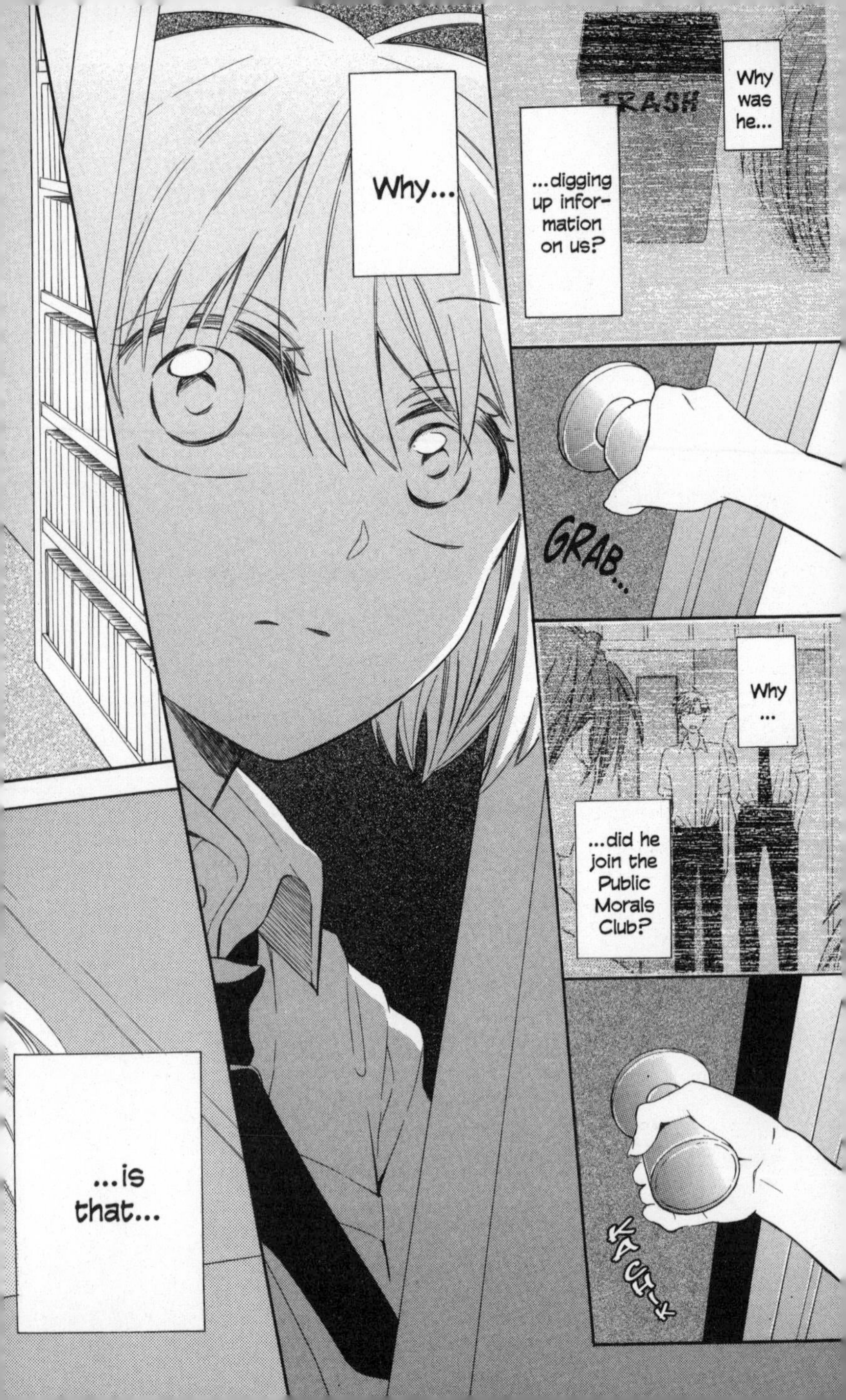
TRASH
Why was he...
...digging up information on us?
GRAB...
Why ...
...did he join the Public Morals Club?
KACHI-K
Why...
...is that...

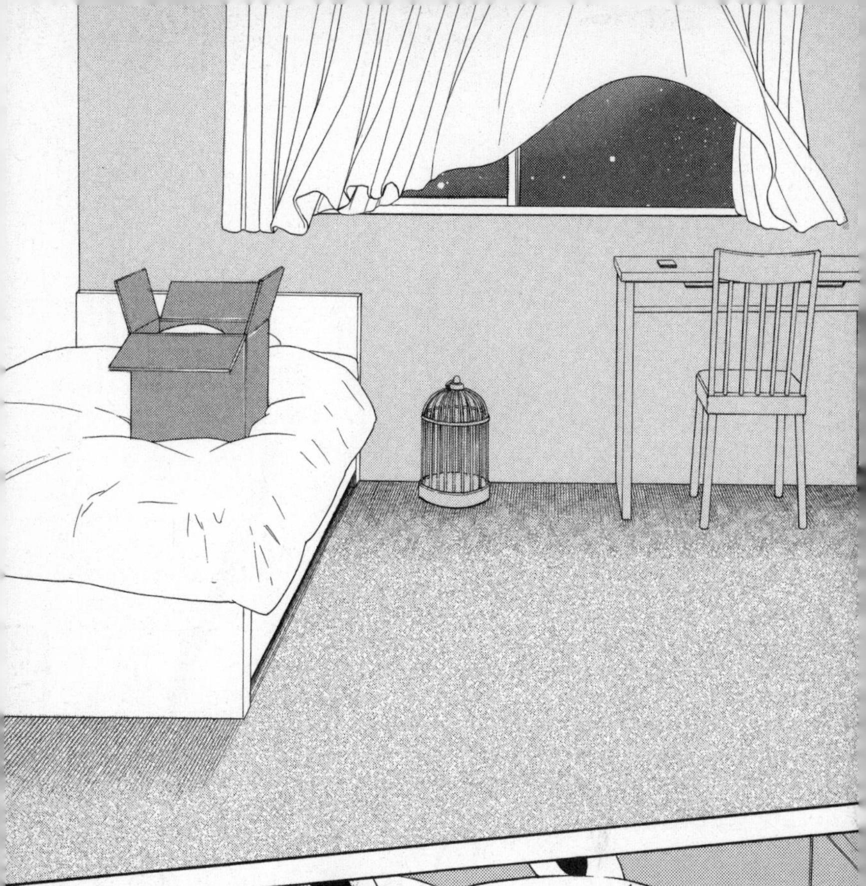

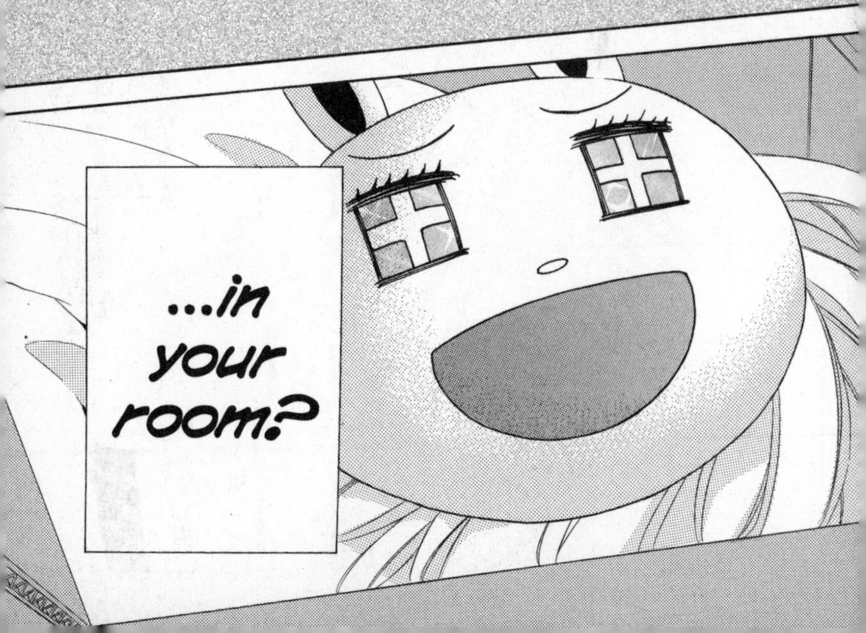
...in your room?

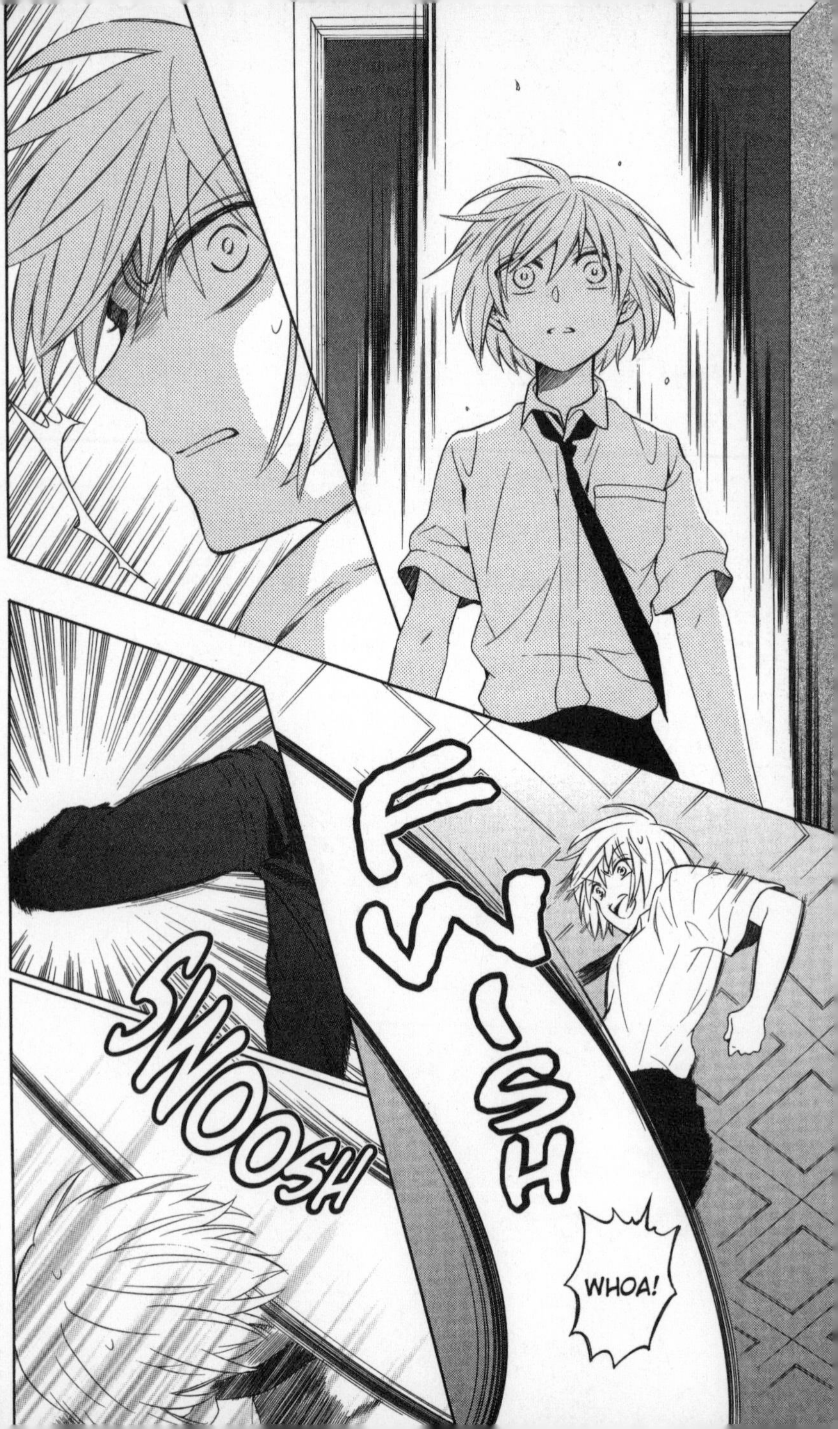
FWISH
WHOA!
SWOOSH

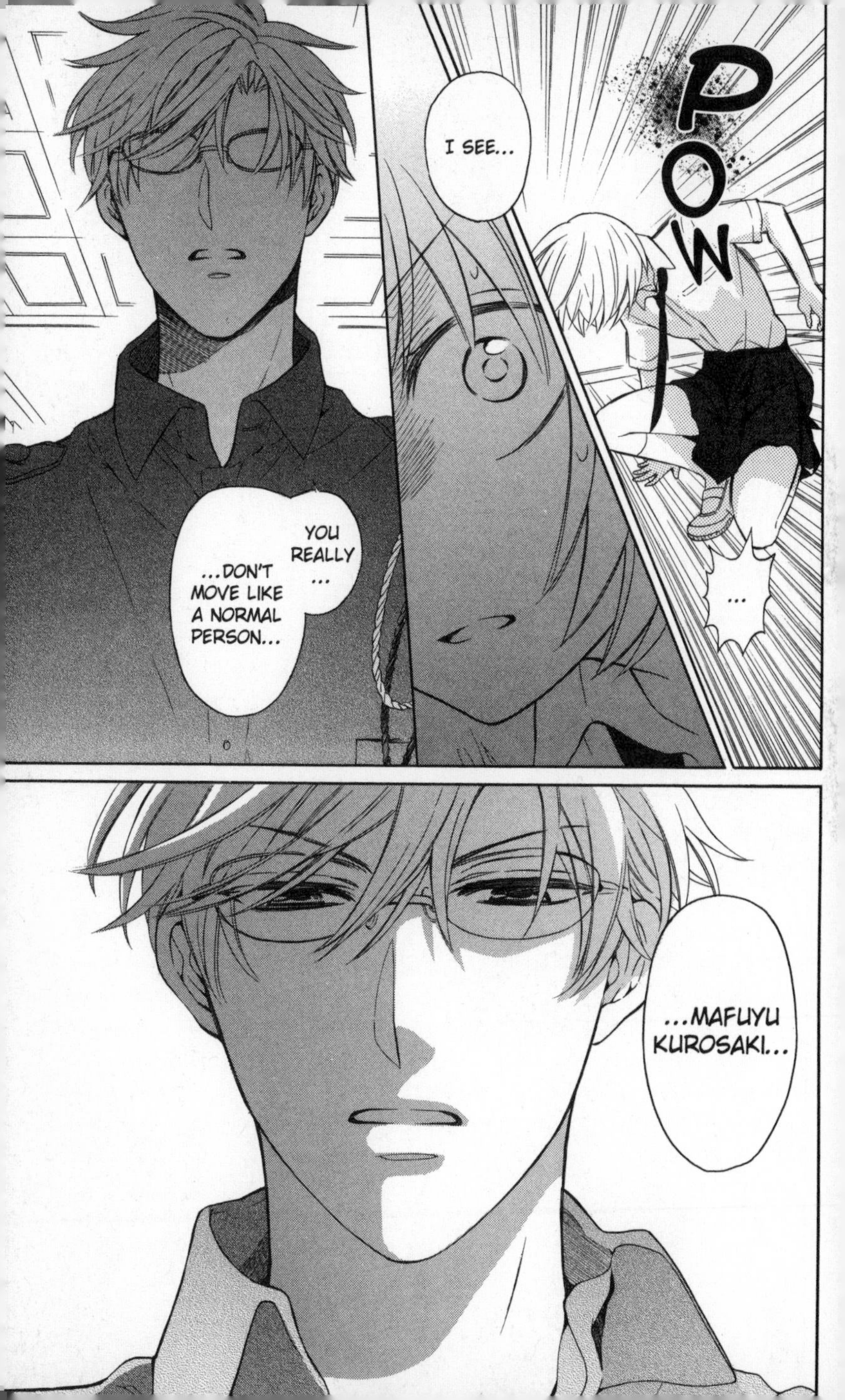
POW
...
I SEE...
YOU REALLY ...
...DON'T MOVE LIKE A NORMAL PERSON...
...MAFUYU KUROSAKI...

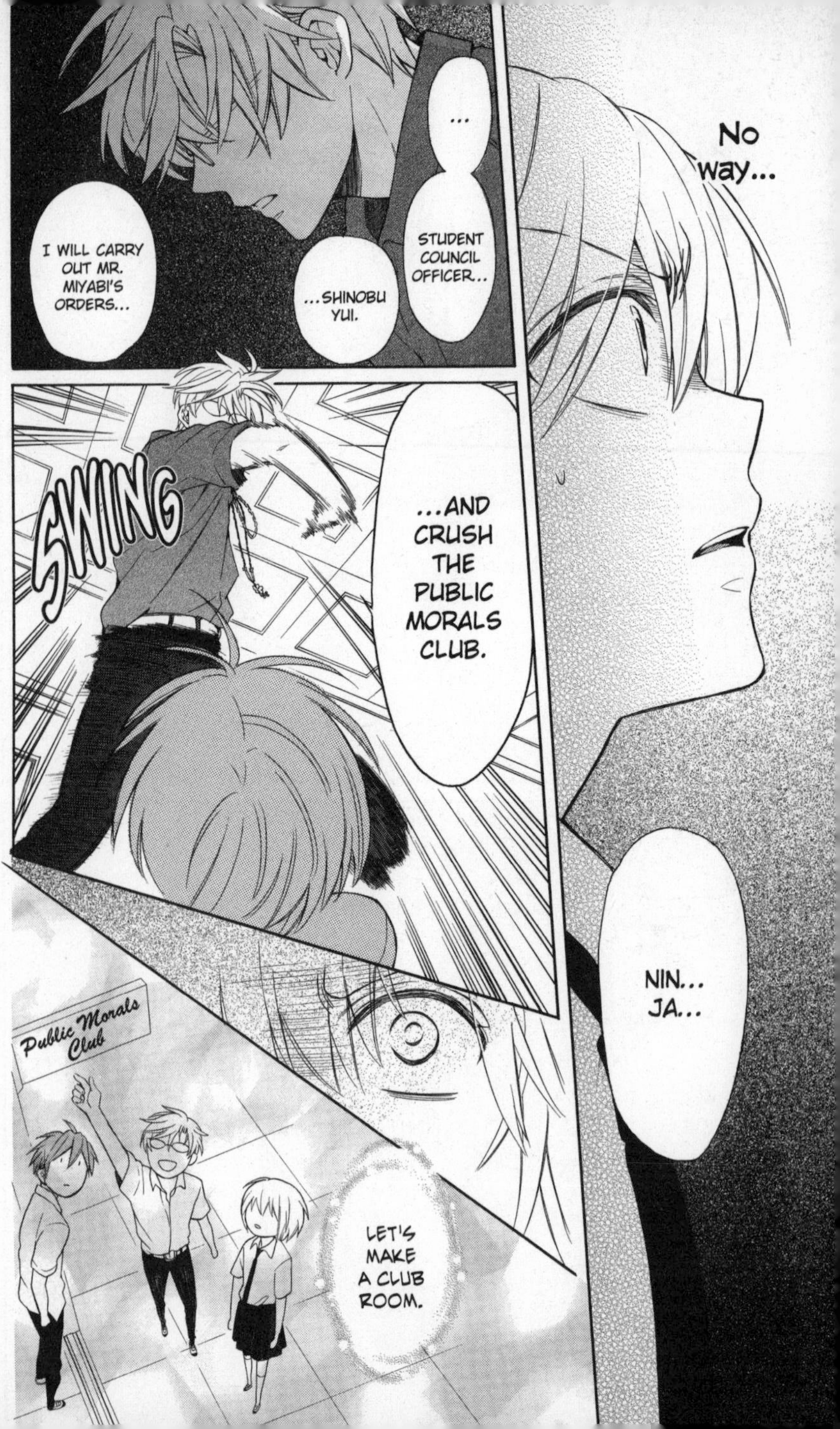
No way...
NIN... JA...
...
STUDENT COUNCIL OFFICER...
...SHINOBU YUI.
I WILL CARRY OUT MR. MIYABI'S ORDERS...
...AND CRUSH THE PUBLIC MORALS CLUB.
SWING
LET'S MAKE A CLUB ROOM.
Public Morals Club

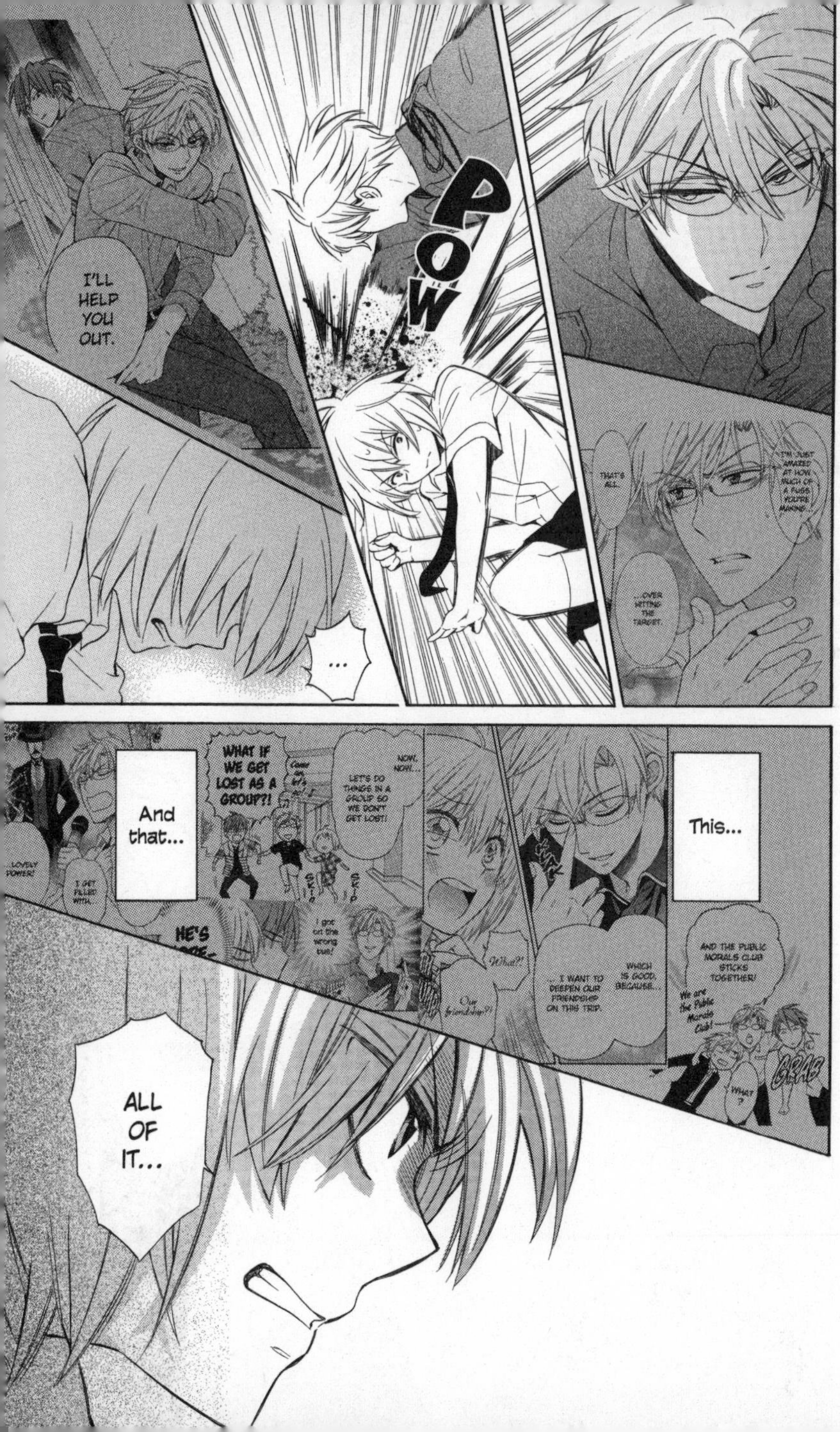
I'M JUST AMAZED AT HOW MUCH OF A FUSS YOU'RE MAKING...
THAT'S ALL.
...OVER HITTING THE TARGET.
POW
I'LL HELP YOU OUT.
...
This...
AND THE PUBLIC MORALS CLUB STICKS TOGETHER!
We are the Public Morals Club!
WHAT?
WHICH IS GOOD, BECAUSE...
...I WANT TO DEEPEN OUR FRIENDSHIP ON THIS TRIP.
What?!
Our friendship?!
NOW, NOW...
LET'S DO THINGS IN A GROUP SO WE DON'T GET LOST!
Come on, let's go!
WHAT IF WE GET LOST AS A GROUP?!
SKIP
SKIP
I got on the wrong bus!
And that...
I GET FILLED WITH...
...LOVELY POWER!
HE'S
ALL OF IT...

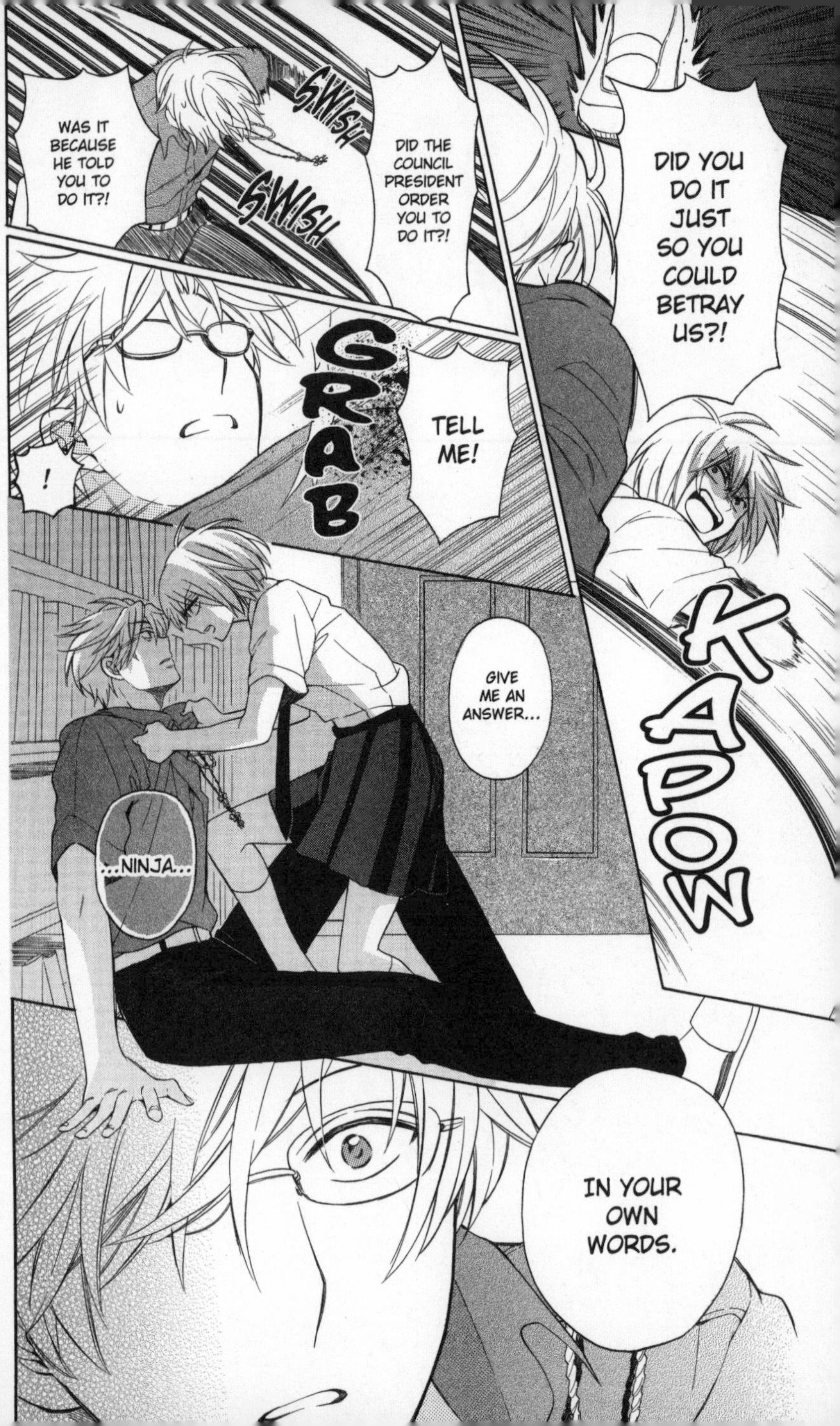

DID YOU DO IT JUST SO YOU COULD BETRAY US?!
KAPOW
DID THE COUNCIL PRESIDENT ORDER YOU TO DO IT?!
SWISH
SWISH
WAS IT BECAUSE HE TOLD YOU TO DO IT?!
GRAB
TELL ME!
!
GIVE ME AN ANSWER...
...NINJA...
IN YOUR OWN WORDS.

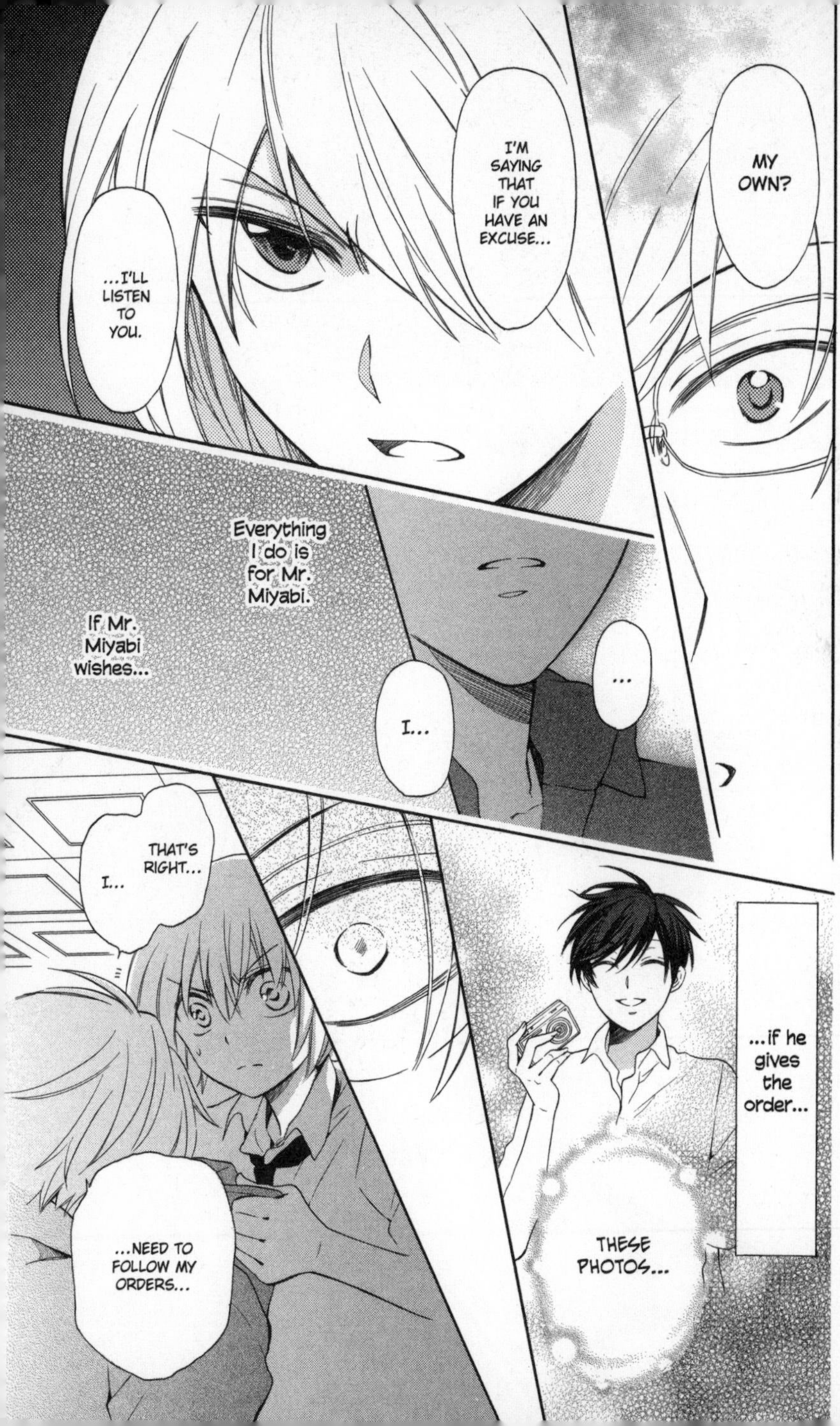
MY OWN?
I'M SAYING THAT IF YOU HAVE AN EXCUSE...
...I'LL LISTEN TO YOU.
...
I...
Everything I do is for Mr. Miyabi.
If Mr. Miyabi wishes...
...if he gives the order...
THESE PHOTOS...
THAT'S RIGHT... I...
...NEED TO FOLLOW MY ORDERS...

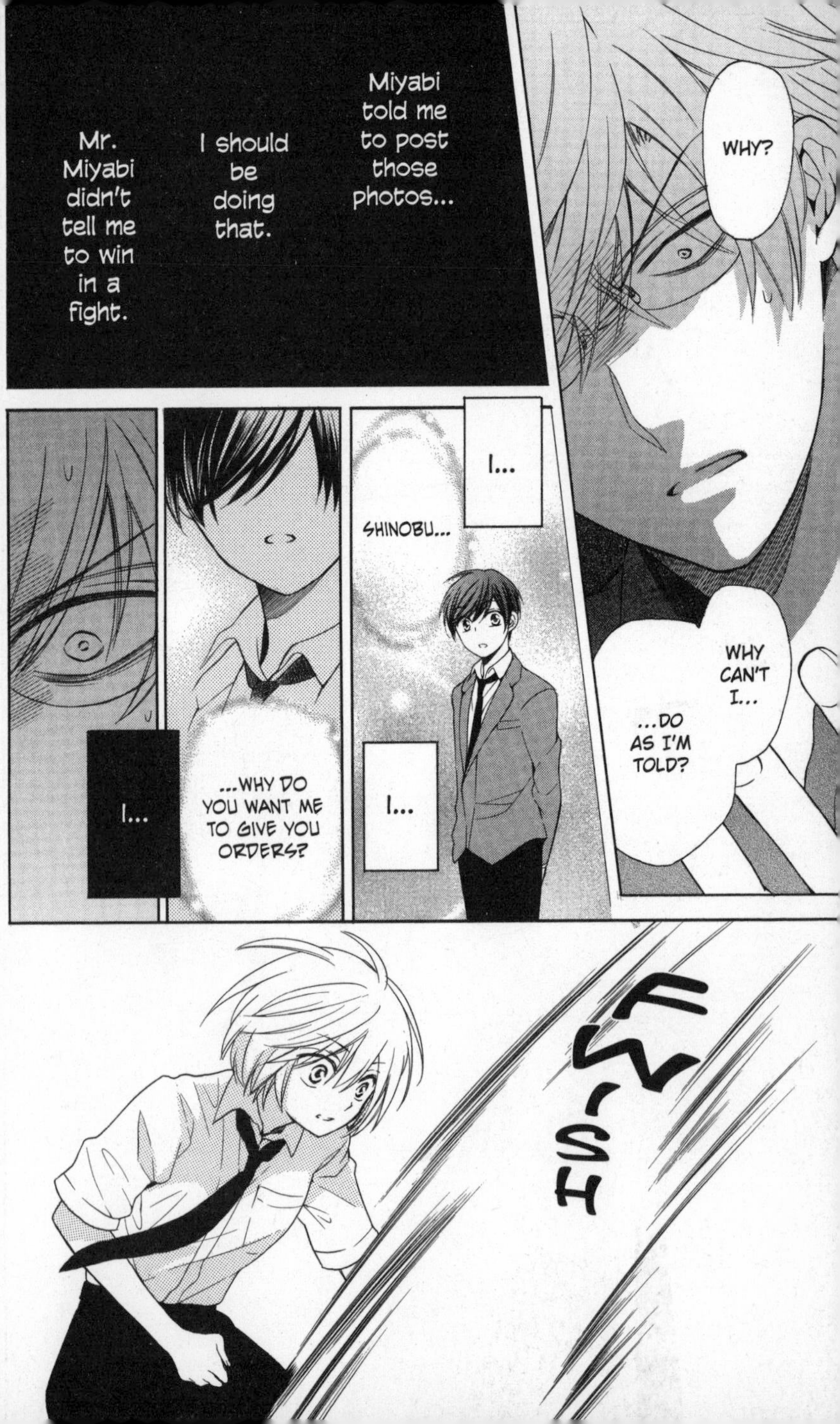
WHY?
WHY CAN'T I...
...DO AS I'M TOLD?
Miyabi told me to post those photos...
I should be doing that.
Mr. Miyabi didn't tell me to win in a fight.
I...
SHINOBU...
I...
...WHY DO YOU WANT ME TO GIVE YOU ORDERS?
I...
FWISH

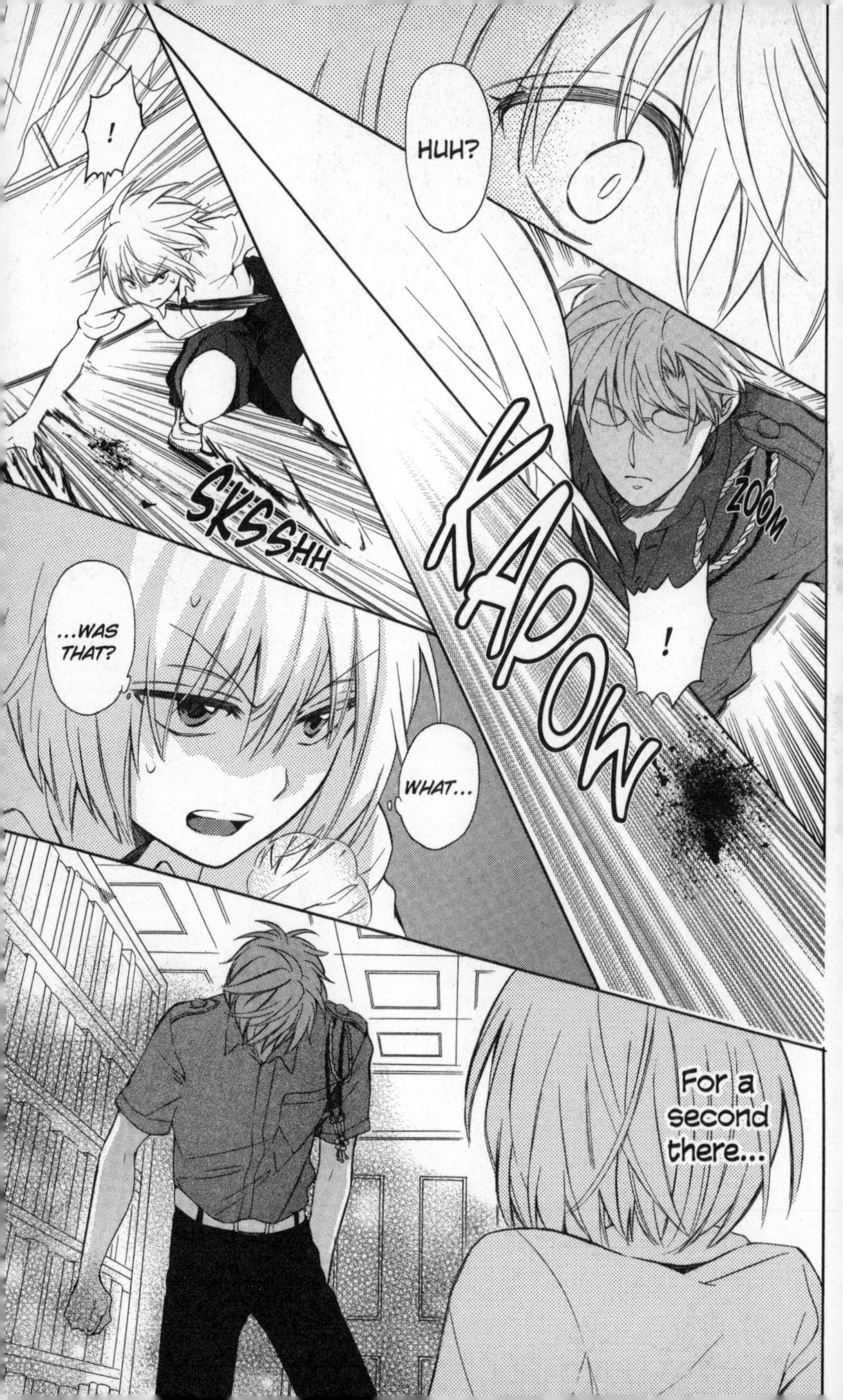
HUH?
ZOOM
!
KAPOW
!
SKSSHH
WHAT...
...WAS THAT?
For a second there...

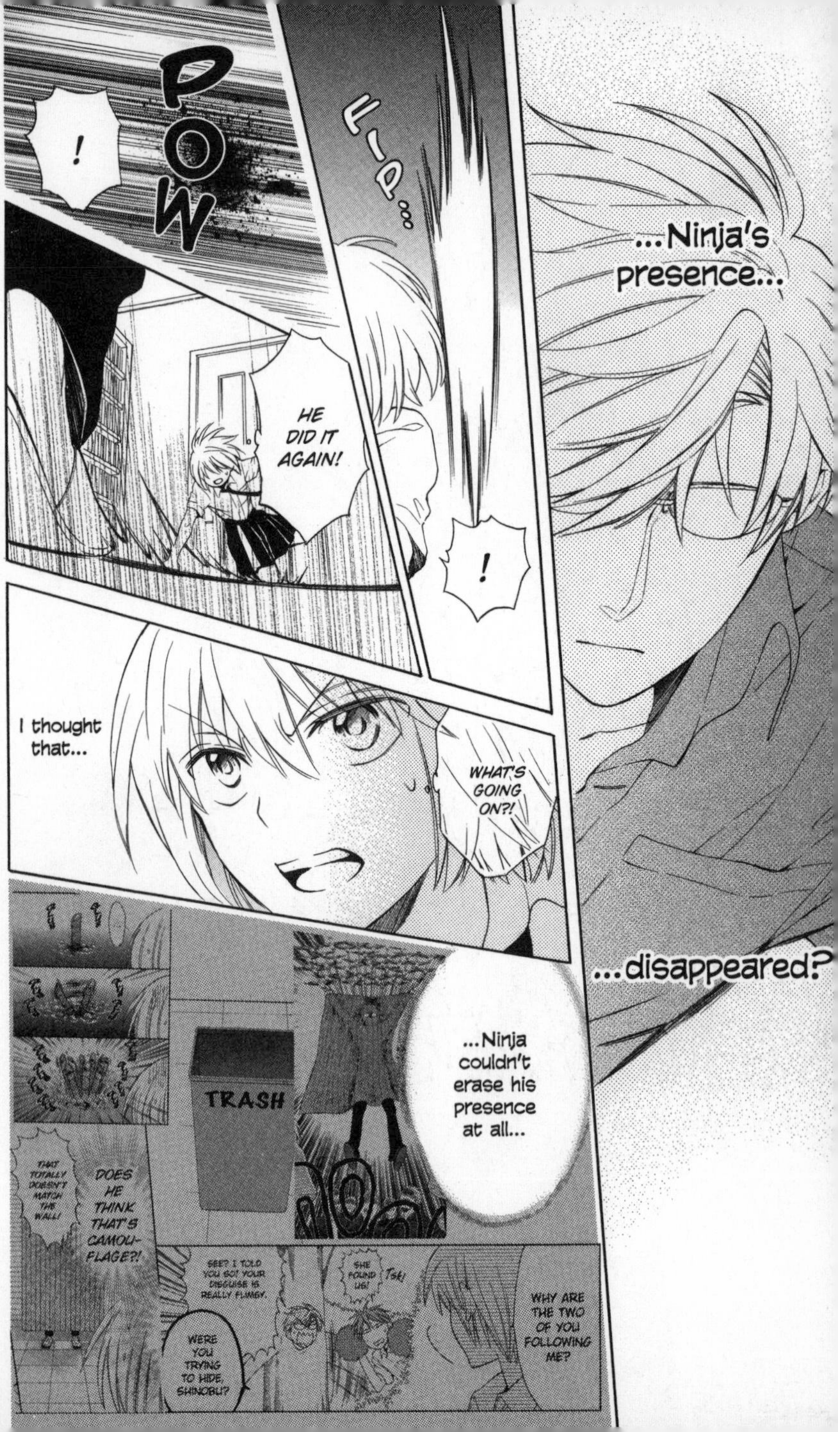
FLIP...
!
POW
!
HE DID IT AGAIN!
WHAT'S GOING ON?!
I thought that...
...Ninja couldn't erase his presence at all...
DOES HE THINK THAT'S CAMOUFLAGE?!
THAT TOTALLY DOESN'T MATCH THE WALL!
TRASH
WHY ARE THE TWO OF YOU FOLLOWING ME?
SHE FOUND US!
Tsk!
SEE? I TOLD YOU SO! YOUR DISGUISE IS REALLY FLIMSY.
WERE YOU TRYING TO HIDE, SHINOBU?
...Ninja's presence...
...disappeared?

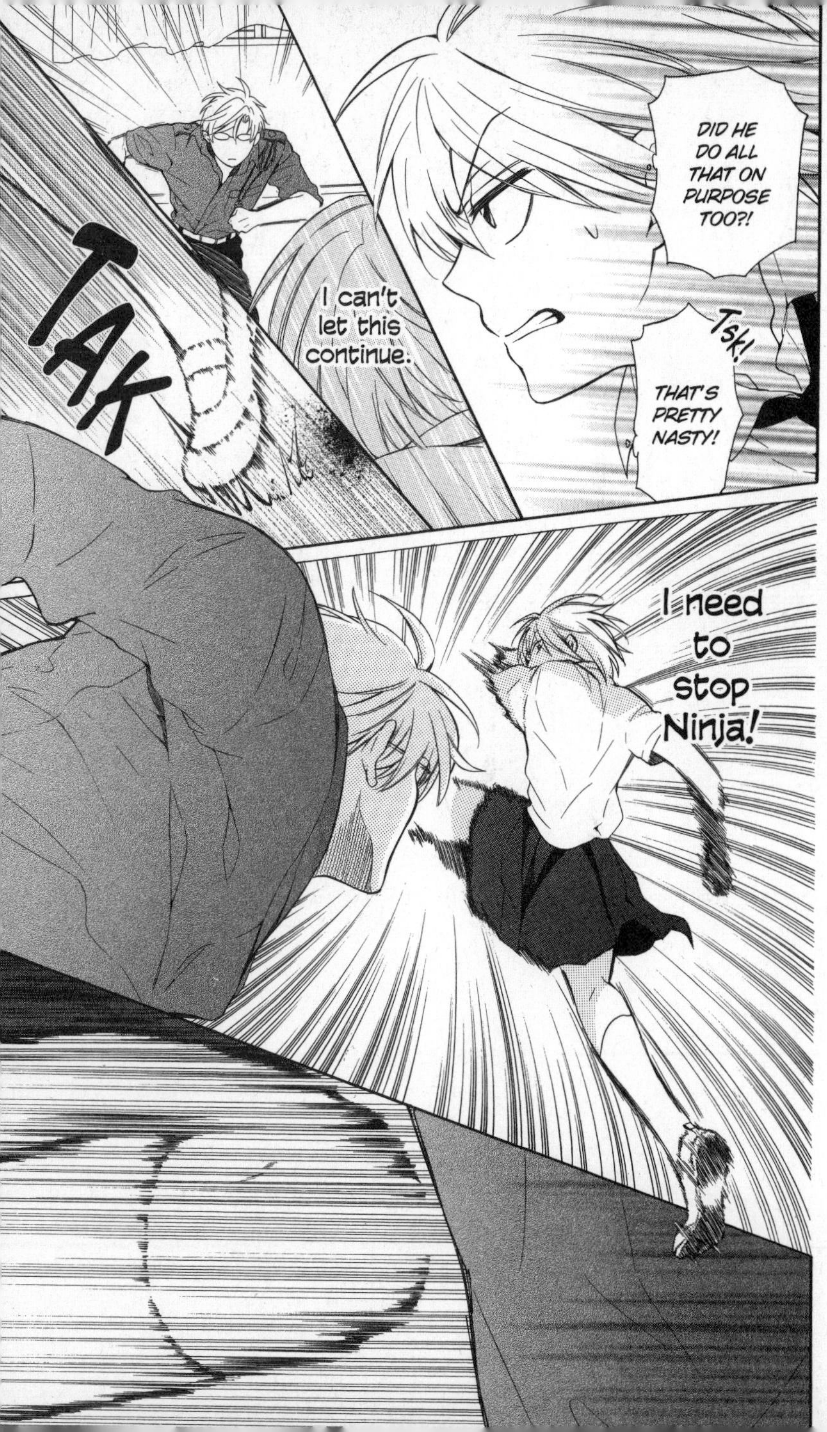
DID HE DO ALL THAT ON PURPOSE TOO?!
Tsk!
THAT'S PRETTY NASTY!
I can't let this continue.
TAK
I need to stop Ninja!

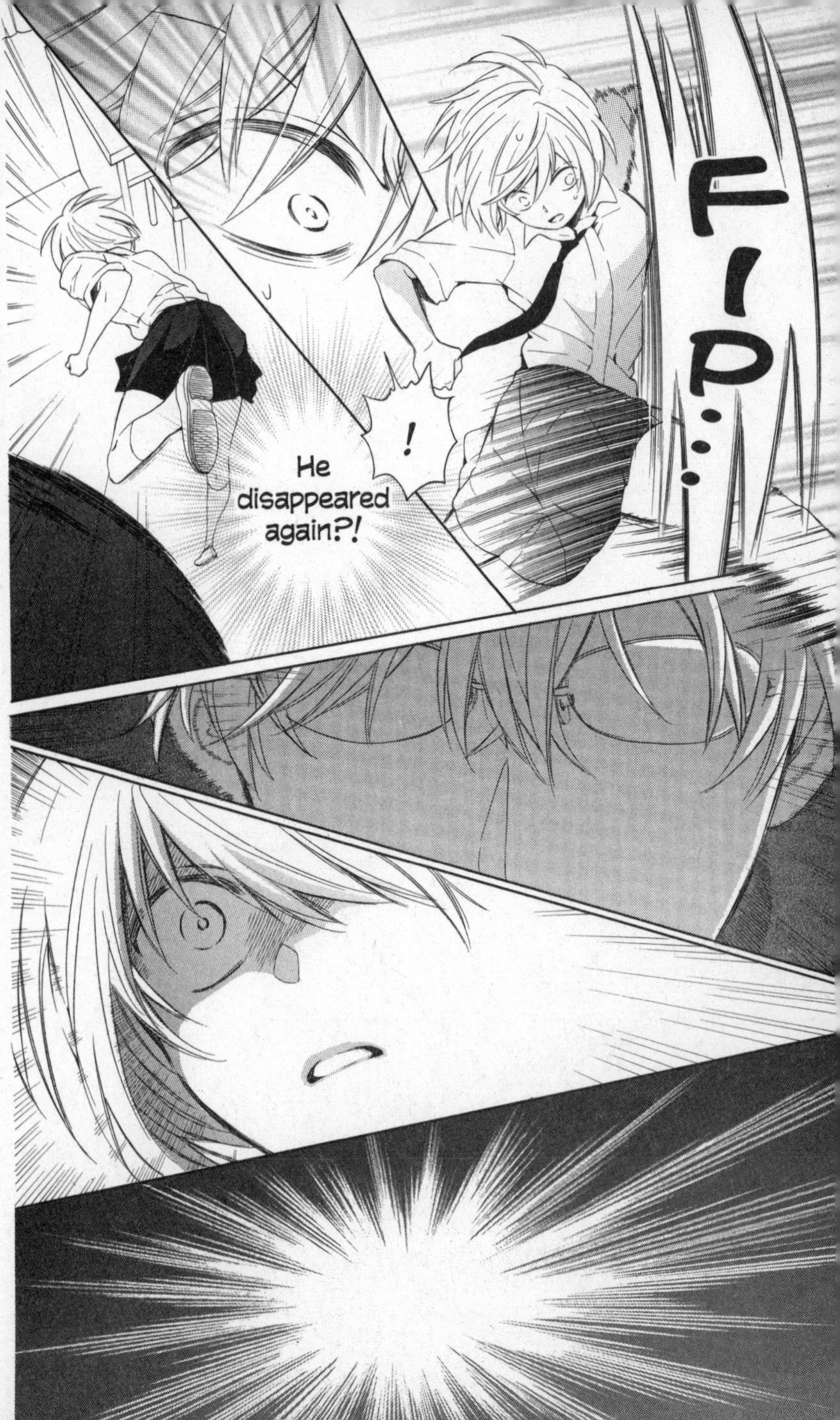
FIP...
!
He disappeared again?!

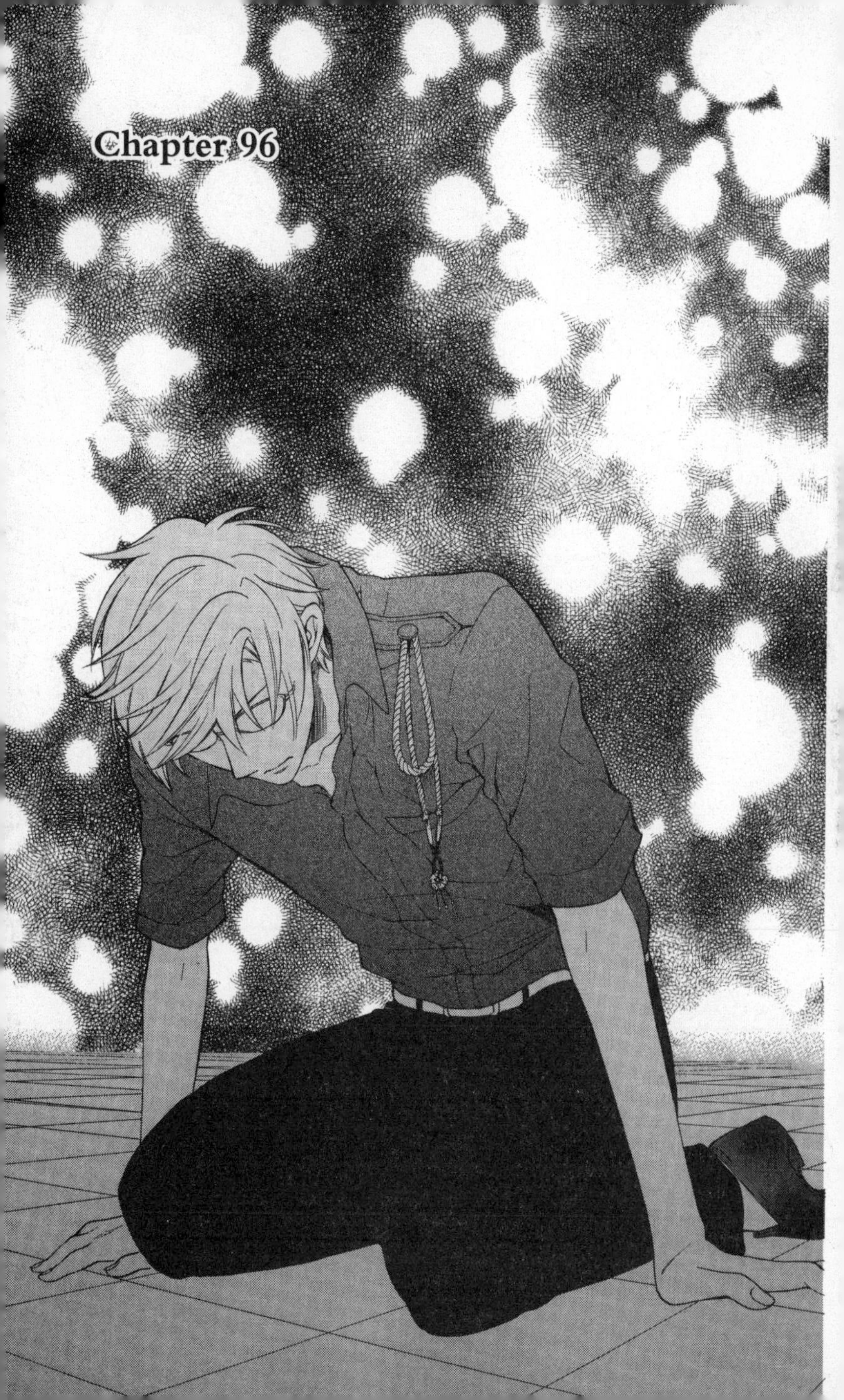
Chapter 96

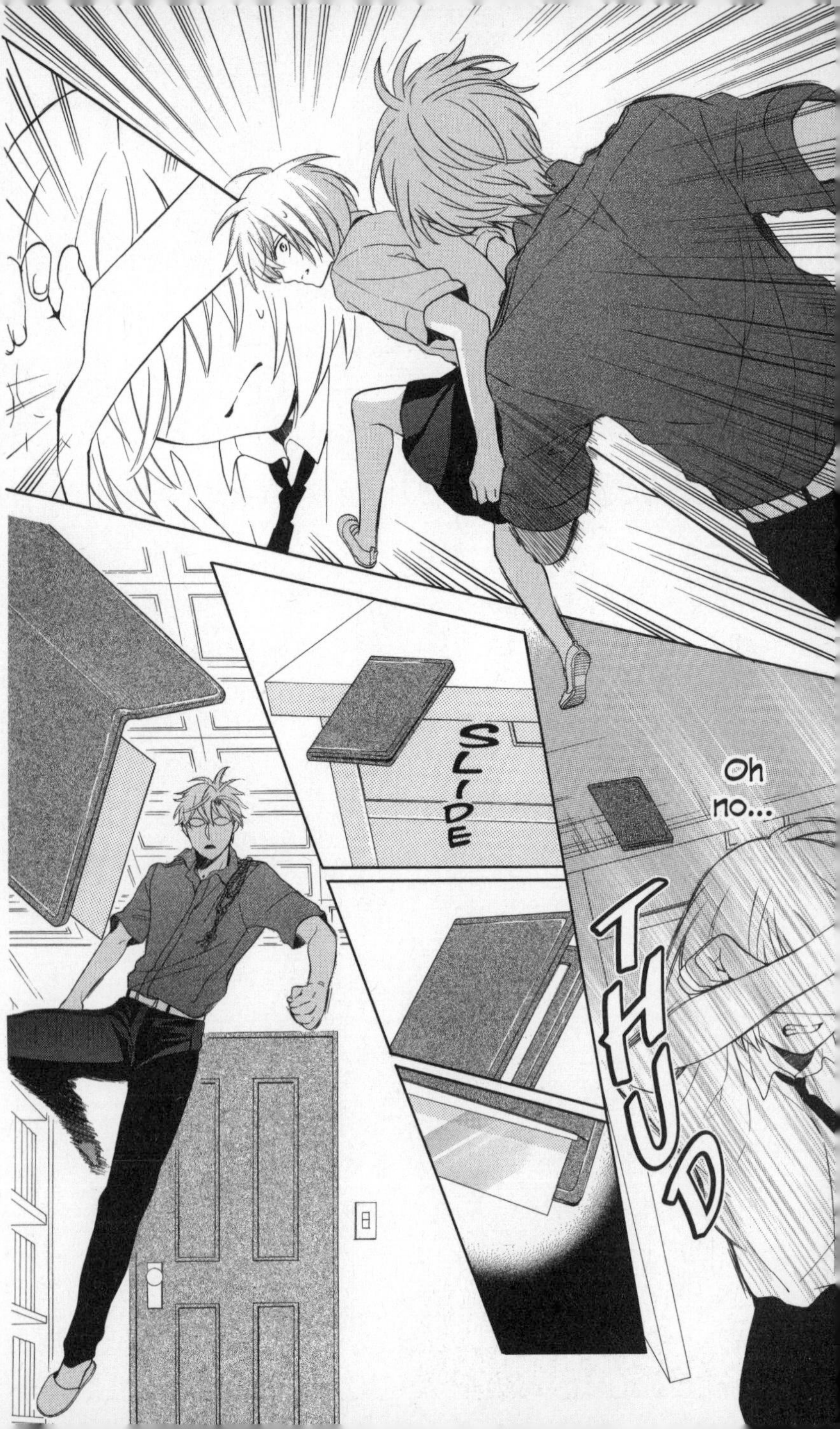
SLIDE
Oh no...
THUD

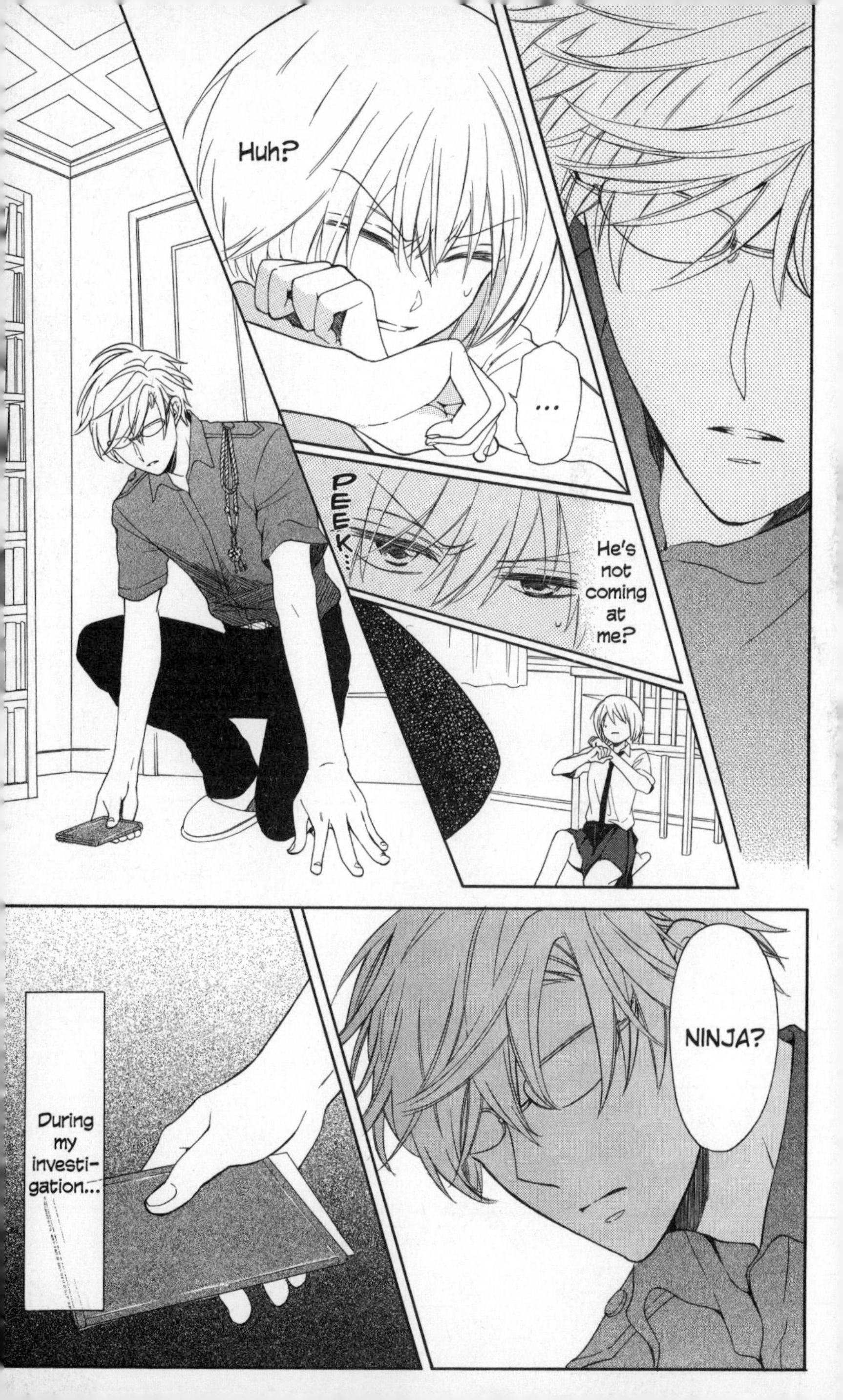

Huh?
...
PEEEK...
He's not coming at me?
NINJA?
During my investigation...

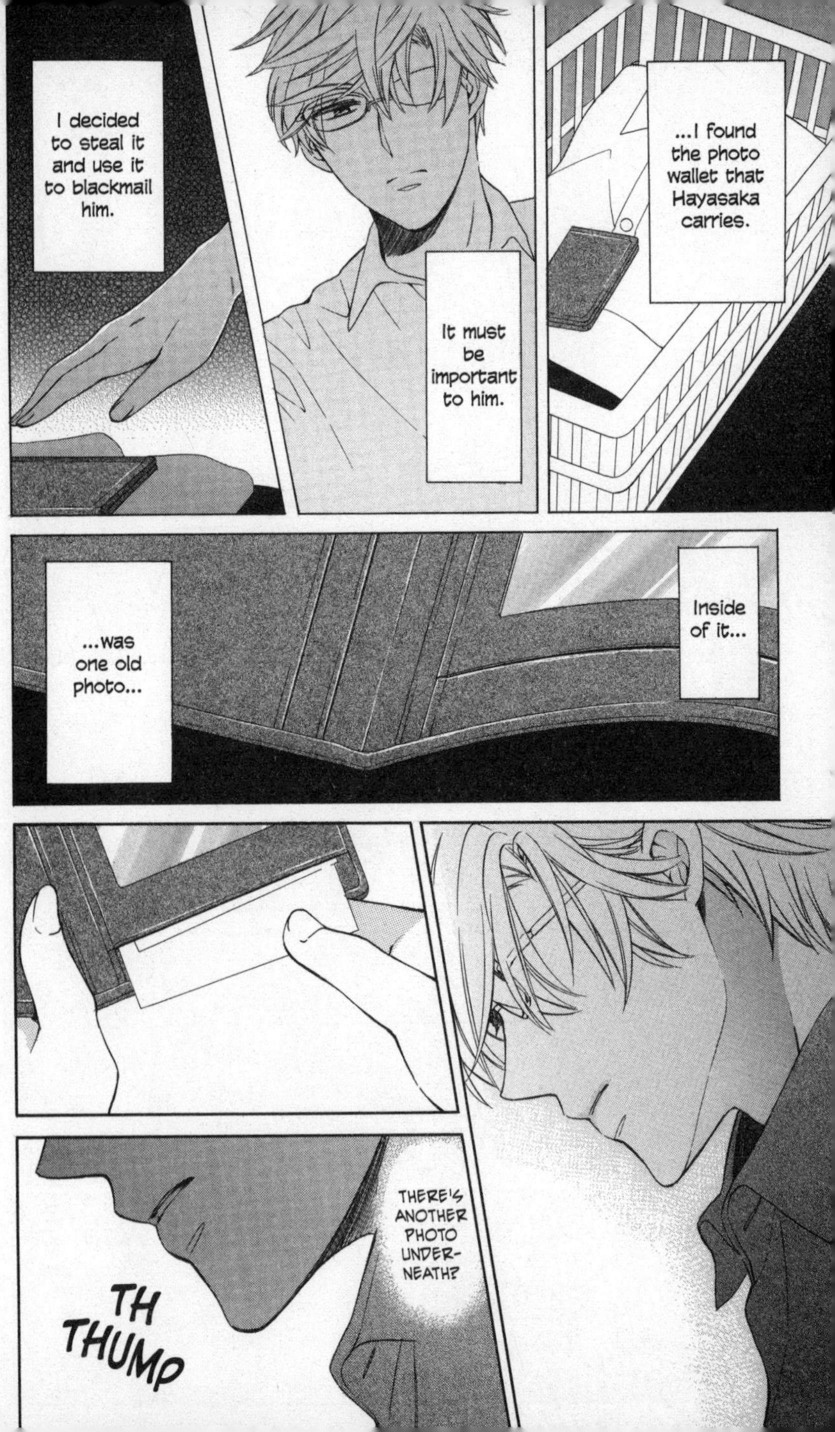
...I found the photo wallet that Hayasaka carries.
It must be important to him.
I decided to steal it and use it to blackmail him.
Inside of it...
...was one old photo...
THERE'S ANOTHER PHOTO UNDER-NEATH?
TH THUMP

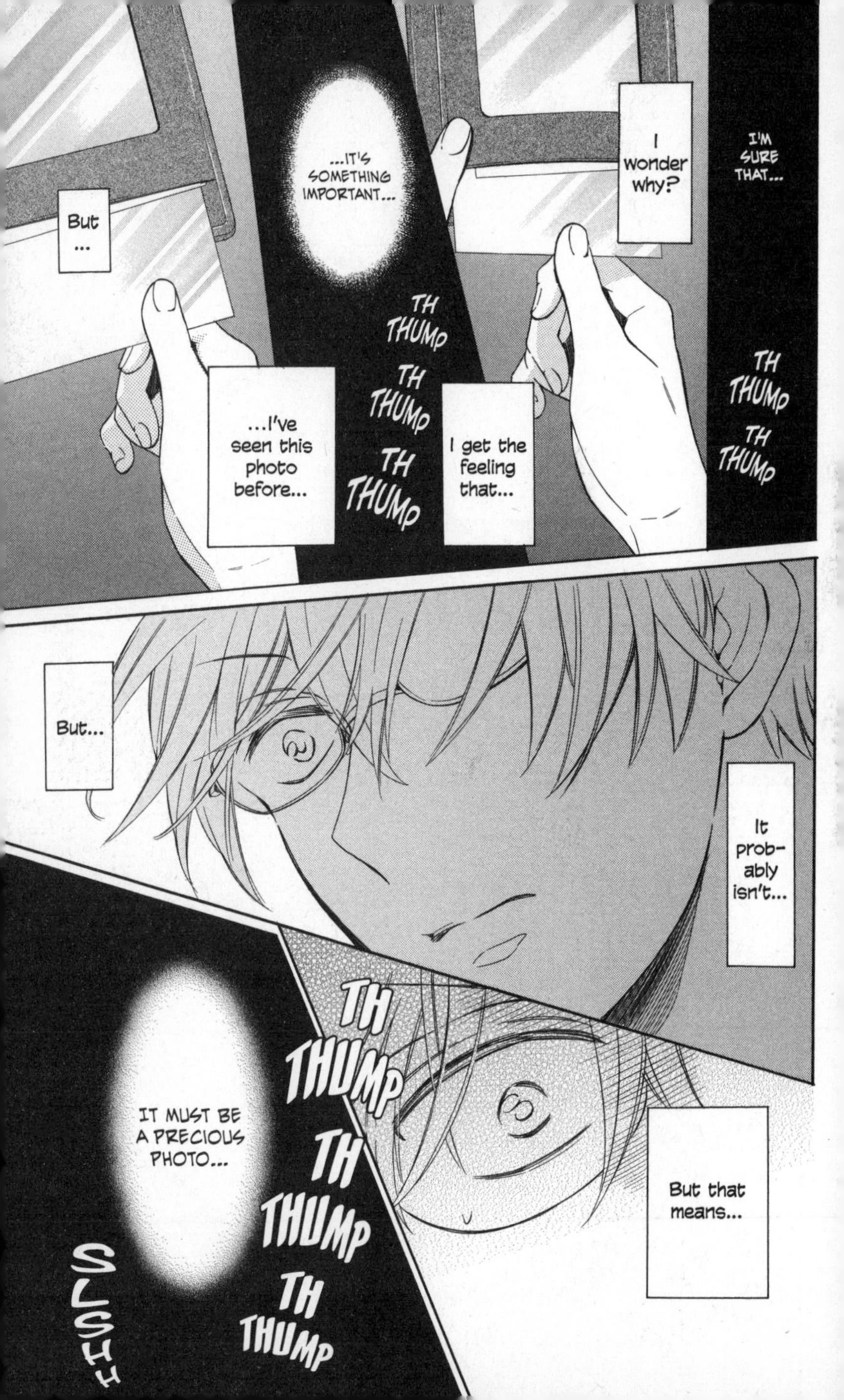
I'M SURE THAT...
TH THUMP
TH THUMP
I wonder why?
I get the feeling that...
...IT'S SOMETHING IMPORTANT...
TH THUMP
TH THUMP
TH THUMP
...I've seen this photo before...
But ...
It probably isn't...
But...
But that means...
TH THUMP
TH THUMP
TH THUMP
IT MUST BE A PRECIOUS PHOTO...
SLSHH

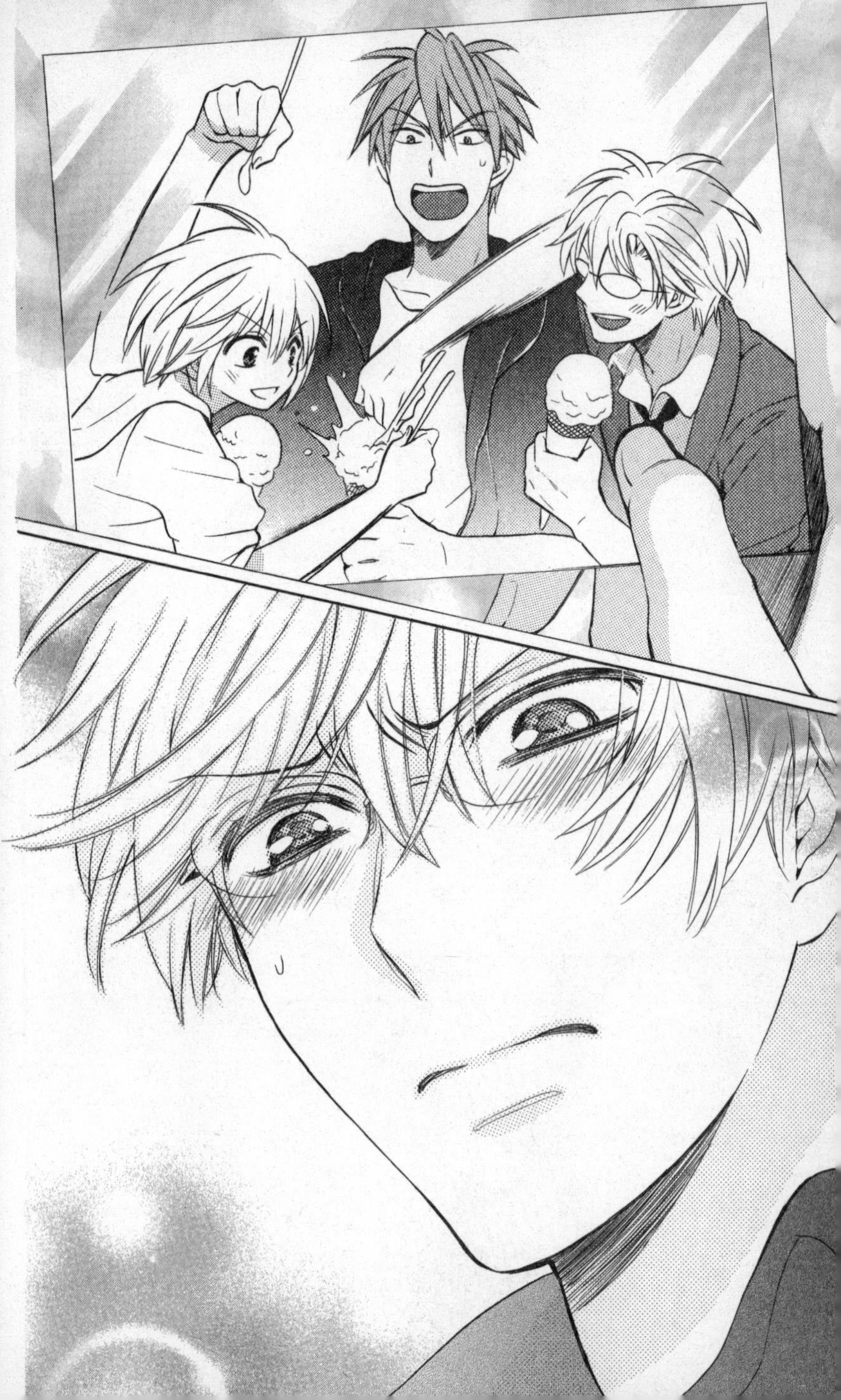

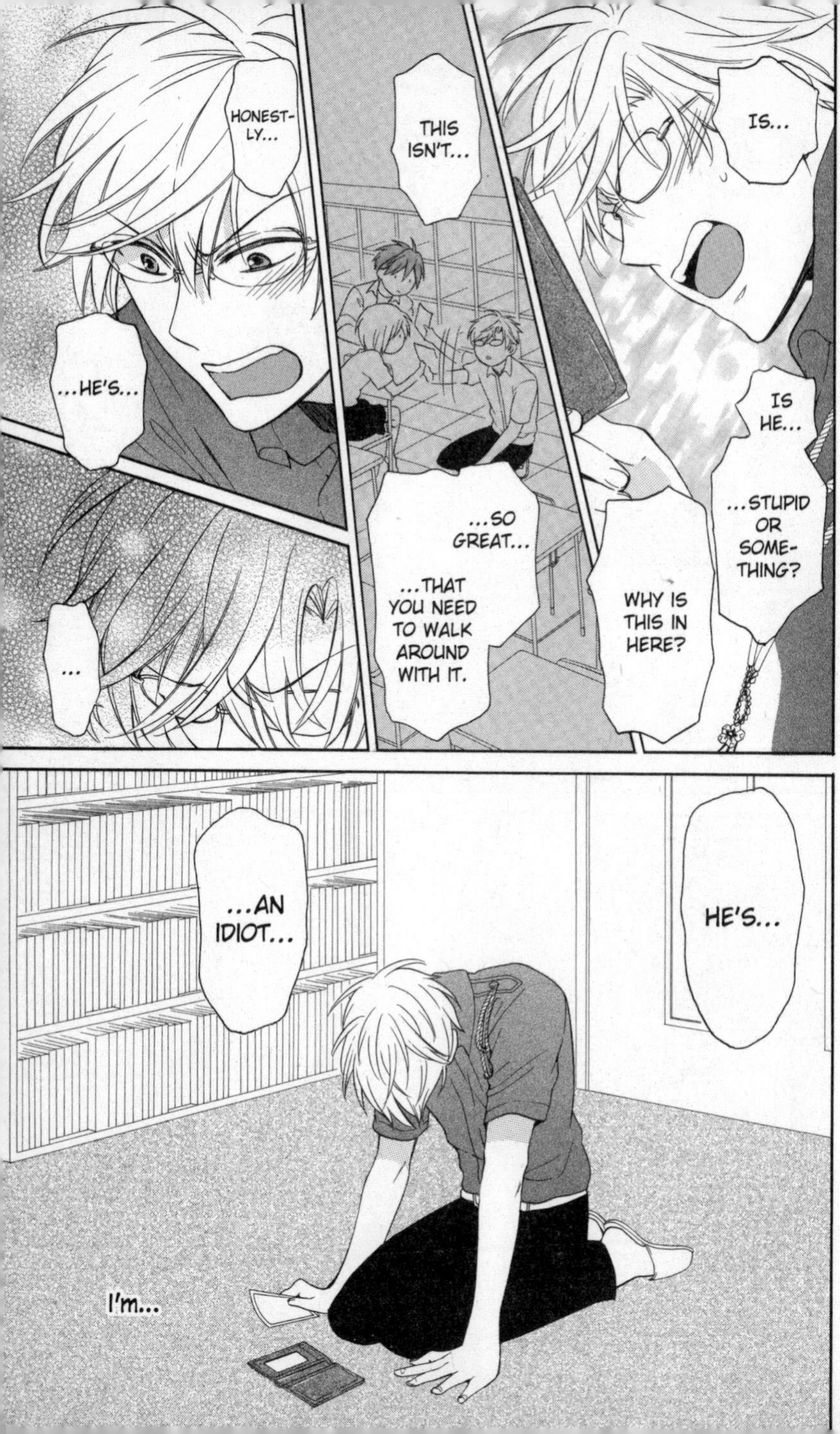
IS...
IS HE...
...STUPID OR SOMETHING?
WHY IS THIS IN HERE?
THIS ISN'T...
...SO GREAT...
...THAT YOU NEED TO WALK AROUND WITH IT.
HONESTLY...
...HE'S...
...
HE'S...
...AN IDIOT...
I'm...

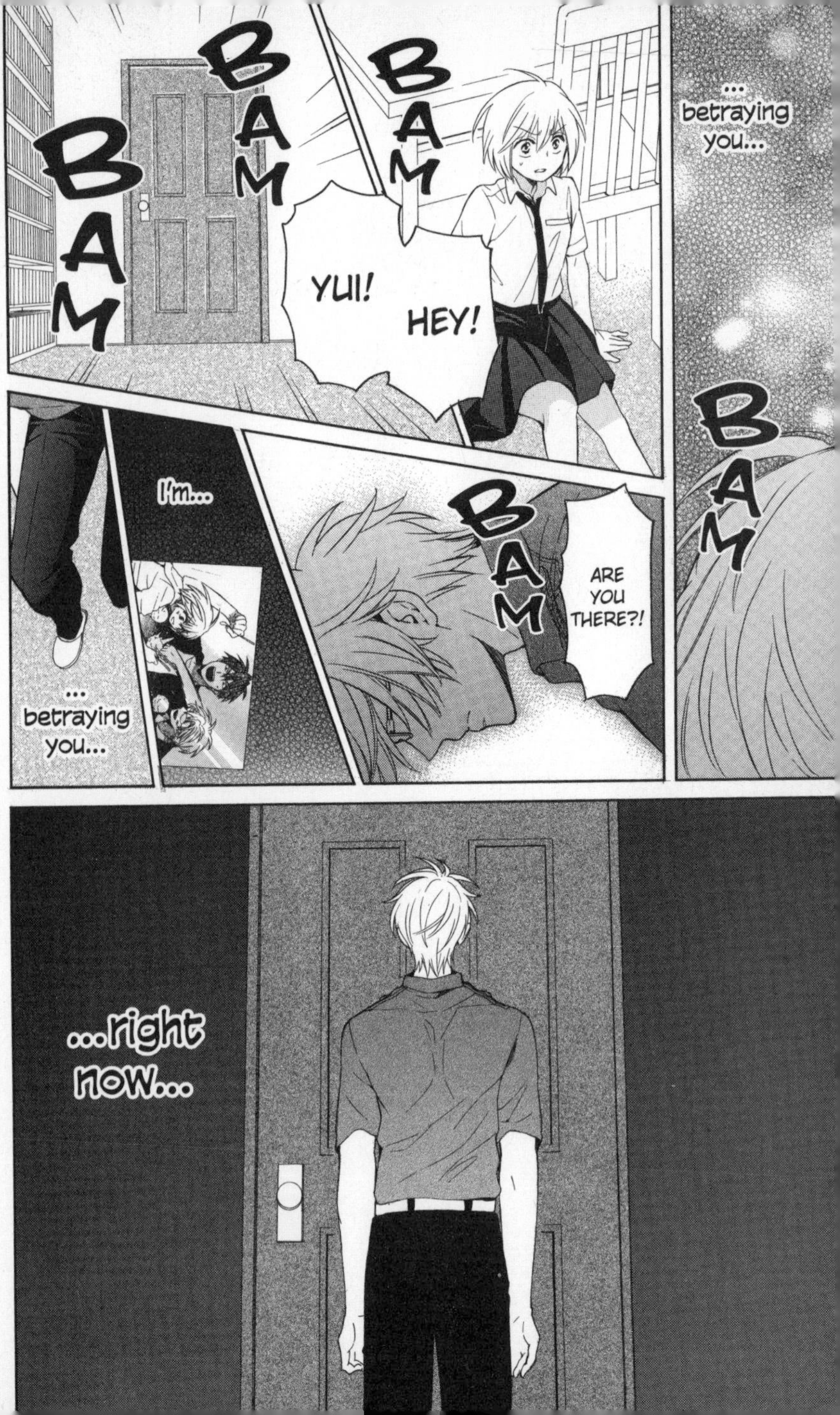

... betraying you...
BAM
BAM
YUI! HEY!
BAM
BAM
ARE YOU THERE?!
BAM
I'm...
... betraying you...
...right now...

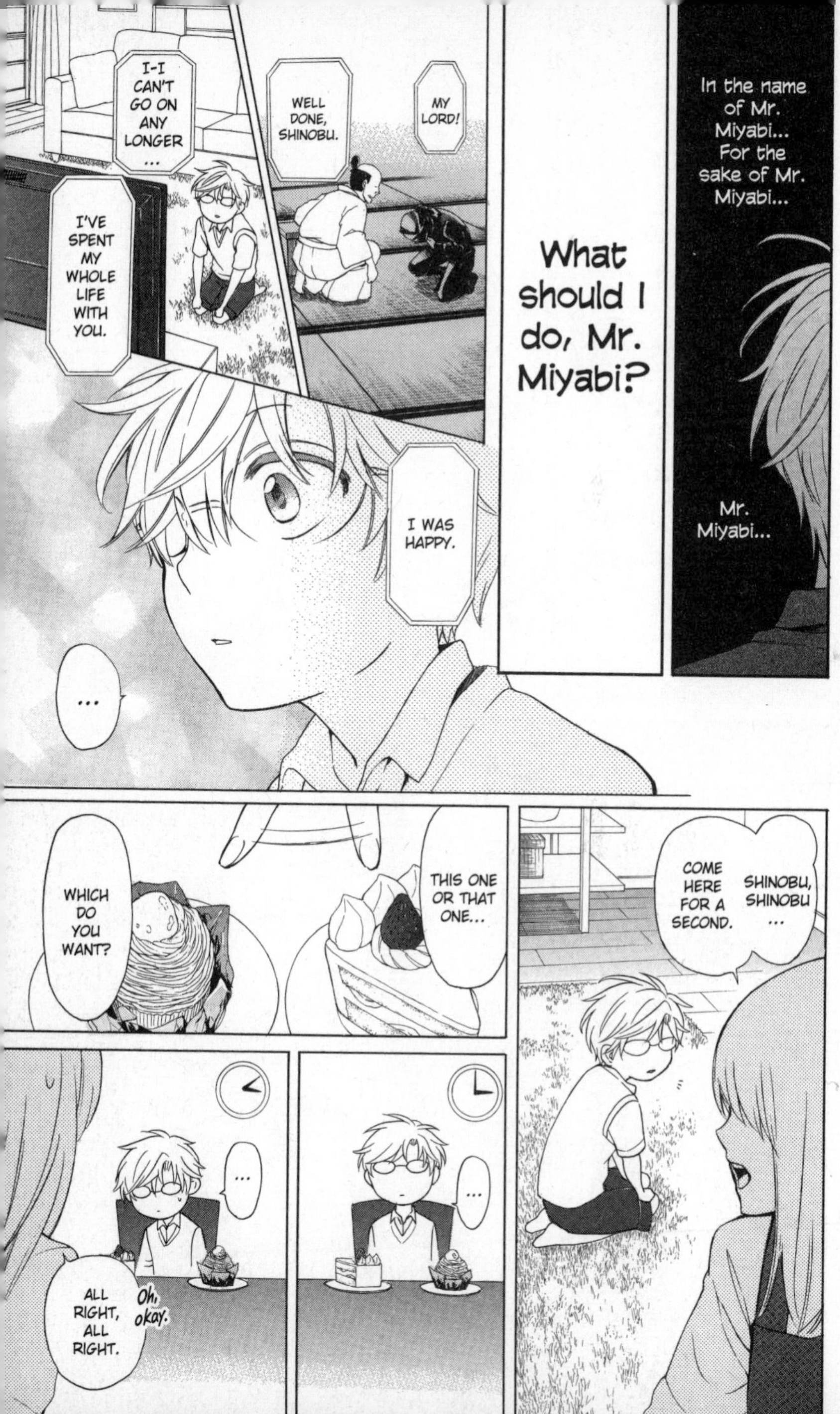

In the name of Mr. Miyabi... For the sake of Mr. Miyabi...
Mr. Miyabi...
What should I do, Mr. Miyabi?
MY LORD!
WELL DONE, SHINOBU.
I-I CAN'T GO ON ANY LONGER...
I'VE SPENT MY WHOLE LIFE WITH YOU.
I WAS HAPPY.
...
SHINOBU, SHINOBU...
COME HERE FOR A SECOND.
THIS ONE OR THAT ONE...
WHICH DO YOU WANT?
...
...
Oh, okay.
ALL RIGHT, ALL RIGHT.

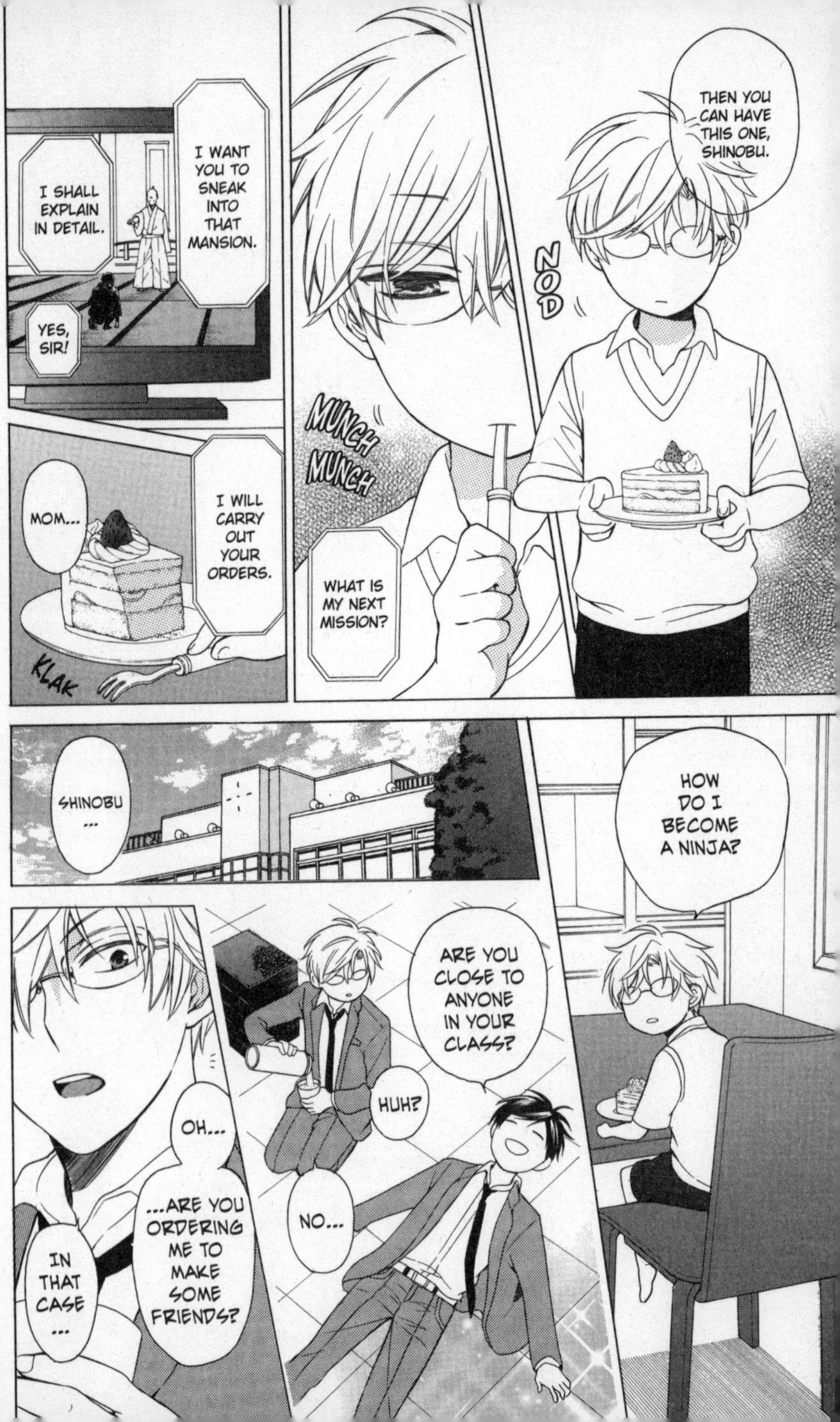
THEN YOU CAN HAVE THIS ONE, SHINOBU.
NOD
MUNCH MUNCH
WHAT IS MY NEXT MISSION?
I WANT YOU TO SNEAK INTO THAT MANSION.
I SHALL EXPLAIN IN DETAIL.
YES, SIR!
I WILL CARRY OUT YOUR ORDERS.
MOM...
KLAK
HOW DO I BECOME A NINJA?
SHINOBU...
ARE YOU CLOSE TO ANYONE IN YOUR CLASS?
HUH?
NO...
OH...
...ARE YOU ORDERING ME TO MAKE SOME FRIENDS?
IN THAT CASE...

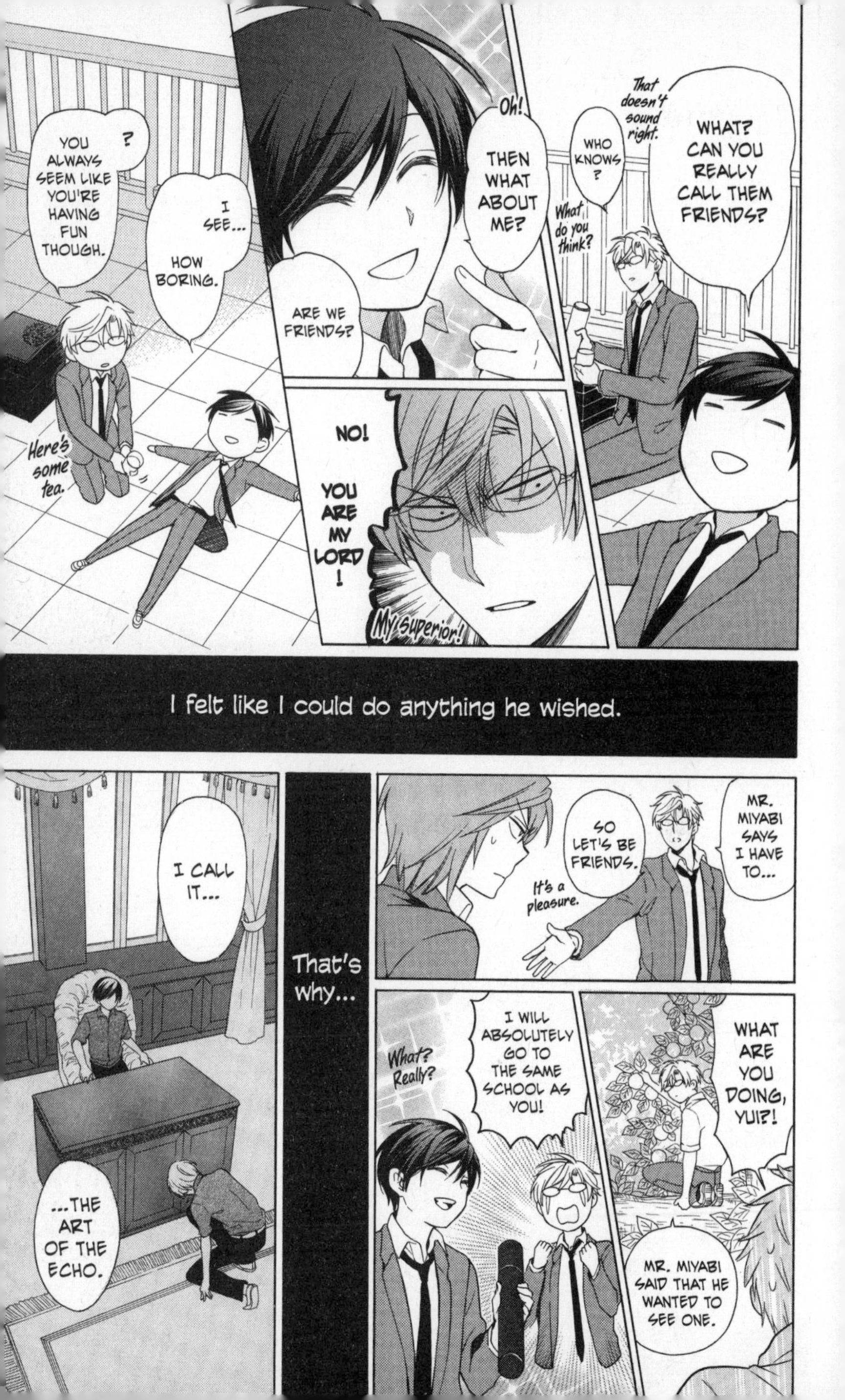
WHAT? CAN YOU REALLY CALL THEM FRIENDS?
That doesn't sound right.
WHO KNOWS?
What do you think?
Oh!
THEN WHAT ABOUT ME?
ARE WE FRIENDS?
NO!
YOU ARE MY LORD!
My superior!
?
YOU ALWAYS SEEM LIKE YOU'RE HAVING FUN THOUGH.
I SEE...
HOW BORING.
Here's some tea.
I felt like I could do anything he wished.
MR. MIYABI SAYS I HAVE TO...
SO LET'S BE FRIENDS.
It's a pleasure.
WHAT ARE YOU DOING, YUI?!
MR. MIYABI SAID THAT HE WANTED TO SEE ONE.
I WILL ABSOLUTELY GO TO THE SAME SCHOOL AS YOU!
What? Really?
That's why...
I CALL IT...
...THE ART OF THE ECHO.

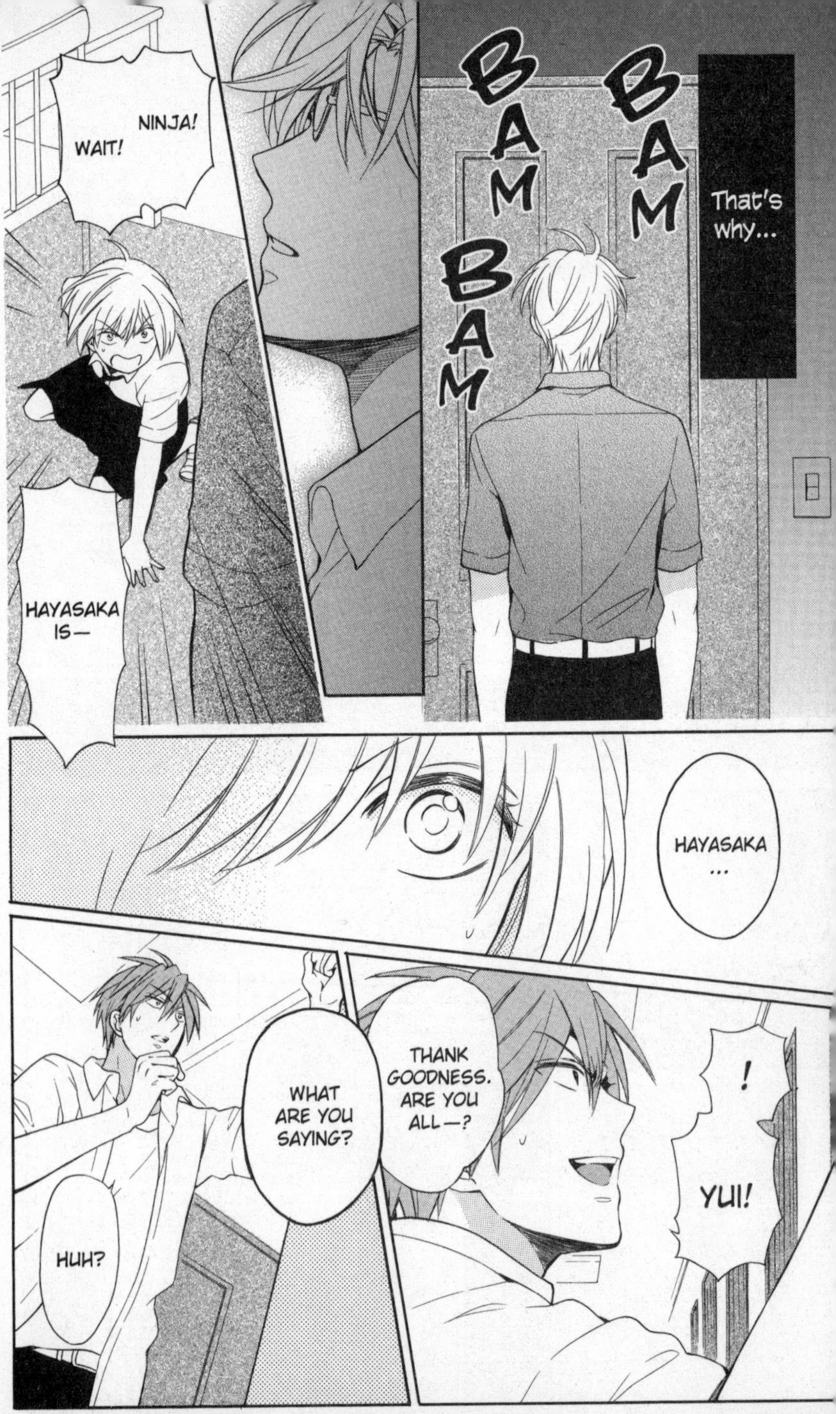

BAM
BAM
BAM
BAM
That's why...
NINJA! WAIT!
HAYASAKA IS—
HAYASAKA...
!
YUI!
THANK GOODNESS. ARE YOU ALL—?
WHAT ARE YOU SAYING?
HUH?

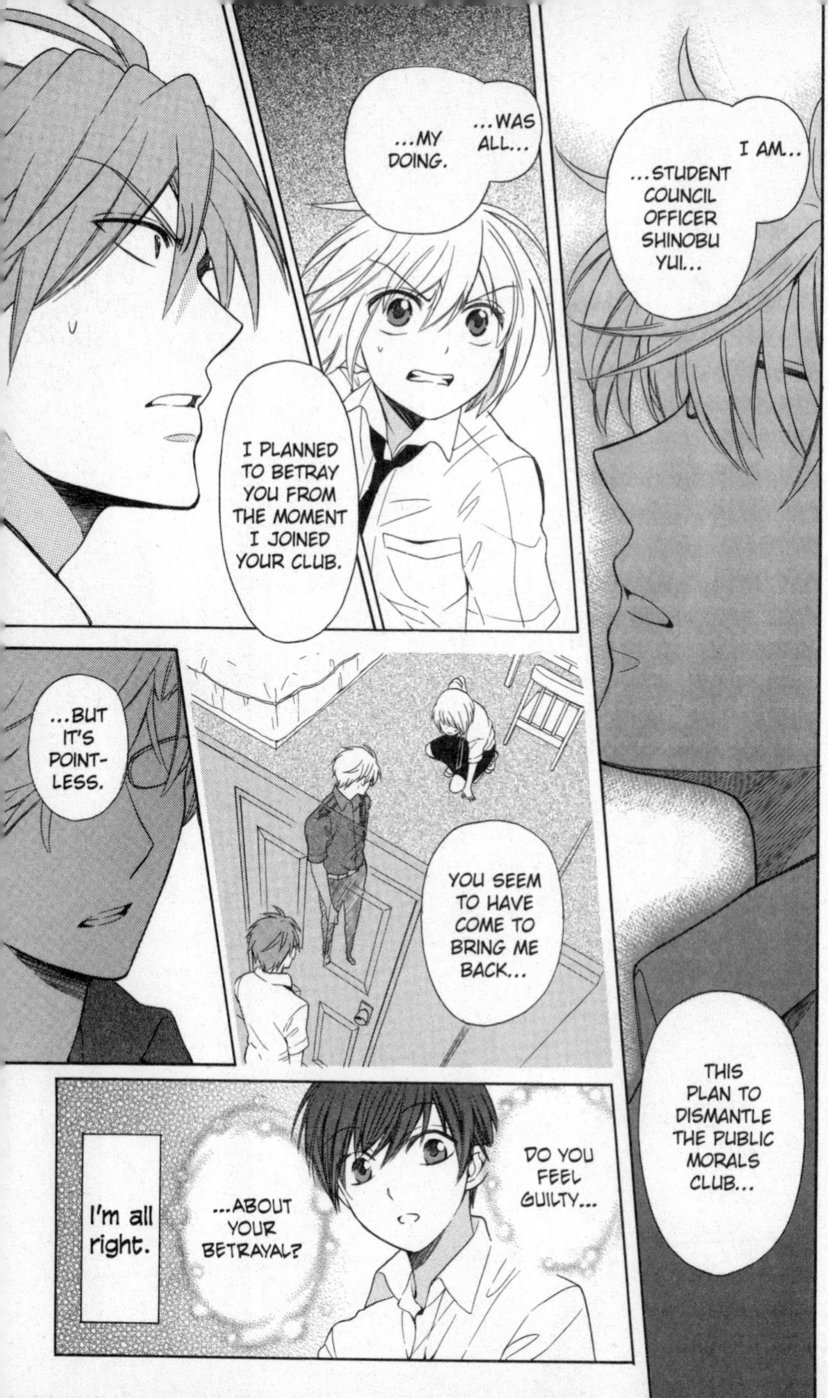
I AM...
...STUDENT COUNCIL OFFICER SHINOBU YUI...
THIS PLAN TO DISMANTLE THE PUBLIC MORALS CLUB...
...WAS ALL...
...MY DOING.
I PLANNED TO BETRAY YOU FROM THE MOMENT I JOINED YOUR CLUB.
YOU SEEM TO HAVE COME TO BRING ME BACK...
...BUT IT'S POINT-LESS.
DO YOU FEEL GUILTY...
...ABOUT YOUR BETRAYAL?
I'm all right.

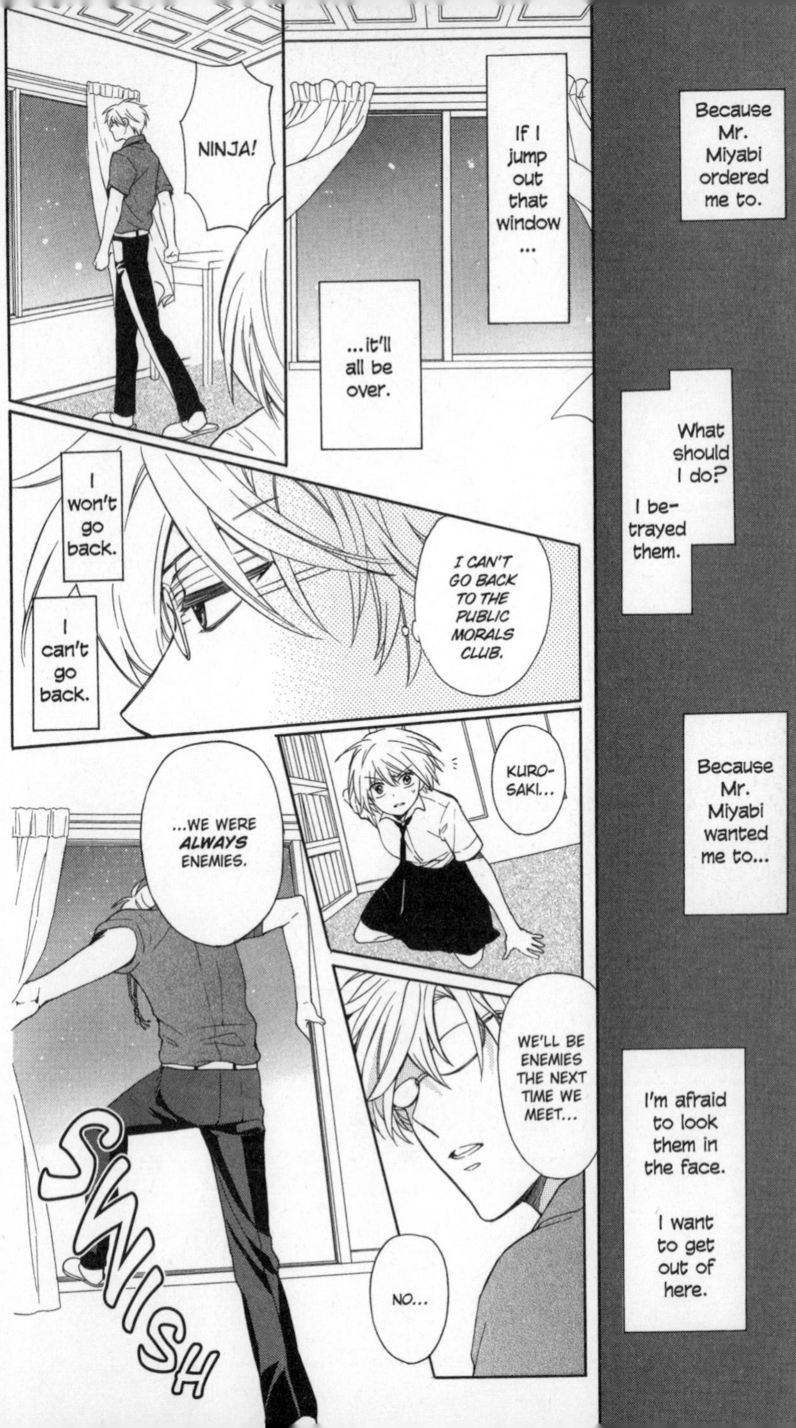
Because Mr. Miyabi ordered me to.
What should I do?
I be-trayed them.
Because Mr. Miyabi wanted me to...
I'm afraid to look them in the face.
I want to get out of here.
If I jump out that window...
...it'll all be over.
NINJA!
I CAN'T GO BACK TO THE PUBLIC MORALS CLUB.
I won't go back.
I can't go back.
KURO-SAKI...
WE'LL BE ENEMIES THE NEXT TIME WE MEET...
NO...
...WE WERE ALWAYS ENEMIES.
SWISH

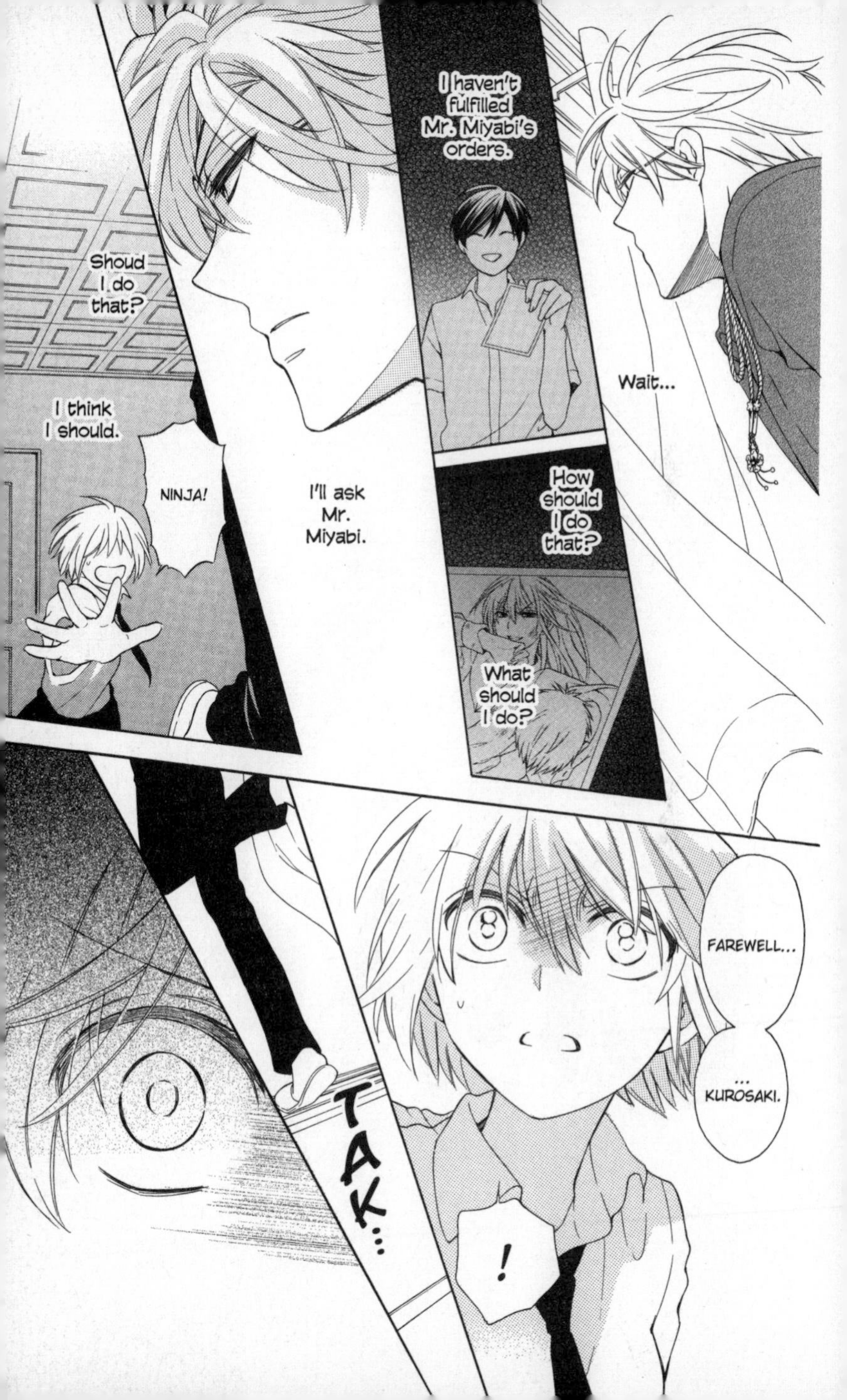
Wait...
I haven't fulfilled Mr. Miyabi's orders.
How should I do that?
What should I do?
I'll ask Mr. Miyabi.
Shoud I do that?
I think I should.
NINJA!
FAREWELL...
...KUROSAKI.
!
TAK...

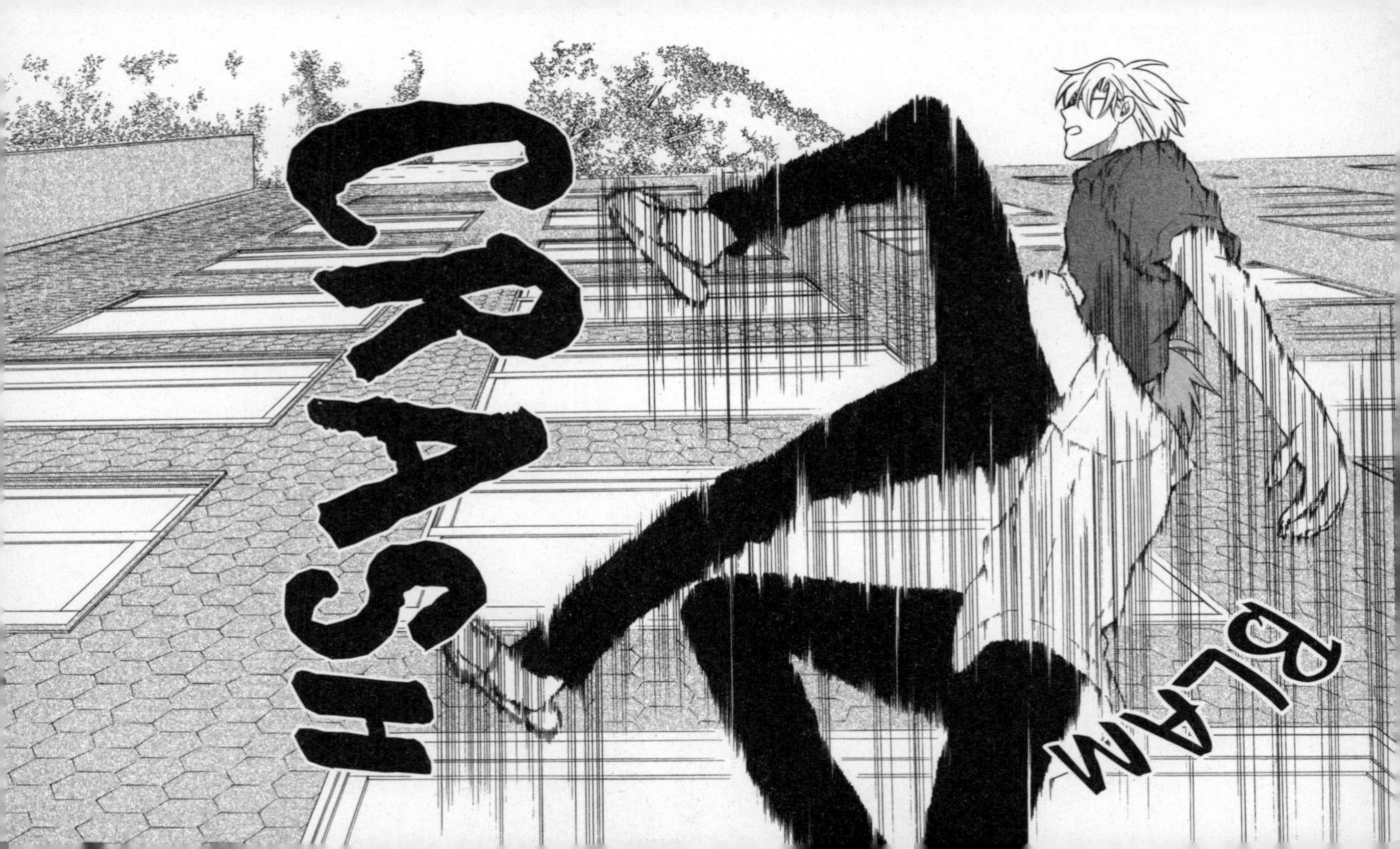
BLAM
CRASH

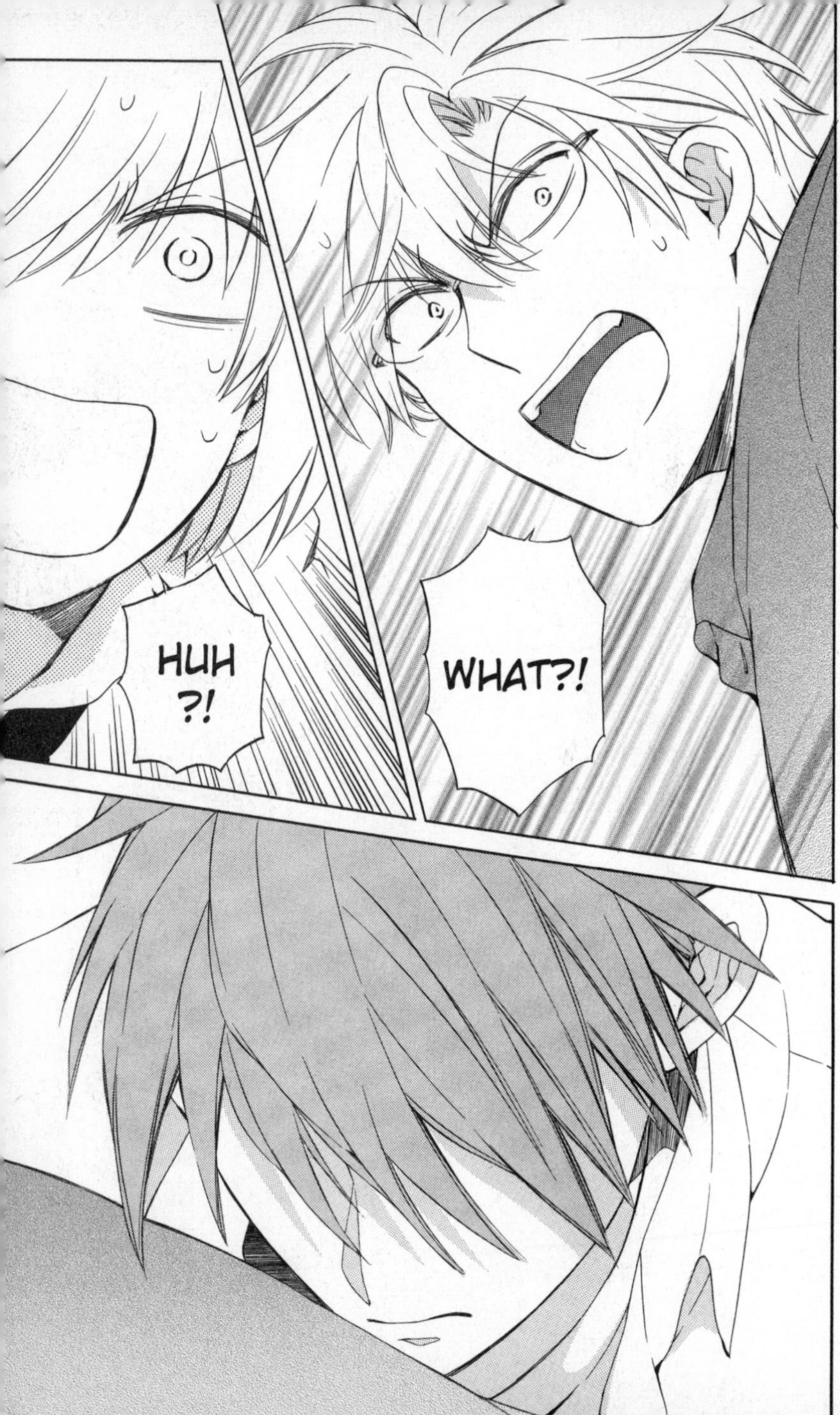
WHAT?!
HUH ?!

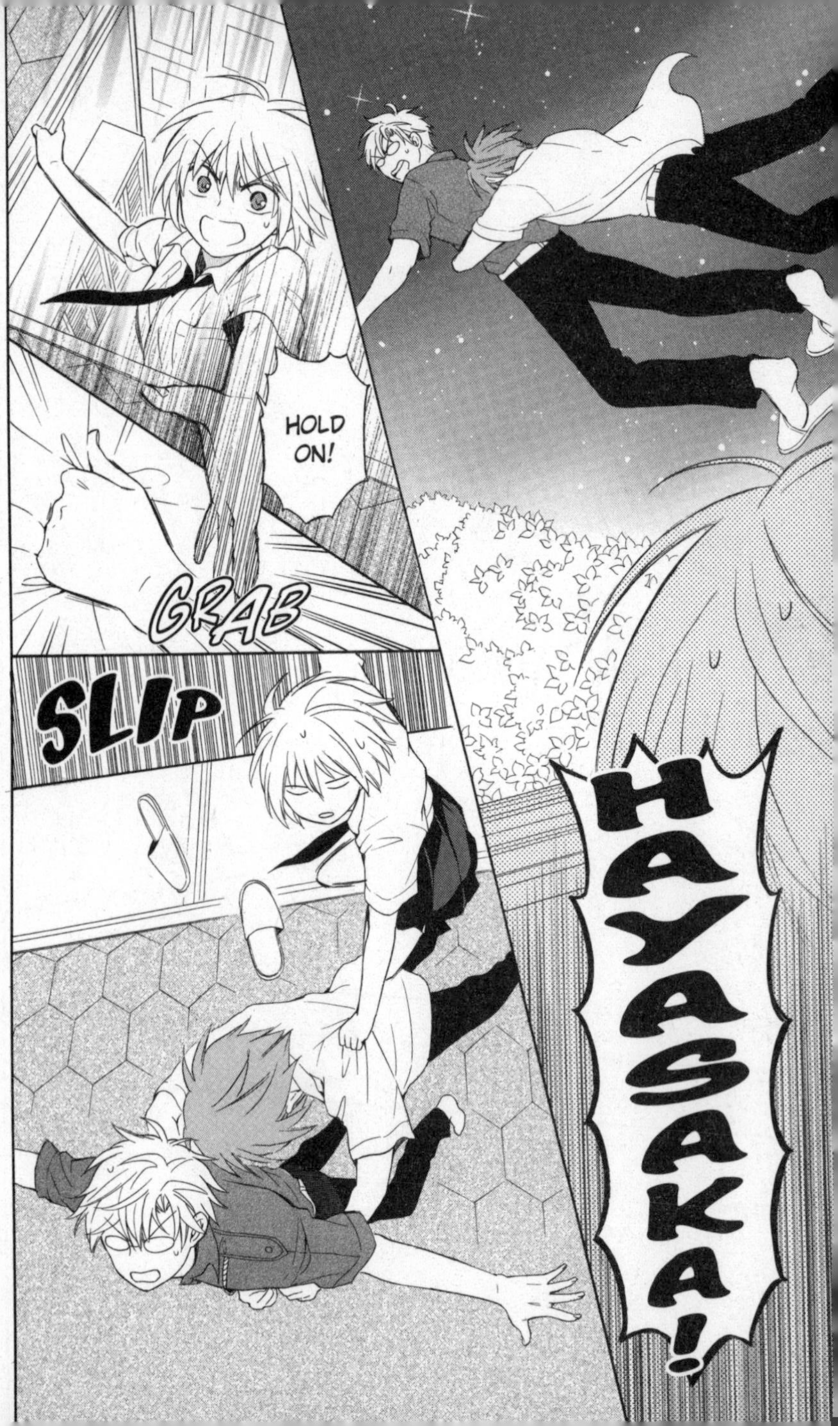
HAYASAKA!
HOLD ON!
GRAB
SLIP

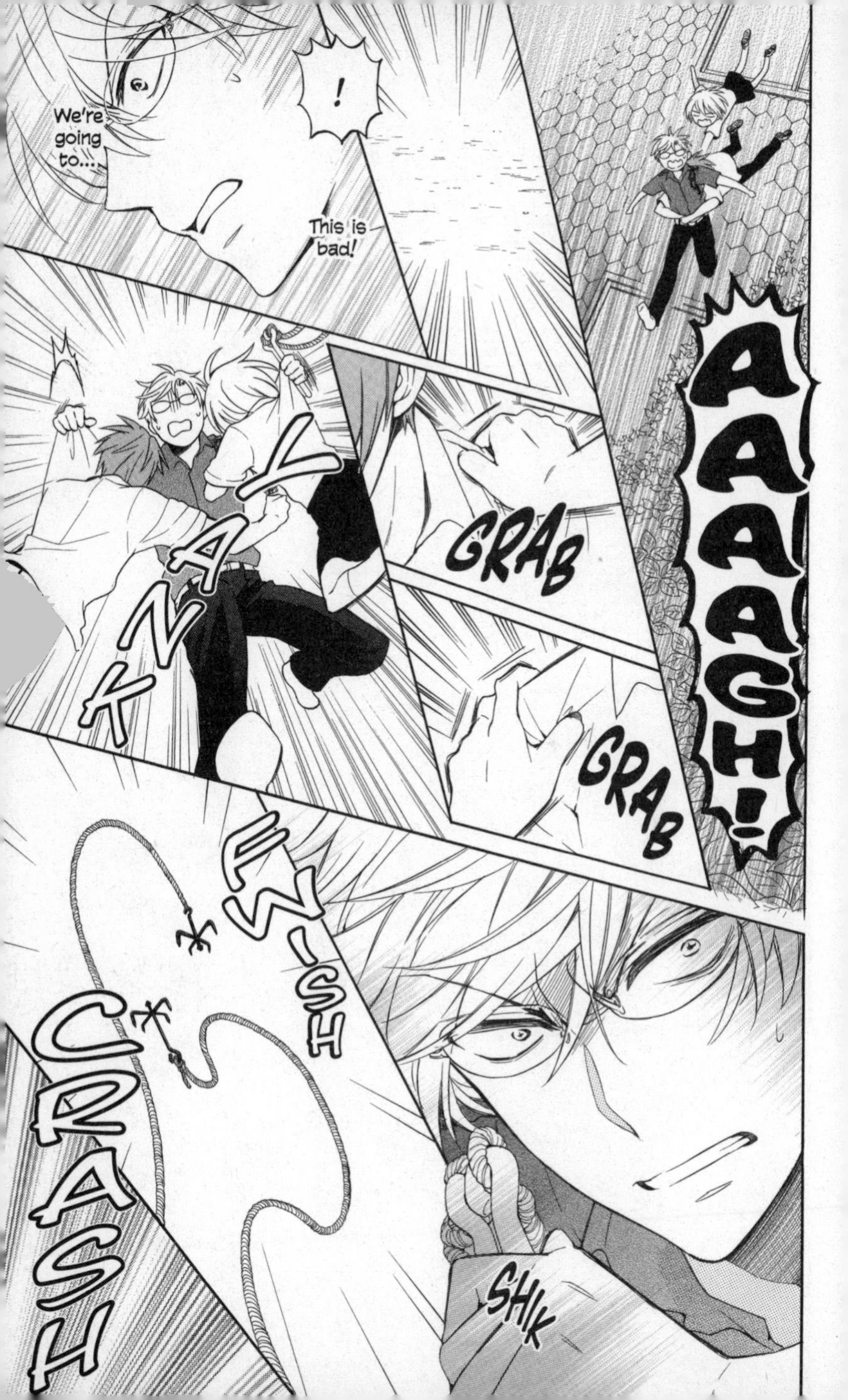
AAAAGH!
!
This is bad!
We're going to...
GRAB
GRAB
YANK
SHIK
FWISH
CRASH

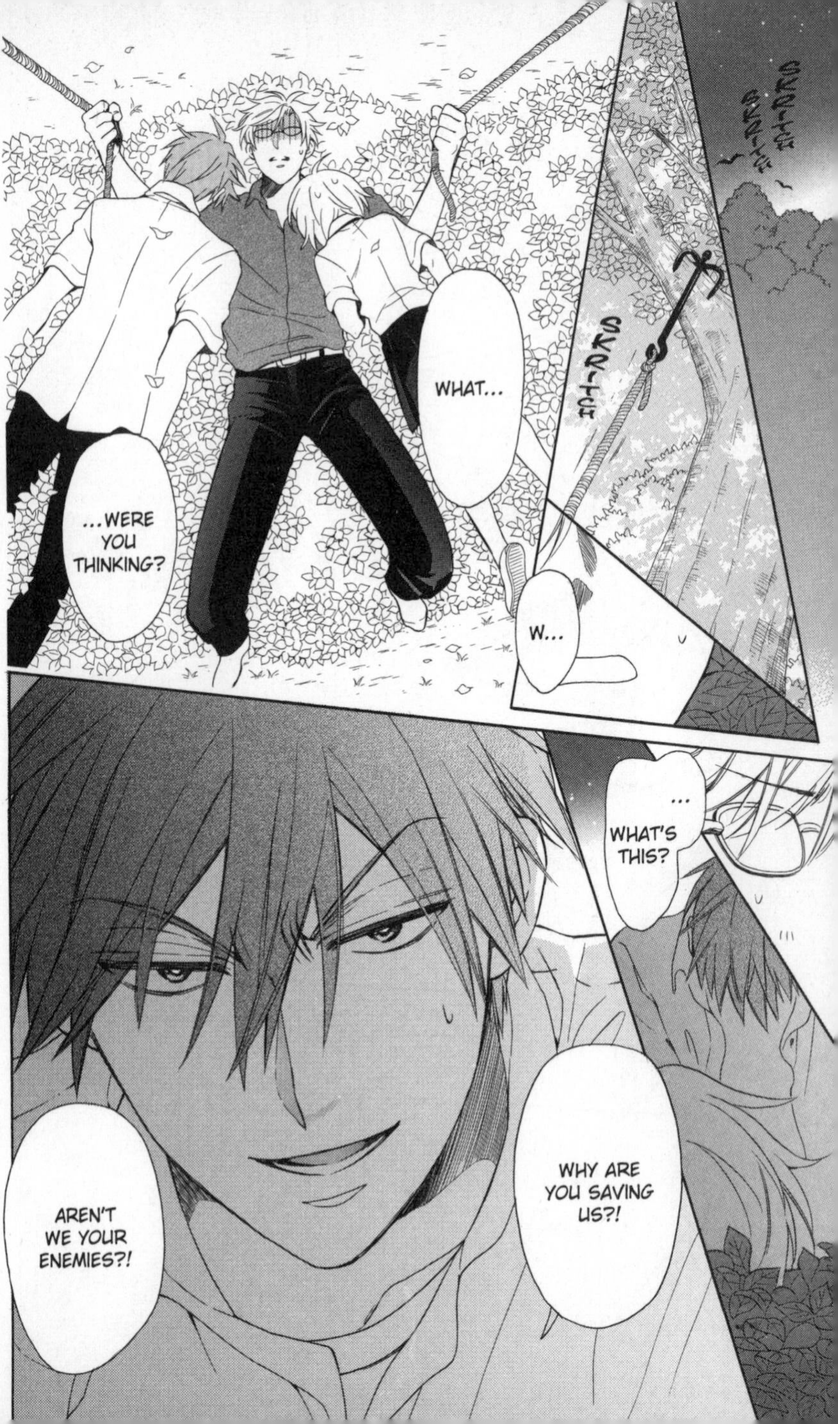
SKRITCH
SKRITCH
SKRITCH
W...
WHAT...
...WERE YOU THINKING?
...WHAT'S THIS?
WHY ARE YOU SAVING US?!
AREN'T WE YOUR ENEMIES?!

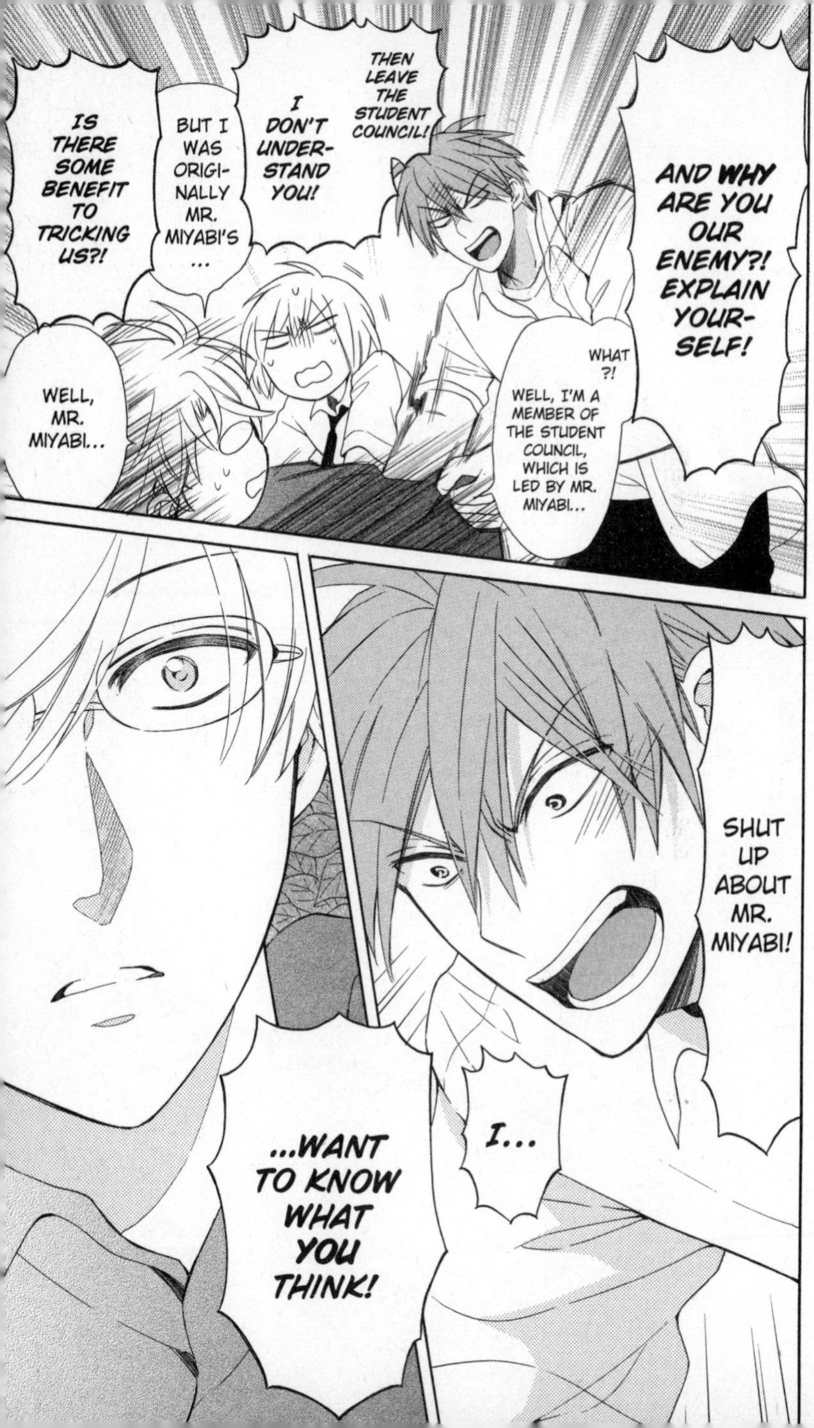
AND WHY ARE YOU OUR ENEMY?! EXPLAIN YOURSELF!
THEN LEAVE THE STUDENT COUNCIL!
I DON'T UNDERSTAND YOU!
BUT I WAS ORIGINALLY MR. MIYABI'S ...
IS THERE SOME BENEFIT TO TRICKING US?!
WHAT?!
WELL, I'M A MEMBER OF THE STUDENT COUNCIL, WHICH IS LED BY MR. MIYABI...
WELL, MR. MIYABI...
SHUT UP ABOUT MR. MIYABI!
I...
...WANT TO KNOW WHAT YOU THINK!

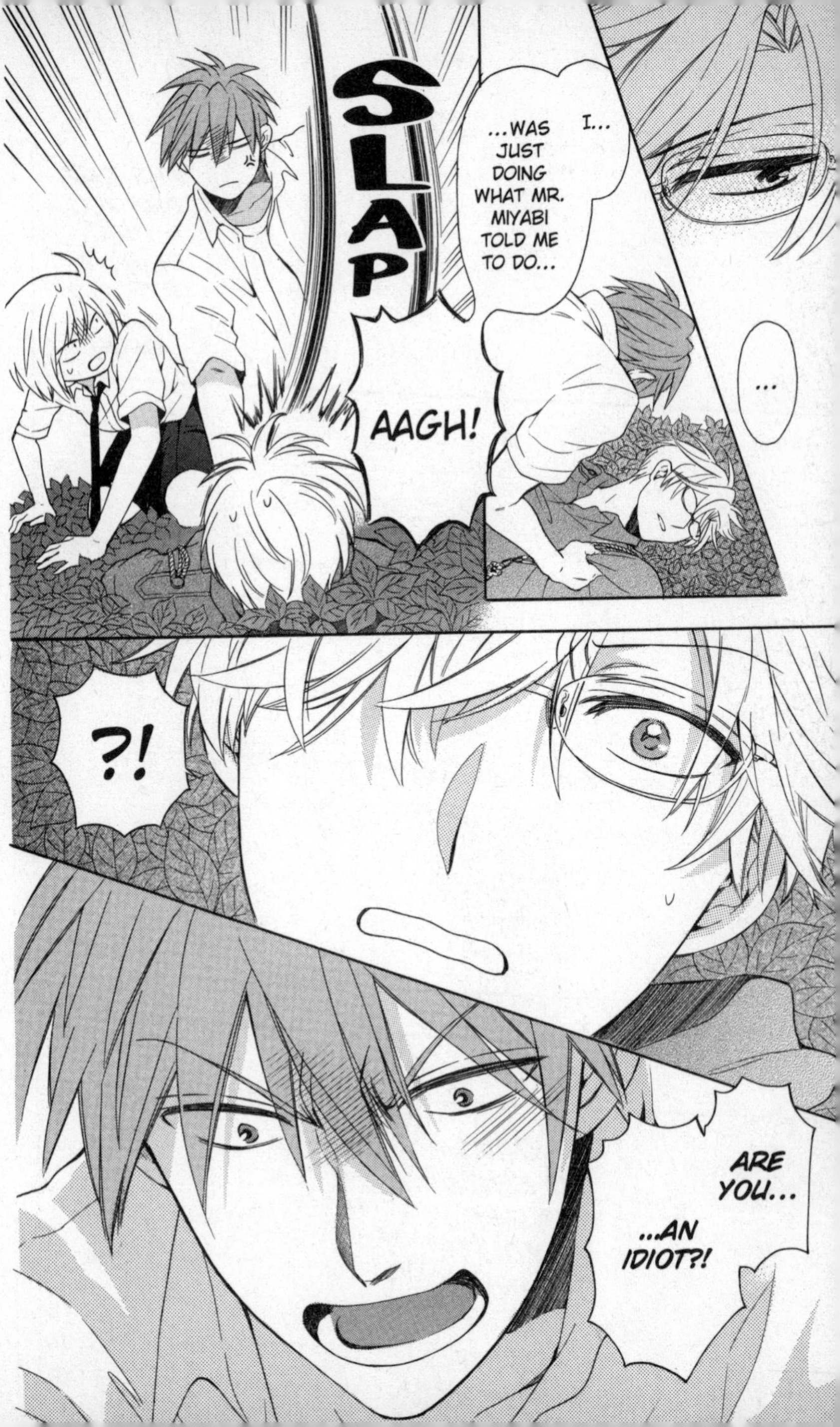

I... ...WAS JUST DOING WHAT MR. MIYABI TOLD ME TO DO...
...
SLAP
AAGH!
?!
ARE YOU...
...AN IDIOT?!

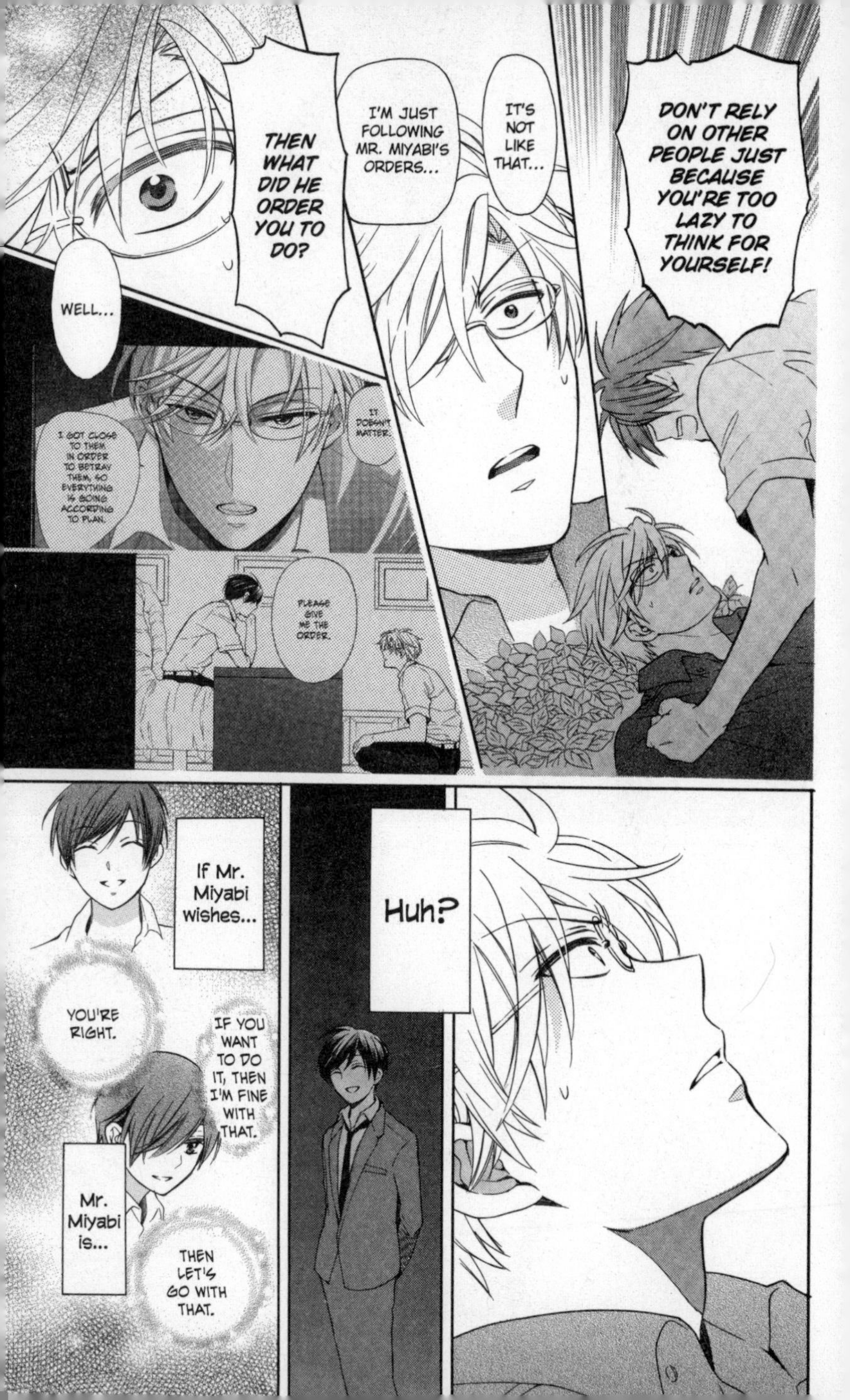
DON'T RELY ON OTHER PEOPLE JUST BECAUSE YOU'RE TOO LAZY TO THINK FOR YOURSELF!
IT'S NOT LIKE THAT...
I'M JUST FOLLOWING MR. MIYABI'S ORDERS...
THEN WHAT DID HE ORDER YOU TO DO?
WELL...
IT DOESN'T MATTER.
I GOT CLOSE TO THEM IN ORDER TO BETRAY THEM, SO EVERYTHING IS GOING ACCORDING TO PLAN.
PLEASE GIVE ME THE ORDER.
Huh?
If Mr. Miyabi wishes...
YOU'RE RIGHT.
IF YOU WANT TO DO IT, THEN I'M FINE WITH THAT.
Mr. Miyabi is...
THEN LET'S GO WITH THAT.

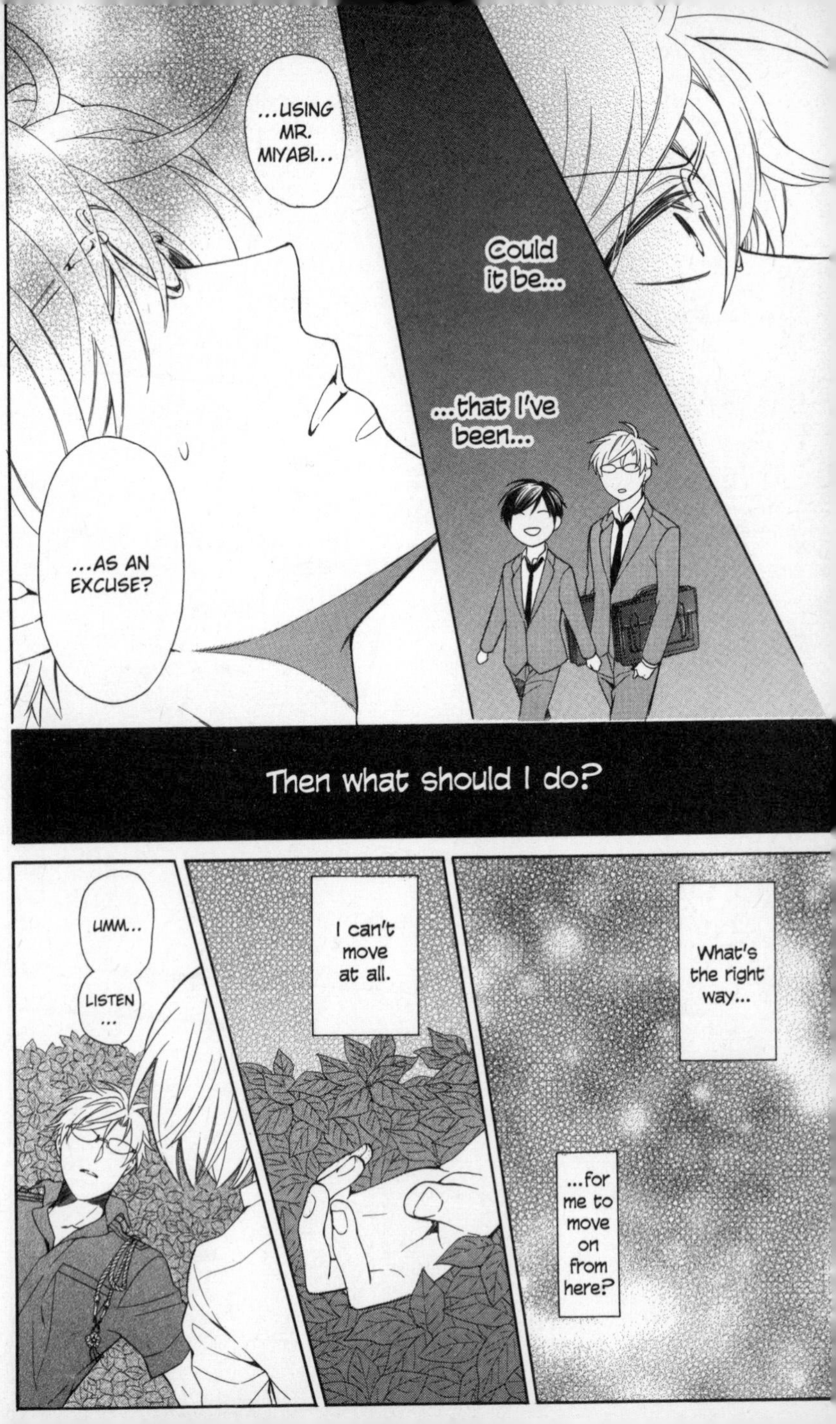
Could it be...
...that I've been...
...USING MR. MIYABI...
...AS AN EXCUSE?
Then what should I do?
What's the right way...
...for me to move on from here?
I can't move at all.
UMM...
LISTEN...

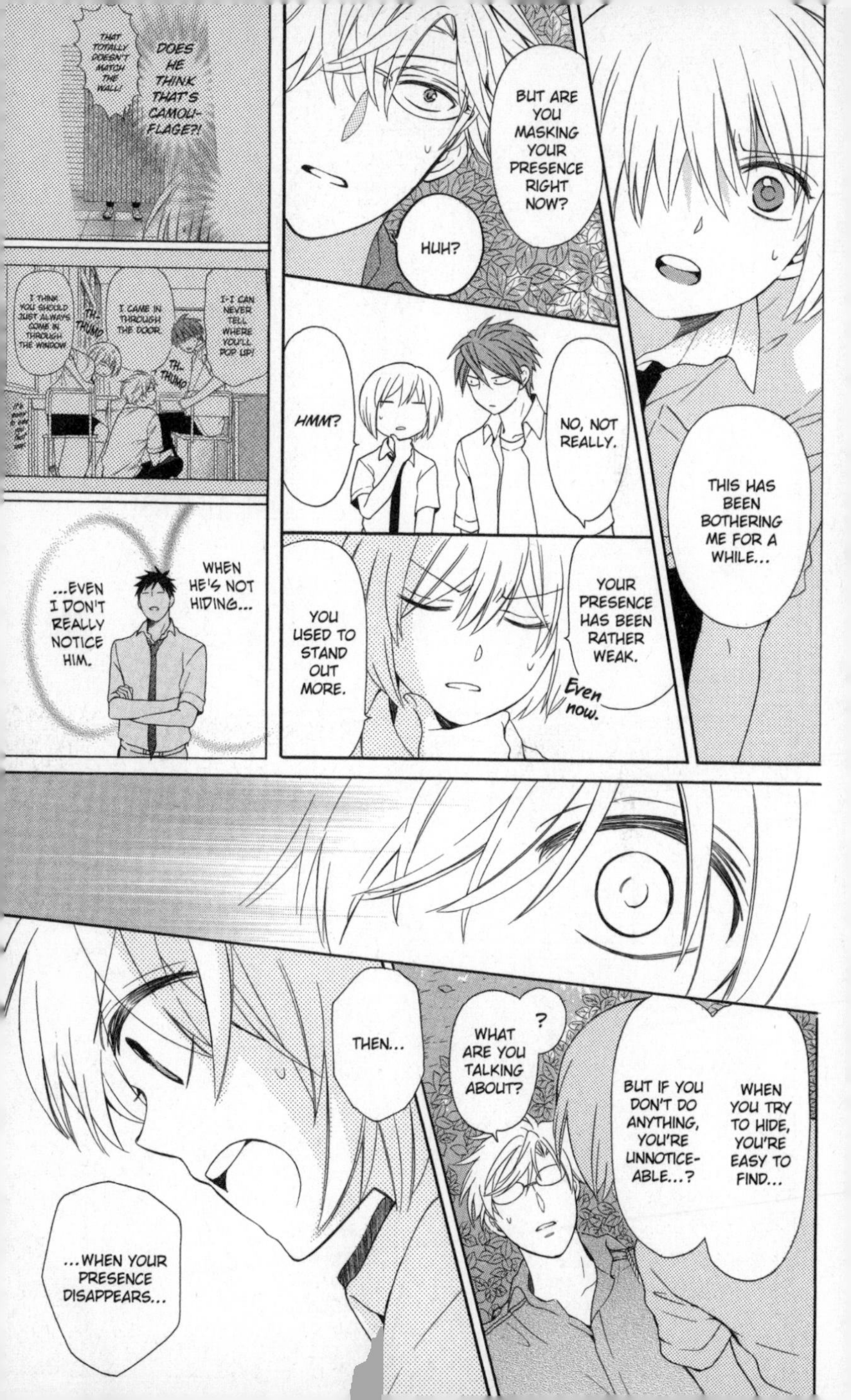
THIS HAS BEEN BOTHERING ME FOR A WHILE...
BUT ARE YOU MASKING YOUR PRESENCE RIGHT NOW?
HUH?
NO, NOT REALLY.
HMM?
YOUR PRESENCE HAS BEEN RATHER WEAK.
Even now.
YOU USED TO STAND OUT MORE.
DOES HE THINK THAT'S CAMOUFLAGE?!
THAT TOTALLY DOESN'T MATCH THE WALL!
I-I CAN NEVER TELL WHERE YOU'LL POP UP!
TH-THUMP
I CAME IN THROUGH THE DOOR.
TH-THUMP
I THINK YOU SHOULD JUST ALWAYS COME IN THROUGH THE WINDOW.
It's easy to see you that way.
WHEN HE'S NOT HIDING...
...EVEN I DON'T REALLY NOTICE HIM.
WHEN YOU TRY TO HIDE, YOU'RE EASY TO FIND...
BUT IF YOU DON'T DO ANYTHING, YOU'RE UNNOTICE-ABLE...?
?
WHAT ARE YOU TALKING ABOUT?
THEN...
...WHEN YOUR PRESENCE DISAPPEARS...

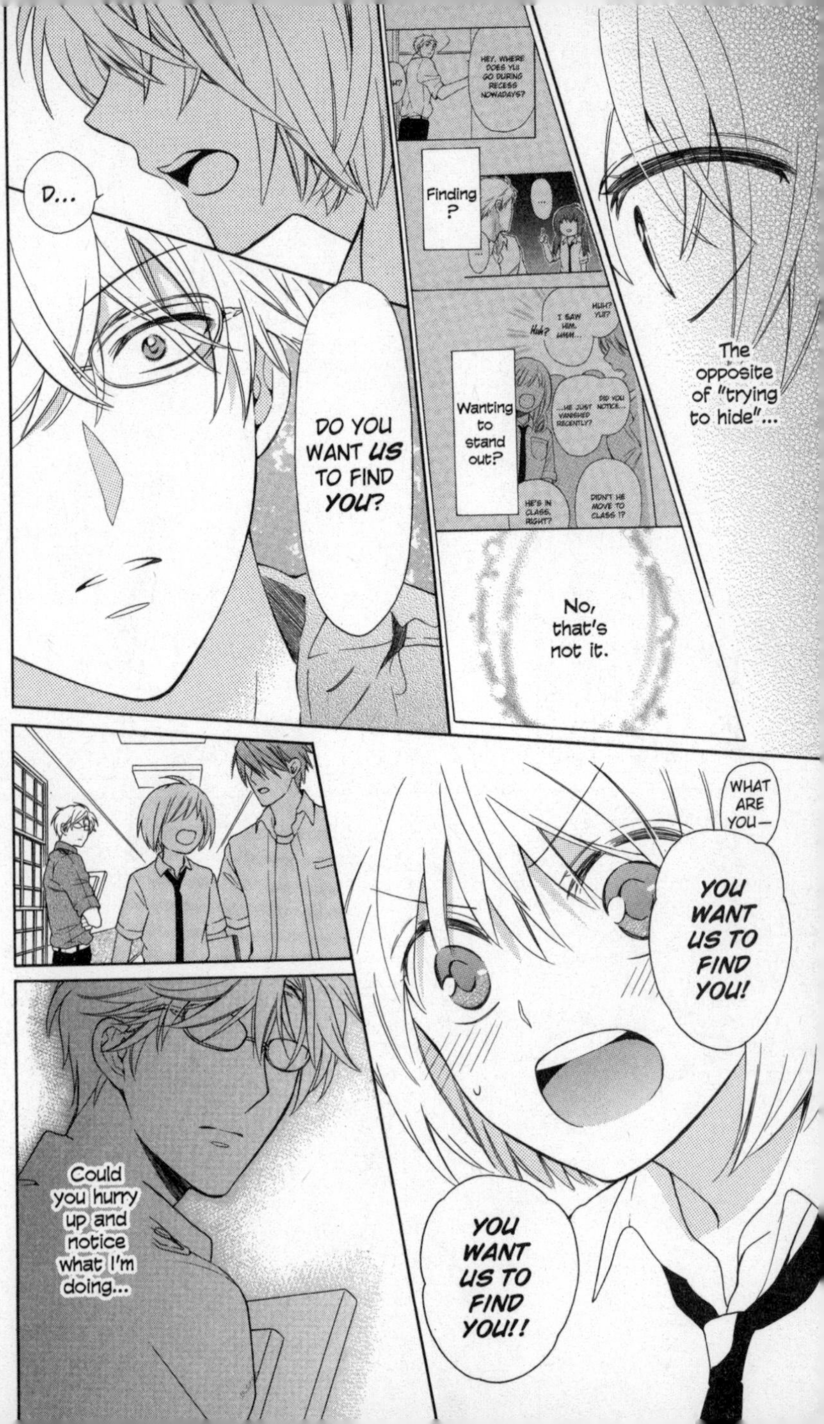
The opposite of "trying to hide"...
HEY, WHERE DOES YUI GO DURING RECESS NOWADAYS?
...
Finding?
...
HUH? YUI?
I SAW HIM. UMM...
Huh?
DID YOU NOTICE... ...HE JUST VANISHED RECENTLY?
Wanting to stand out?
DIDN'T HE MOVE TO CLASS 1?
HE'S IN CLASS, RIGHT?
No, that's not it.
D...
DO YOU WANT US TO FIND YOU?
WHAT ARE YOU—
YOU WANT US TO FIND YOU!
YOU WANT US TO FIND YOU!!
Could you hurry up and notice what I'm doing...

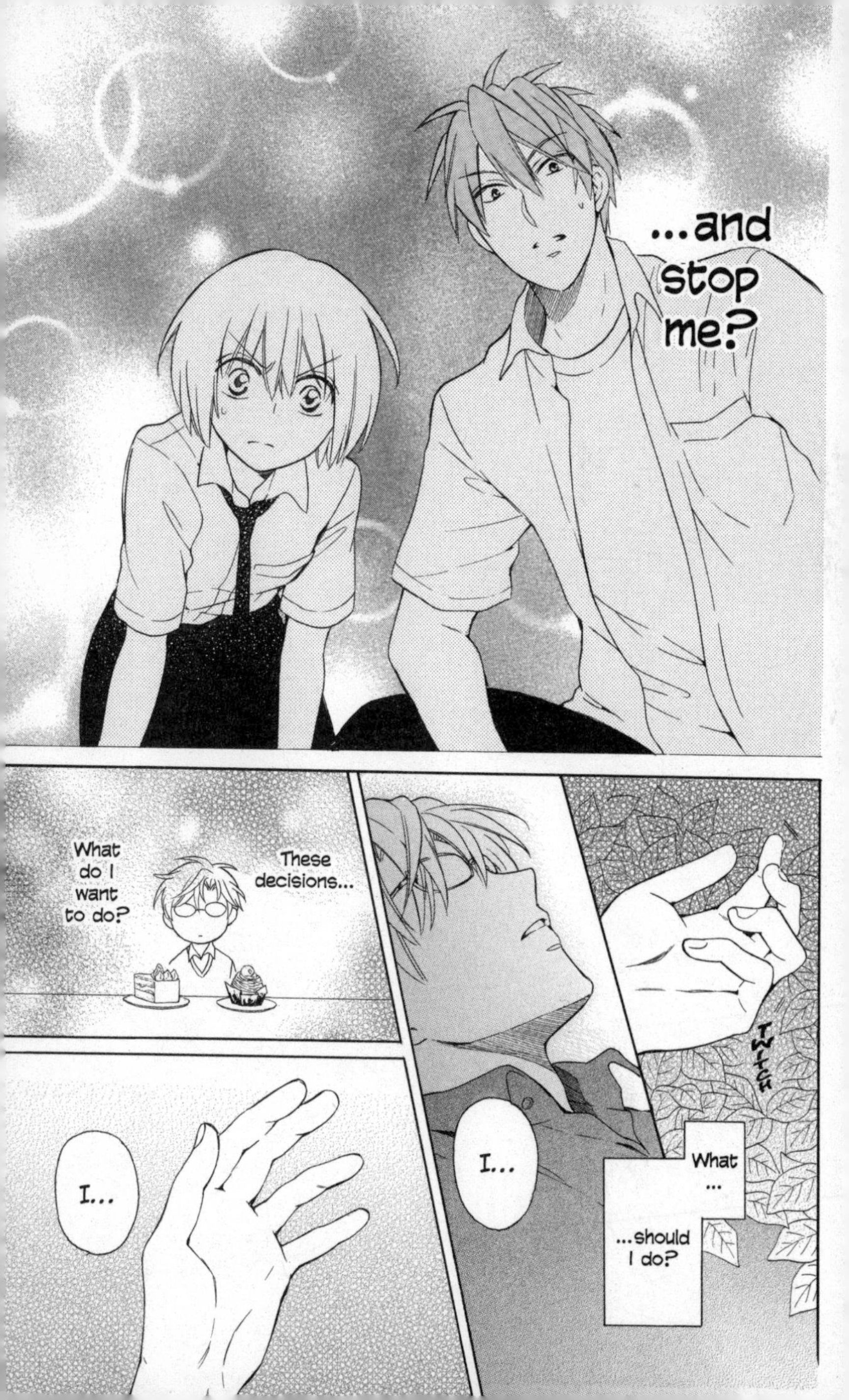
...and stop me?
TWITCH
What ...
...should I do?
I...
These decisions...
What do I want to do?
I...

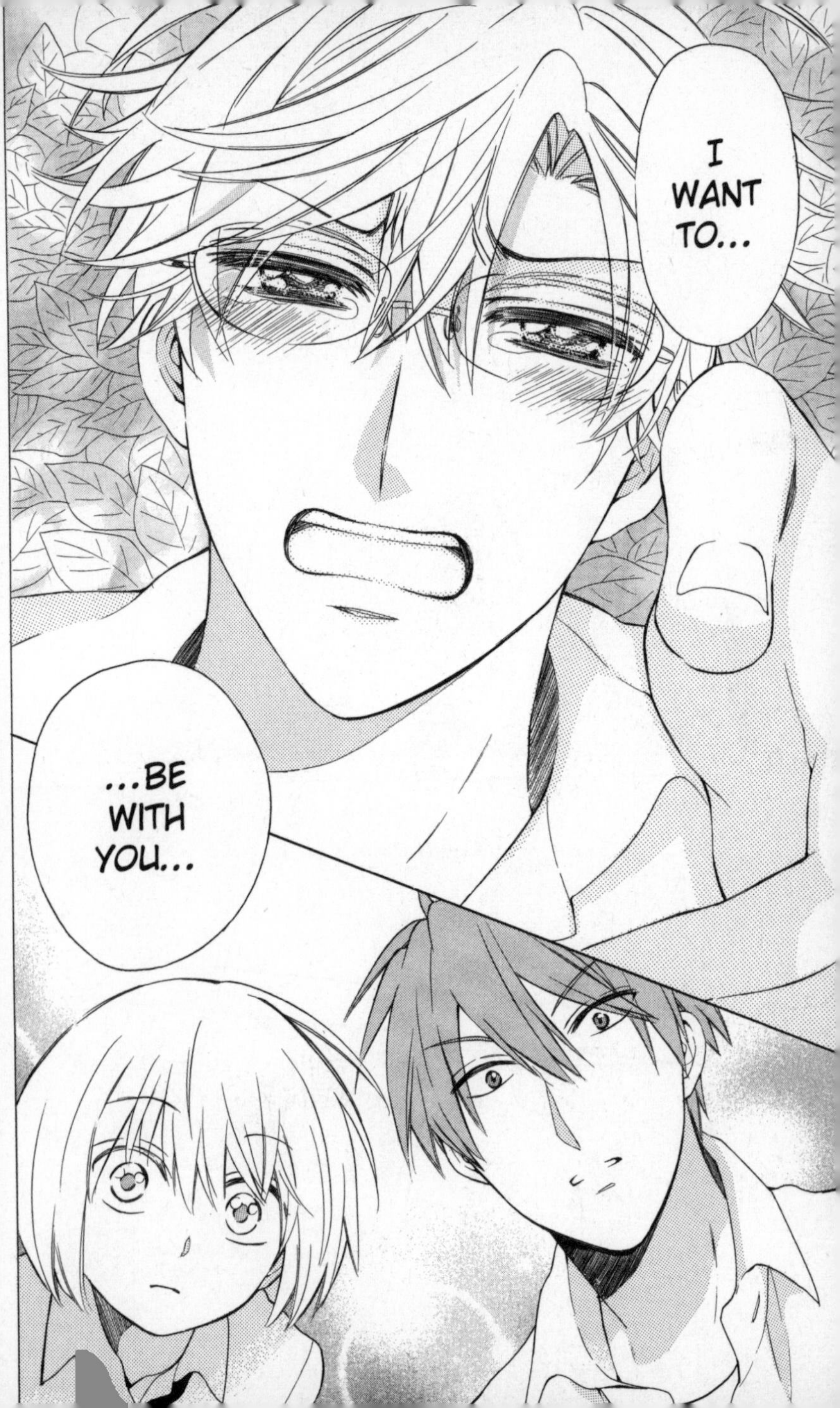
I WANT TO...
...BE WITH YOU...

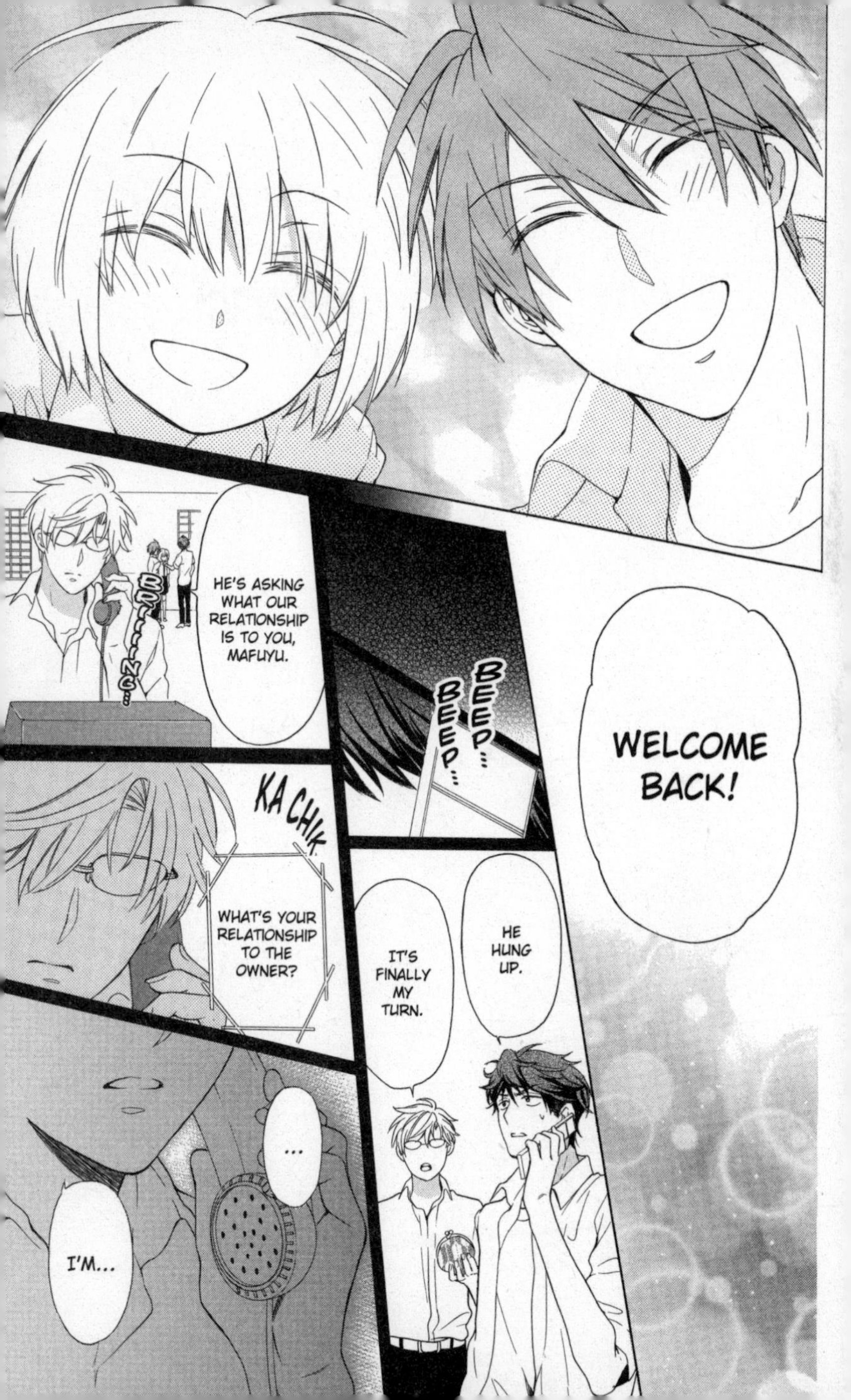
WELCOME BACK!
BEEP... BEEP...
HE HUNG UP.
IT'S FINALLY MY TURN.
HE'S ASKING WHAT OUR RELATIONSHIP IS TO YOU, MAFUYU.
BRIIIING...
KA CHIK
WHAT'S YOUR RELATIONSHIP TO THE OWNER?
...
I'M...

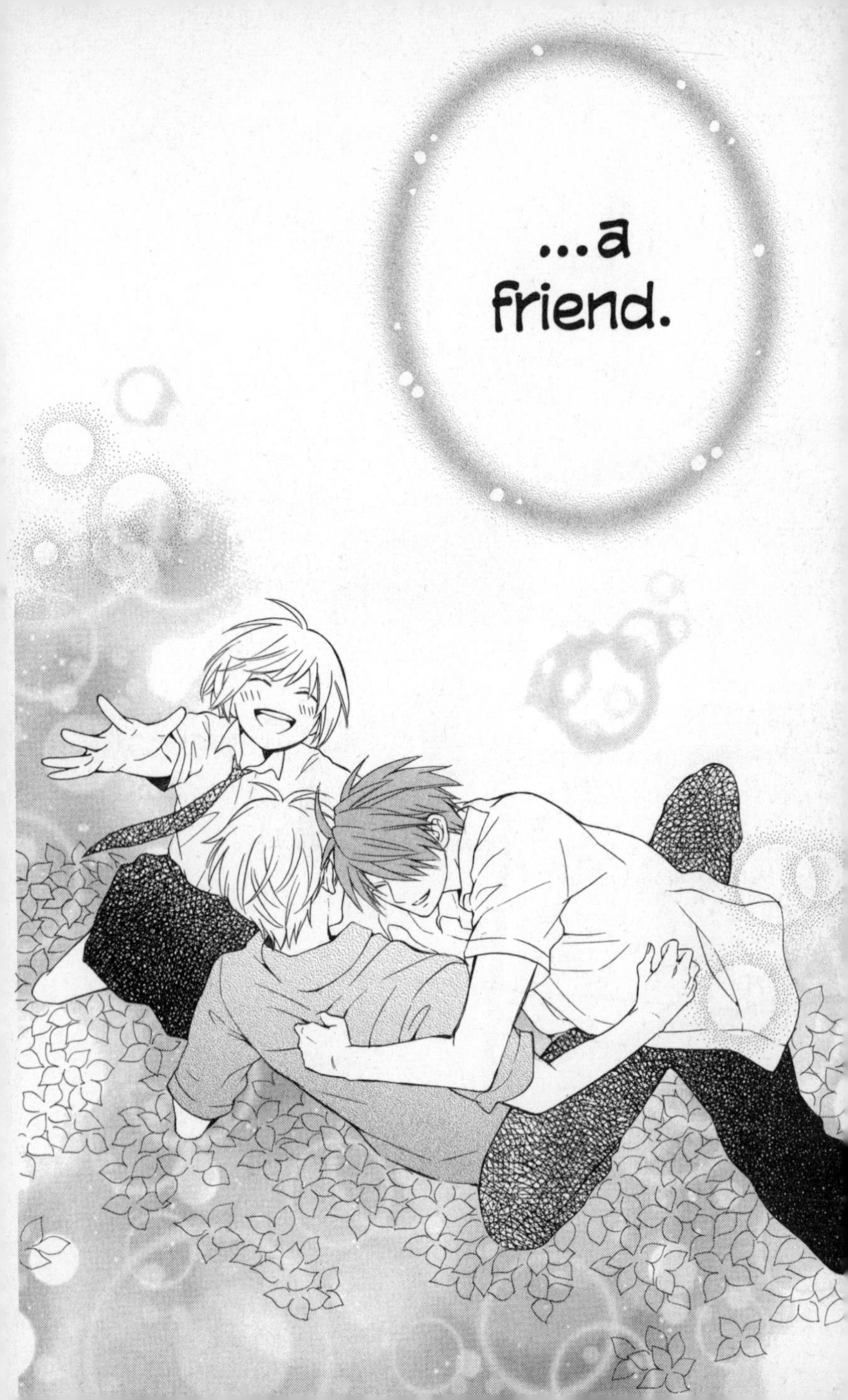
...a
friend.

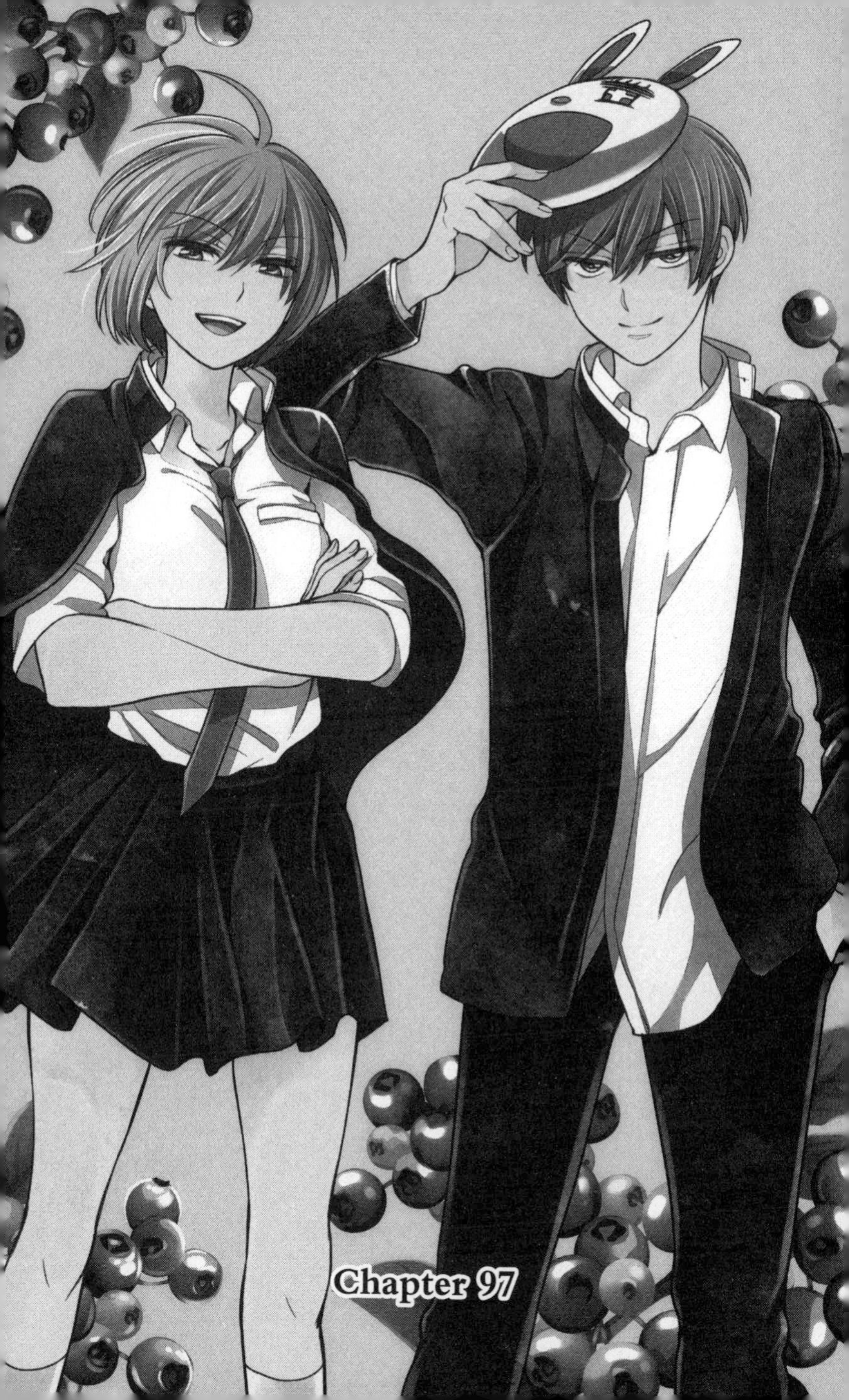
Chapter 97

Character PROFILE

THIS SEGMENT IS WHERE WE INTRODUCE THINGS ABOUT THE MAIN CHARACTERS THAT YOU WOULDN'T KNOW FROM THE MAIN STORY, LIKE THEIR BIRTHDAY, BLOOD TYPE, LIKES AND DISLIKES, AND OTHER THINGS!

"PERSONALITY PREFERENCE" ISN'T ABOUT THE CHARACTERS THEMSELVES, BUT RATHER ABOUT WHO THEY WOULD POTENTIALLY LIKE. THEY MAY NOT EVEN REALIZE IT. "INTERESTS" ARE HIDDEN INTERESTS THAT AREN'T SHOWN IN THE MAIN STORY. "WEAKNESSES AND DISLIKES" ARE ONE OR THE OTHER. "CLOSE RELATIONSHIPS" REFER TO THE PEOPLE CLOSEST TO THE CHARACTER.

Data

BIRTHDAY / DECEMBER 21

BLOOD TYPE / TYPE O

HEIGHT / 5'1"

CLASS / SECOND YEAR, CLASS 1

FAMILY / FATHER, MOTHER

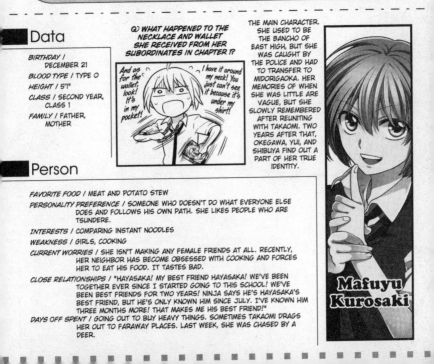

Q) WHAT HAPPENED TO THE NECKLACE AND WALLET SHE RECEIVED FROM HER SUBORDINATES IN CHAPTER 1?

I have it around my neck! You just can't see it because it's under my shirt!
And as for the wallet, look! It's in my pocket!

THE MAIN CHARACTER. SHE USED TO BE THE BANCHO OF EAST HIGH, BUT SHE WAS CAUGHT BY THE POLICE AND HAD TO TRANSFER TO MIDORIGAOKA. HER MEMORIES OF WHEN SHE WAS LITTLE ARE VAGUE, BUT SHE SLOWLY REMEMBERED AFTER REUNITING WITH TAKAOMI. TWO YEARS AFTER THAT, OKEGAWA, YUI, AND SHIBUYA FIND OUT A PART OF HER TRUE IDENTITY.

Mafuyu Kurosaki

Person

FAVORITE FOOD / MEAT AND POTATO STEW

PERSONALITY PREFERENCE / SOMEONE WHO DOESN'T DO WHAT EVERYONE ELSE DOES AND FOLLOWS HIS OWN PATH. SHE LIKES PEOPLE WHO ARE TSUNDERE.

INTERESTS / COMPARING INSTANT NOODLES

WEAKNESS / GIRLS, COOKING

CURRENT WORRIES / SHE ISN'T MAKING ANY FEMALE FRIENDS AT ALL. RECENTLY, HER NEIGHBOR HAS BECOME OBSESSED WITH COOKING AND FORCES HER TO EAT HIS FOOD. IT TASTES BAD.

CLOSE RELATIONSHIPS / "HAYASAKA! MY BEST FRIEND HAYASAKA! WE'VE BEEN TOGETHER EVER SINCE I STARTED GOING TO THIS SCHOOL! WE'VE BEEN BEST FRIENDS FOR TWO YEARS! NINJA SAYS HE'S HAYASAKA'S BEST FRIEND, BUT HE'S ONLY KNOWN HIM SINCE JULY. I'VE KNOWN HIM THREE MONTHS MORE! THAT MAKES ME HIS BEST FRIEND!"

DAYS OFF SPENT / GOING OUT TO BUY HEAVY THINGS. SOMETIMES TAKAOMI DRAGS HER OUT TO FARAWAY PLACES. LAST WEEK, SHE WAS CHASED BY A DEER.

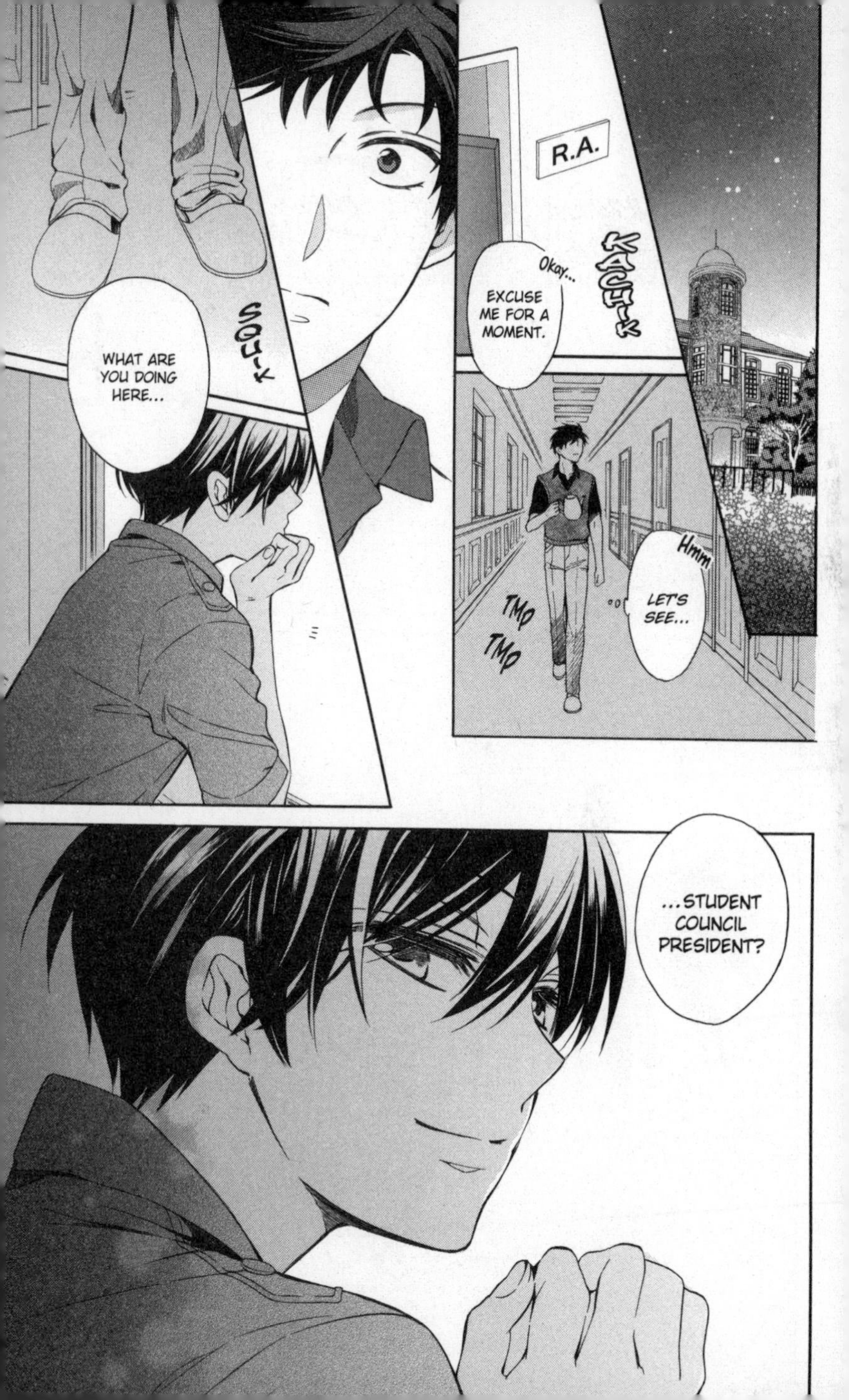
R.A.
KACHI-K
Okay...
EXCUSE ME FOR A MOMENT.
Hmm
LET'S SEE...
TMP
TMP
SQUI-K
WHAT ARE YOU DOING HERE...
...STUDENT COUNCIL PRESIDENT?

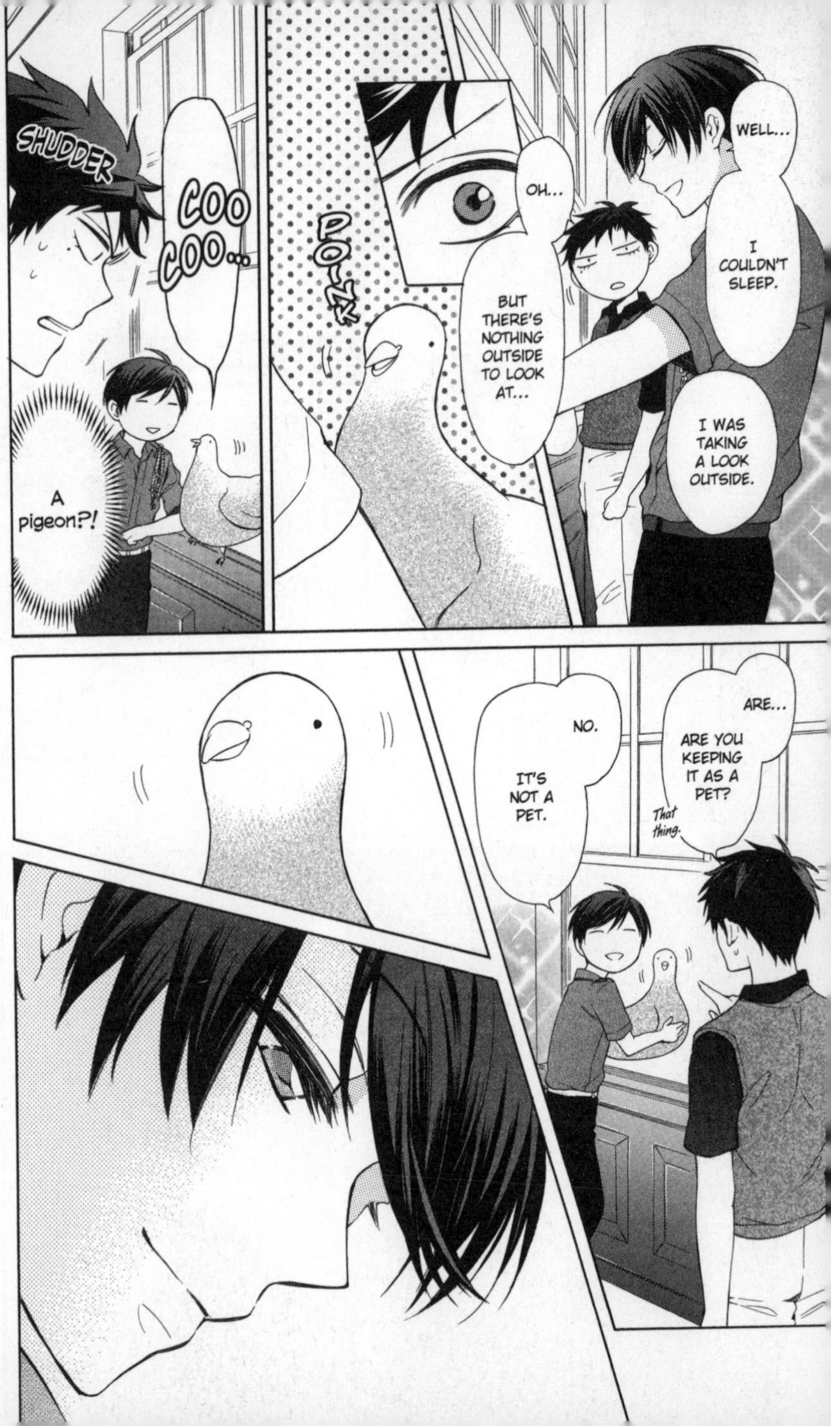
WELL...
I COULDN'T SLEEP.
I WAS TAKING A LOOK OUTSIDE.
OH...
BUT THERE'S NOTHING OUTSIDE TO LOOK AT...
POINK
SHUDDER
COO COO...
A pigeon?!
ARE...
ARE YOU KEEPING IT AS A PET?
That thing.
NO.
IT'S NOT A PET.

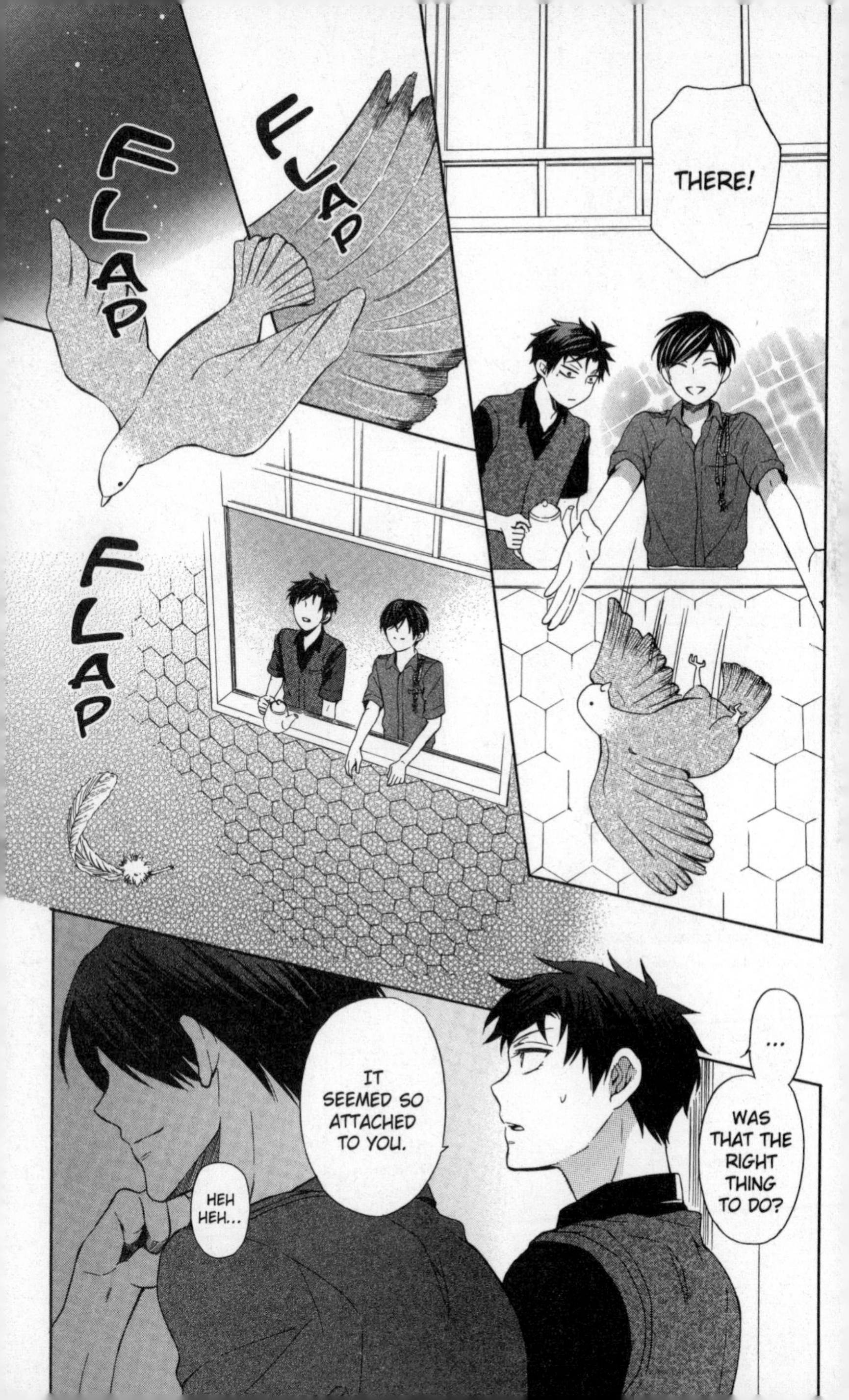

THERE!
FLAP
FLAP
FLAP
FLAP
...
WAS THAT THE RIGHT THING TO DO?
IT SEEMED SO ATTACHED TO YOU.
HEH HEH...

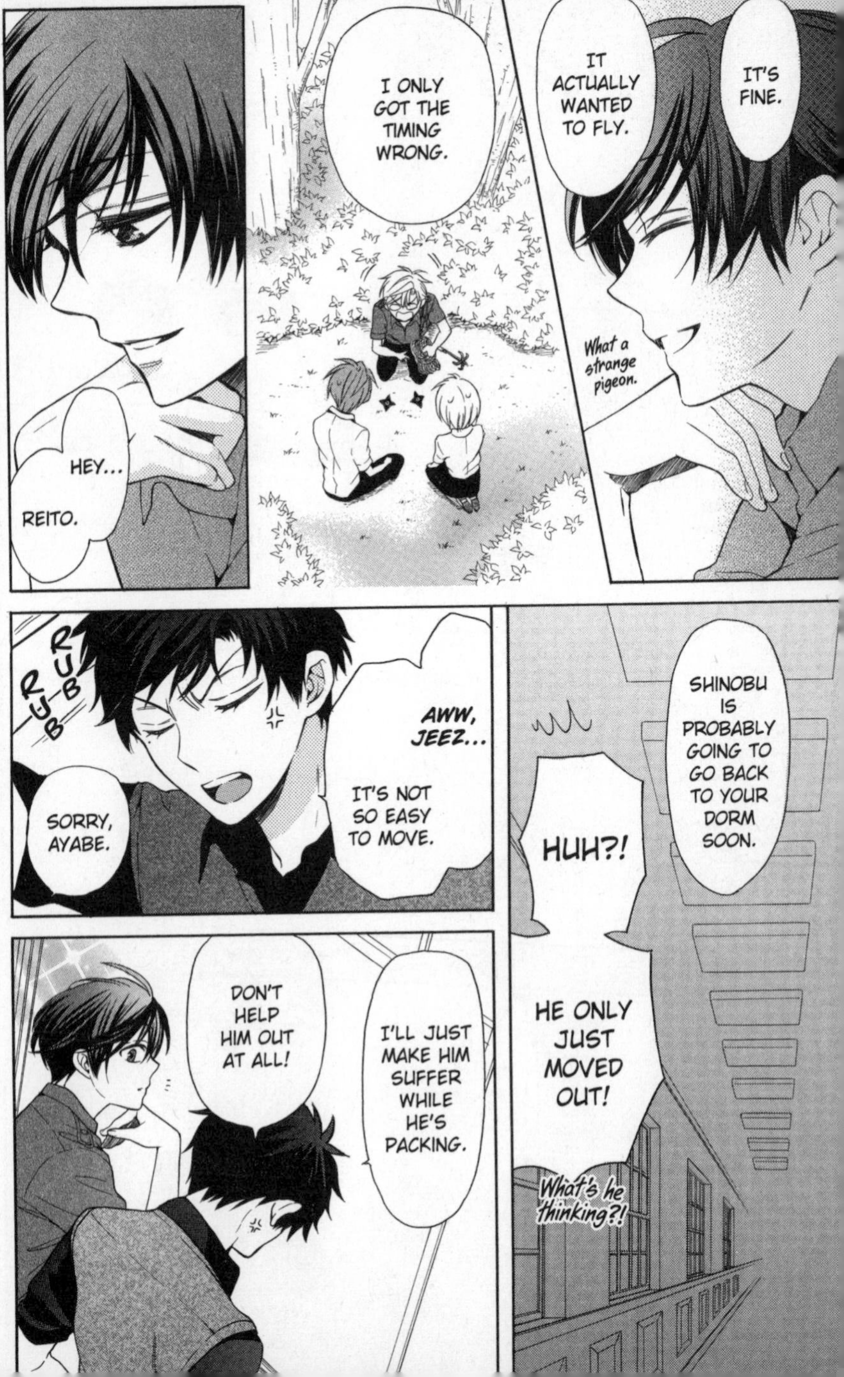
IT'S FINE.
IT ACTUALLY WANTED TO FLY.
What a strange pigeon.
I ONLY GOT THE TIMING WRONG.
HEY...
REITO.
SHINOBU IS PROBABLY GOING TO GO BACK TO YOUR DORM SOON.
HUH?!
HE ONLY JUST MOVED OUT!
What's he thinking?!
AWW, JEEZ...
IT'S NOT SO EASY TO MOVE.
SORRY, AYABE.
RUB RUB
I'LL JUST MAKE HIM SUFFER WHILE HE'S PACKING.
DON'T HELP HIM OUT AT ALL!

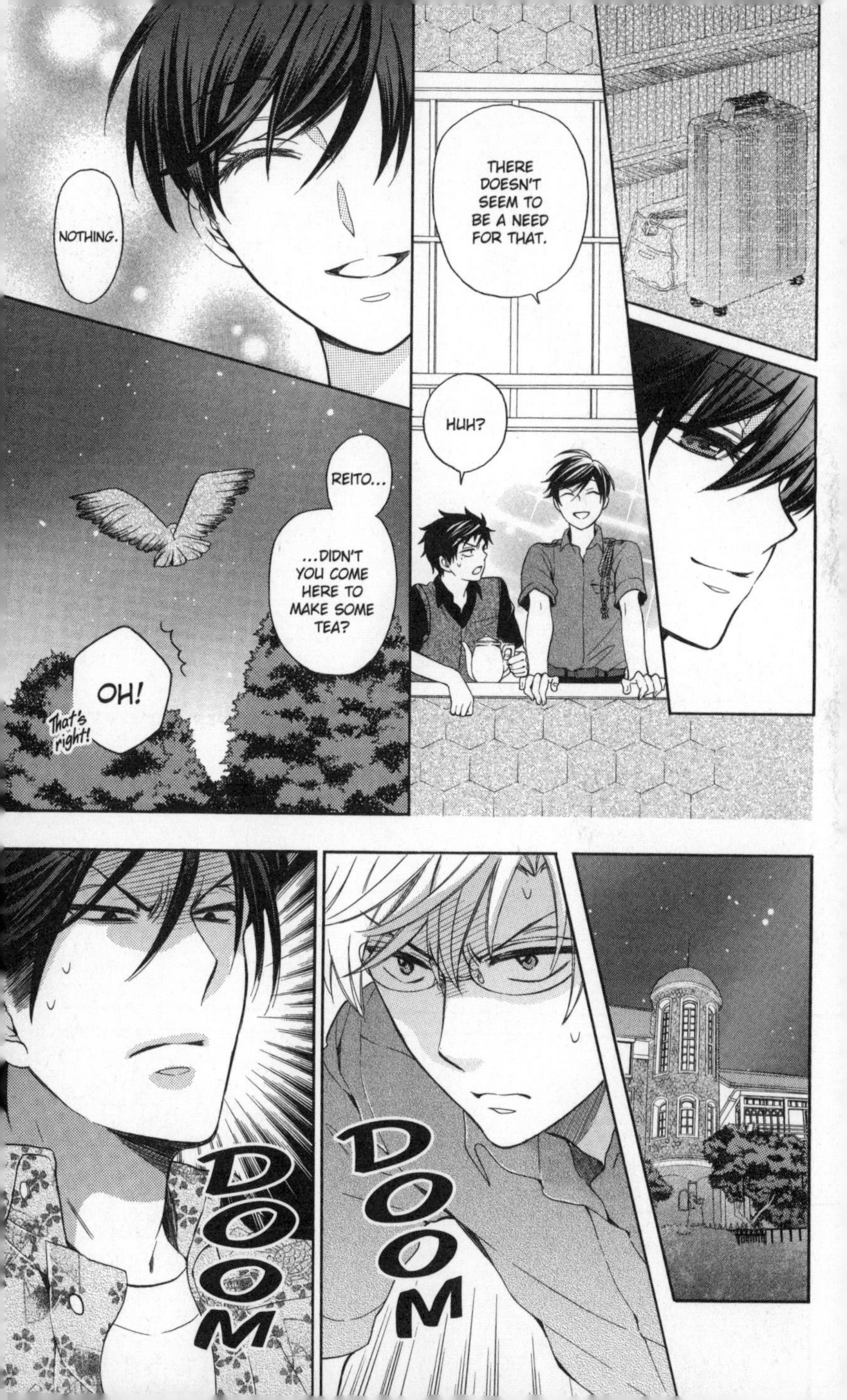
THERE DOESN'T SEEM TO BE A NEED FOR THAT.
HUH?
NOTHING.
REITO...
...DIDN'T YOU COME HERE TO MAKE SOME TEA?
OH!
That's right!
DOOOM
DOOOM

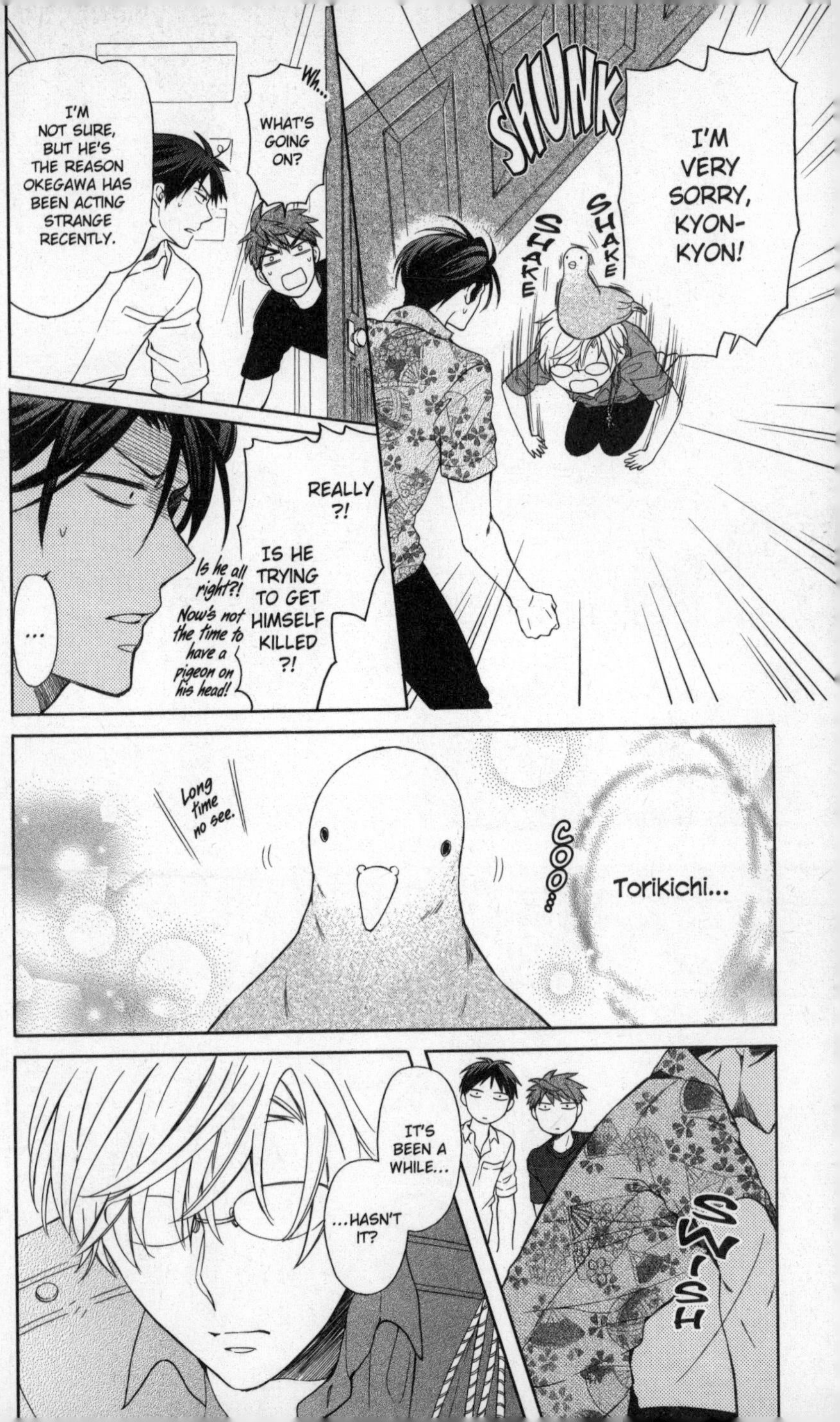
SHUNK
I'M VERY SORRY, KYON-KYON!
SHAKE SHAKE
Wh...
WHAT'S GOING ON?
I'M NOT SURE, BUT HE'S THE REASON OKEGAWA HAS BEEN ACTING STRANGE RECENTLY.
REALLY?!
IS HE TRYING TO GET HIMSELF KILLED?!
Is he all right?! Now's not the time to have a pigeon on his head!
...
Torikichi...
COO...
Long time no see.
SWISH
IT'S BEEN A WHILE...
...HASN'T IT?

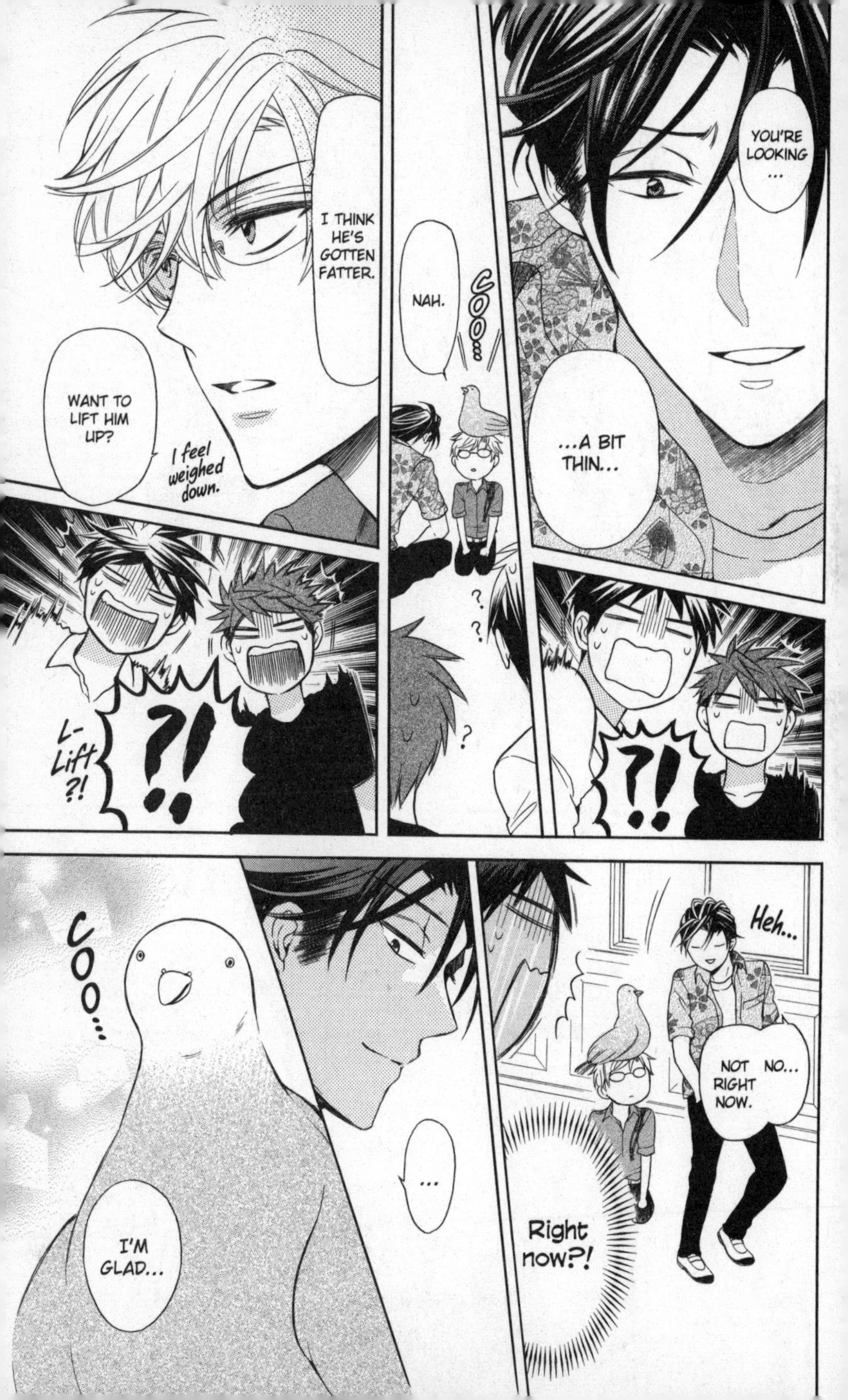
YOU'RE LOOKING ...
...A BIT THIN...
NAH.
COO...
I THINK HE'S GOTTEN FATTER.
WANT TO LIFT HIM UP?
I feel weighed down.
?!!
?
?
?
L-Lift?!
?!!
Heh...
NO... NOT RIGHT NOW.
Right now?!
...
COO...
I'M GLAD...

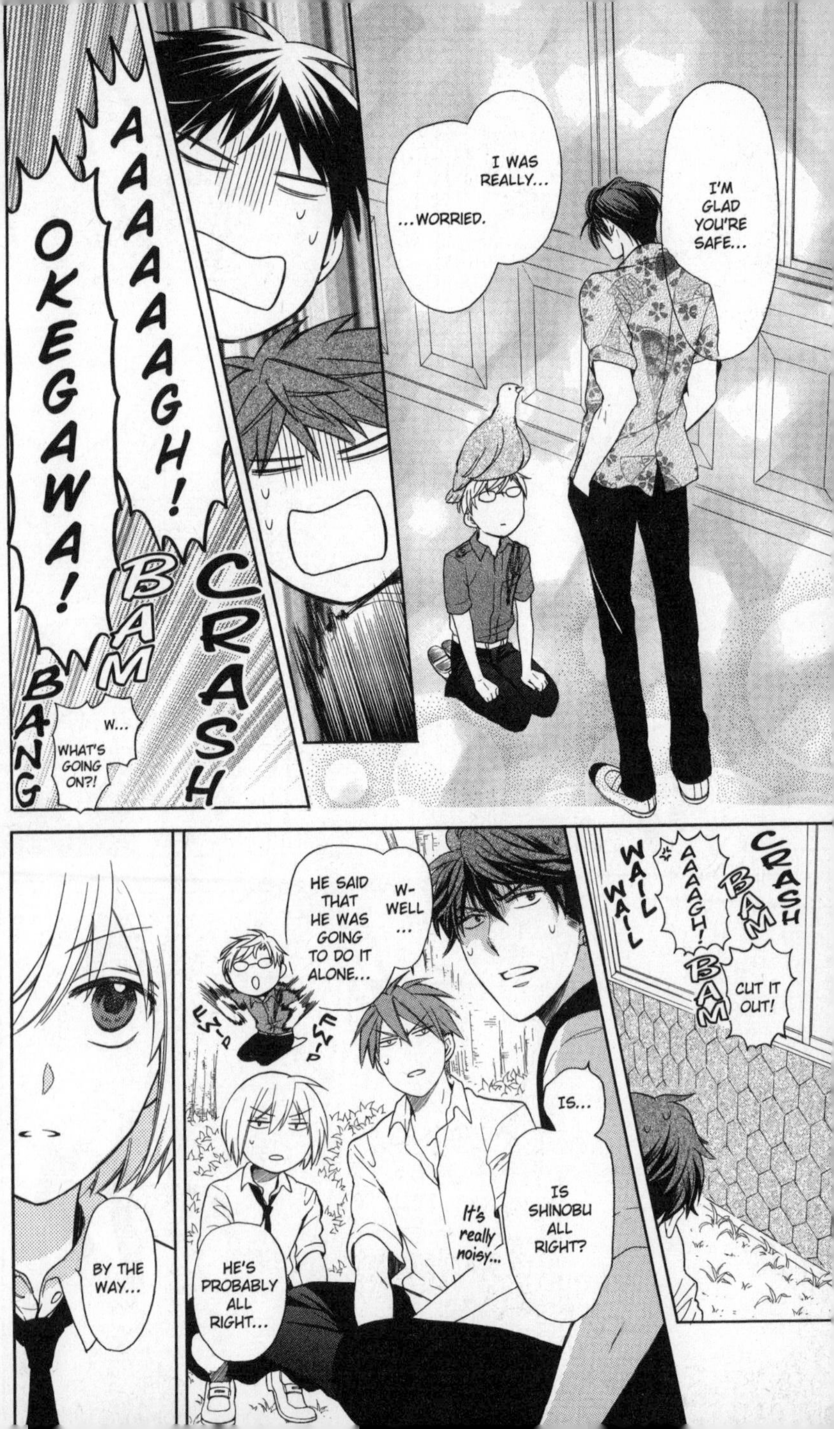
I'M GLAD YOU'RE SAFE...
I WAS REALLY...
...WORRIED.
CRASH
BAM BAM
BANG
AAAAAAAAGH!
OKEGAWA!
W... WHAT'S GOING ON?!
CRASH
BAM
AAAAGH!
BAM
WAIL WAIL
CUT IT OUT!
W-WELL...
HE SAID THAT HE WAS GOING TO DO IT ALONE...
IS...
IS SHINOBU ALL RIGHT?
It's really noisy...
HE'S PROBABLY ALL RIGHT...
BY THE WAY...

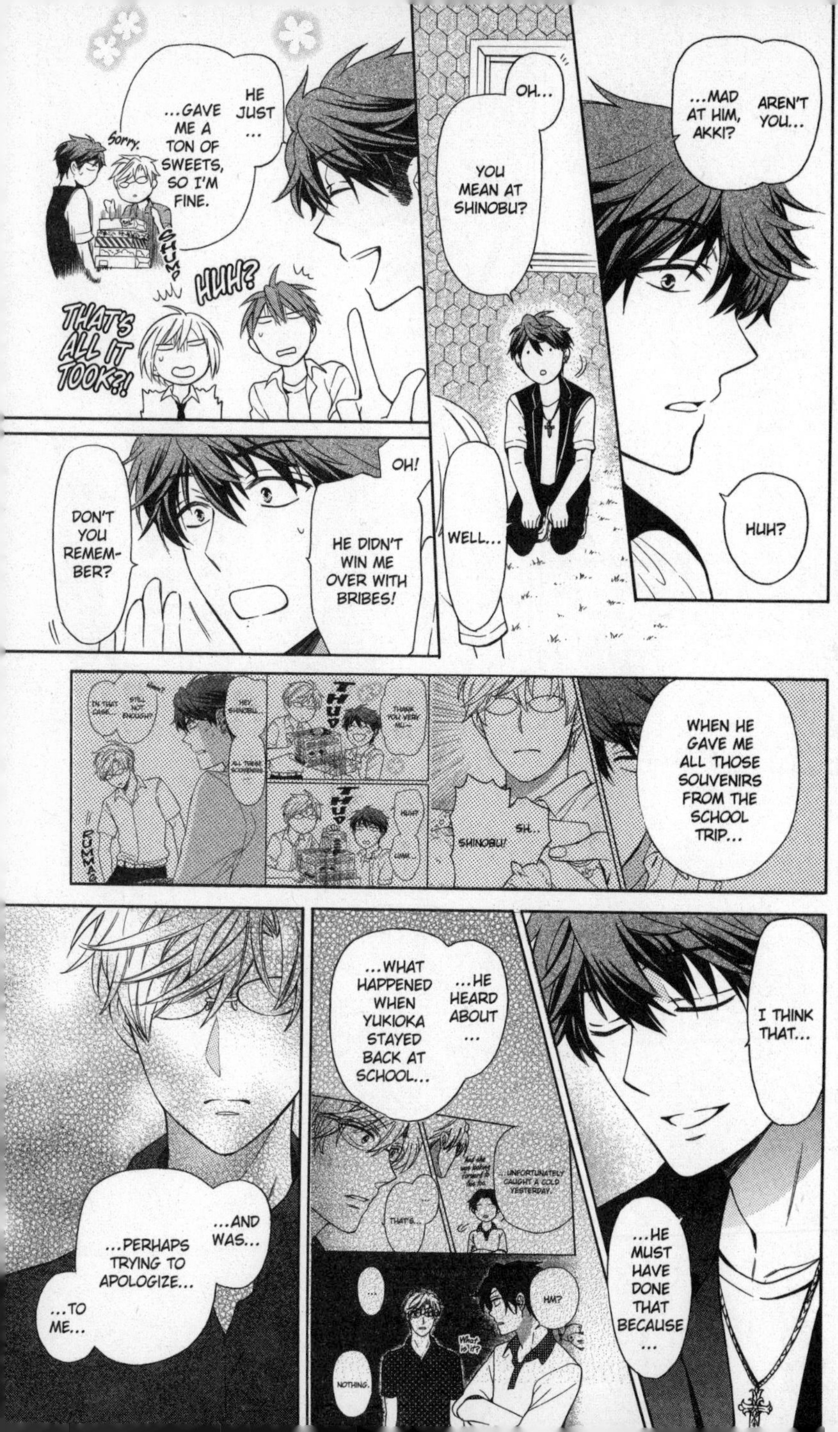
AREN'T YOU...
...MAD AT HIM, AKKI?
HUH?
OH...
YOU MEAN AT SHINOBU?
WELL...
HE JUST ...
...GAVE ME A TON OF SWEETS, SO I'M FINE.
Sorry.
SHUMP
HUH?
THAT'S ALL IT TOOK?!
OH!
HE DIDN'T WIN ME OVER WITH BRIBES!
DON'T YOU REMEMBER?
WHEN HE GAVE ME ALL THOSE SOUVENIRS FROM THE SCHOOL TRIP...
SH...
SHINOBU!
THANK YOU VERY MU—
THUD
HUH?
UMM...
THUD
HEY SHINOBU...
ALL THESE SOUVENIRS
STILL NOT ENOUGH?
IN THAT CASE...
RUMMAGE
I THINK THAT...
...HE MUST HAVE DONE THAT BECAUSE ...
...HE HEARD ABOUT ...
...WHAT HAPPENED WHEN YUKIOKA STAYED BACK AT SCHOOL...
...UNFORTUNATELY CAUGHT A COLD YESTERDAY.
THAT'S...
HM?
What is it?
...
NOTHING.
...AND WAS...
...PERHAPS TRYING TO APOLOGIZE...
...TO ME...

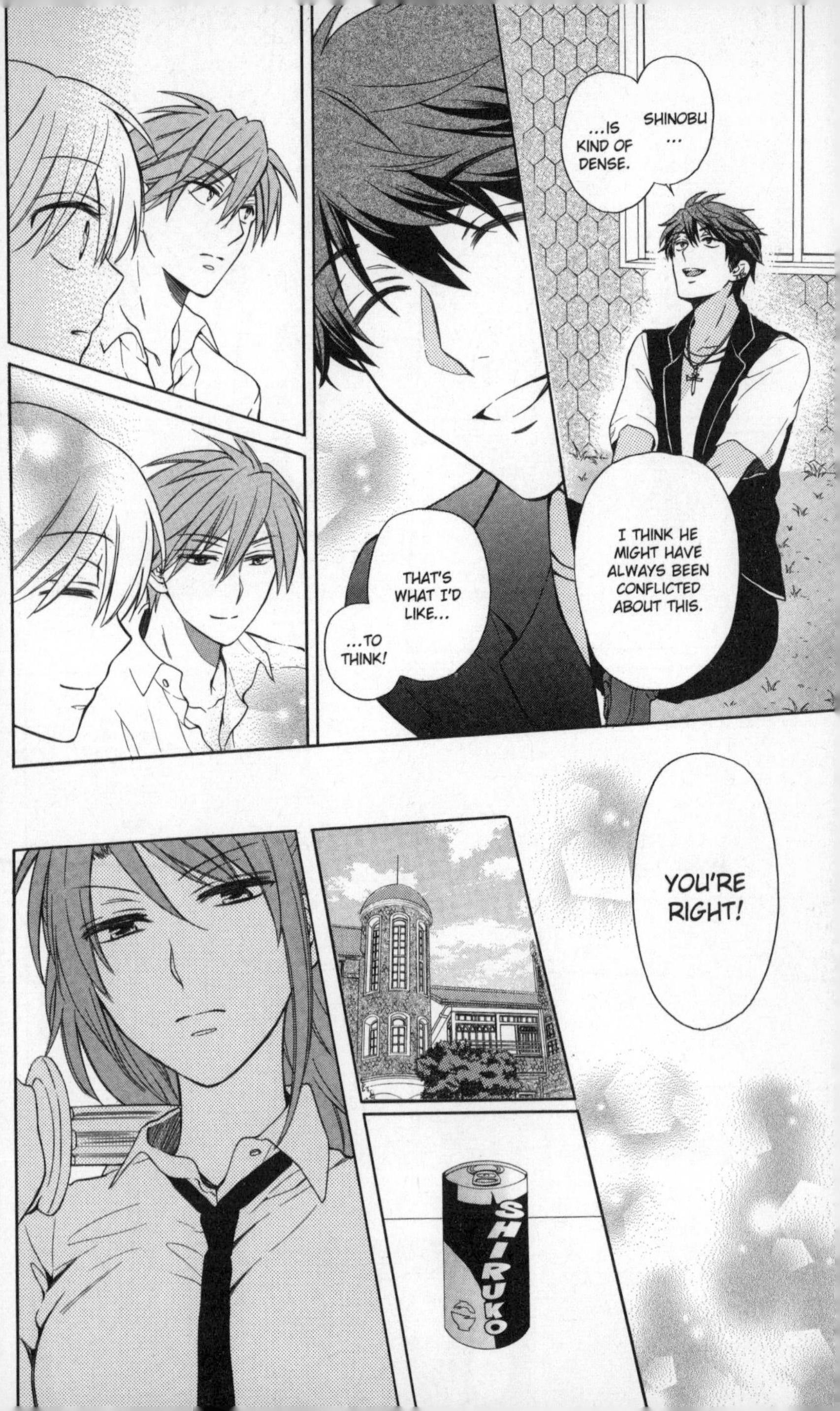
SHINOBU ...
...IS KIND OF DENSE.
I THINK HE MIGHT HAVE ALWAYS BEEN CONFLICTED ABOUT THIS.
THAT'S WHAT I'D LIKE...
...TO THINK!
YOU'RE RIGHT!
SHIRUKO

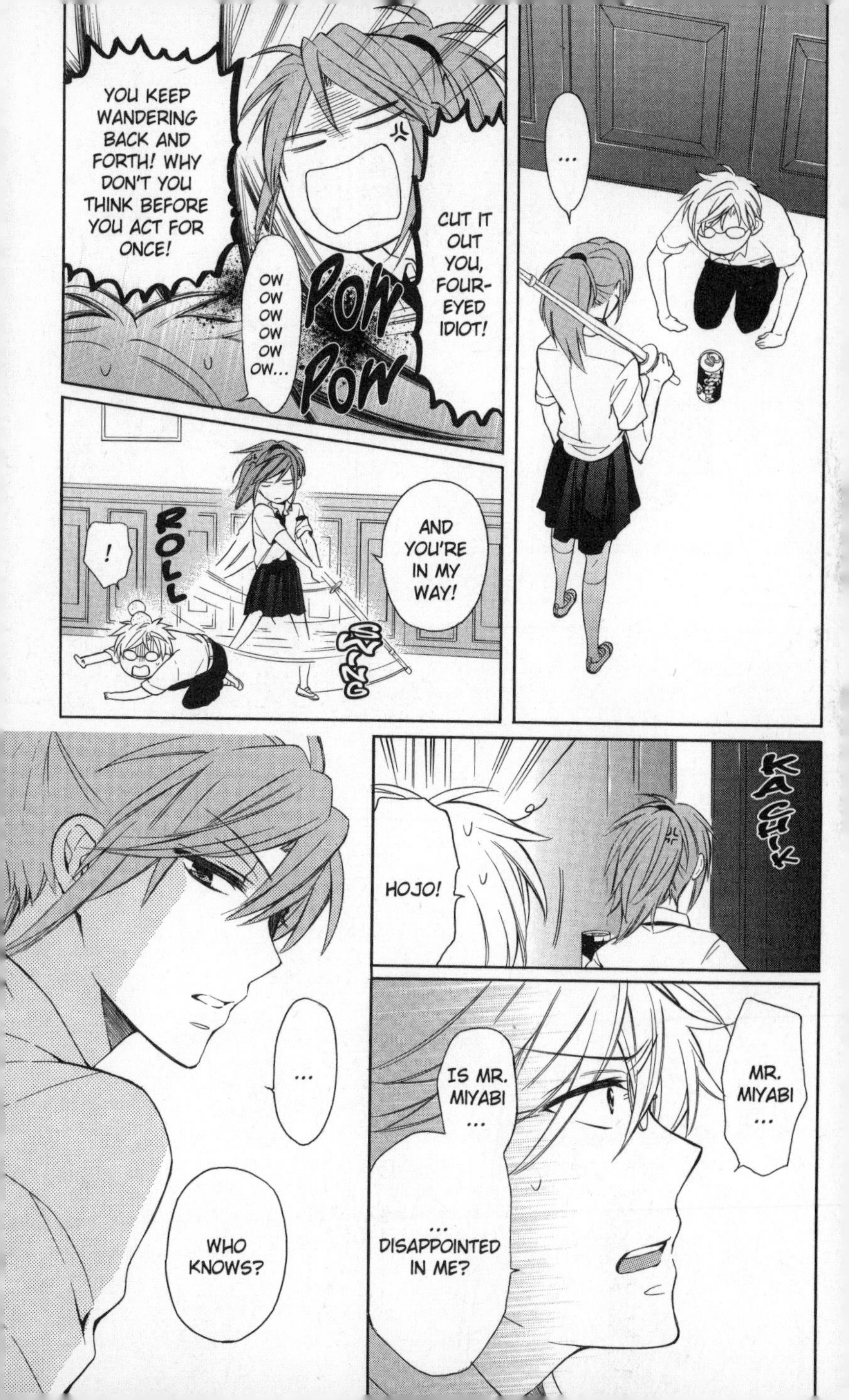
...
CUT IT OUT YOU, FOUR-EYED IDIOT!
YOU KEEP WANDERING BACK AND FORTH! WHY DON'T YOU THINK BEFORE YOU ACT FOR ONCE!
POW POW
OW OW OW OW OW OW...
AND YOU'RE IN MY WAY!
SWING
ROLL
!
KACHIK
HOJO!
MR. MIYABI ...
IS MR. MIYABI ...
... DISAPPOINTED IN ME?
...
WHO KNOWS?

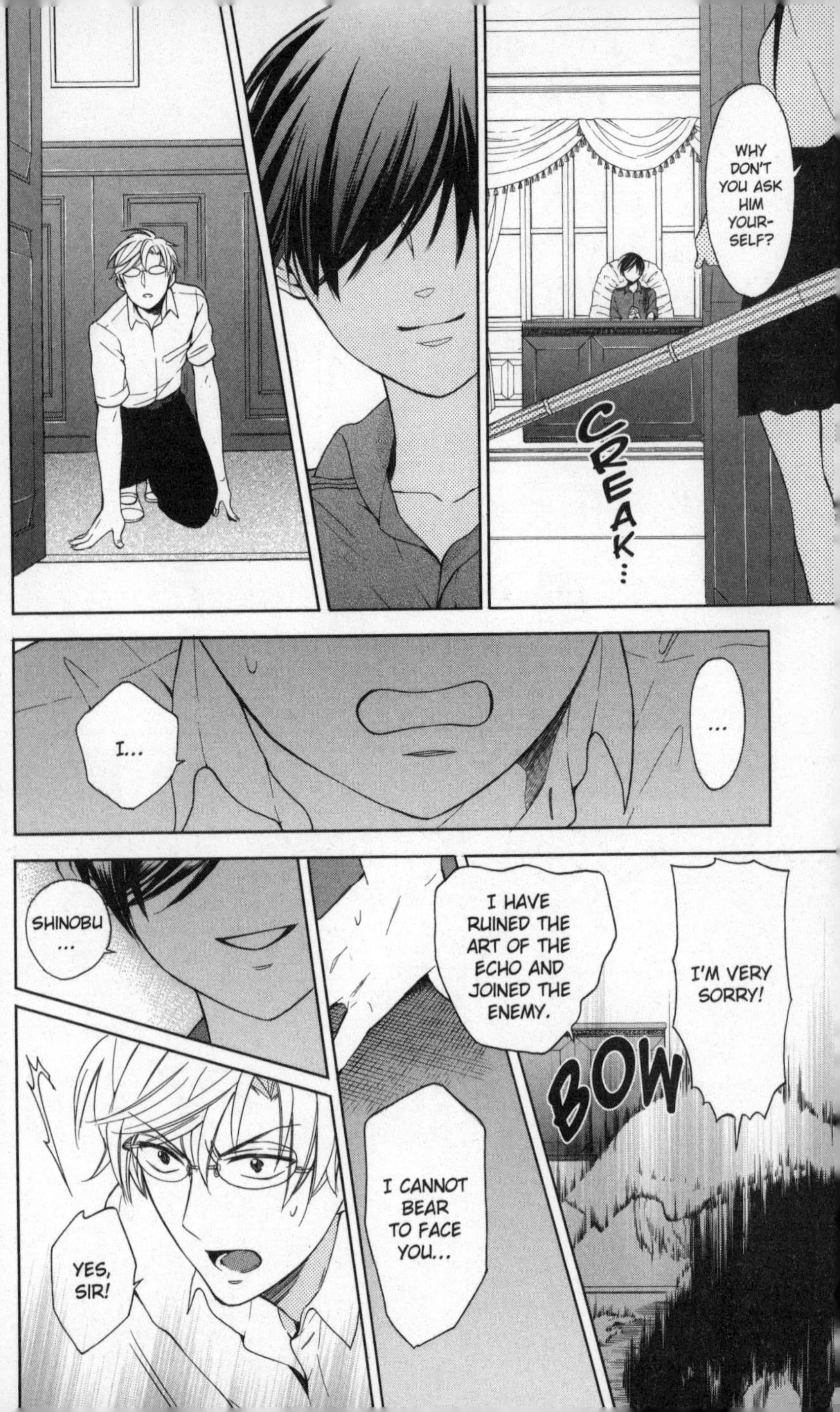
WHY DON'T YOU ASK HIM YOUR-SELF?
CREAK...
...
I...
I'M VERY SORRY!
BOW
I HAVE RUINED THE ART OF THE ECHO AND JOINED THE ENEMY.
SHINOBU...
I CANNOT BEAR TO FACE YOU...
YES, SIR!

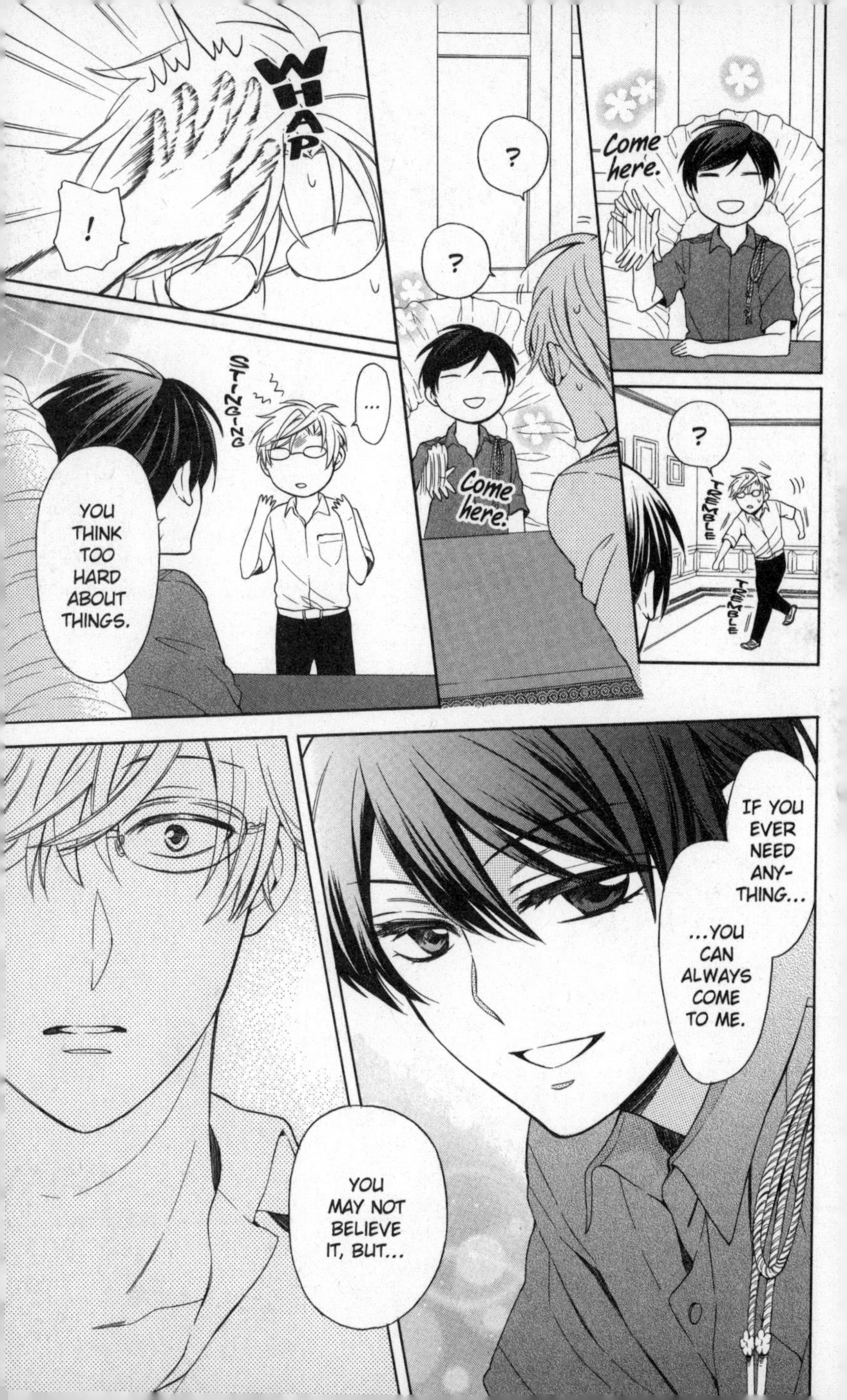
Come here.
?
TREMBLE
TREMBLE
?
?
Come here.
WHAP
!
STINGING
...
YOU THINK TOO HARD ABOUT THINGS.
IF YOU EVER NEED ANYTHING...
...YOU CAN ALWAYS COME TO ME.
YOU MAY NOT BELIEVE IT, BUT...

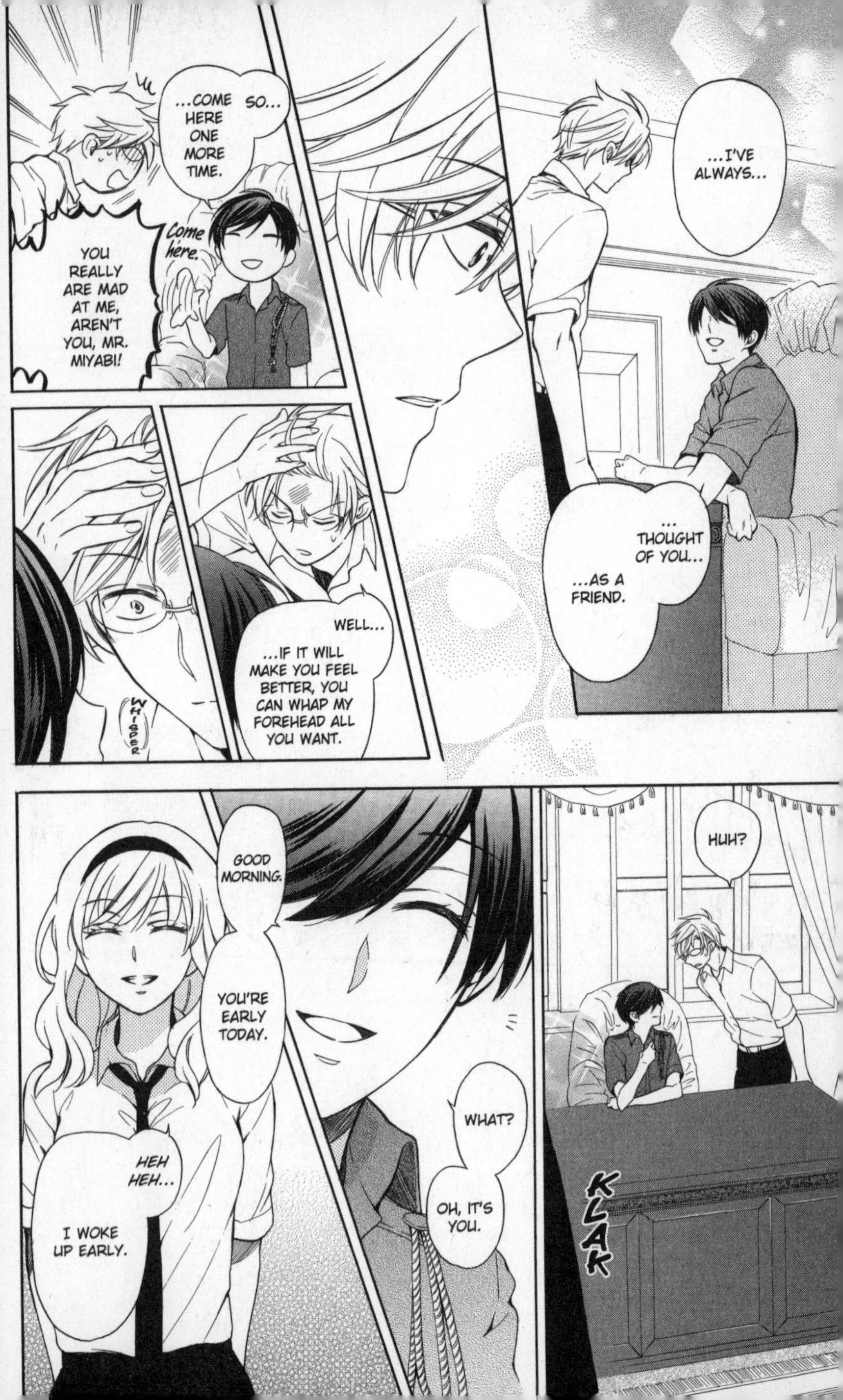

...I'VE ALWAYS...
... THOUGHT OF YOU...
...AS A FRIEND.
SO...
...COME HERE ONE MORE TIME.
Come here.
YOU REALLY ARE MAD AT ME, AREN'T YOU, MR. MIYABI!
WELL...
...IF IT WILL MAKE YOU FEEL BETTER, YOU CAN WHAP MY FOREHEAD ALL YOU WANT.
WHISPER
HUH?
KLAK
WHAT?
OH, IT'S YOU.
GOOD MORNING.
YOU'RE EARLY TODAY.
HEH HEH...
I WOKE UP EARLY.

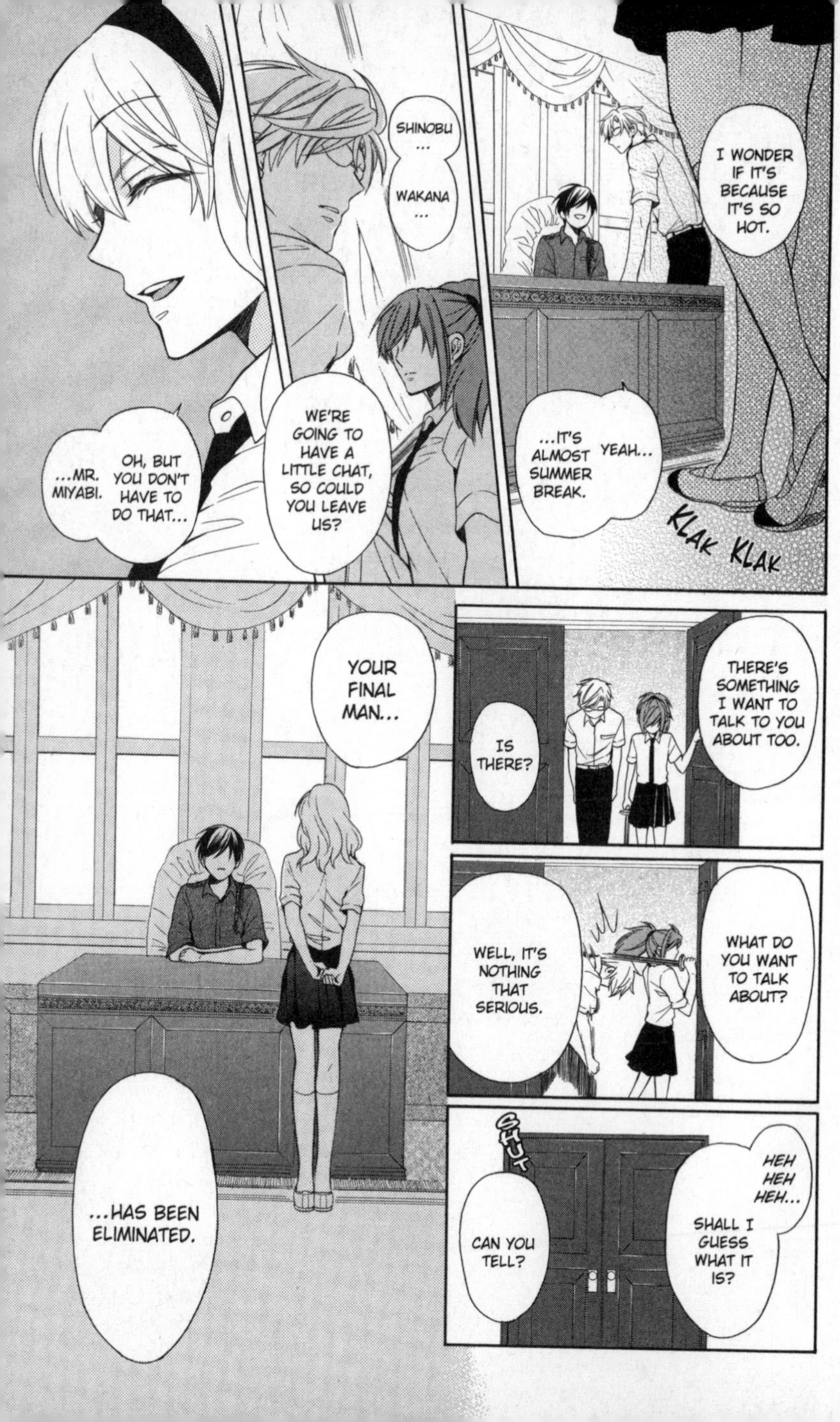
I WONDER IF IT'S BECAUSE IT'S SO HOT.
YEAH...
...IT'S ALMOST SUMMER BREAK.
KLAK KLAK
SHINOBU...
WAKANA...
WE'RE GOING TO HAVE A LITTLE CHAT, SO COULD YOU LEAVE US?
OH, BUT YOU DON'T HAVE TO DO THAT...
...MR. MIYABI.
THERE'S SOMETHING I WANT TO TALK TO YOU ABOUT TOO.
IS THERE?
WHAT DO YOU WANT TO TALK ABOUT?
WELL, IT'S NOTHING THAT SERIOUS.
SHUT
HEH HEH HEH...
SHALL I GUESS WHAT IT IS?
CAN YOU TELL?
YOUR FINAL MAN...
...HAS BEEN ELIMINATED.

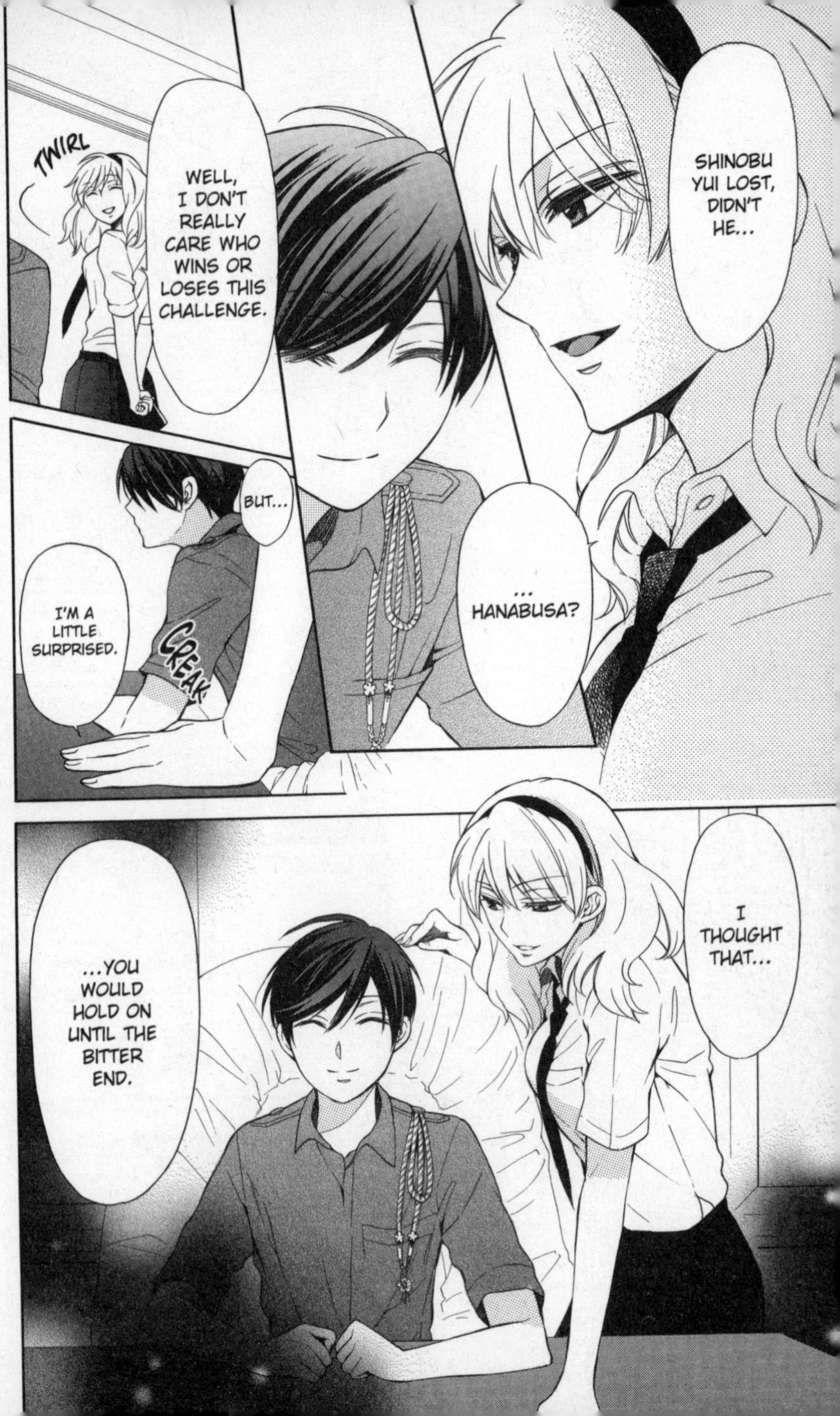
SHINOBU YUI LOST, DIDN'T HE...
... HANABUSA?
WELL, I DON'T REALLY CARE WHO WINS OR LOSES THIS CHALLENGE.
TWIRL
BUT...
I'M A LITTLE SURPRISED.
CREAK
I THOUGHT THAT...
...YOU WOULD HOLD ON UNTIL THE BITTER END.

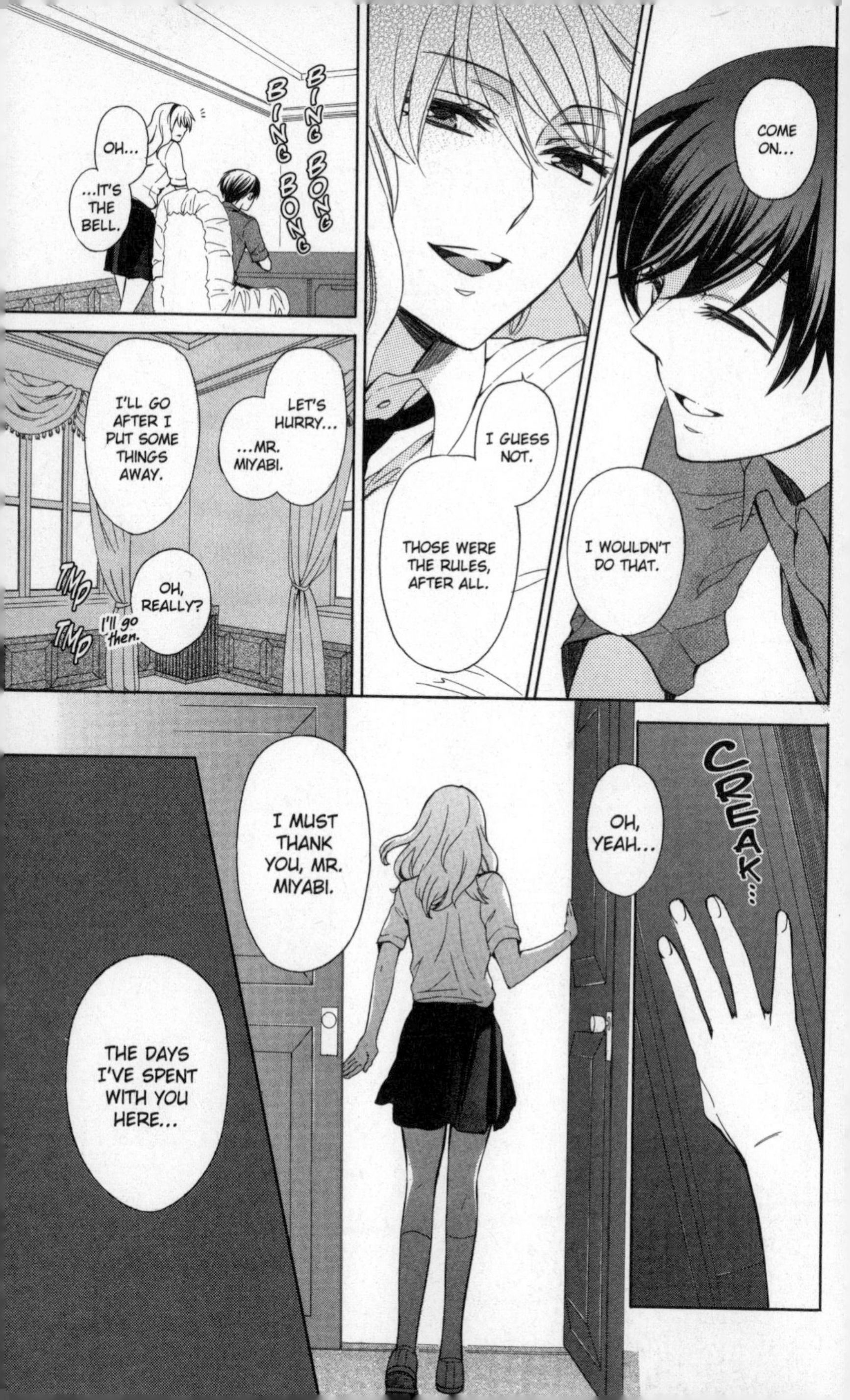
COME ON...
I WOULDN'T DO THAT.
I GUESS NOT.
THOSE WERE THE RULES, AFTER ALL.
BING BONG
BING BONG
OH...
...IT'S THE BELL.
LET'S HURRY...
...MR. MIYABI.
I'LL GO AFTER I PUT SOME THINGS AWAY.
OH, REALLY?
I'll go then.
TMP
TMP
CREAK...
OH, YEAH...
I MUST THANK YOU, MR. MIYABI.
THE DAYS I'VE SPENT WITH YOU HERE...

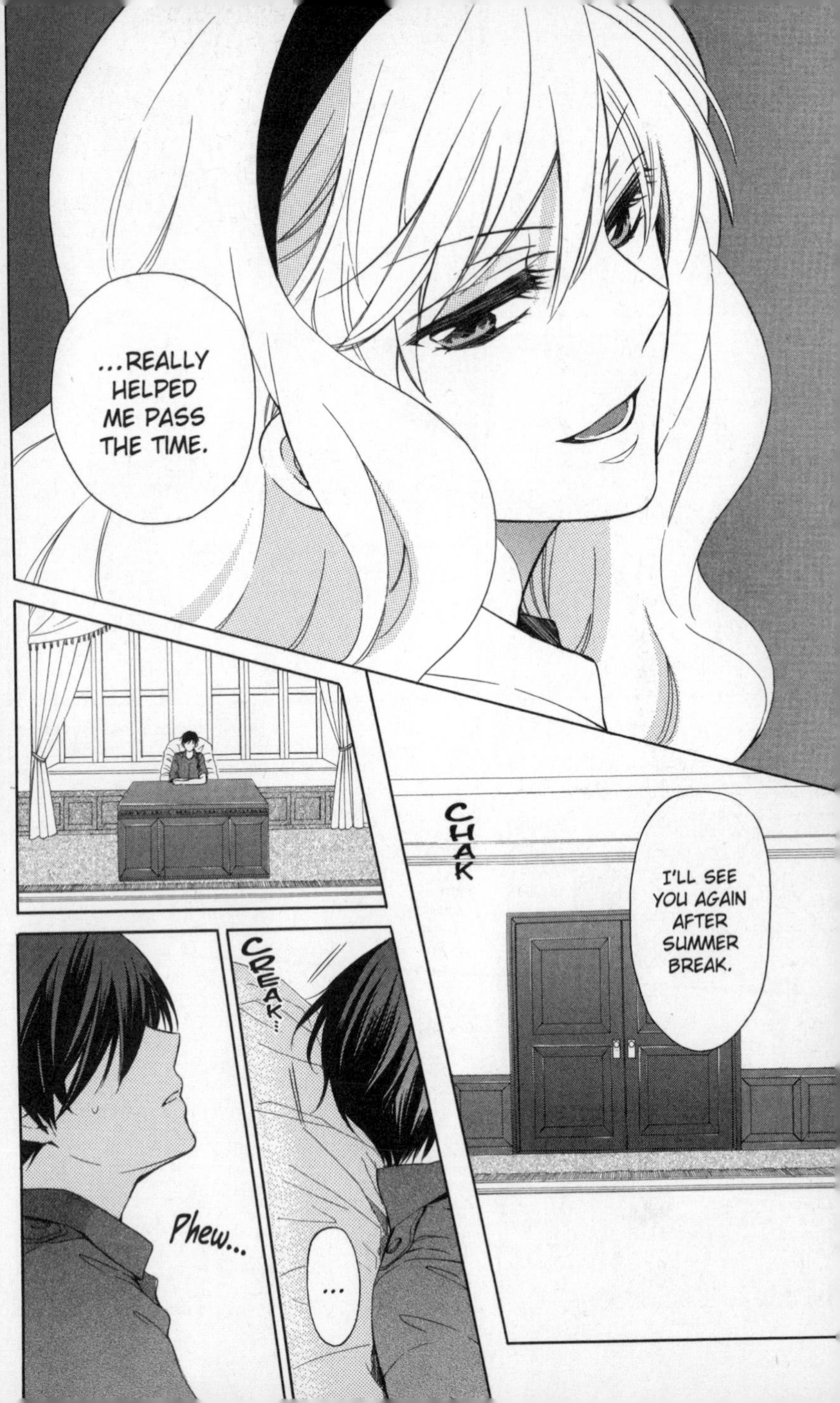
...REALLY HELPED ME PASS THE TIME.
CHAK
I'LL SEE YOU AGAIN AFTER SUMMER BREAK.
CREAK...
...
Phew...

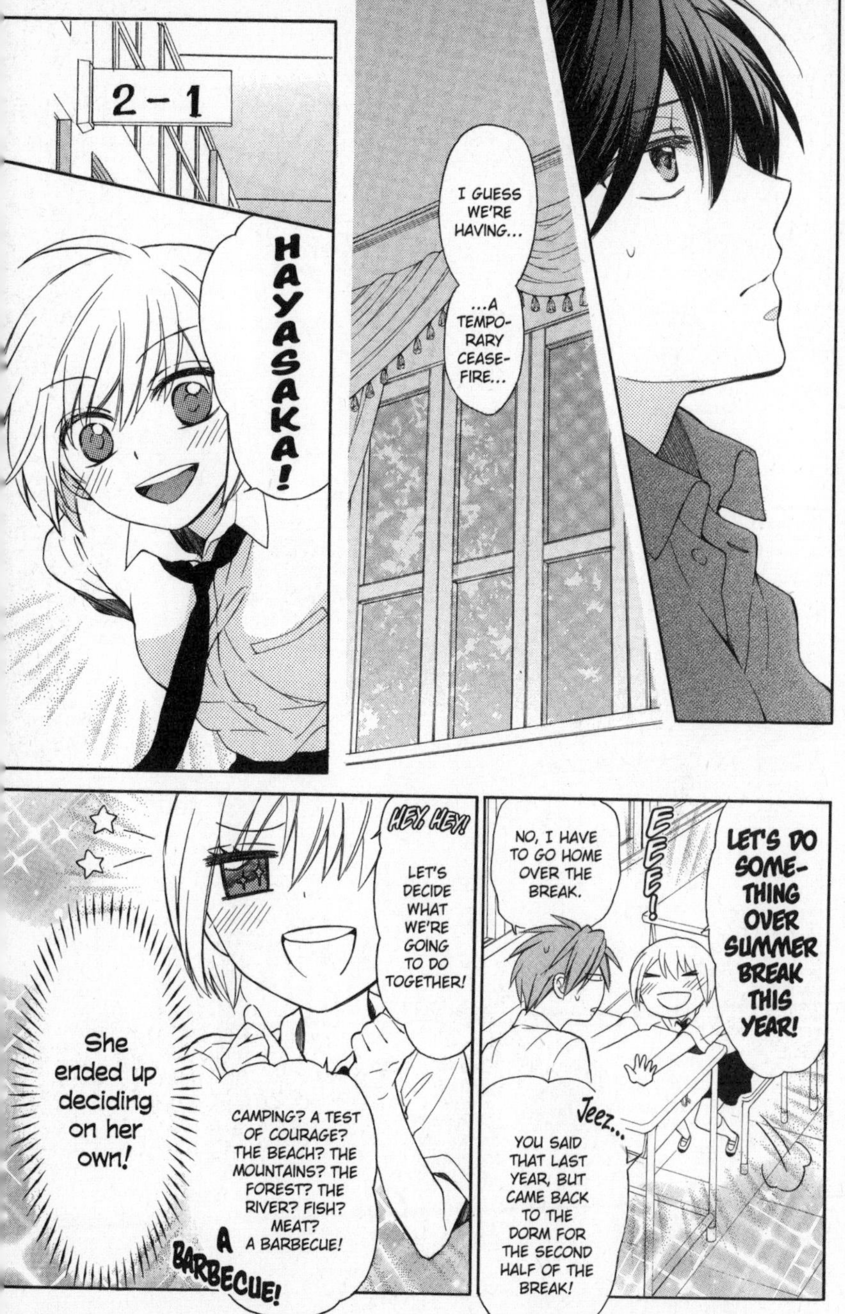
I GUESS WE'RE HAVING...
...A TEMPORARY CEASE-FIRE...
2-1
HAYASAKA!
LET'S DO SOMETHING OVER SUMMER BREAK THIS YEAR!
EEE!
NO, I HAVE TO GO HOME OVER THE BREAK.
Jeez...
YOU SAID THAT LAST YEAR, BUT CAME BACK TO THE DORM FOR THE SECOND HALF OF THE BREAK!
HEY, HEY!
LET'S DECIDE WHAT WE'RE GOING TO DO TOGETHER!
CAMPING? A TEST OF COURAGE? THE BEACH? THE MOUNTAINS? THE FOREST? THE RIVER? FISH? MEAT? A BARBECUE!
A BARBECUE!
She ended up deciding on her own!

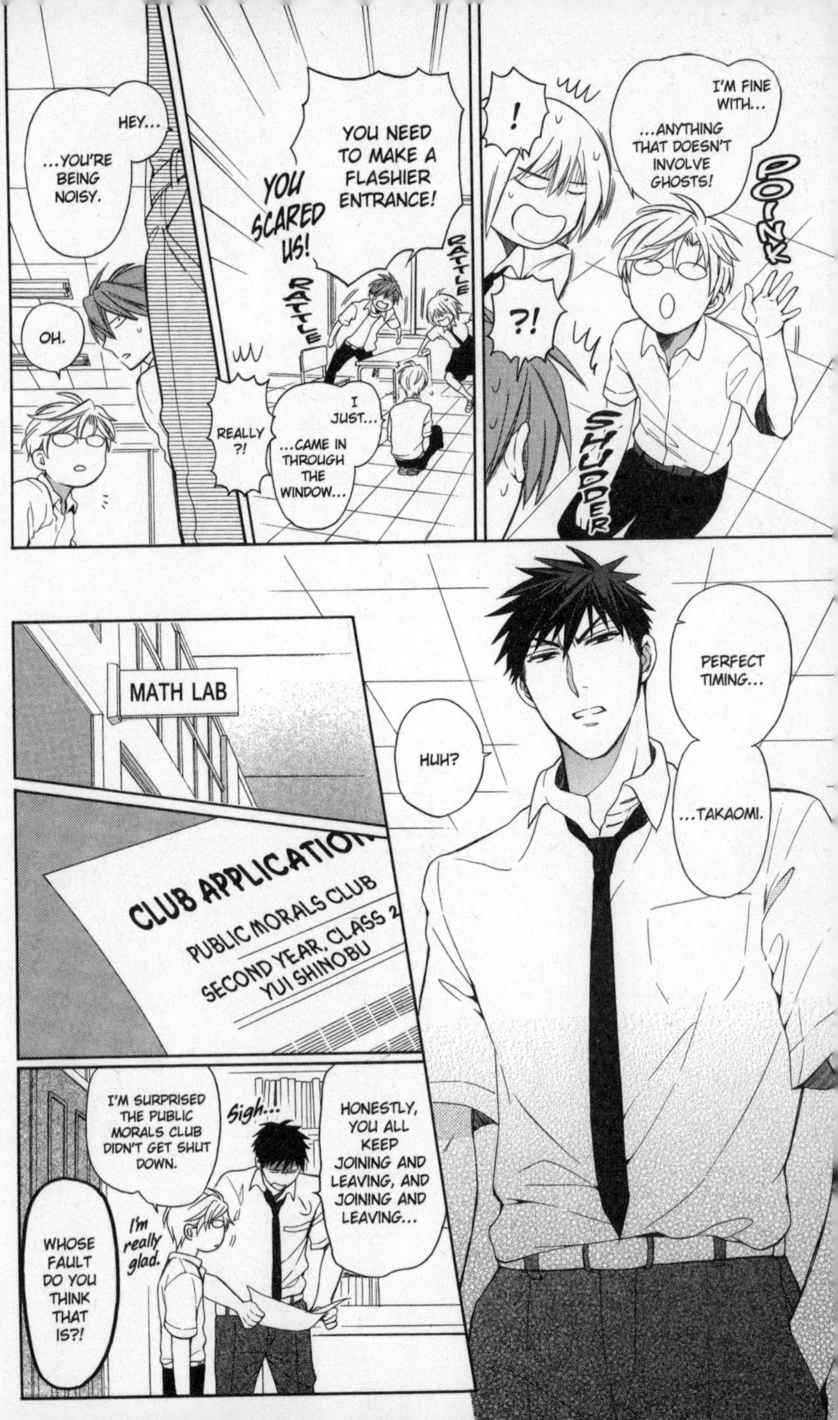
I'M FINE WITH...
...ANYTHING THAT DOESN'T INVOLVE GHOSTS!
POINK
!
?!
SHUDDER
YOU NEED TO MAKE A FLASHIER ENTRANCE!
YOU SCARED US!
RATTLE
RATTLE
HEY...
...YOU'RE BEING NOISY.
OH.
I JUST...
...CAME IN THROUGH THE WINDOW...
REALLY ?!
PERFECT TIMING...
...TAKAOMI.
HUH?
MATH LAB
CLUB APPLICATION
PUBLIC MORALS CLUB
SECOND YEAR, CLASS 2
YUI SHINOBU
HONESTLY, YOU ALL KEEP JOINING AND LEAVING, AND JOINING AND LEAVING...
Sigh...!
I'M SURPRISED THE PUBLIC MORALS CLUB DIDN'T GET SHUT DOWN.
I'm really glad.
WHOSE FAULT DO YOU THINK THAT IS?!

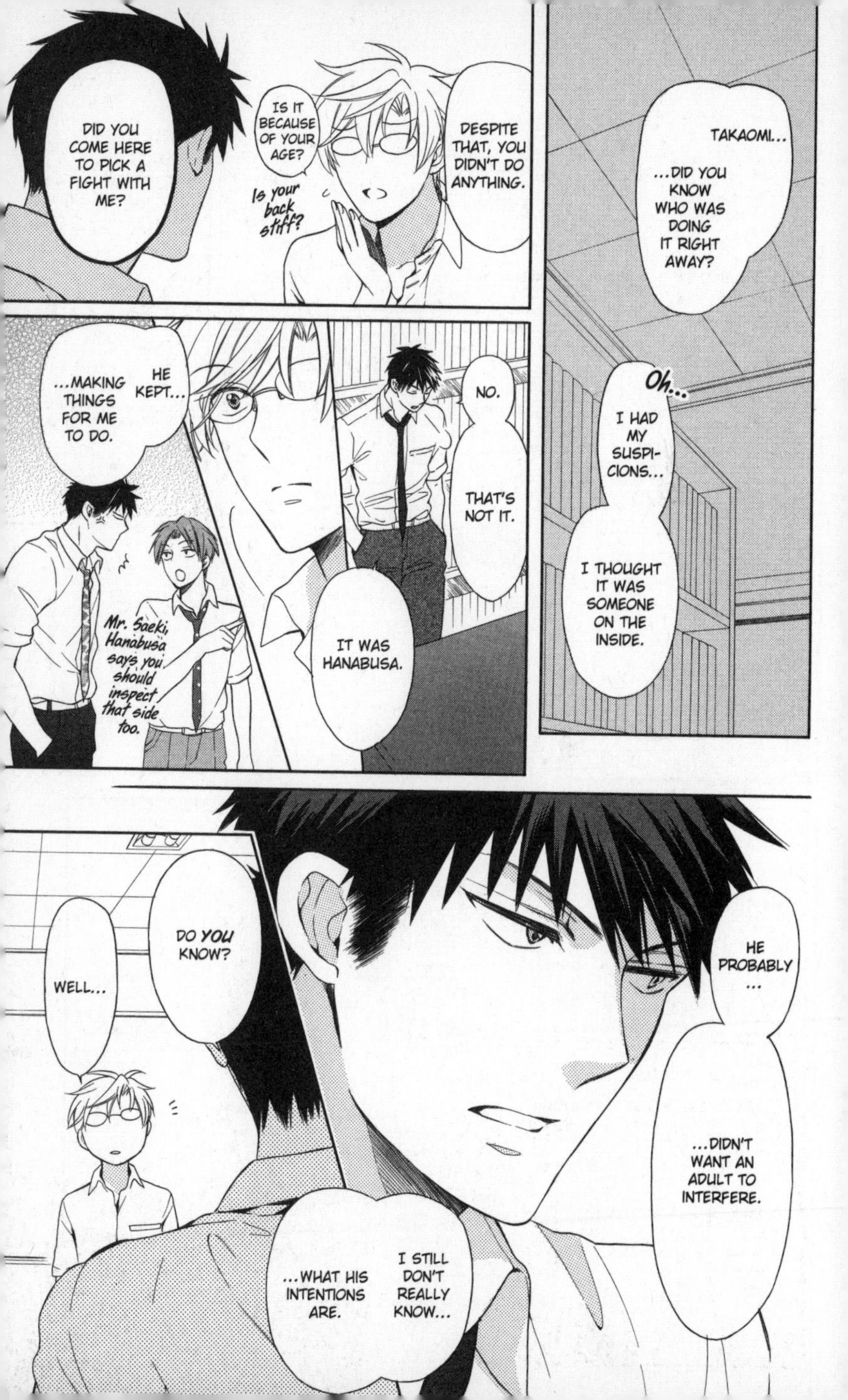
TAKAOMI...
...DID YOU KNOW WHO WAS DOING IT RIGHT AWAY?
Oh...
I HAD MY SUSPICIONS...
I THOUGHT IT WAS SOMEONE ON THE INSIDE.
DESPITE THAT, YOU DIDN'T DO ANYTHING.
IS IT BECAUSE OF YOUR AGE?
Is your back stiff?
DID YOU COME HERE TO PICK A FIGHT WITH ME?
NO.
THAT'S NOT IT.
IT WAS HANABUSA.
HE KEPT...
...MAKING THINGS FOR ME TO DO.
Mr. Saeki, Hanabusa says you should inspect that side too.
HE PROBABLY...
...DIDN'T WANT AN ADULT TO INTERFERE.
I STILL DON'T REALLY KNOW...
...WHAT HIS INTENTIONS ARE.
DO YOU KNOW?
WELL...

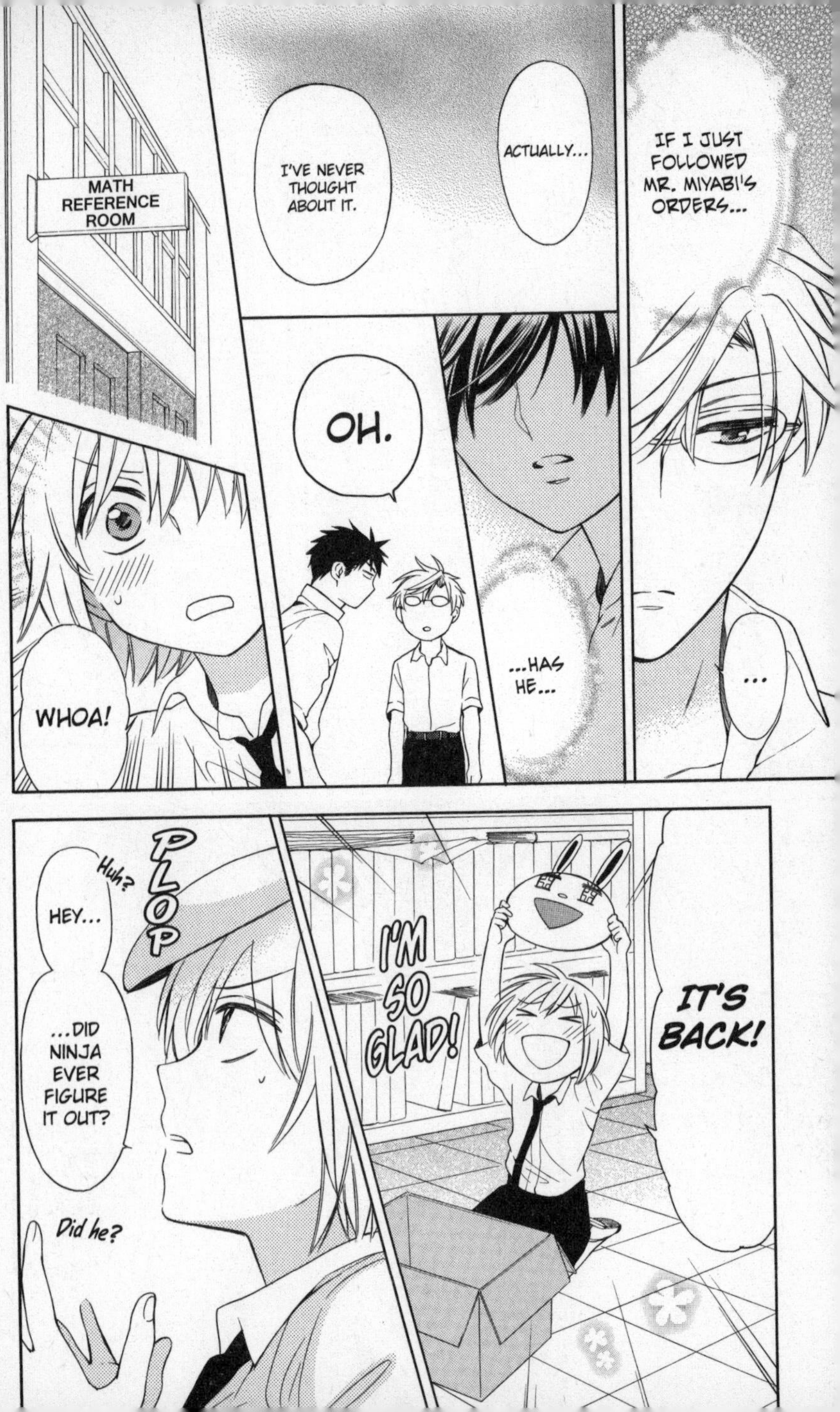
IF I JUST FOLLOWED MR. MIYABI'S ORDERS...
...
ACTUALLY...
I'VE NEVER THOUGHT ABOUT IT.
MATH REFERENCE ROOM
...HAS HE...
OH.
WHOA!
IT'S BACK!
I'M SO GLAD!
PLOP
Huh?
HEY...
...DID NINJA EVER FIGURE IT OUT?
Did he?

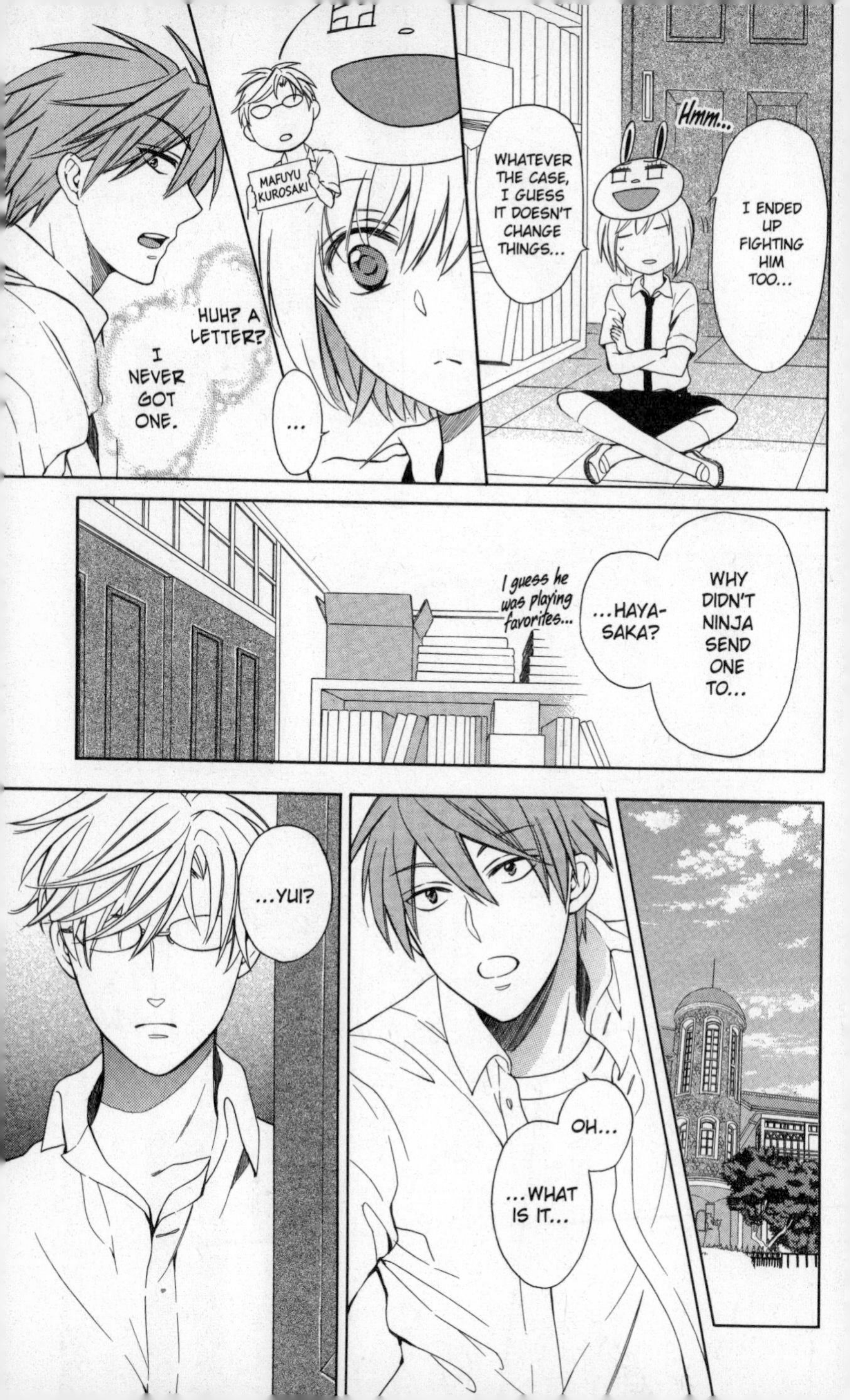
Hmm...
I ENDED UP FIGHTING HIM TOO...
WHATEVER THE CASE, I GUESS IT DOESN'T CHANGE THINGS...
MAFUYU KUROSAKI
...
HUH? A LETTER?
I NEVER GOT ONE.
WHY DIDN'T NINJA SEND ONE TO...
...HAYA-SAKA?
I guess he was playing favorites...
OH...
...WHAT IS IT...
...YUI?

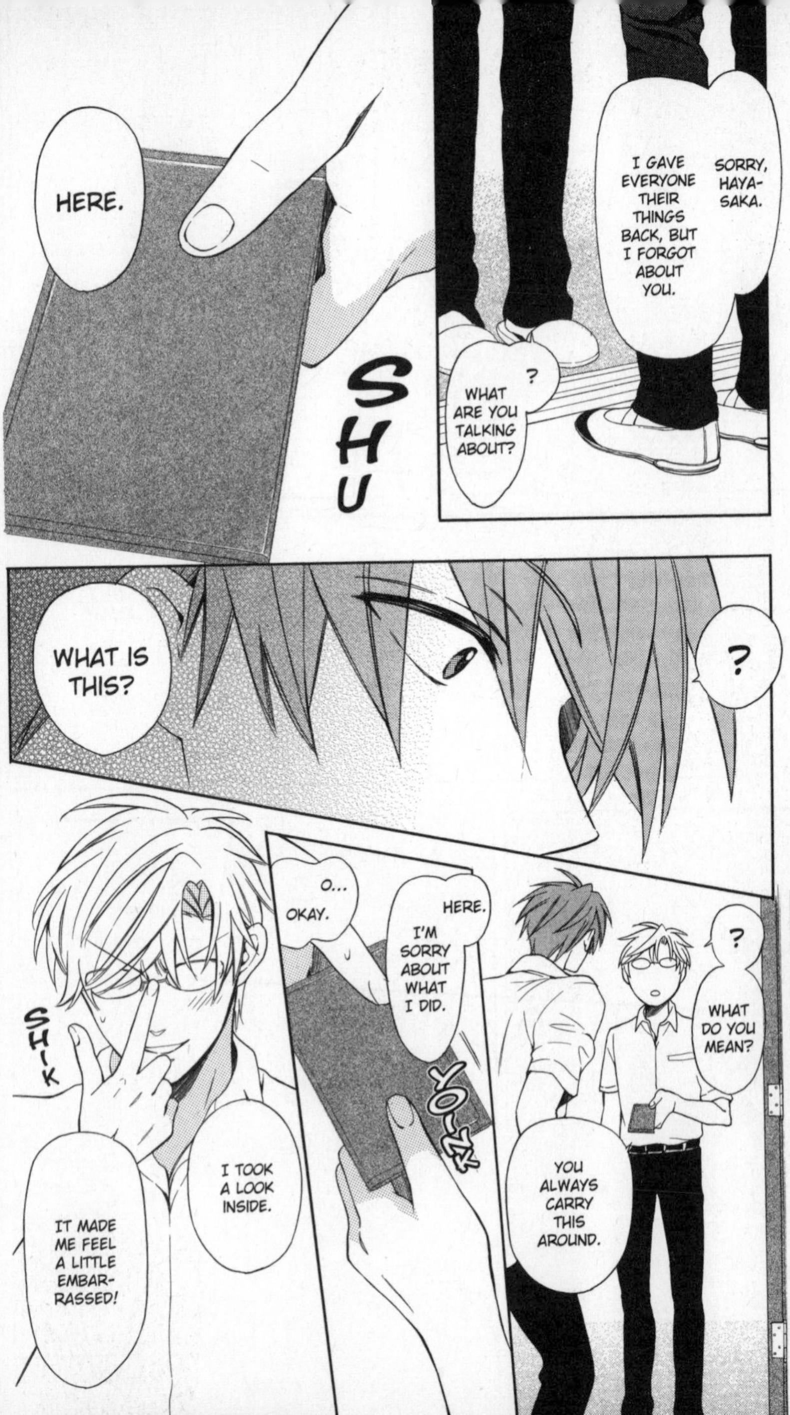
SORRY, HAYASAKA.
I GAVE EVERYONE THEIR THINGS BACK, BUT I FORGOT ABOUT YOU.
? WHAT ARE YOU TALKING ABOUT?
SHU
HERE.
?
WHAT IS THIS?
?
WHAT DO YOU MEAN?
YOU ALWAYS CARRY THIS AROUND.
HERE.
I'M SORRY ABOUT WHAT I DID.
O... OKAY.
YOINK
SHIK
I TOOK A LOOK INSIDE.
IT MADE ME FEEL A LITTLE EMBARRASSED!

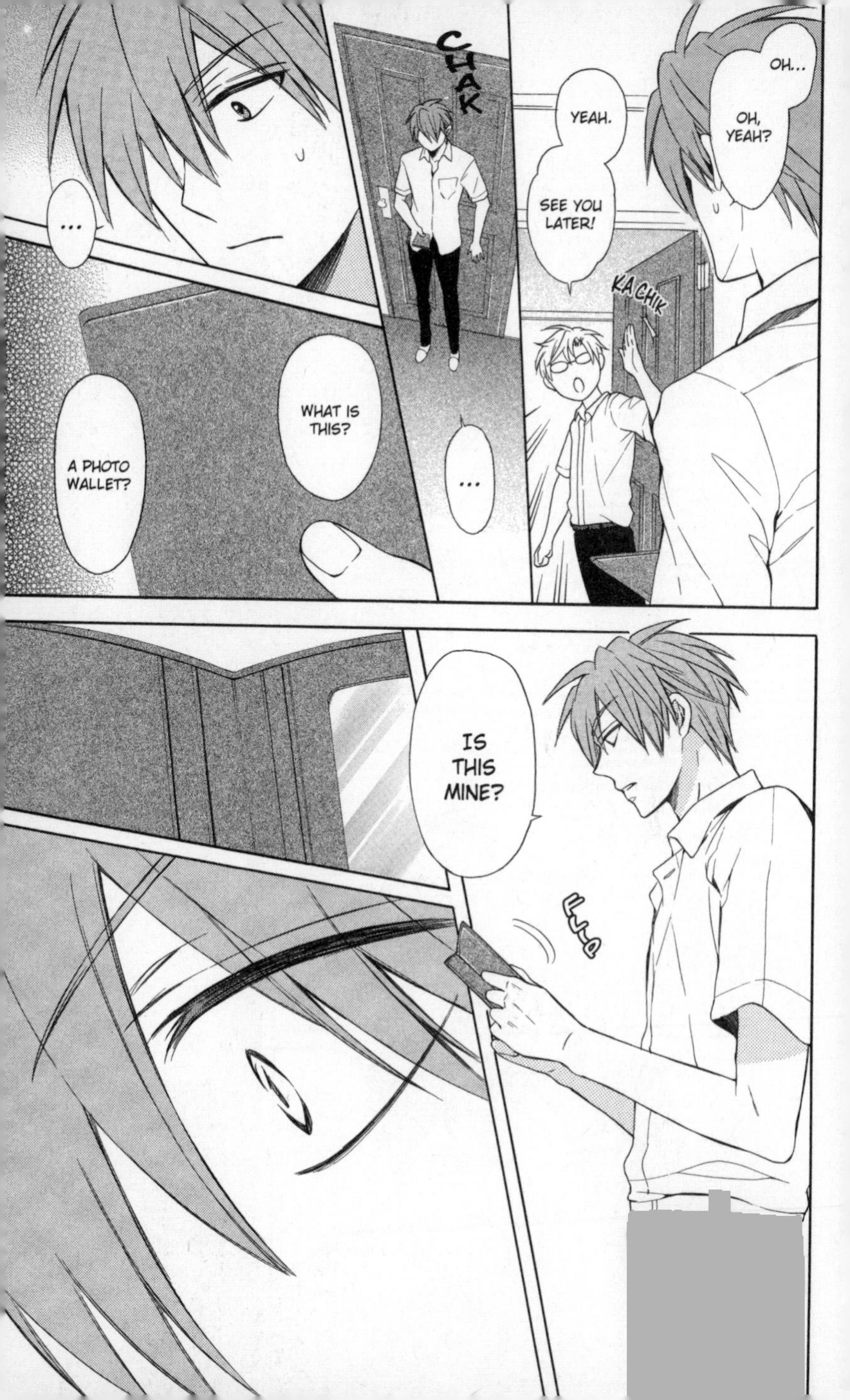
OH...
OH, YEAH?
YEAH.
SEE YOU LATER!
KA CHIK
CHAK
...
...
WHAT IS THIS?
A PHOTO WALLET?
IS THIS MINE?
FLIP

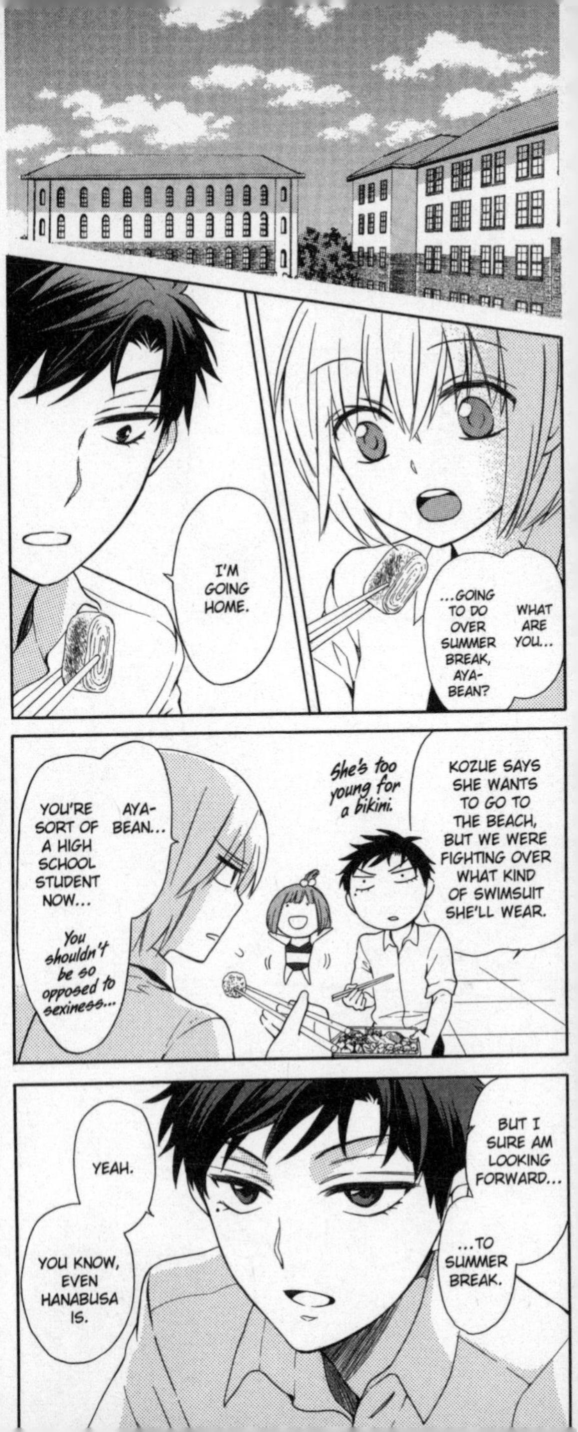
WHAT ARE YOU...
...GOING TO DO OVER SUMMER BREAK, AYA-BEAN?
I'M GOING HOME.
KOZUE SAYS SHE WANTS TO GO TO THE BEACH, BUT WE WERE FIGHTING OVER WHAT KIND OF SWIMSUIT SHE'LL WEAR.
She's too young for a bikini.
AYA-BEAN...
YOU'RE SORT OF A HIGH SCHOOL STUDENT NOW...
You shouldn't be so opposed to sexiness...
BUT I SURE AM LOOKING FORWARD...
...TO SUMMER BREAK.
YEAH.
YOU KNOW, EVEN HANABUSA IS.

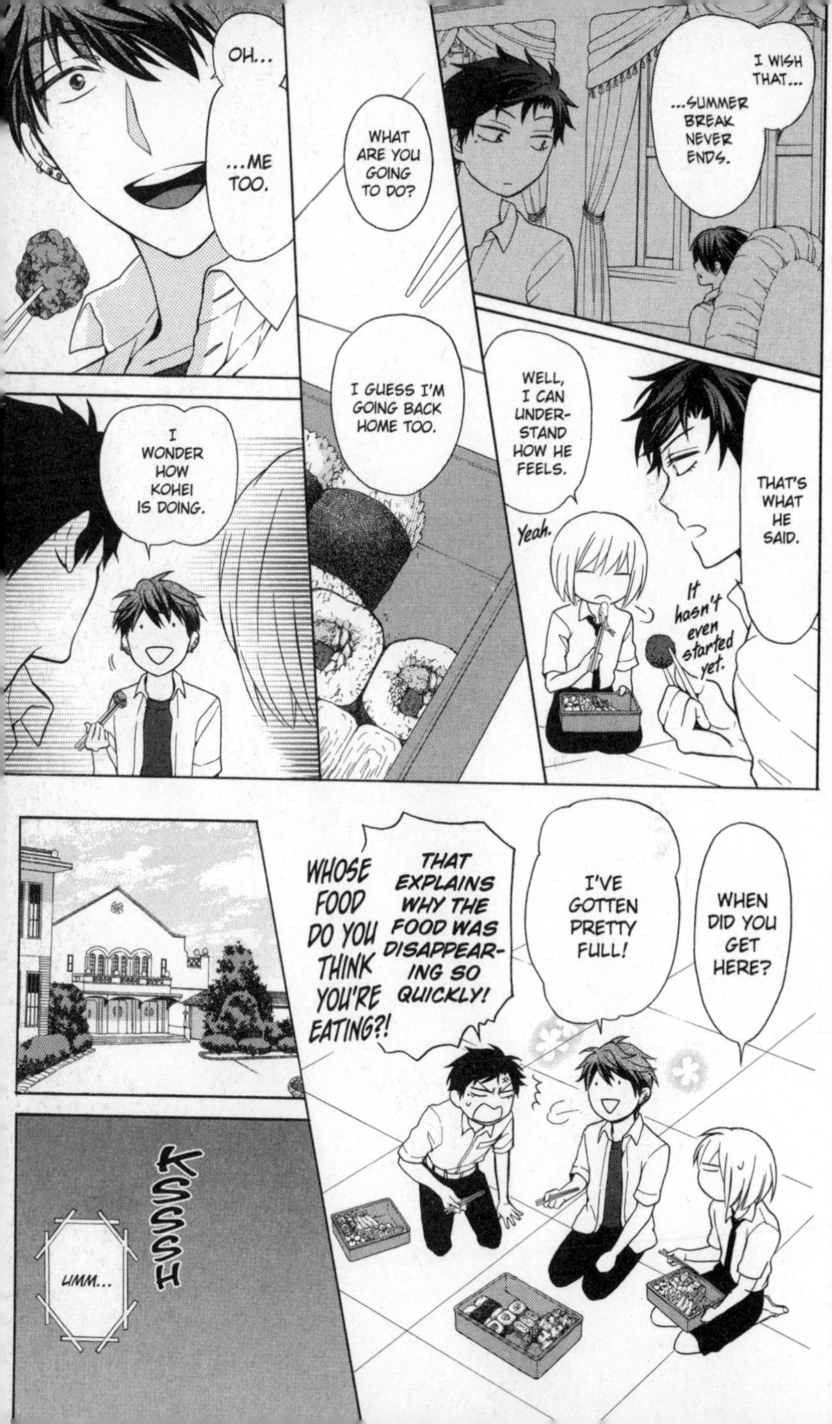
I WISH THAT...
...SUMMER BREAK NEVER ENDS.
WHAT ARE YOU GOING TO DO?
OH...
...ME TOO.
WELL, I CAN UNDER-STAND HOW HE FEELS.
Yeah.
THAT'S WHAT HE SAID.
It hasn't even started yet.
I GUESS I'M GOING BACK HOME TOO.
I WONDER HOW KOHEI IS DOING.
WHEN DID YOU GET HERE?
I'VE GOTTEN PRETTY FULL!
THAT EXPLAINS WHY THE FOOD WAS DISAPPEAR-ING SO QUICKLY!
WHOSE FOOD DO YOU THINK YOU'RE EATING?!
KSSSSH
UMM...

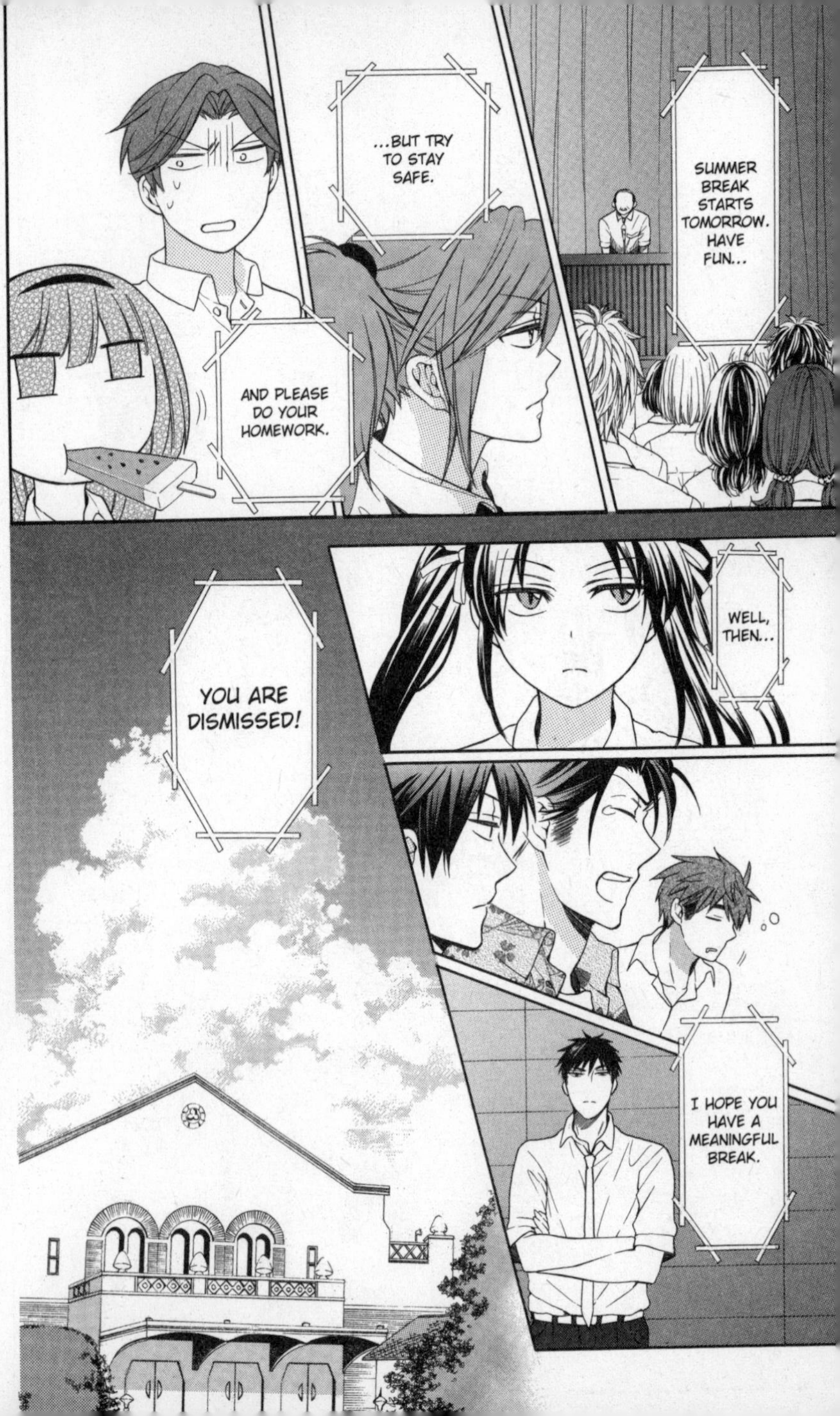
SUMMER BREAK STARTS TOMORROW. HAVE FUN...
...BUT TRY TO STAY SAFE.
AND PLEASE DO YOUR HOMEWORK.
WELL, THEN...
I HOPE YOU HAVE A MEANINGFUL BREAK.
YOU ARE DISMISSED!

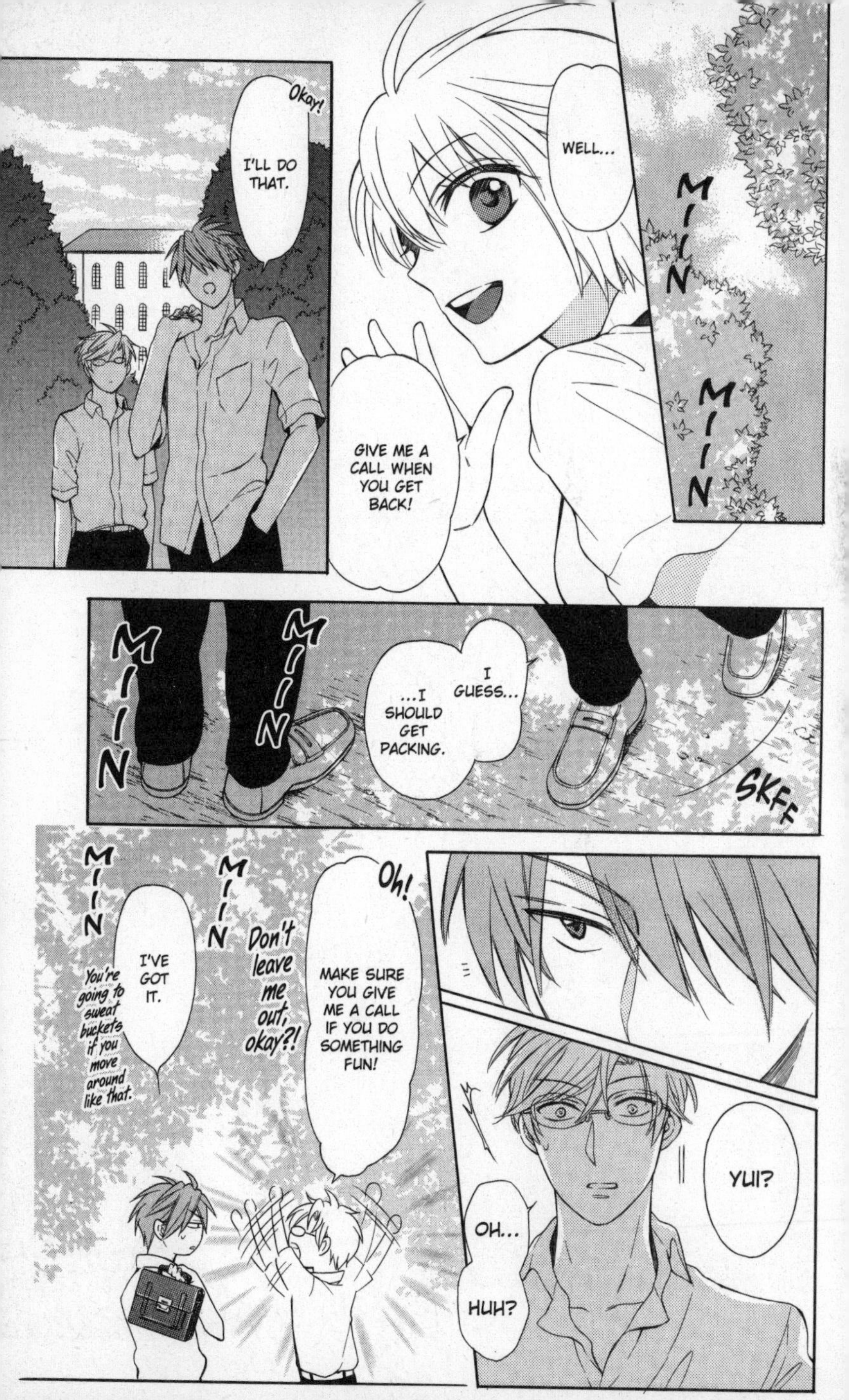

MIIN
MIIN
WELL...
GIVE ME A CALL WHEN YOU GET BACK!
Okay!
I'LL DO THAT.
I GUESS...
...I SHOULD GET PACKING.
SKFF
MIIN
MIIN
YUI?
OH...
HUH?
Oh!
MAKE SURE YOU GIVE ME A CALL IF YOU DO SOMETHING FUN!
Don't leave me out, okay?!
MIIN
I'VE GOT IT.
You're going to sweat buckets if you move around like that.
MIIN

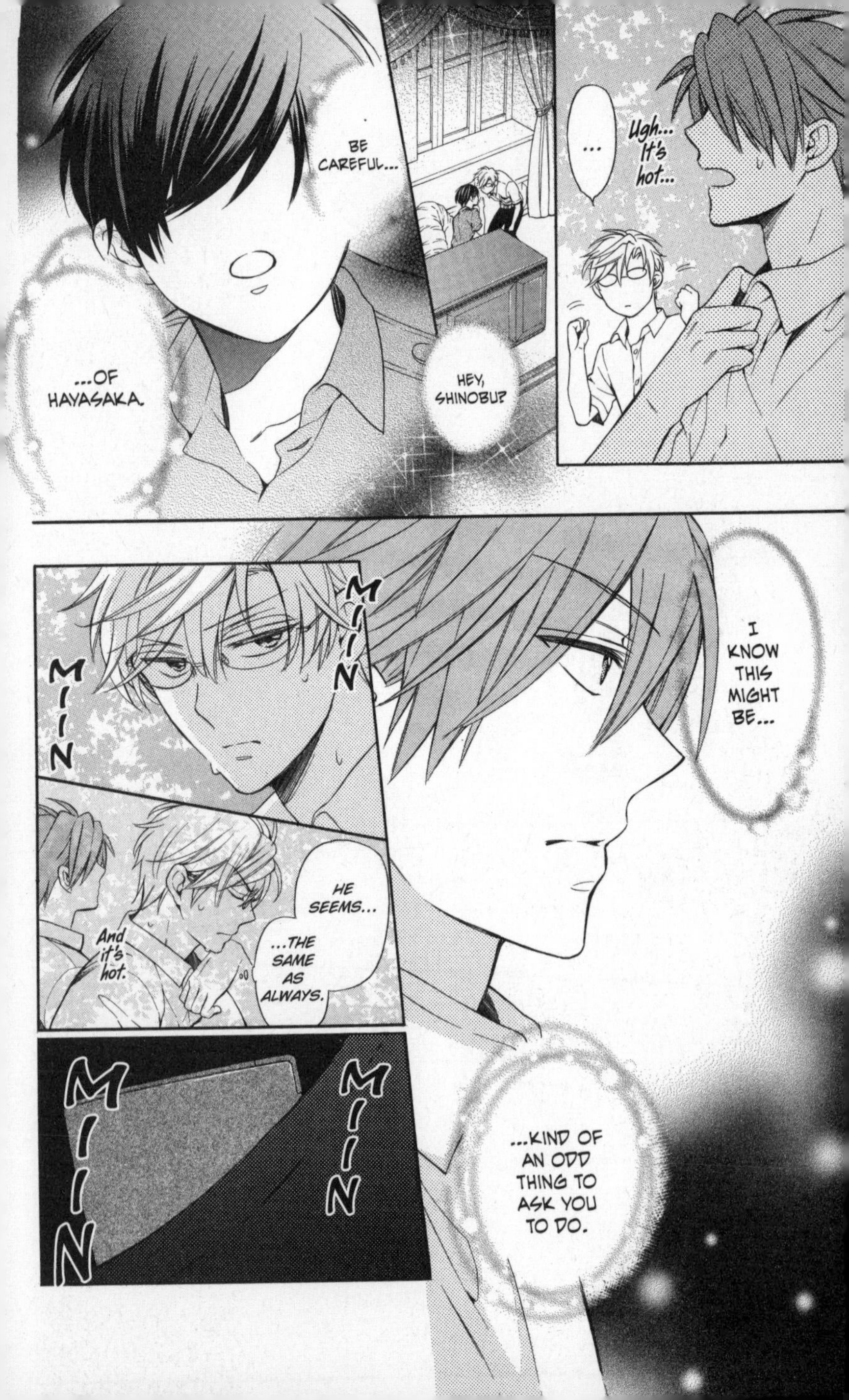
Ugh... It's hot...
...
HEY, SHINOBU?
BE CAREFUL...
...OF HAYASAKA.
I KNOW THIS MIGHT BE...
...KIND OF AN ODD THING TO ASK YOU TO DO.
MIIN
MIIN
HE SEEMS...
...THE SAME AS ALWAYS.
And it's hot.
MIIN
MIIN

ORESAMA TEACHER

Chapter 98

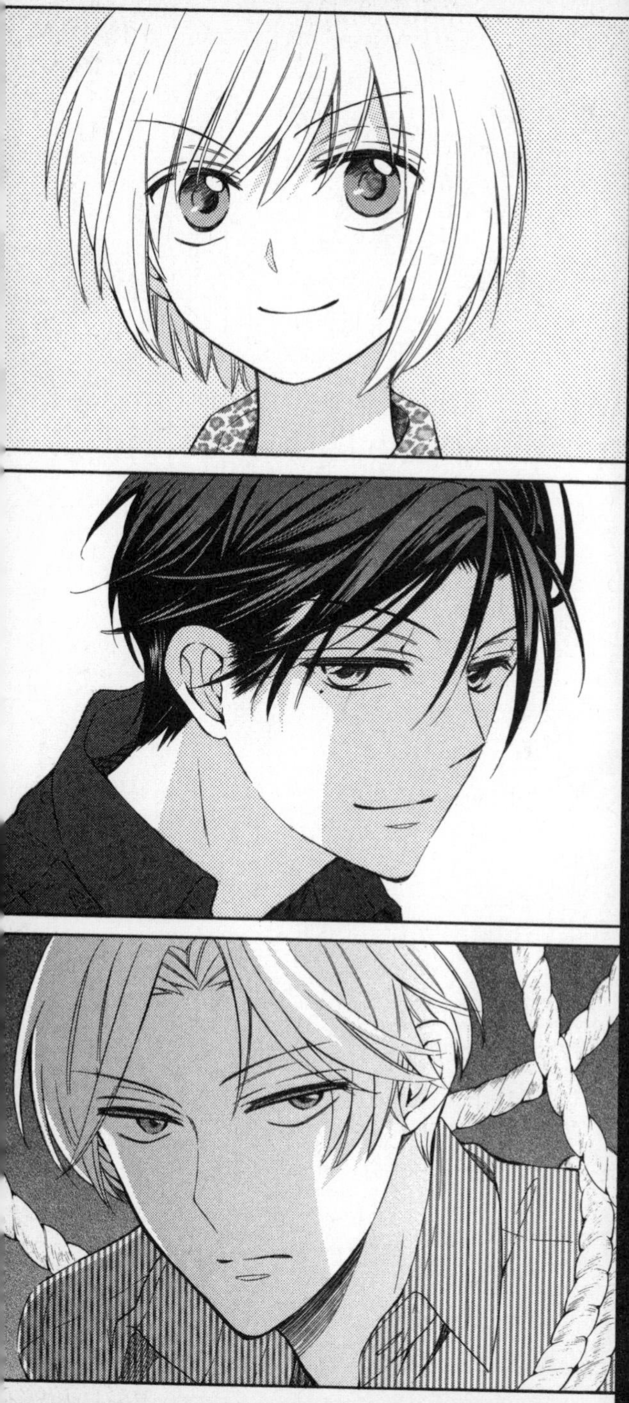

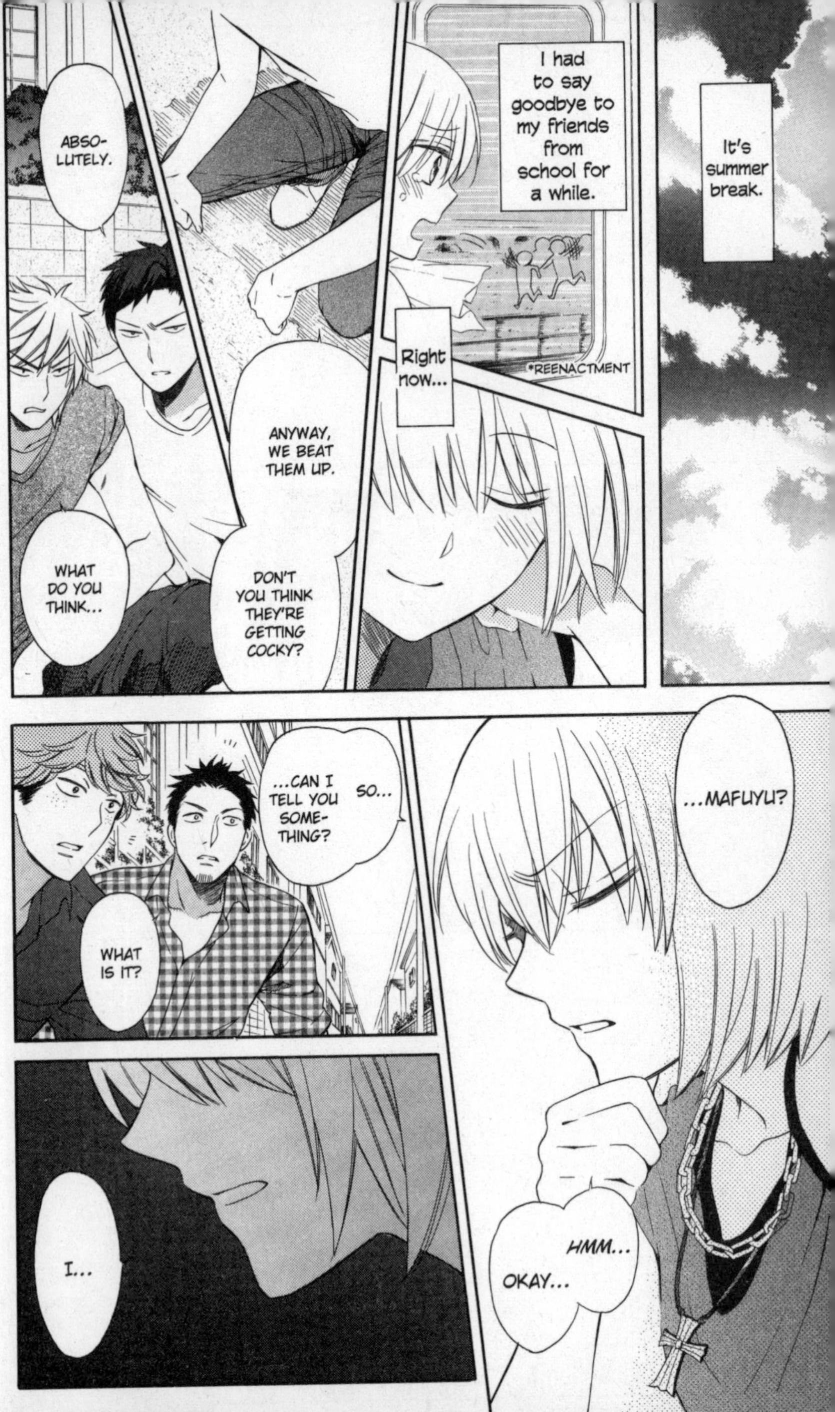
It's summer break.
I had to say goodbye to my friends from school for a while.
*REENACTMENT
Right now...
ANYWAY, WE BEAT THEM UP.
DON'T YOU THINK THEY'RE GETTING COCKY?
ABSO-LUTELY.
WHAT DO YOU THINK...
...MAFUYU?
HMM... OKAY...
SO...
...CAN I TELL YOU SOME-THING?
WHAT IS IT?
I...

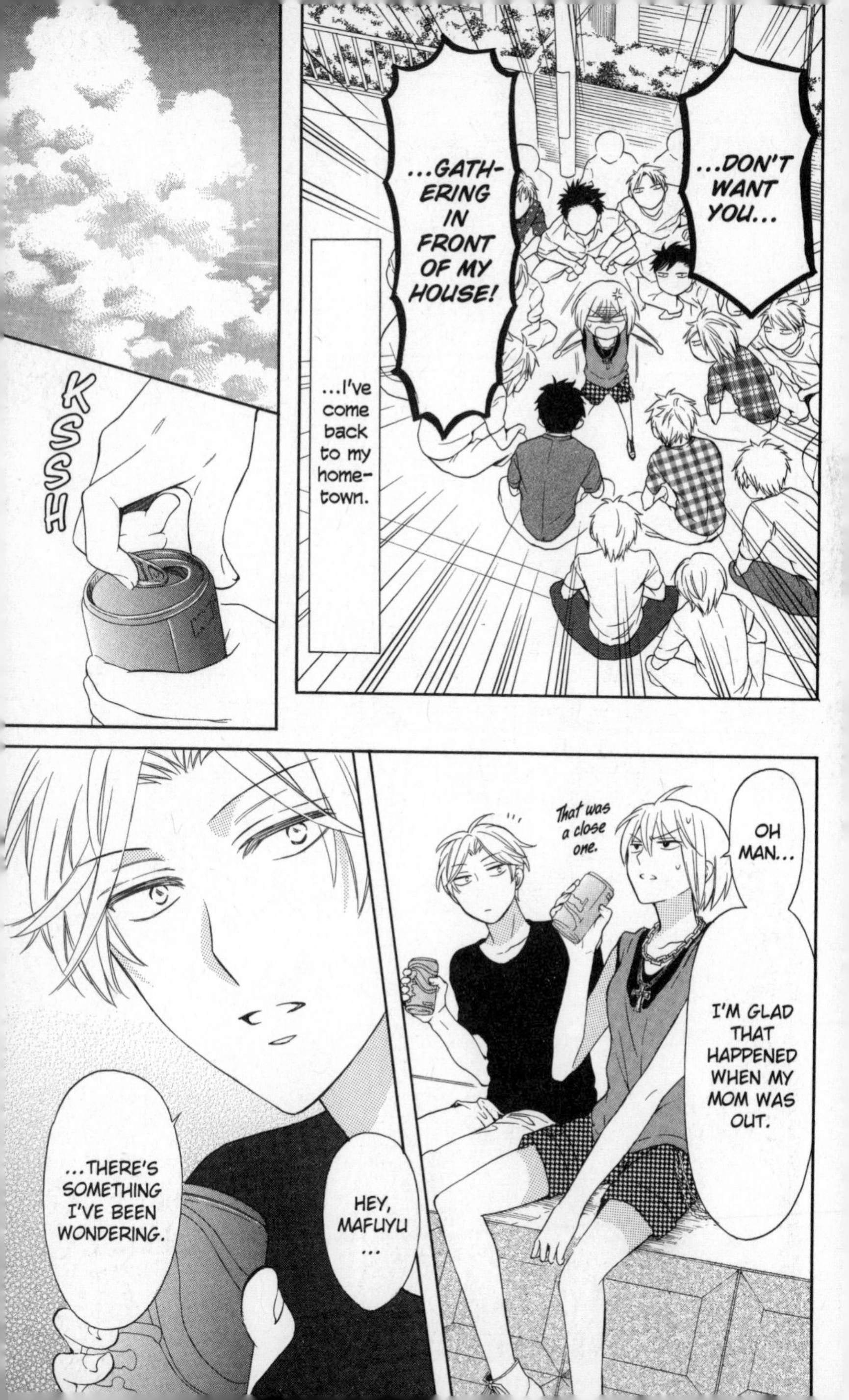

...DON'T WANT YOU...
...GATH-ERING IN FRONT OF MY HOUSE!
...I've come back to my home-town.
KSSH
OH MAN...
That was a close one.
I'M GLAD THAT HAPPENED WHEN MY MOM WAS OUT.
HEY, MAFUYU...
...THERE'S SOMETHING I'VE BEEN WONDERING.

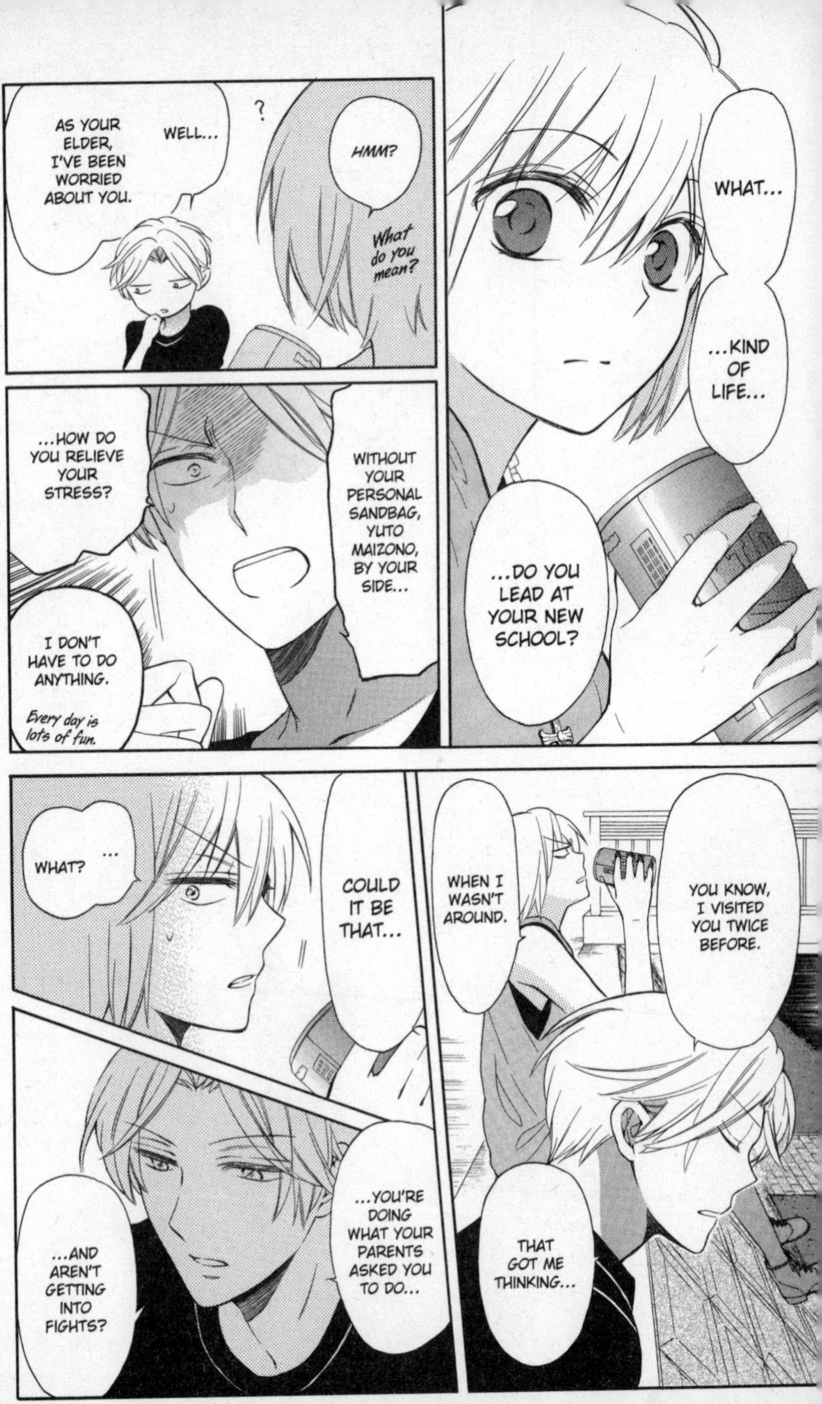
WHAT...
...KIND OF LIFE...
...DO YOU LEAD AT YOUR NEW SCHOOL?
HMM?
What do you mean?
?
WELL...
AS YOUR ELDER, I'VE BEEN WORRIED ABOUT YOU.
WITHOUT YOUR PERSONAL SANDBAG, YUTO MAIZONO, BY YOUR SIDE...
...HOW DO YOU RELIEVE YOUR STRESS?
I DON'T HAVE TO DO ANYTHING.
Every day is lots of fun.
YOU KNOW, I VISITED YOU TWICE BEFORE.
WHEN I WASN'T AROUND.
THAT GOT ME THINKING...
COULD IT BE THAT...
...
WHAT?
...YOU'RE DOING WHAT YOUR PARENTS ASKED YOU TO DO...
...AND AREN'T GETTING INTO FIGHTS?

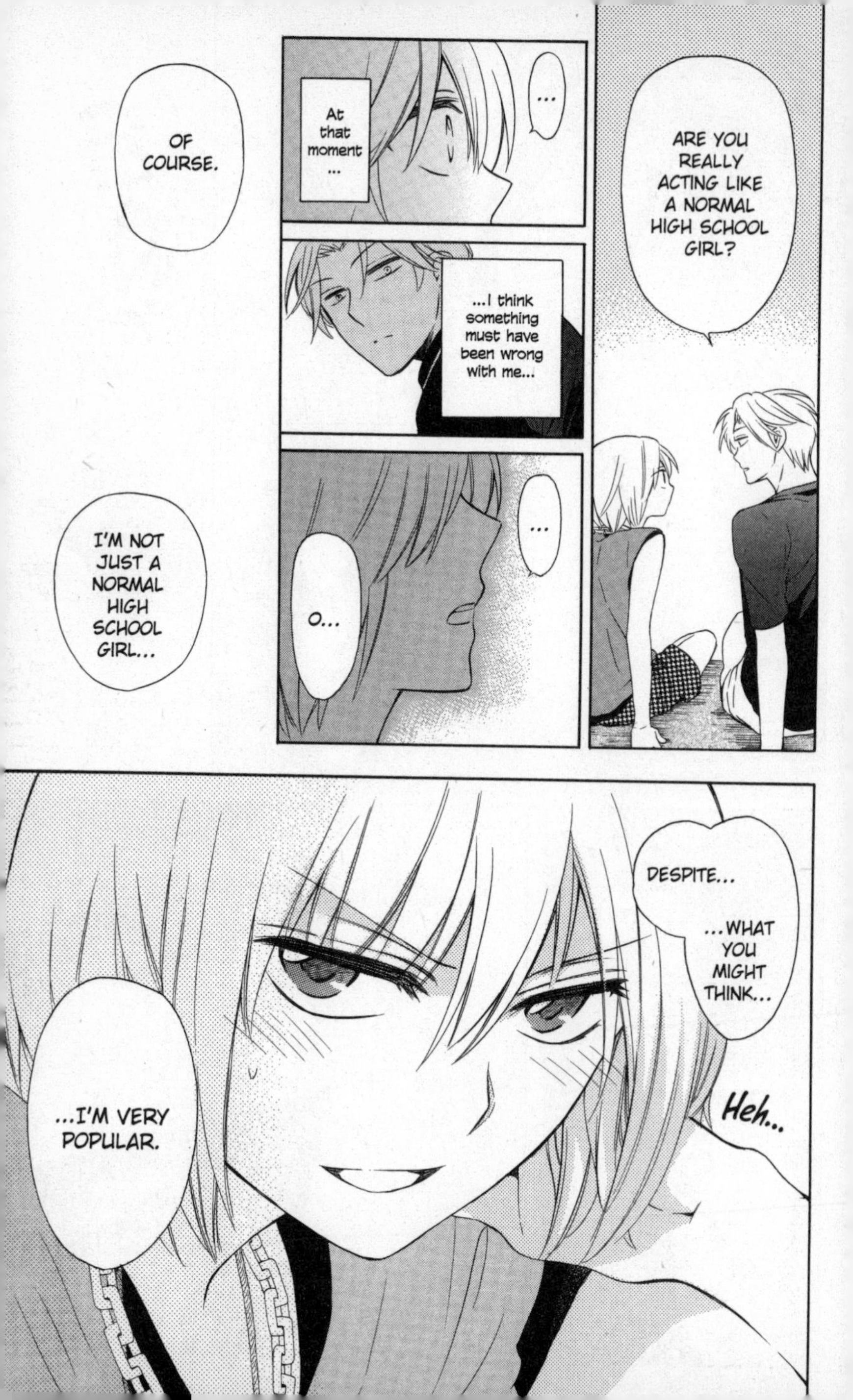
ARE YOU REALLY ACTING LIKE A NORMAL HIGH SCHOOL GIRL?
...
At that moment ...
OF COURSE.
...I think something must have been wrong with me...
...
O...
I'M NOT JUST A NORMAL HIGH SCHOOL GIRL...
DESPITE...
...WHAT YOU MIGHT THINK...
Heh...
...I'M VERY POPULAR.

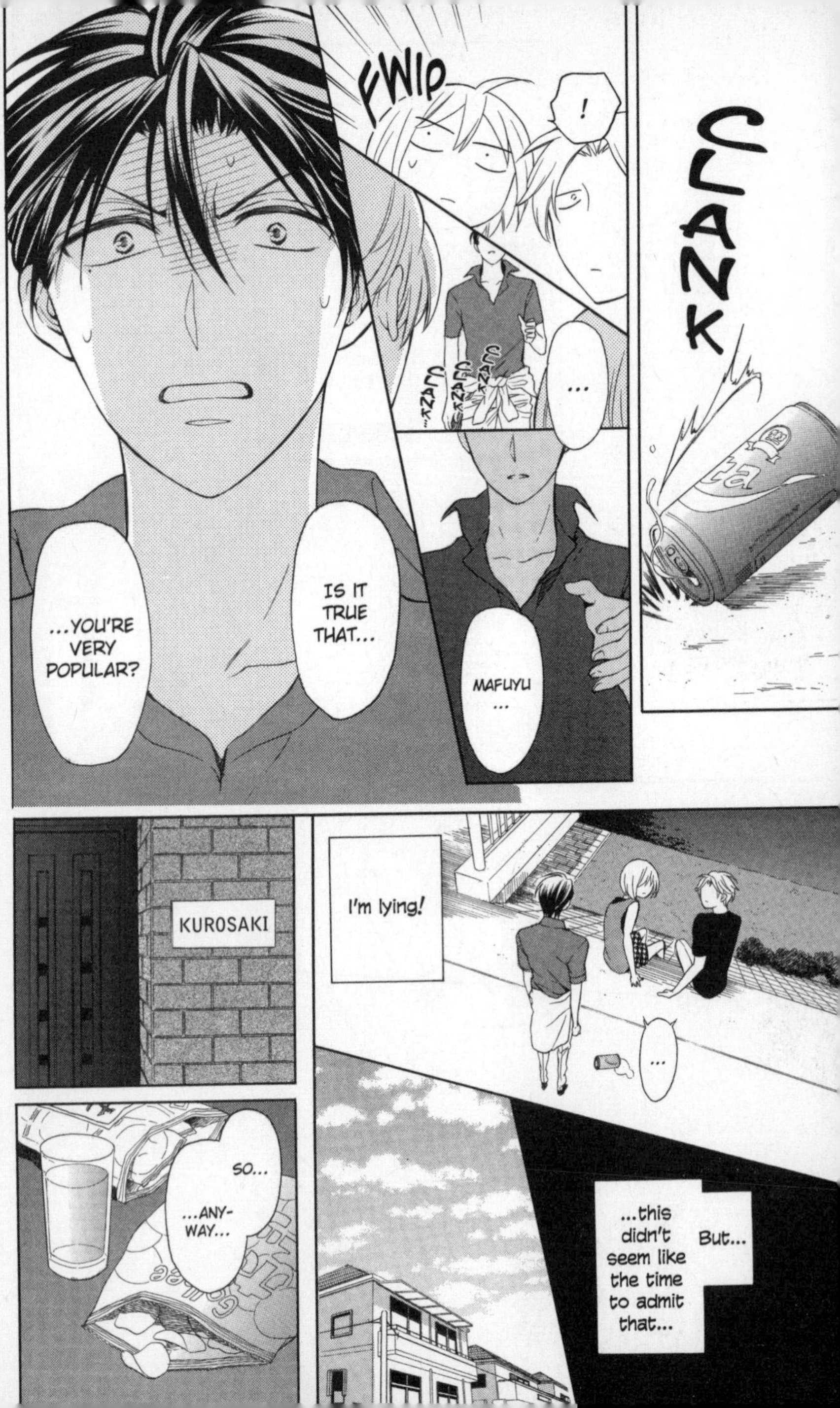
CLANK
FWIP
!
CLANK CLANK CLANK...
...
MAFUYU...
IS IT TRUE THAT...
...YOU'RE VERY POPULAR?
I'm lying!
...
KUROSAKI
But...
...this didn't seem like the time to admit that...
SO...
...ANY-WAY...

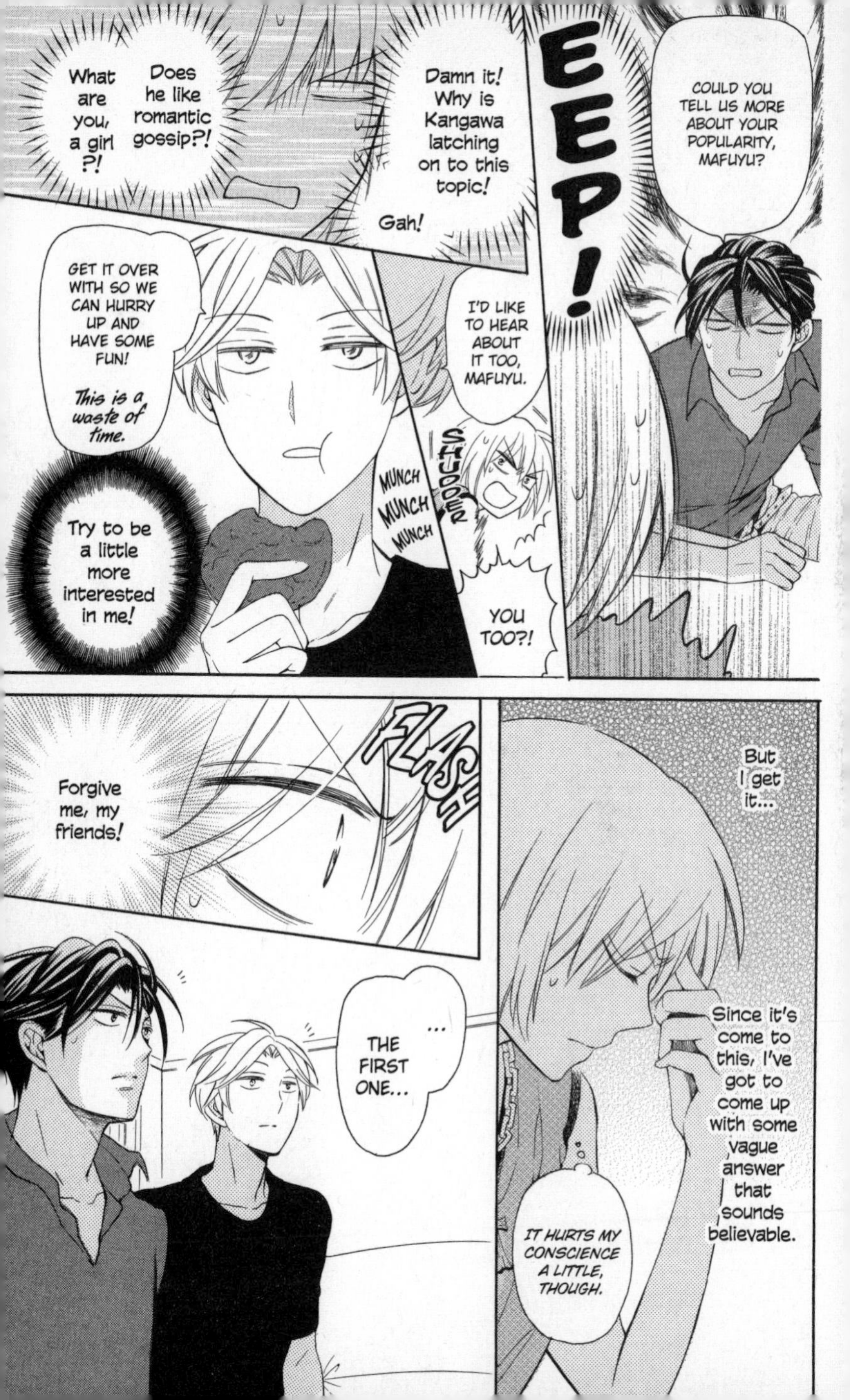
COULD YOU TELL US MORE ABOUT YOUR POPULARITY, MAFUYU?
EEP!
Damn it! Why is Kangawa latching on to this topic!
Gah!
Does he like romantic gossip?!
What are you, a girl?!
I'D LIKE TO HEAR ABOUT IT TOO, MAFUYU.
SHUDDER
YOU TOO?!
MUNCH MUNCH MUNCH
GET IT OVER WITH SO WE CAN HURRY UP AND HAVE SOME FUN!
This is a waste of time.
Try to be a little more interested in me!
But I get it...
Since it's come to this, I've got to come up with some vague answer that sounds believable.
IT HURTS MY CONSCIENCE A LITTLE, THOUGH.
FLASH
Forgive me, my friends!
...
THE FIRST ONE...

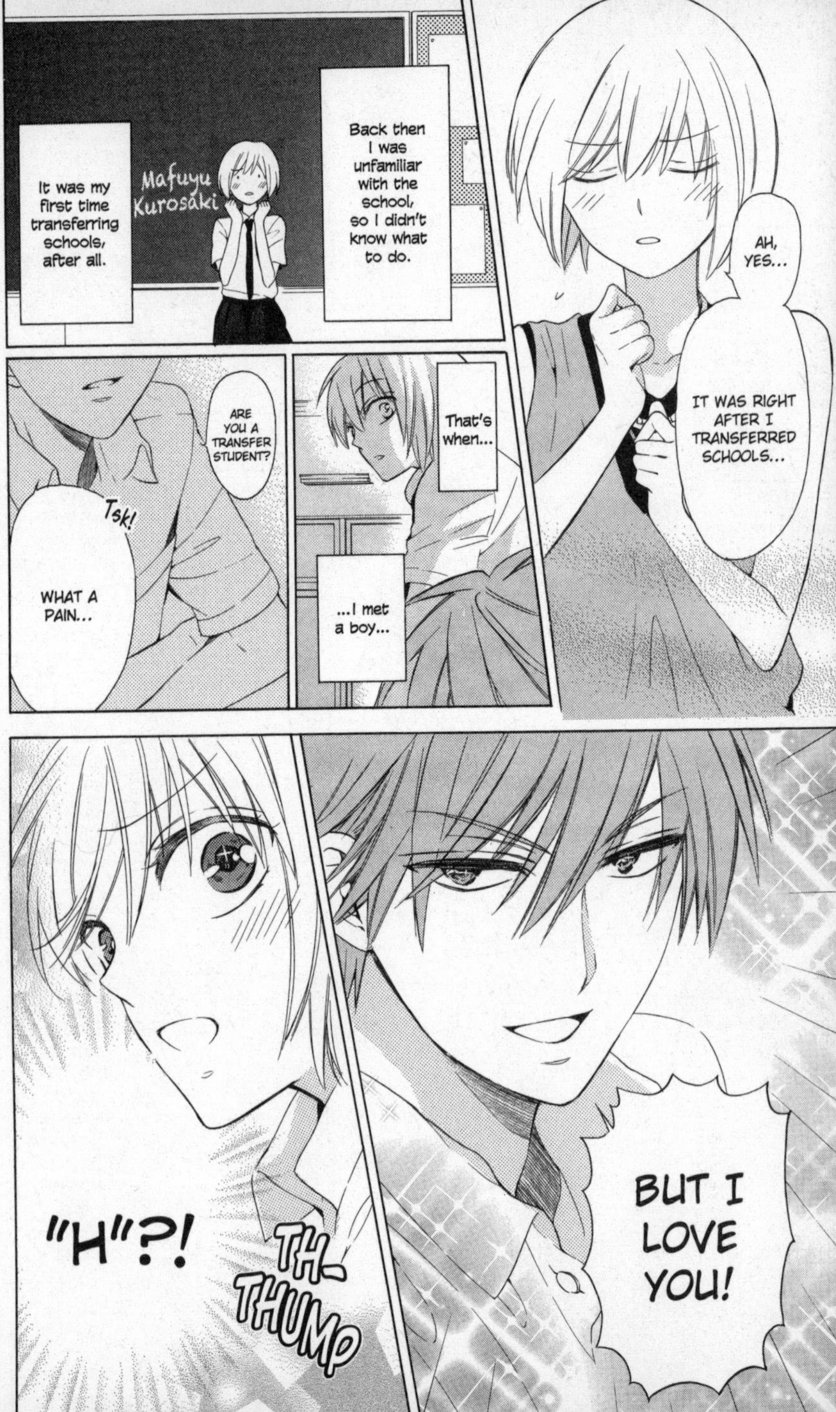
AH, YES...
IT WAS RIGHT AFTER I TRANSFERRED SCHOOLS...
Back then I was unfamiliar with the school, so I didn't know what to do.
Mafuyu Kurosaki
It was my first time transferring schools, after all.
That's when...
...I met a boy...
ARE YOU A TRANSFER STUDENT?
Tsk!
WHAT A PAIN...
BUT I LOVE YOU!
TH-THUMP
"H"?!

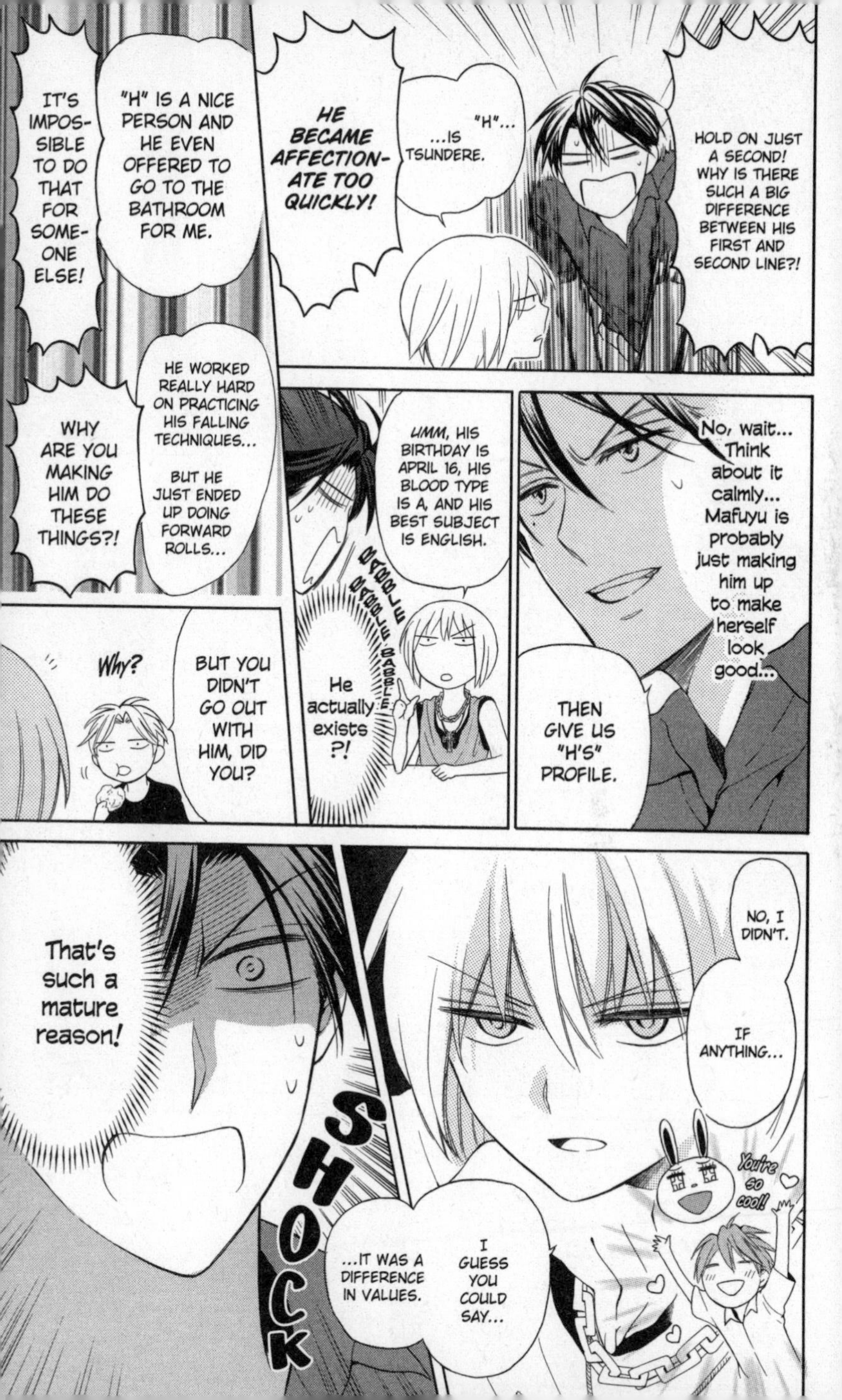

"H"... ...IS TSUNDERE.
HOLD ON JUST A SECOND! WHY IS THERE SUCH A BIG DIFFERENCE BETWEEN HIS FIRST AND SECOND LINE?!
HE BECAME AFFECTIONATE TOO QUICKLY!
"H" IS A NICE PERSON AND HE EVEN OFFERED TO GO TO THE BATHROOM FOR ME.
IT'S IMPOSSIBLE TO DO THAT FOR SOMEONE ELSE!
No, wait... Think about it calmly... Mafuyu is probably just making him up to make herself look good...
THEN GIVE US "H'S" PROFILE.
UMM, HIS BIRTHDAY IS APRIL 16, HIS BLOOD TYPE IS A, AND HIS BEST SUBJECT IS ENGLISH.
BABBLE BABBLE BABBLE
He actually exists?!
HE WORKED REALLY HARD ON PRACTICING HIS FALLING TECHNIQUES...
BUT HE JUST ENDED UP DOING FORWARD ROLLS...
WHY ARE YOU MAKING HIM DO THESE THINGS?!
BUT YOU DIDN'T GO OUT WITH HIM, DID YOU?
Why?
NO, I DIDN'T.
IF ANYTHING...
I GUESS YOU COULD SAY...
...IT WAS A DIFFERENCE IN VALUES.
You're so cool!
SHOCK
That's such a mature reason!

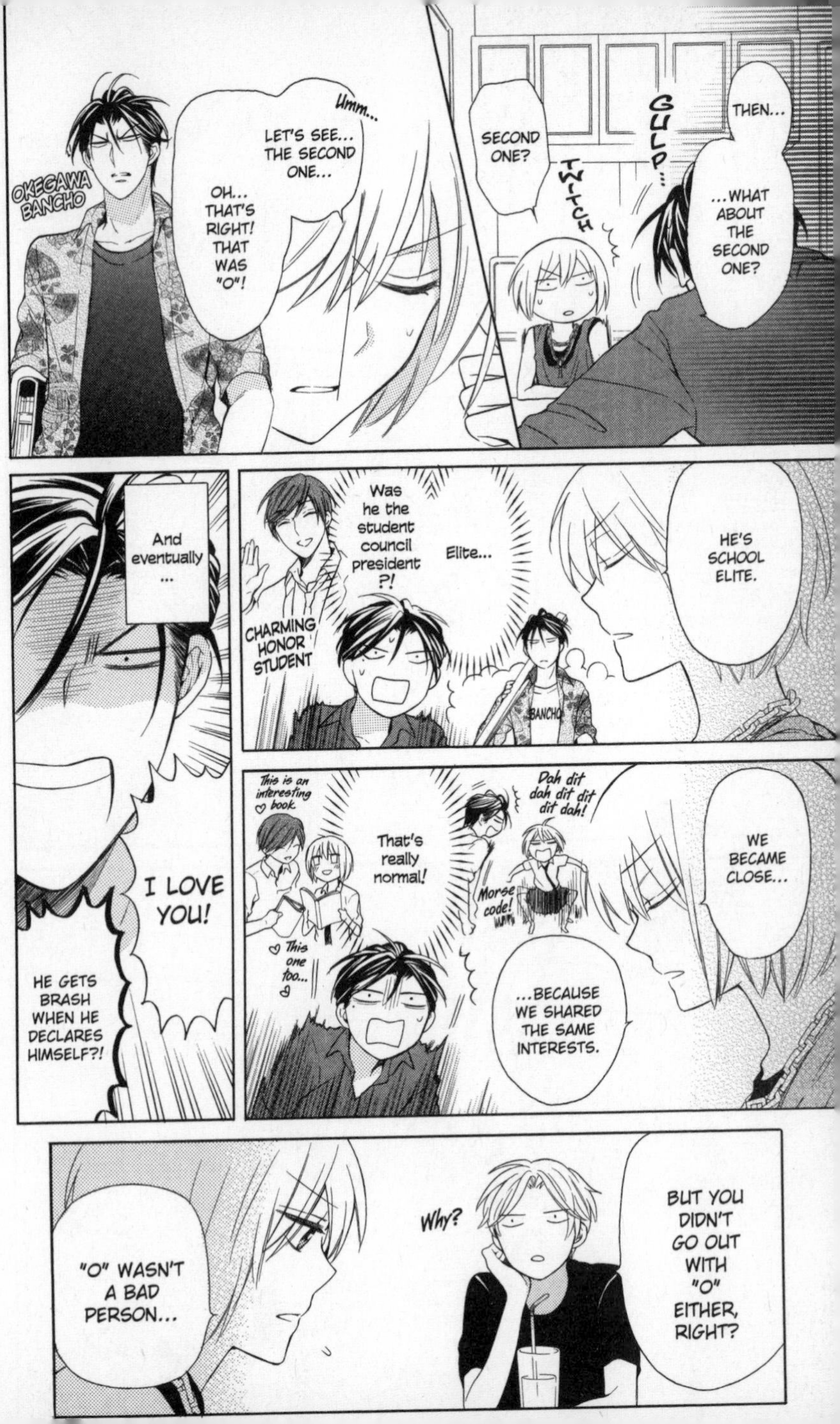
THEN...
...WHAT ABOUT THE SECOND ONE?
GULP...
SECOND ONE?
TWITCH
Umm...
LET'S SEE... THE SECOND ONE...
OH... THAT'S RIGHT! THAT WAS "O"!
OKEGAWA BANCHO
HE'S SCHOOL ELITE.
Elite...
Was he the student council president?!
CHARMING HONOR STUDENT
BANCHO
WE BECAME CLOSE...
...BECAUSE WE SHARED THE SAME INTERESTS.
Dah dit dah dit dit dit dah!
Morse code!
That's really normal!
This is an interesting book
This one too...
And eventually ...
I LOVE YOU!
HE GETS BRASH WHEN HE DECLARES HIMSELF?!
BUT YOU DIDN'T GO OUT WITH "O" EITHER, RIGHT?
Why?
"O" WASN'T A BAD PERSON...

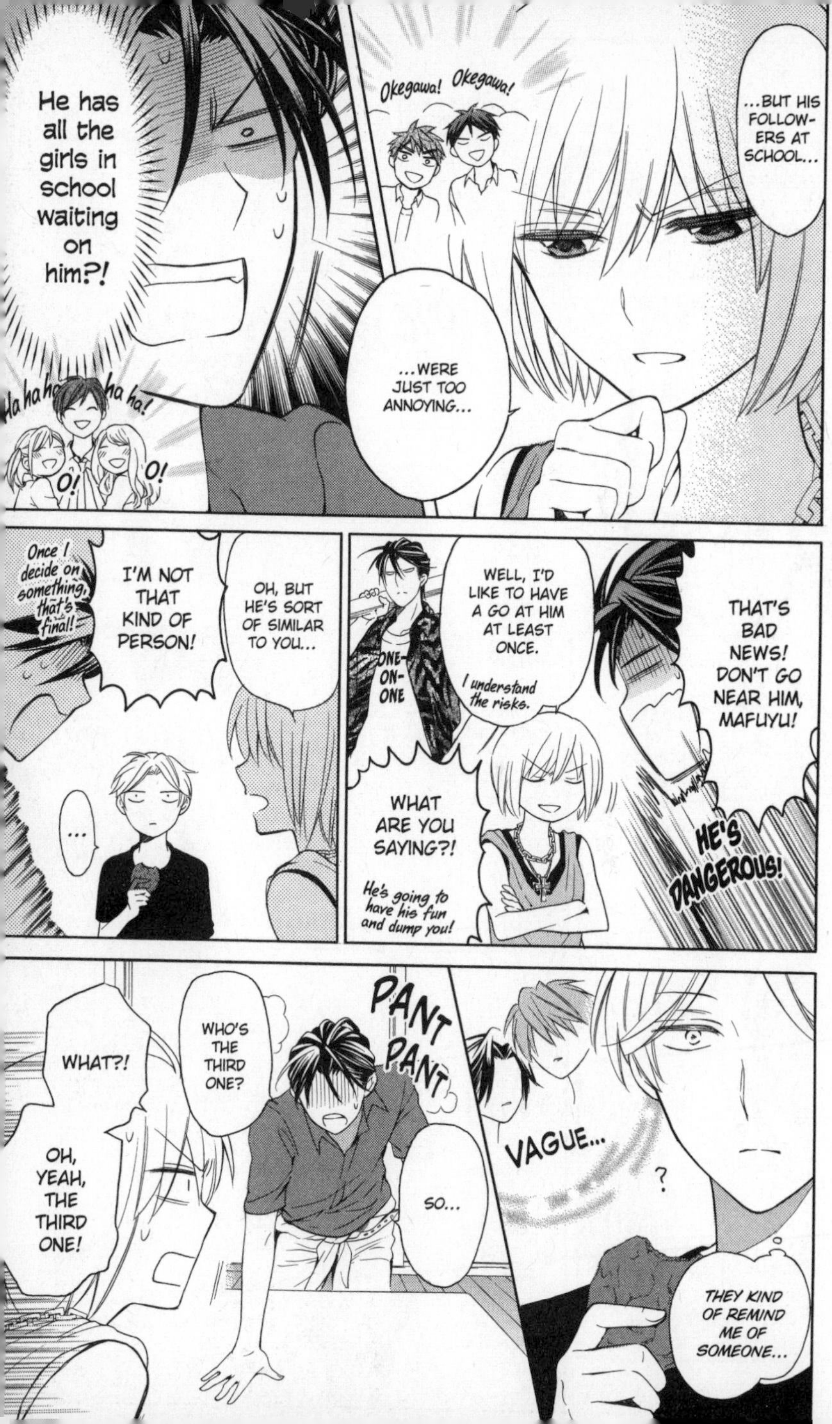
...BUT HIS FOLLOWERS AT SCHOOL...
Okegawa! Okegawa!
...WERE JUST TOO ANNOYING...
He has all the girls in school waiting on him?!
Ha ha ha ha ha!
O! O!
THAT'S BAD NEWS! DON'T GO NEAR HIM, MAFUYU!
WELL, I'D LIKE TO HAVE A GO AT HIM AT LEAST ONCE.
I understand the risks.
ONE-ON-ONE
HE'S DANGEROUS!
WHAT ARE YOU SAYING?!
He's going to have his fun and dump you!
OH, BUT HE'S SORT OF SIMILAR TO YOU...
I'M NOT THAT KIND OF PERSON!
Once I decide on something, that's final!
...
VAGUE...
?
THEY KIND OF REMIND ME OF SOMEONE...
PANT PANT
WHO'S THE THIRD ONE?
WHAT?!
SO...
OH, YEAH, THE THIRD ONE!

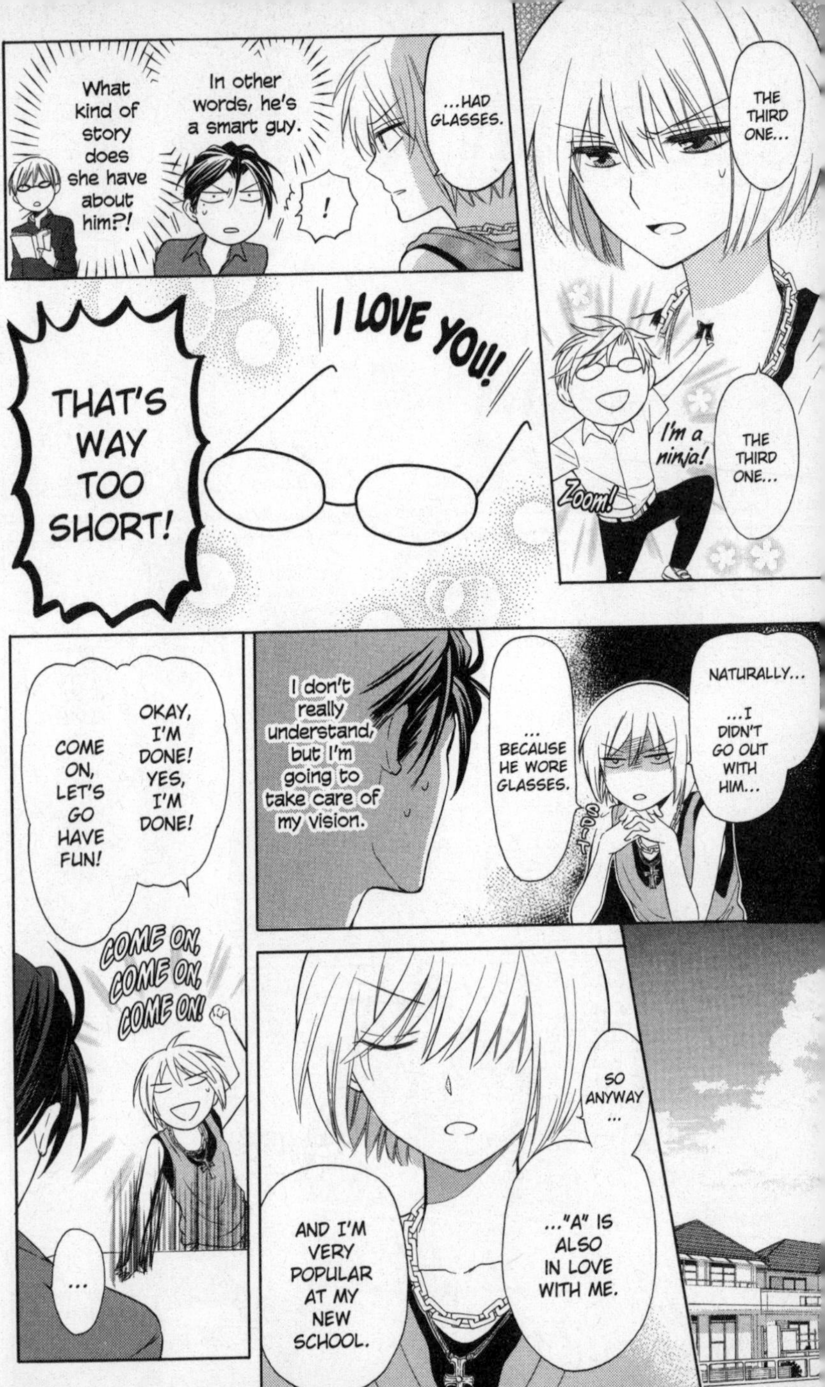
THE THIRD ONE...
THE THIRD ONE...
I'm a ninja!
Zoom!
...HAD GLASSES.
!
In other words, he's a smart guy.
What kind of story does she have about him?!
I LOVE YOU!
THAT'S WAY TOO SHORT!
NATURALLY... ...I DIDN'T GO OUT WITH HIM...
...BECAUSE HE WORE GLASSES.
I don't really understand, but I'm going to take care of my vision.
SO ANYWAY...
..."A" IS ALSO IN LOVE WITH ME.
AND I'M VERY POPULAR AT MY NEW SCHOOL.
OKAY, I'M DONE! YES, I'M DONE!
COME ON, LET'S GO HAVE FUN!
COME ON, COME ON, COME ON!
...

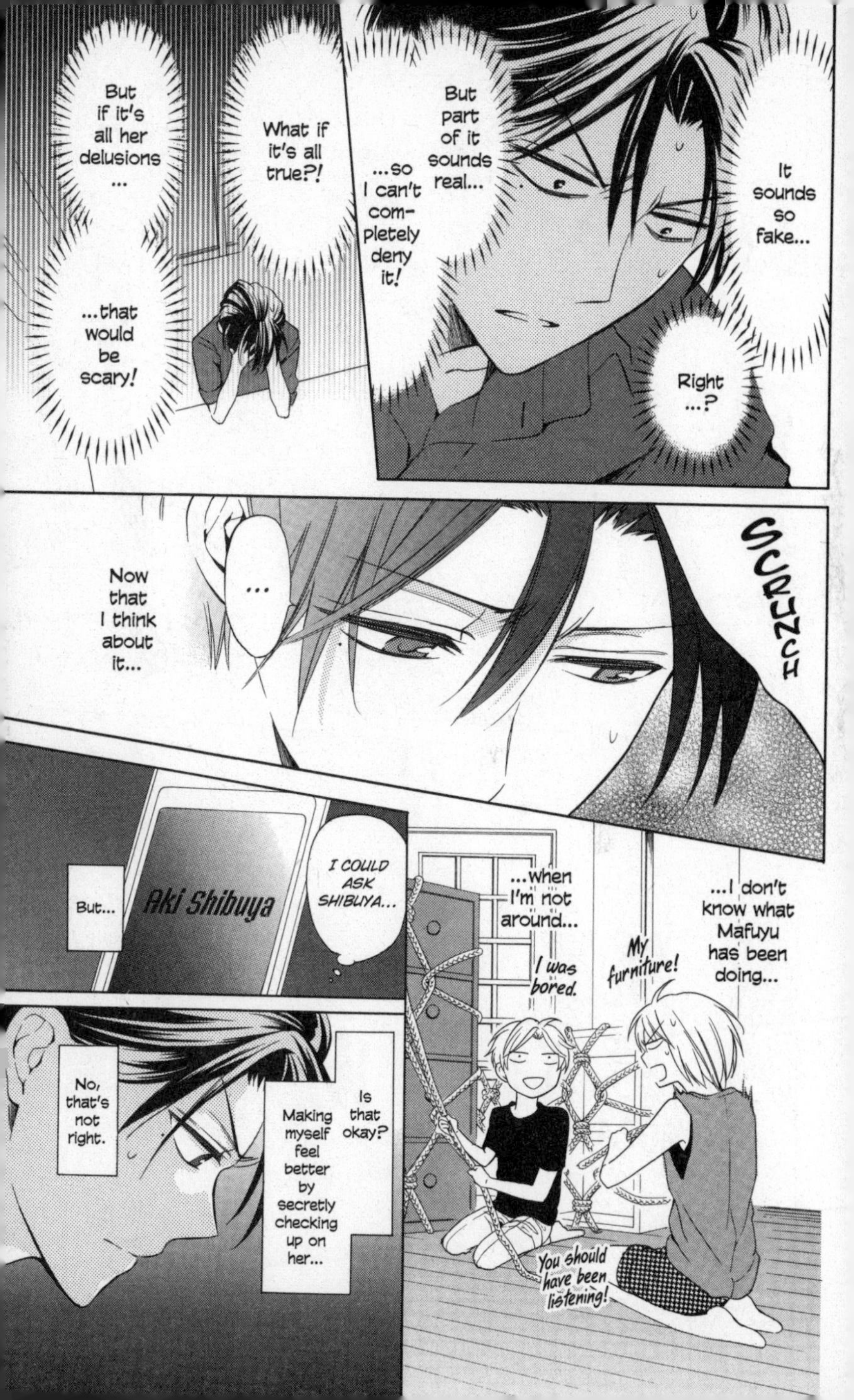
It sounds so fake...
But part of it sounds real...
...so I can't completely deny it!
Right ...?
What if it's all true?!
But if it's all her delusions ...
...that would be scary!
SCRUNCH
...
Now that I think about it...
...I don't know what Mafuyu has been doing...
...when I'm not around...
My furniture!
I was bored.
You should have been listening!
I COULD ASK SHIBUYA...
Aki Shibuya
But...
Is that okay?
Making myself feel better by secretly checking up on her...
No, that's not right.

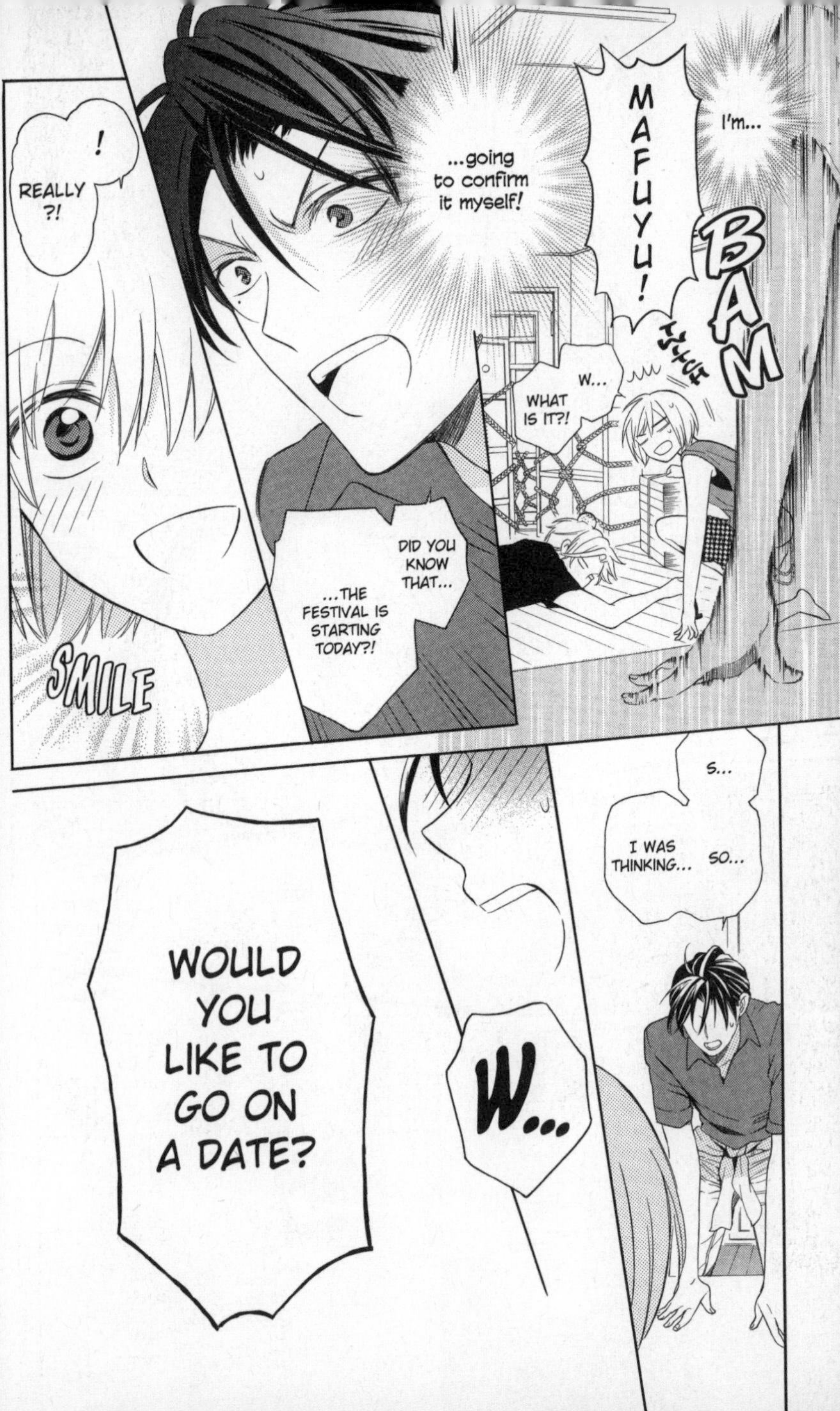
I'm...
...going to confirm it myself!
BAM
MAFUYU!
W... WHAT IS IT?!
DID YOU KNOW THAT...
...THE FESTIVAL IS STARTING TODAY?!
! REALLY ?!
SMILE
S...
SO... I WAS THINKING...
W...
WOULD YOU LIKE TO GO ON A DATE?

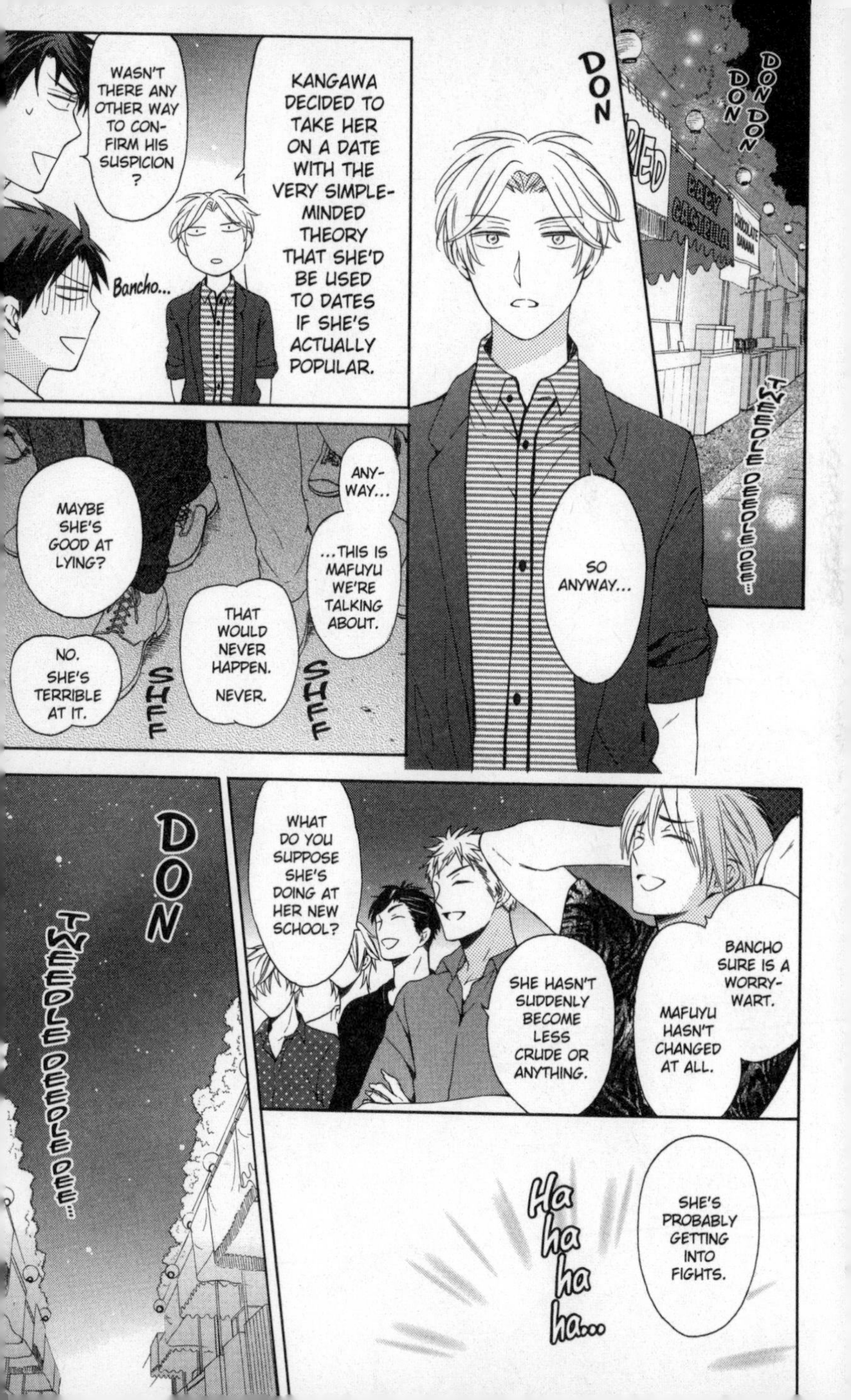
DON
DON DON DON DON
TWEEDLE DEEDLE DEE...
SO ANYWAY...
KANGAWA DECIDED TO TAKE HER ON A DATE WITH THE VERY SIMPLE-MINDED THEORY THAT SHE'D BE USED TO DATES IF SHE'S ACTUALLY POPULAR.
WASN'T THERE ANY OTHER WAY TO CON-FIRM HIS SUSPICION?
Bancho...
ANY-WAY...
...THIS IS MAFUYU WE'RE TALKING ABOUT.
SHEFF
MAYBE SHE'S GOOD AT LYING?
THAT WOULD NEVER HAPPEN. NEVER.
SHEFF
NO. SHE'S TERRIBLE AT IT.
WHAT DO YOU SUPPOSE SHE'S DOING AT HER NEW SCHOOL?
BANCHO SURE IS A WORRY-WART.
MAFUYU HASN'T CHANGED AT ALL.
SHE HASN'T SUDDENLY BECOME LESS CRUDE OR ANYTHING.
SHE'S PROBABLY GETTING INTO FIGHTS.
Ha ha ha ha...
DON
TWEEDLE DEEDLE DEE...

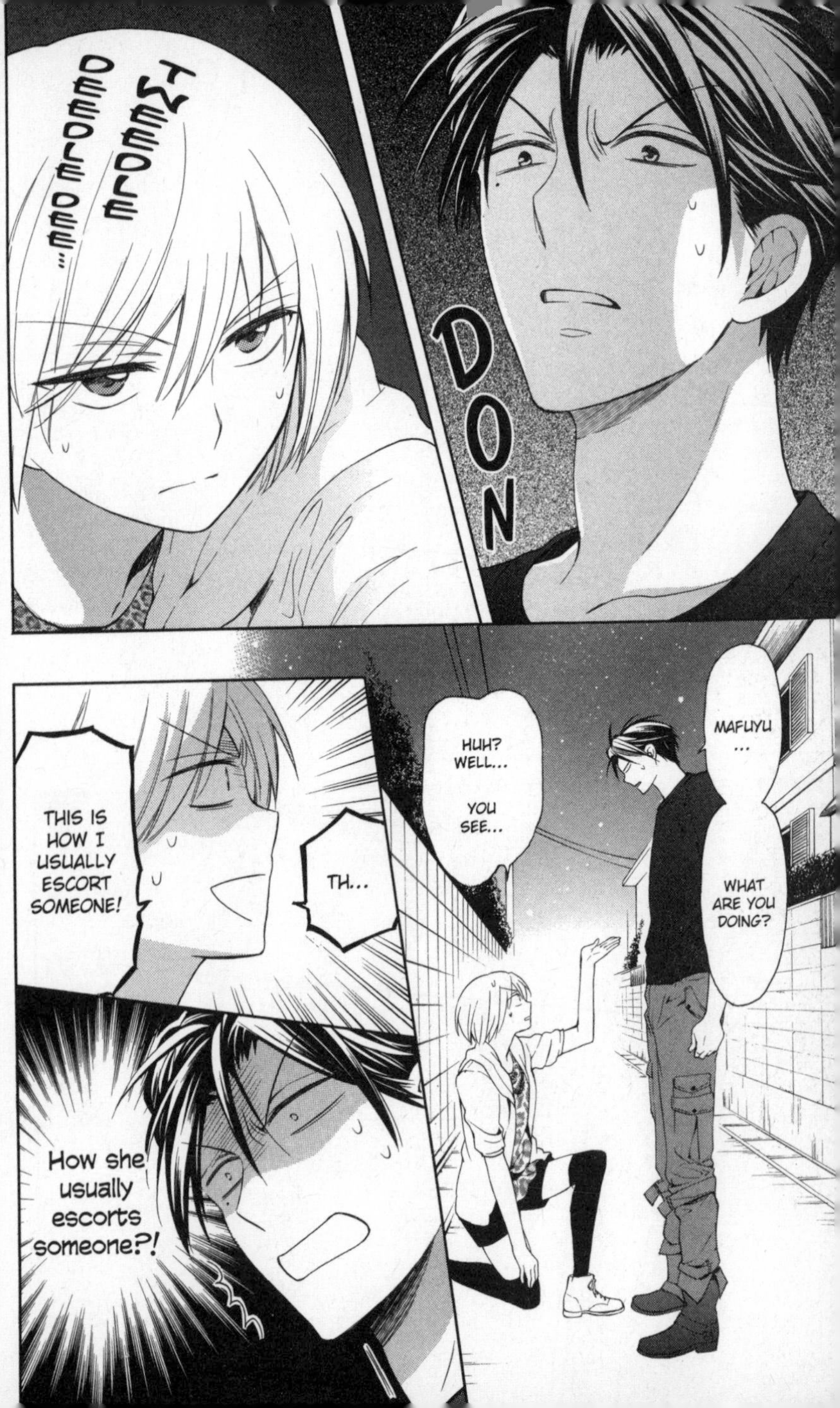
DON
TWEEDLE DEEDLE DEE...
MAFUYU...
WHAT ARE YOU DOING?
HUH? WELL...
YOU SEE...
TH...
THIS IS HOW I USUALLY ESCORT SOMEONE!
How she usually escorts someone?!

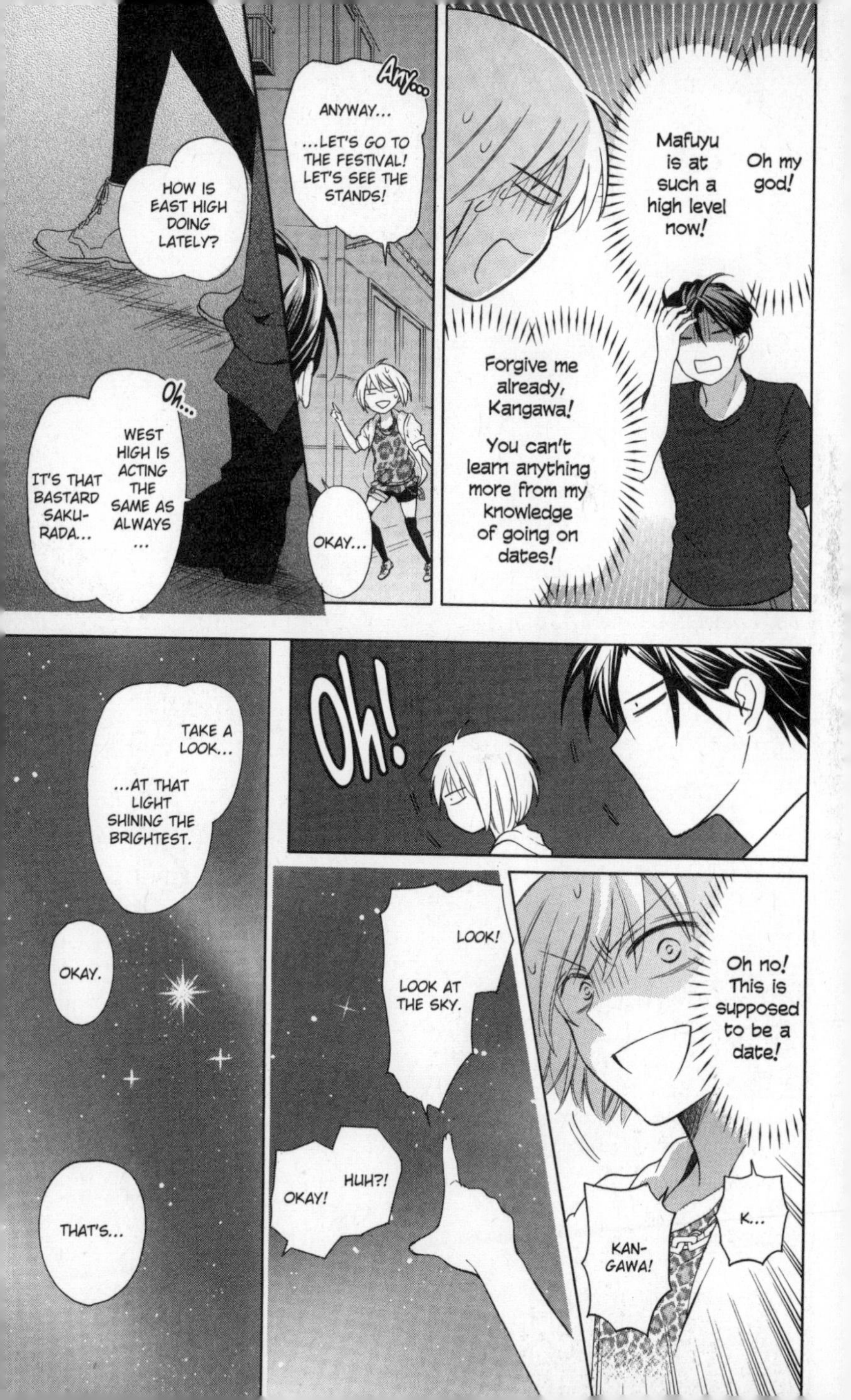
Oh my god!
Mafuyu is at such a high level now!
Forgive me already, Kangawa!
You can't learn anything more from my knowledge of going on dates!
Any...
ANYWAY...
...LET'S GO TO THE FESTIVAL! LET'S SEE THE STANDS!
OKAY...
HOW IS EAST HIGH DOING LATELY?
Oh...
WEST HIGH IS ACTING THE SAME AS ALWAYS...
IT'S THAT BASTARD SAKU-RADA...
Oh!
Oh no! This is supposed to be a date!
K...
KAN-GAWA!
LOOK!
LOOK AT THE SKY.
HUH?!
OKAY!
TAKE A LOOK...
...AT THAT LIGHT SHINING THE BRIGHTEST.
OKAY.
THAT'S...

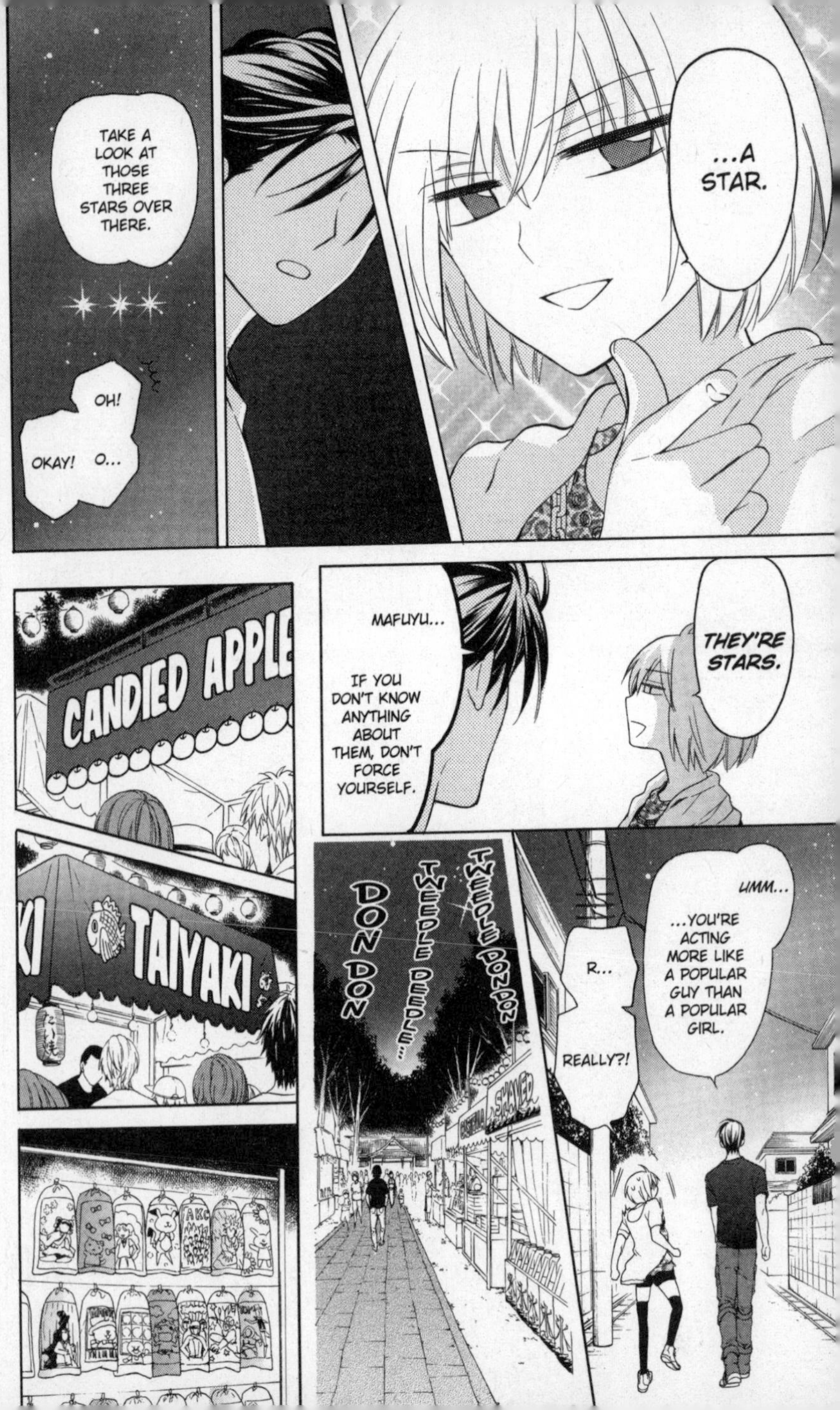
...A STAR.
TAKE A LOOK AT THOSE THREE STARS OVER THERE.
OH!
O...
OKAY!
THEY'RE STARS.
MAFUYU...
IF YOU DON'T KNOW ANYTHING ABOUT THEM, DON'T FORCE YOURSELF.
UMM...
...YOU'RE ACTING MORE LIKE A POPULAR GUY THAN A POPULAR GIRL.
R...
REALLY?!
TWEEDLE DON DON
TWEEDLE DEEDLE...
DON DON
SHAVED
CANDIED APPLE
TAIYAKI

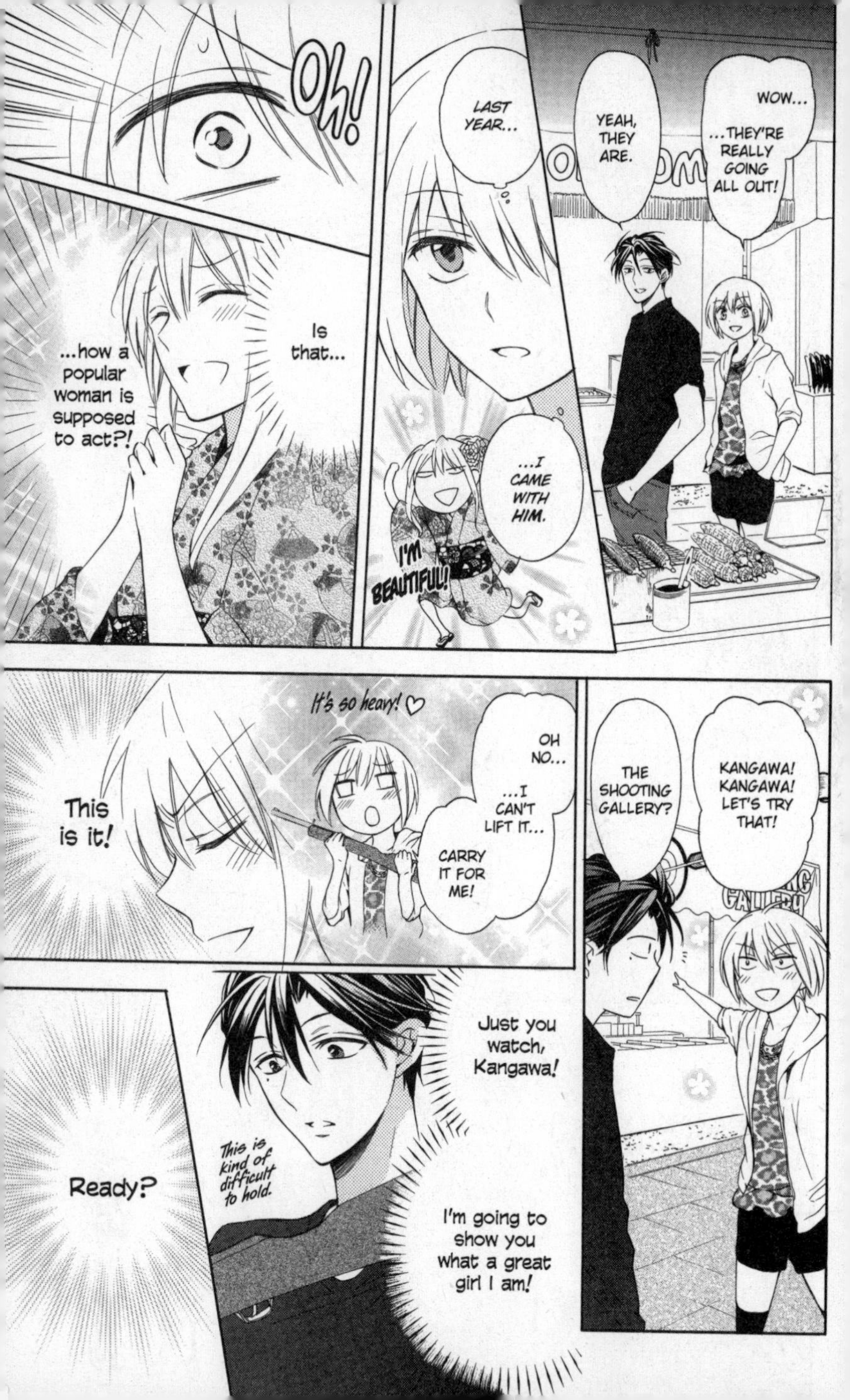
WOW...
...THEY'RE REALLY GOING ALL OUT!
YEAH, THEY ARE.
LAST YEAR...
...I CAME WITH HIM.
I'M BEAUTIFUL!
Oh!
Is that...
...how a popular woman is supposed to act?!
KANGAWA! KANGAWA! LET'S TRY THAT!
THE SHOOTING GALLERY?
It's so heavy! ♡
OH NO...
...I CAN'T LIFT IT...
CARRY IT FOR ME!
This is it!
Just you watch, Kangawa!
I'm going to show you what a great girl I am!
This is kind of difficult to hold.
Ready?

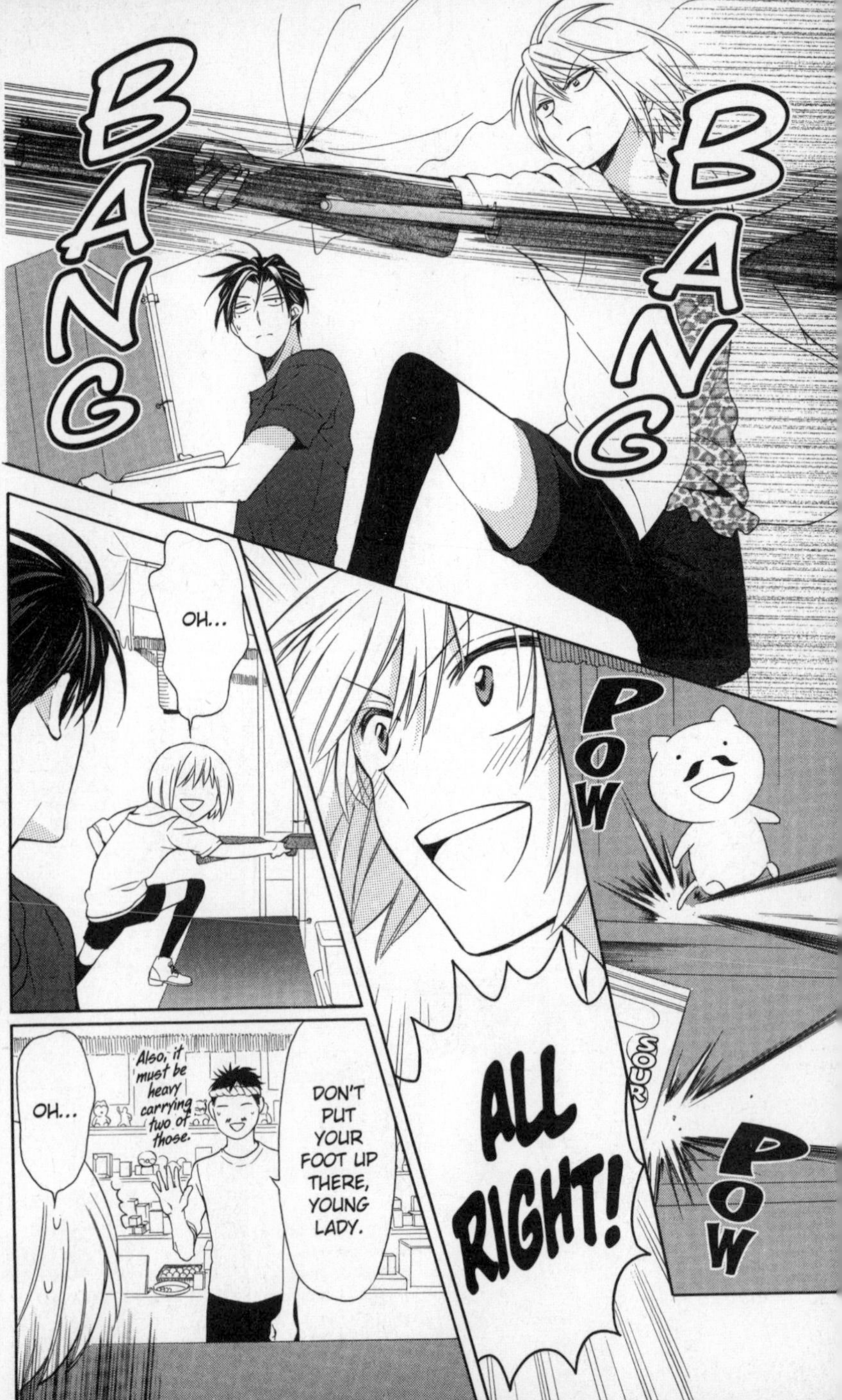
BANG
BANG
POW
POW
ALL RIGHT!
SOUR
OH...
DON'T PUT YOUR FOOT UP THERE, YOUNG LADY.
Also, it must be heavy carrying two of those.
OH...

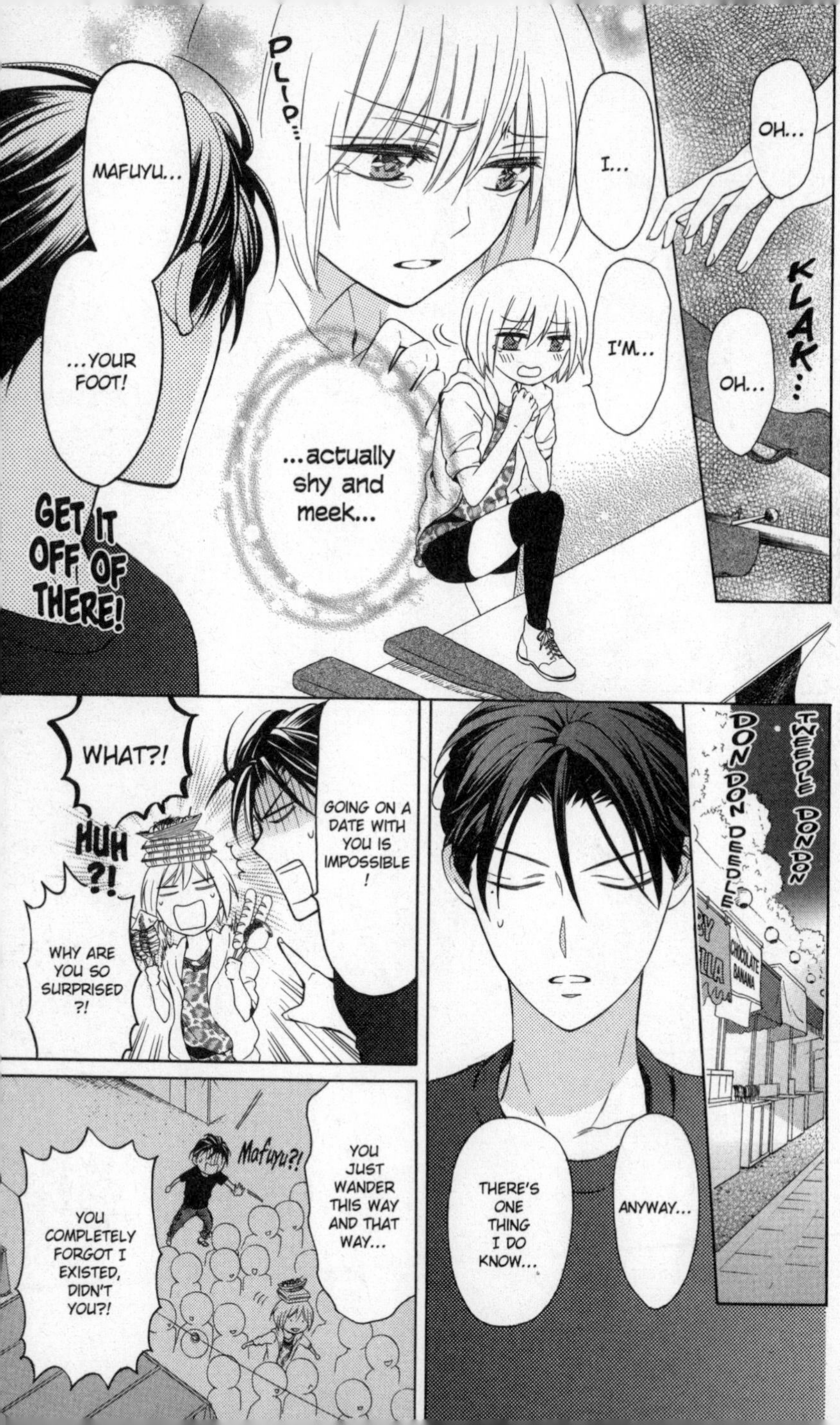
OH...
KLAK...
OH...
PLIP...
I...
I'M...
...actually shy and meek...
MAFUYU...
...YOUR FOOT!
GET IT OFF OF THERE!
TWEEDLE DONDON
DON DON DEEDLE
CHOCOLATE BANANA
ANYWAY...
THERE'S ONE THING I DO KNOW...
GOING ON A DATE WITH YOU IS IMPOSSIBLE!
WHAT?!
HUH?!
WHY ARE YOU SO SURPRISED?!
YOU JUST WANDER THIS WAY AND THAT WAY...
Mafuyu?!
YOU COMPLETELY FORGOT I EXISTED, DIDN'T YOU?!

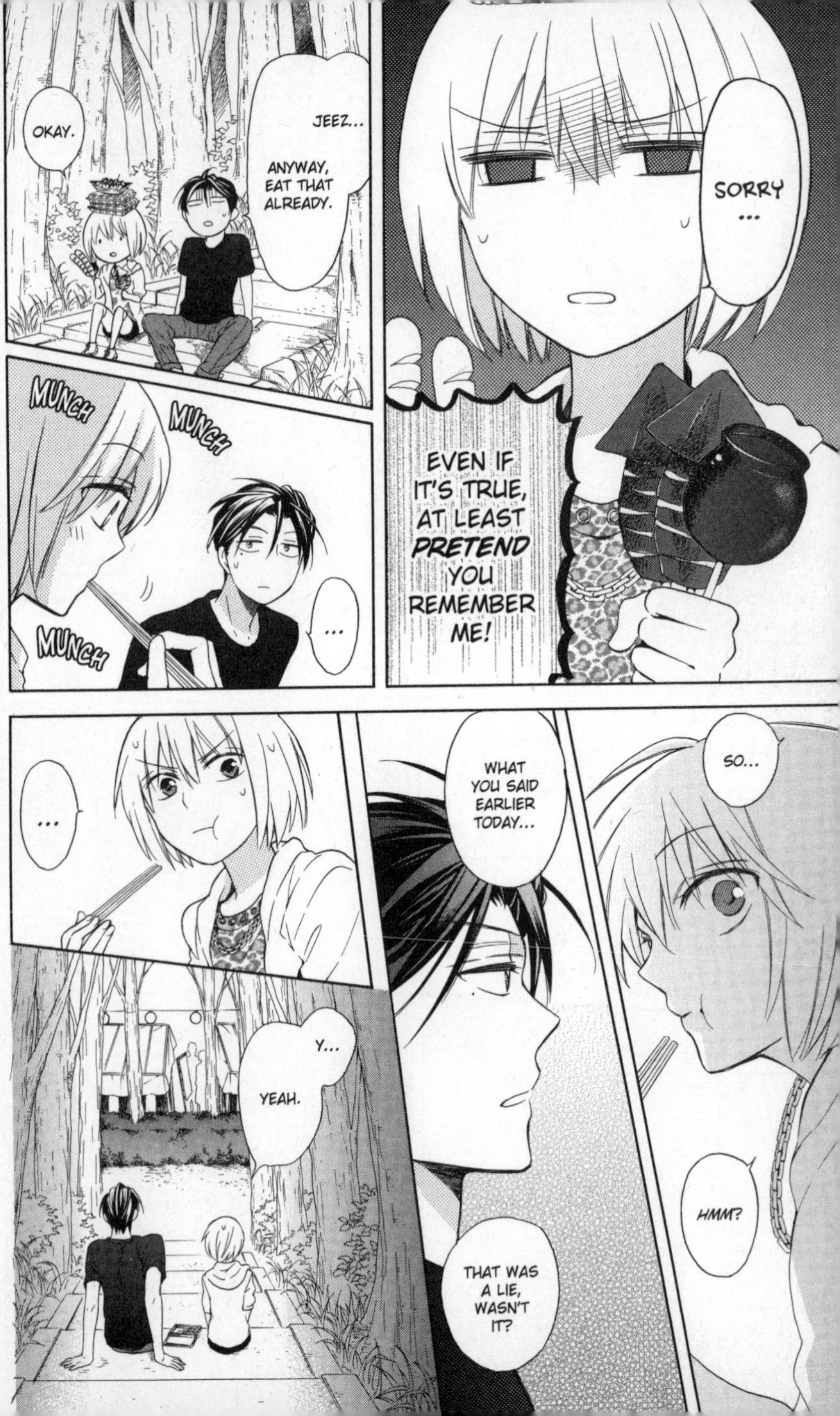
SORRY ...
EVEN IF IT'S TRUE, AT LEAST PRETEND YOU REMEMBER ME!
JEEZ...
ANYWAY, EAT THAT ALREADY.
OKAY.
MUNCH
MUNCH
MUNCH
...
SO...
HMM?
WHAT YOU SAID EARLIER TODAY...
THAT WAS A LIE, WASN'T IT?
...
Y...
YEAH.

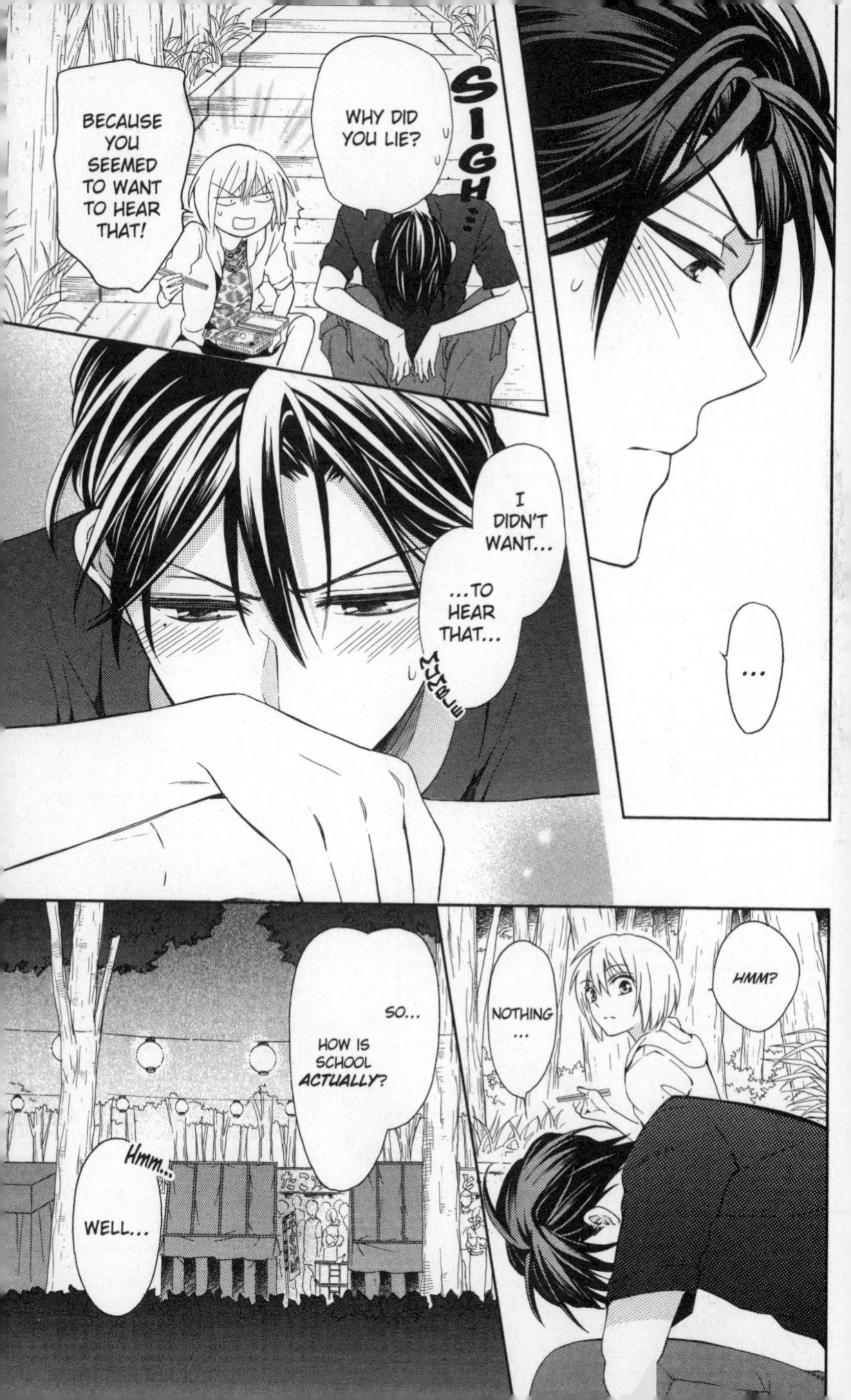
...
WHY DID YOU LIE?
SIGH...
BECAUSE YOU SEEMED TO WANT TO HEAR THAT!
I DIDN'T WANT...
...TO HEAR THAT...
MUMBLE
HMM?
NOTHING...
SO...
HOW IS SCHOOL ACTUALLY?
Hmm...
WELL...

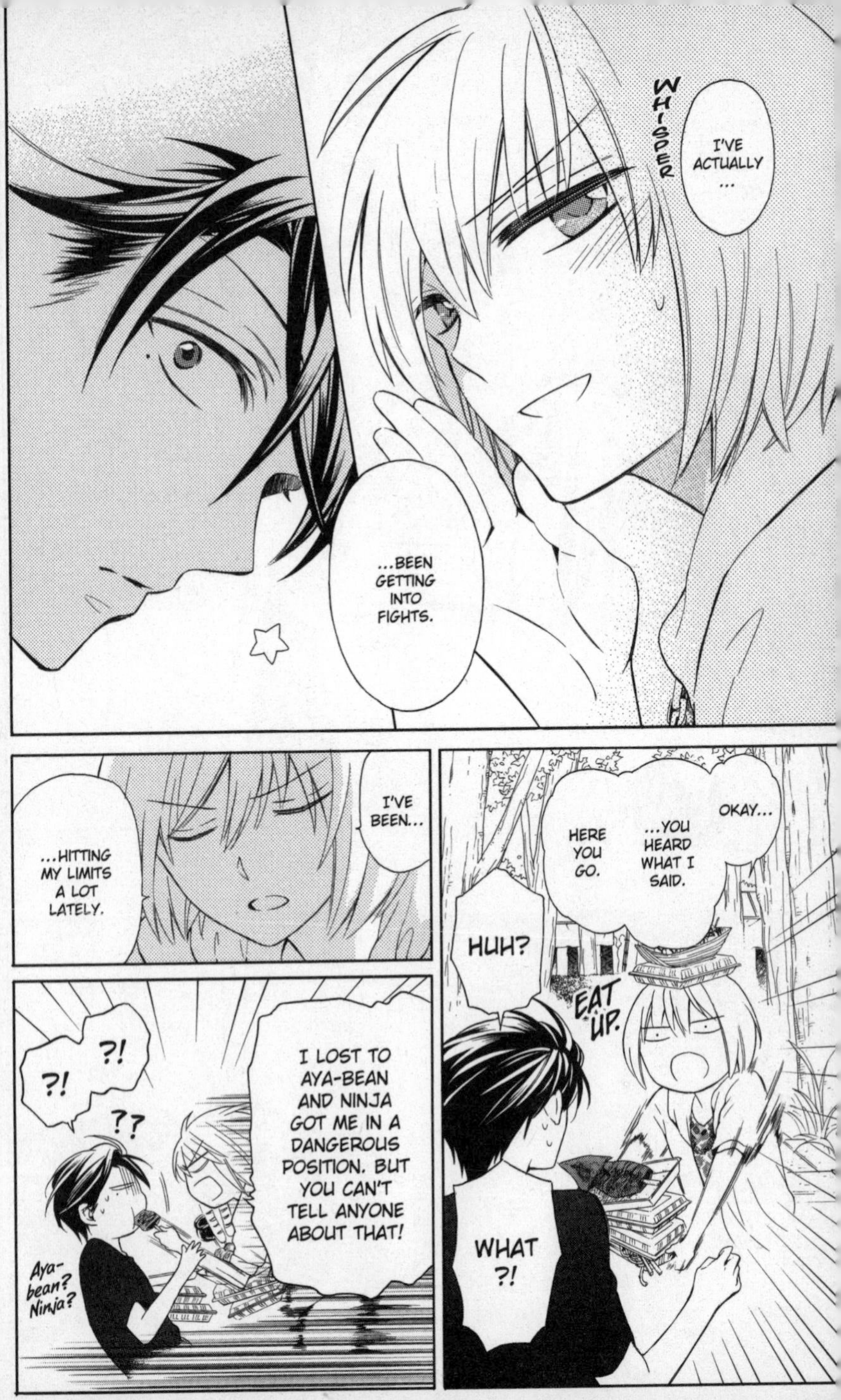
WHISPER
I'VE ACTUALLY ...
...BEEN GETTING INTO FIGHTS.
OKAY...
...YOU HEARD WHAT I SAID.
HERE YOU GO.
HUH?
EAT UP.
WHAT ?!
I'VE BEEN...
...HITTING MY LIMITS A LOT LATELY.
I LOST TO AYA-BEAN AND NINJA GOT ME IN A DANGEROUS POSITION. BUT YOU CAN'T TELL ANYONE ABOUT THAT!
?!
?!
??
Aya-bean? Ninja?

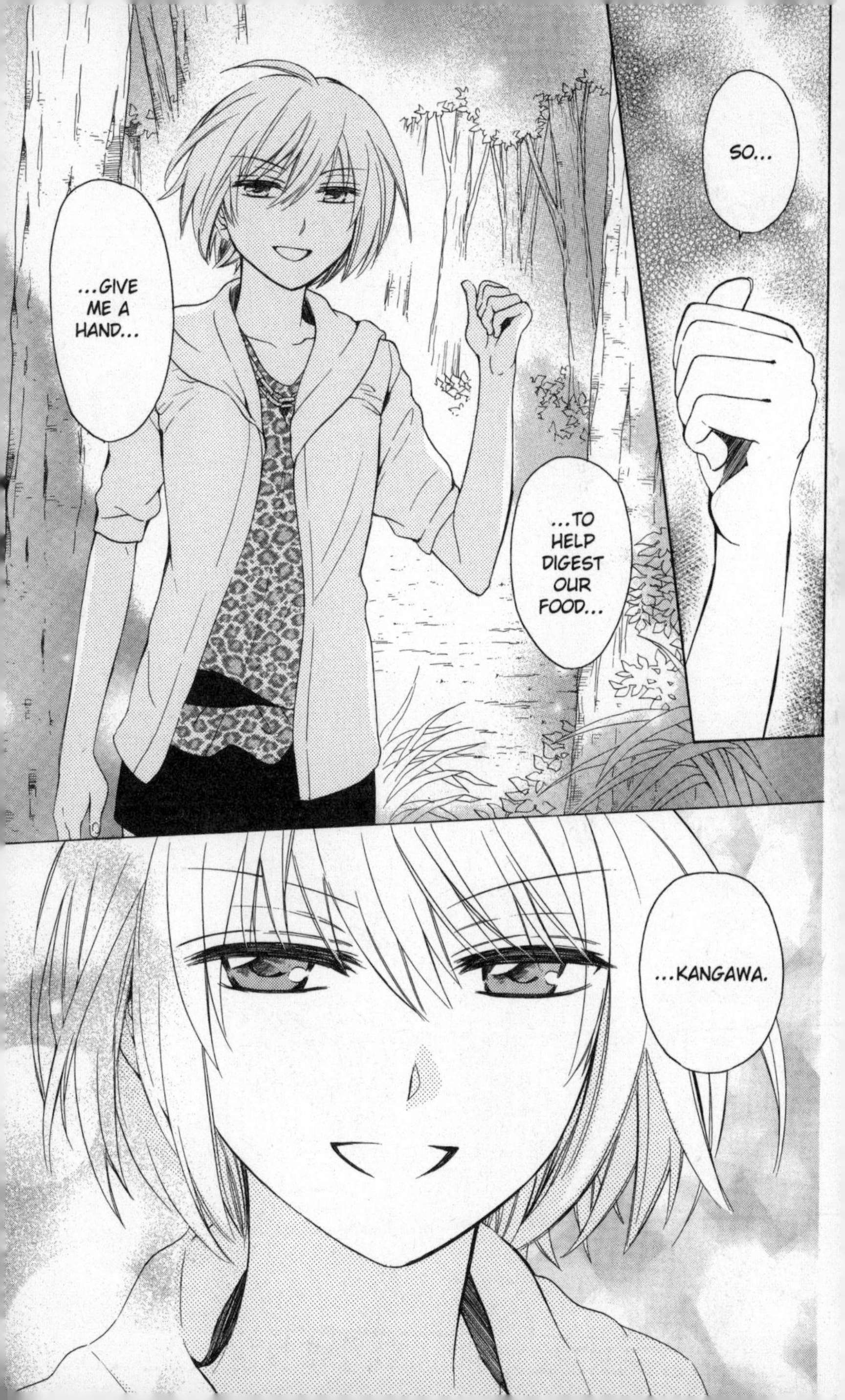
SO...
...TO HELP DIGEST OUR FOOD...
...GIVE ME A HAND...
...KANGAWA.

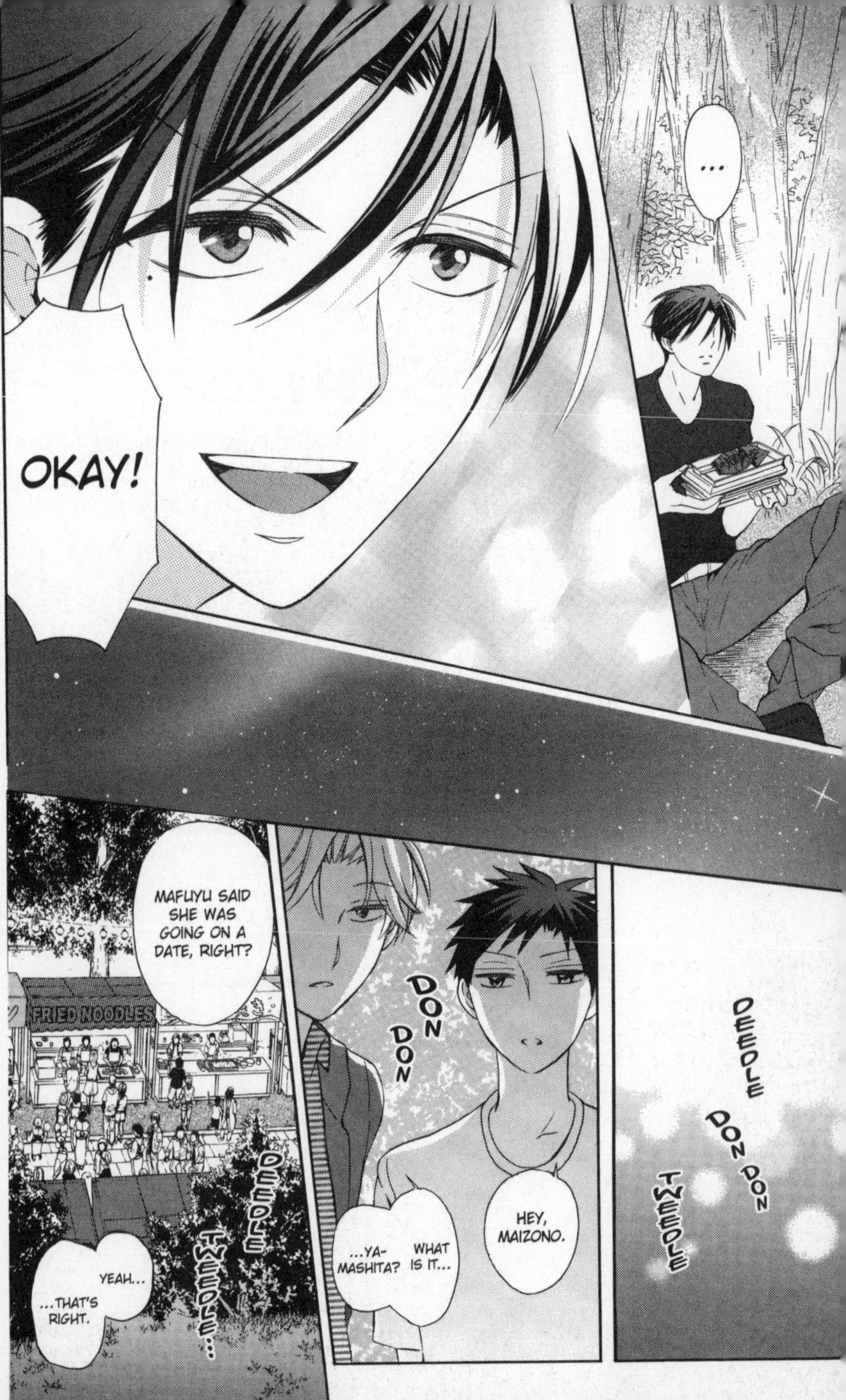
...
OKAY!
DEEDLE
DON DON
TWEEDLE
DON DON
HEY, MAIZONO.
WHAT IS IT...
...YA-MASHITA?
MAFUYU SAID SHE WAS GOING ON A DATE, RIGHT?
FRIED NOODLES
DEEDLE TWEEDLE...
YEAH...
...THAT'S RIGHT.

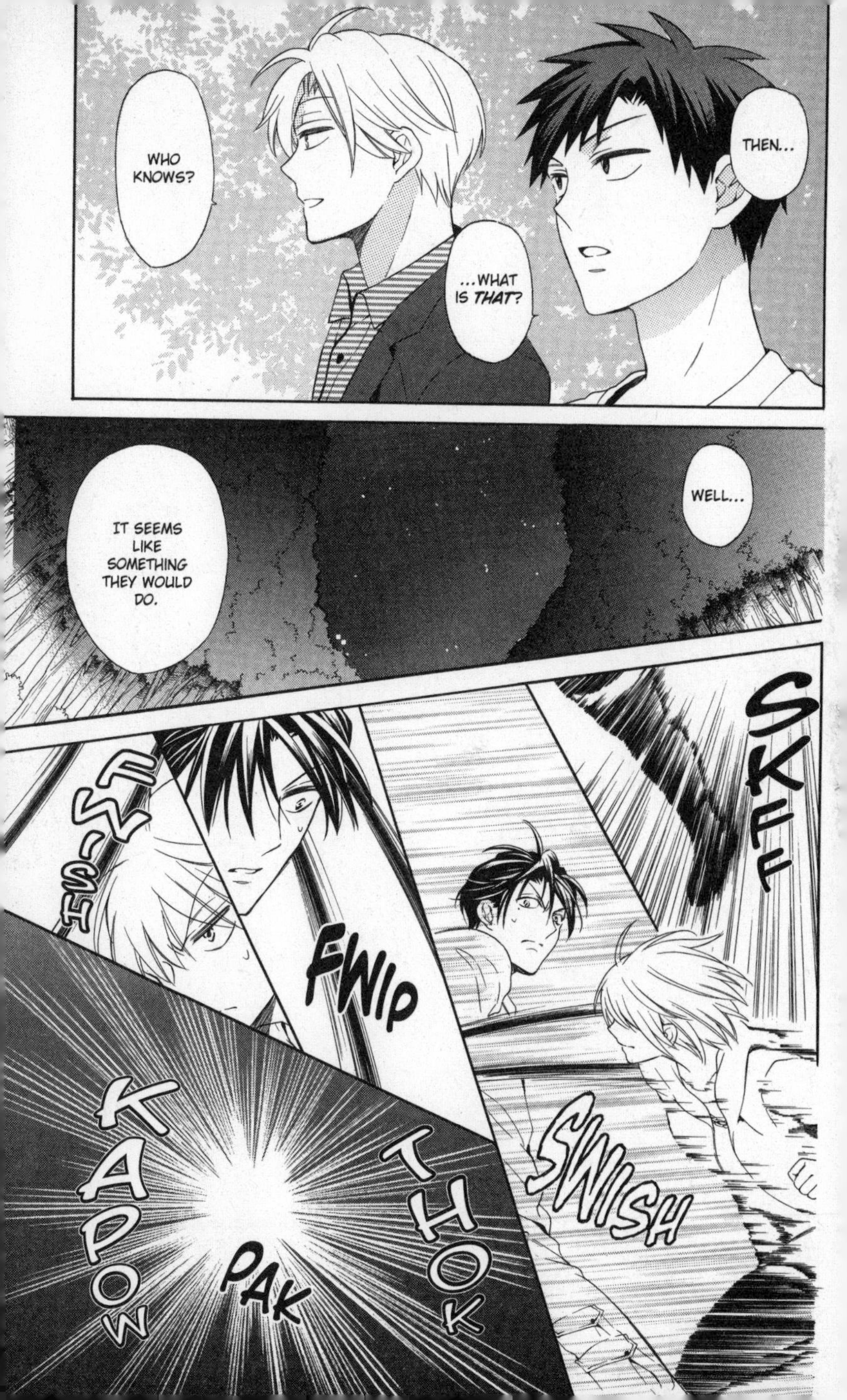
THEN...
...WHAT IS *THAT*?
WHO KNOWS?
WELL...
IT SEEMS LIKE SOMETHING THEY WOULD DO.
SKFF
SWISH
FWIP
THOK
PAK
KAPOW

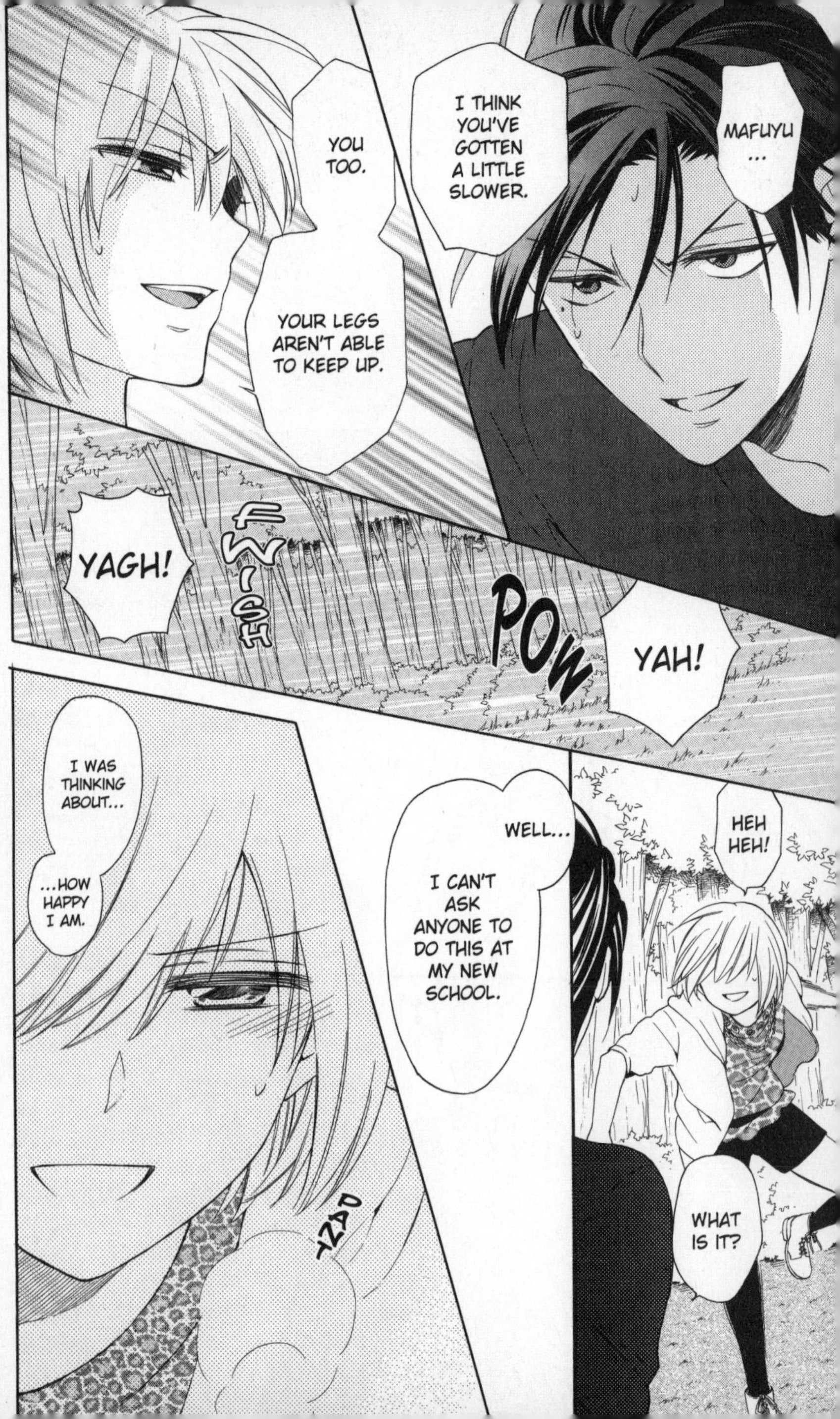
MAFUYU...
I THINK YOU'VE GOTTEN A LITTLE SLOWER.
YOU TOO.
YOUR LEGS AREN'T ABLE TO KEEP UP.
YAH!
POW
FWISH
YAGH!
HEH HEH!
WHAT IS IT?
WELL...
I CAN'T ASK ANYONE TO DO THIS AT MY NEW SCHOOL.
I WAS THINKING ABOUT...
...HOW HAPPY I AM.
TZAP

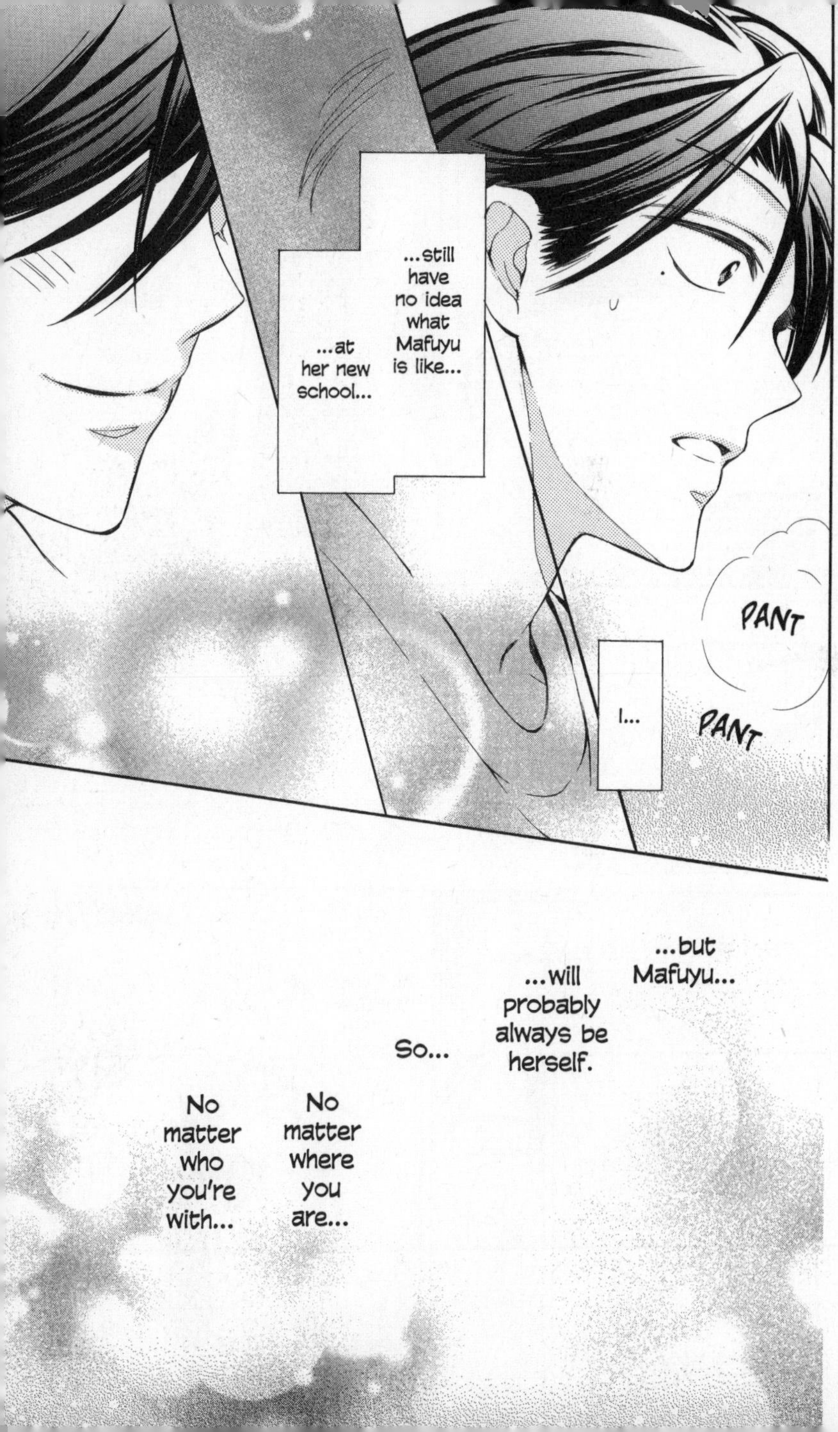

...still have no idea what Mafuyu is like...
...at her new school...
PANT
I...
PANT
...but Mafuyu...
...will probably always be herself.
So...
No matter where you are...
No matter who you're with...

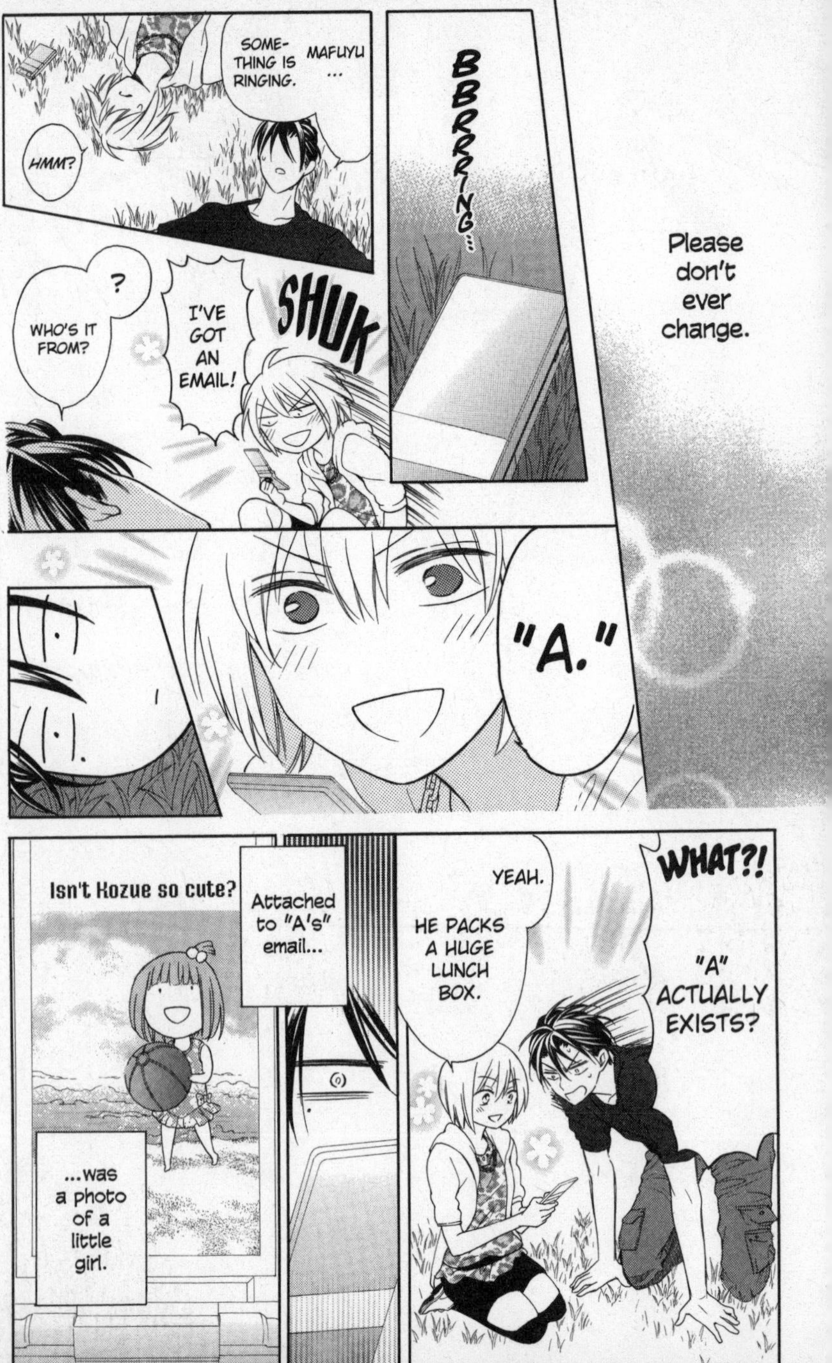
Please don't ever change.
BBRRRING...
MAFUYU ...
SOME-THING IS RINGING.
HMM?
SHUK
I'VE GOT AN EMAIL!
WHO'S IT FROM?
?
"A."
WHAT?!
"A" ACTUALLY EXISTS?
YEAH.
HE PACKS A HUGE LUNCH BOX.
Attached to "A's" email...
Isn't Kozue so cute?
...was a photo of a little girl.

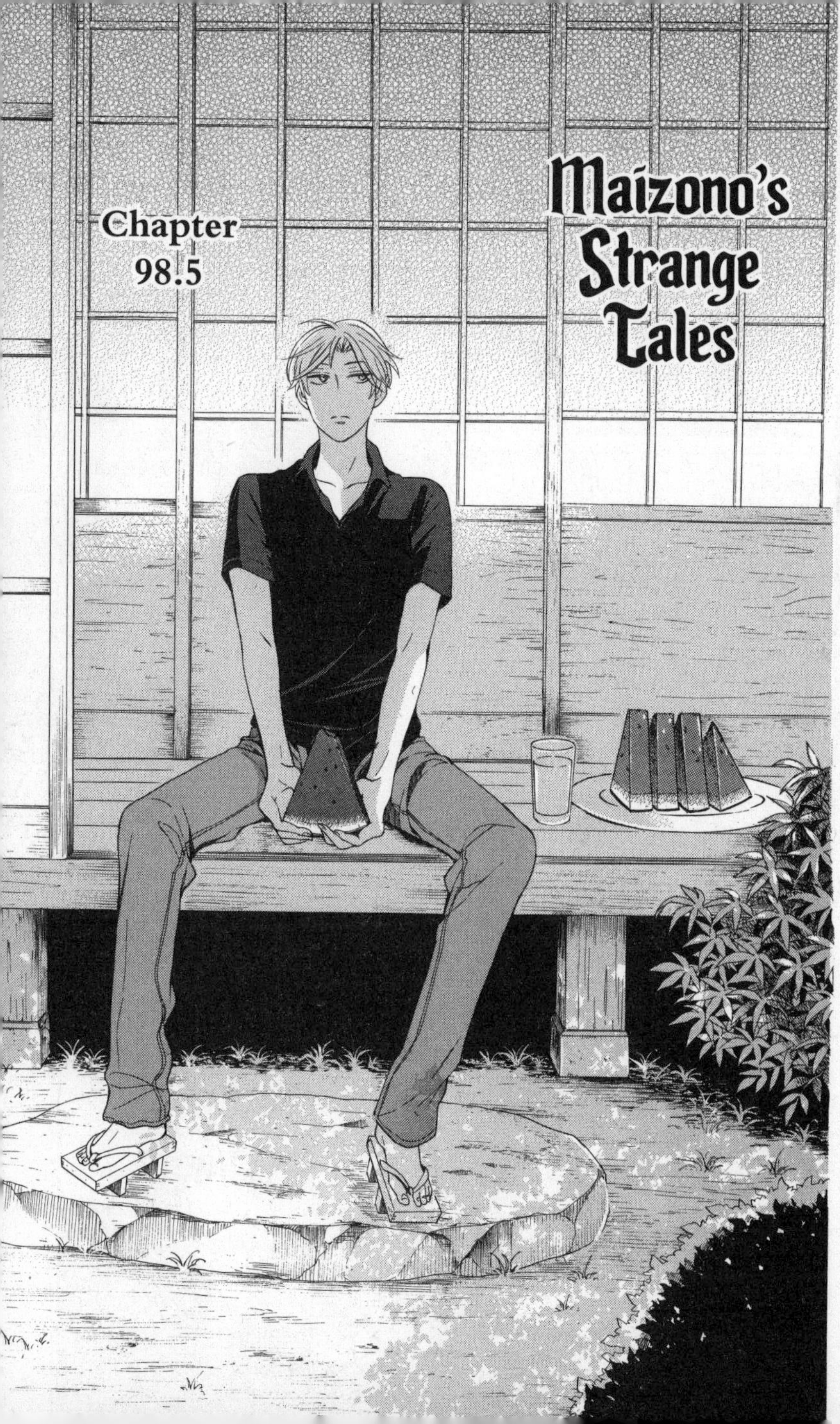
Chapter
98.5
Maizono's
Strange
Tales

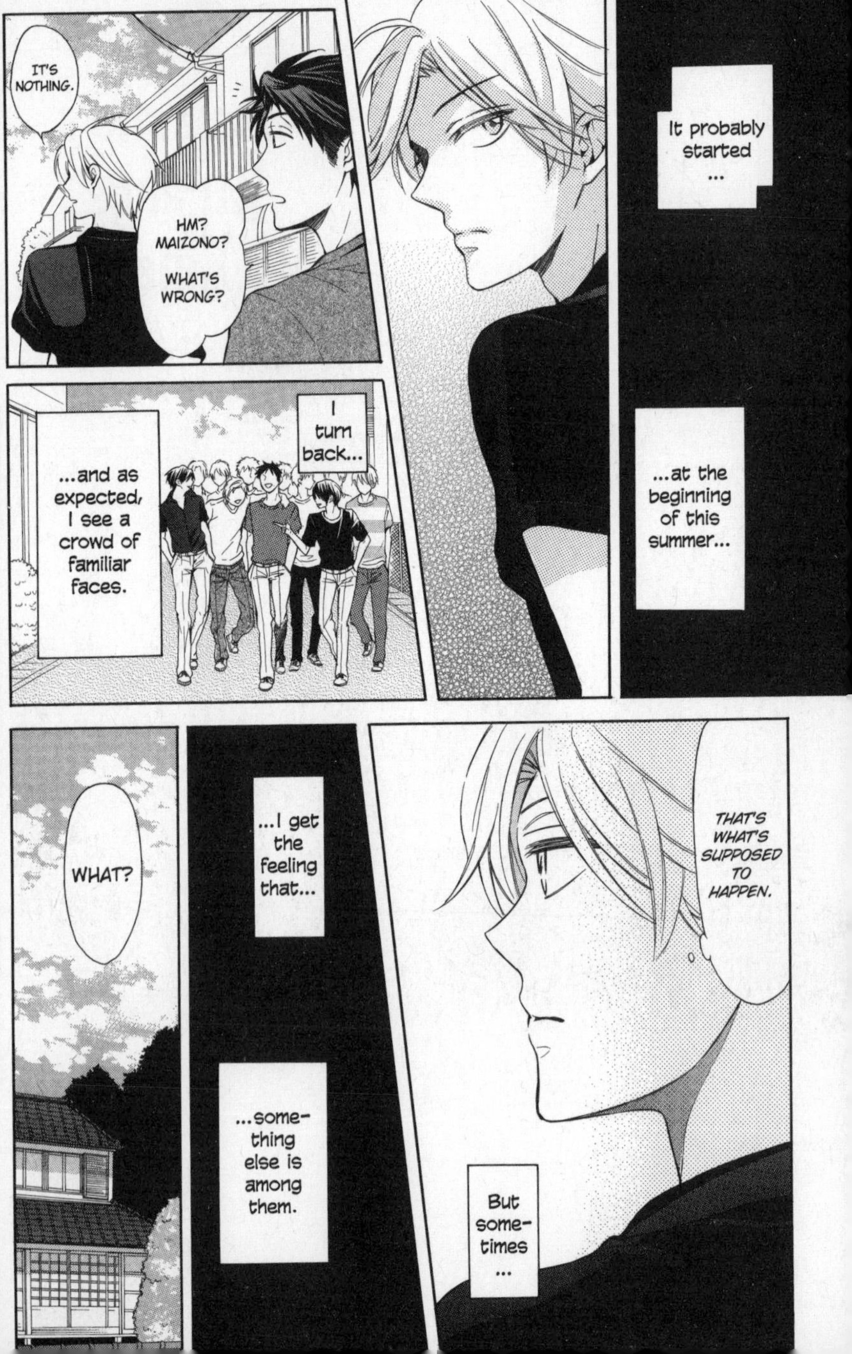
It probably started ...
...at the beginning of this summer...
HM? MAIZONO? WHAT'S WRONG?
IT'S NOTHING.
I turn back...
...and as expected, I see a crowd of familiar faces.
THAT'S WHAT'S SUPPOSED TO HAPPEN.
But some-times ...
...I get the feeling that...
...some-thing else is among them.
WHAT?

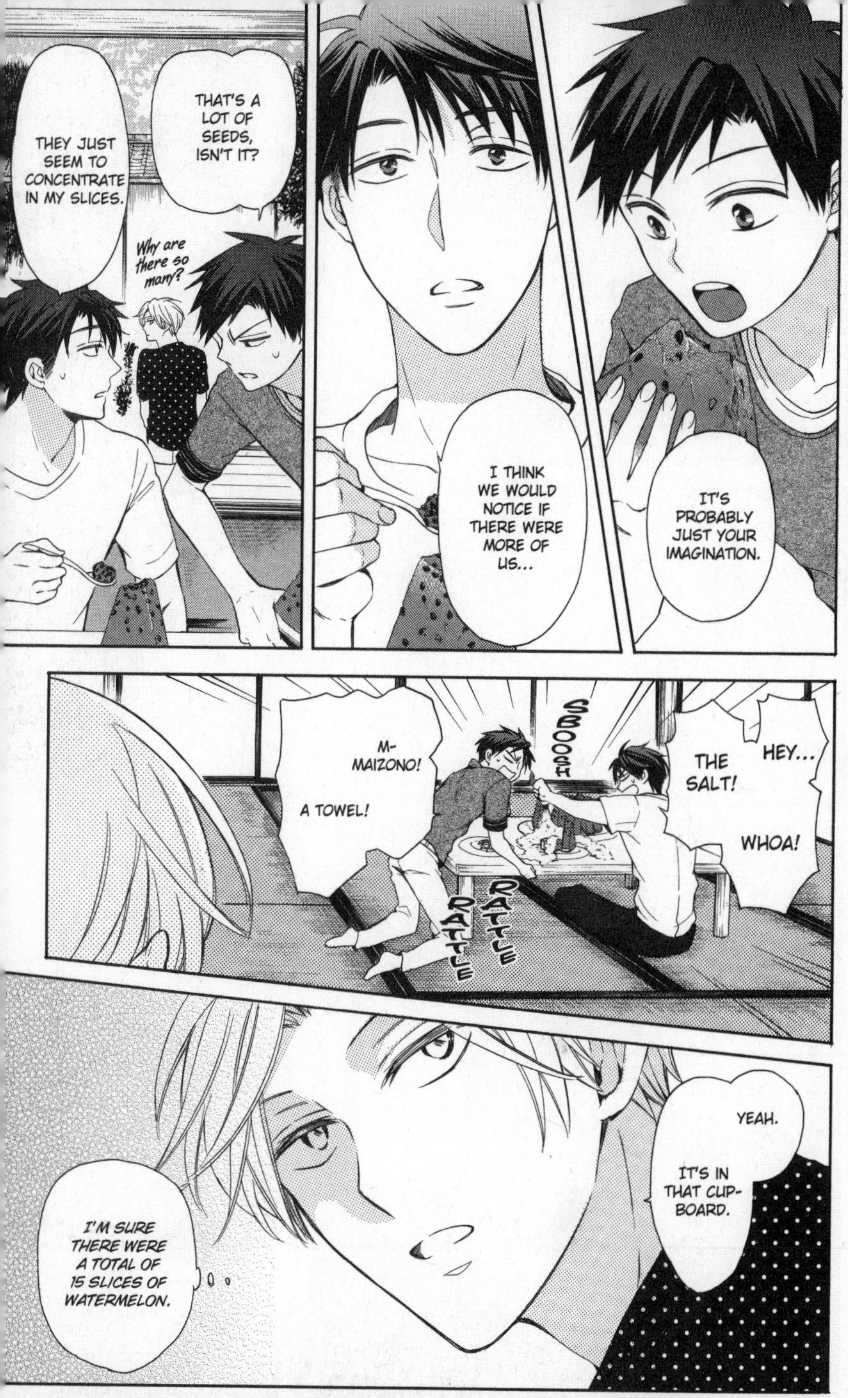
IT'S PROBABLY JUST YOUR IMAGINATION.
I THINK WE WOULD NOTICE IF THERE WERE MORE OF US...
THAT'S A LOT OF SEEDS, ISN'T IT?
THEY JUST SEEM TO CONCENTRATE IN MY SLICES.
Why are there so many?
HEY...
THE SALT!
WHOA!
SBOOSH
M-MAIZONO!
A TOWEL!
RATTLE RATTLE
YEAH.
IT'S IN THAT CUP-BOARD.
I'M SURE THERE WERE A TOTAL OF 15 SLICES OF WATERMELON.

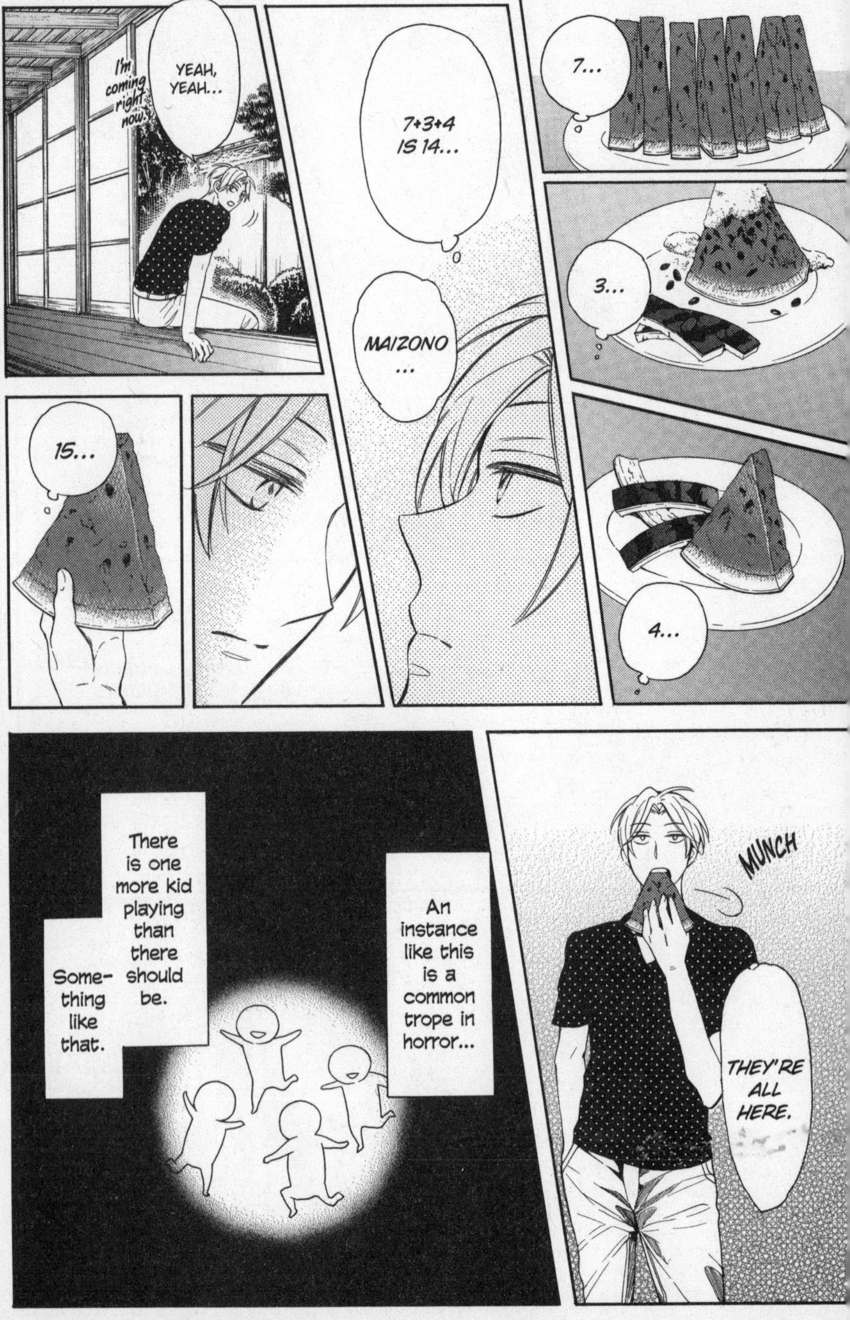
7...
3...
4...
7+3+4 IS 14...
MAIZONO ...
YEAH, YEAH...
I'm coming right now.
15...
MUNCH
THEY'RE ALL HERE.
An instance like this is a common trope in horror...
There is one more kid playing than there should be.
Something like that.

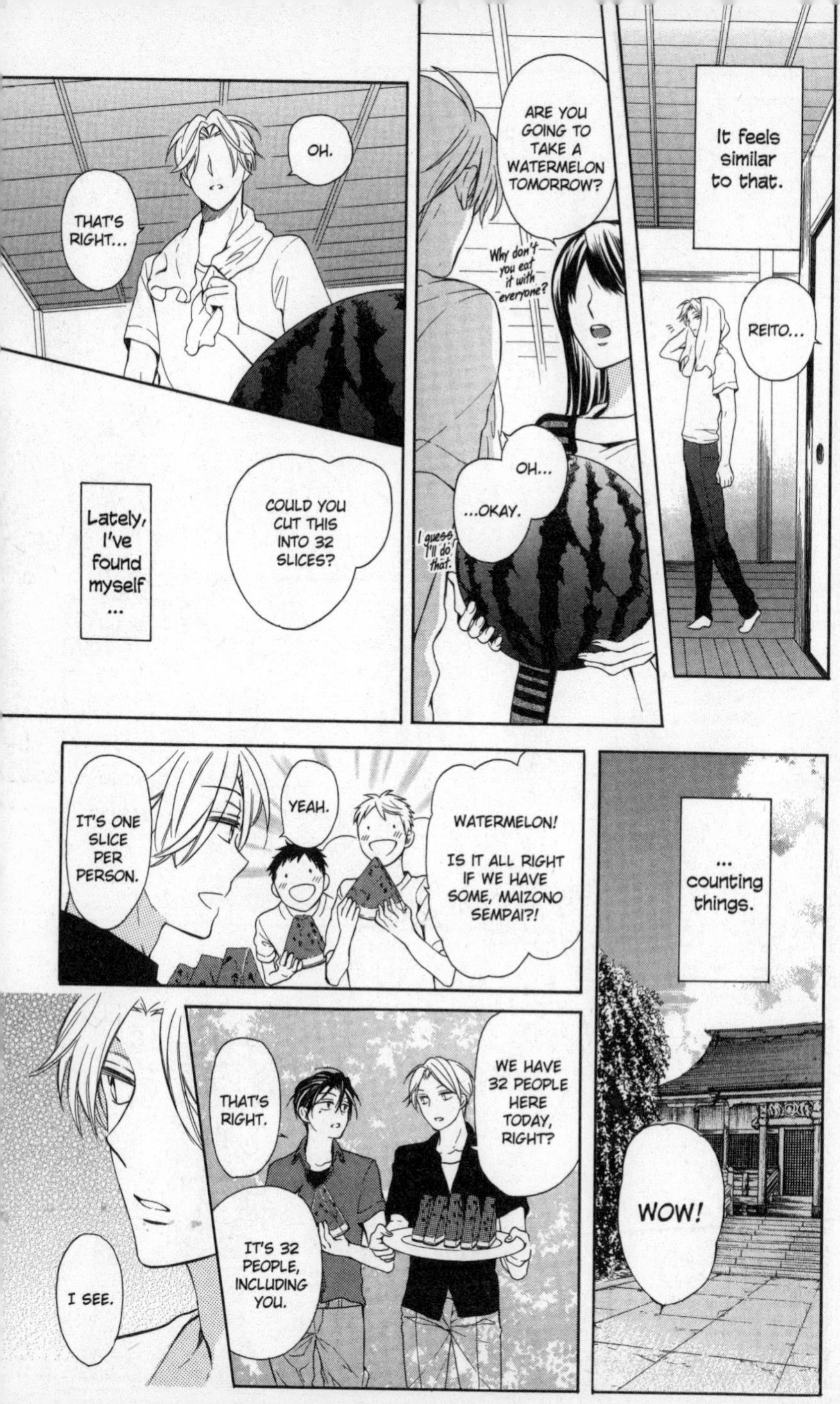
It feels similar to that.
REITO...
ARE YOU GOING TO TAKE A WATERMELON TOMORROW?
Why don't you eat it with everyone?
OH... ...OKAY.
I guess I'll do that.
OH.
THAT'S RIGHT...
COULD YOU CUT THIS INTO 32 SLICES?
Lately, I've found myself ...
... counting things.
WOW!
WATERMELON! IS IT ALL RIGHT IF WE HAVE SOME, MAIZONO SEMPAI?!
YEAH.
IT'S ONE SLICE PER PERSON.
WE HAVE 32 PEOPLE HERE TODAY, RIGHT?
THAT'S RIGHT.
IT'S 32 PEOPLE, INCLUDING YOU.
I SEE.

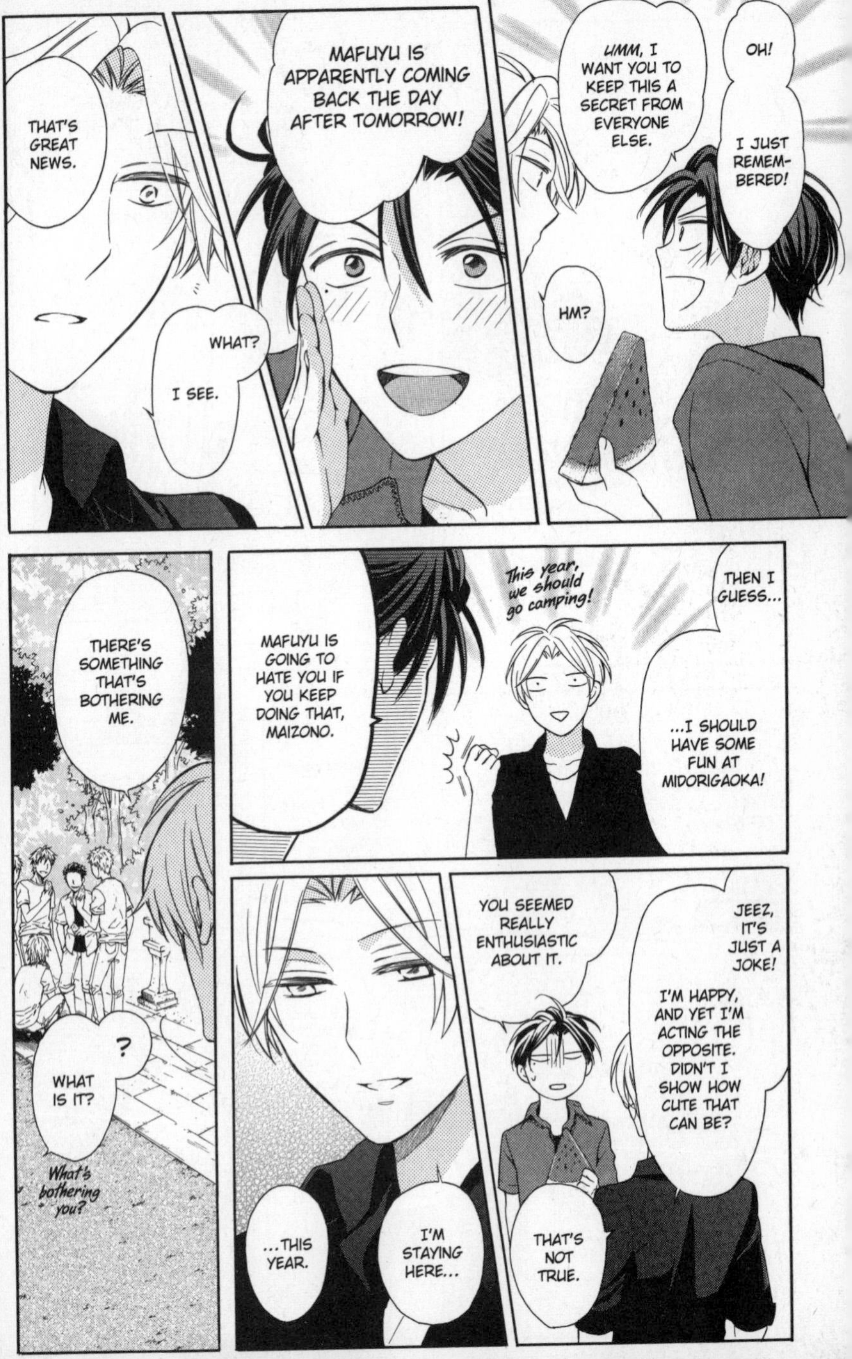
OH!
I JUST REMEMBERED!
UMM, I WANT YOU TO KEEP THIS A SECRET FROM EVERYONE ELSE.
HM?
MAFUYU IS APPARENTLY COMING BACK THE DAY AFTER TOMORROW!
WHAT?
I SEE.
THAT'S GREAT NEWS.
THEN I GUESS...
...I SHOULD HAVE SOME FUN AT MIDORIGAOKA!
This year, we should go camping!
MAFUYU IS GOING TO HATE YOU IF YOU KEEP DOING THAT, MAIZONO.
JEEZ, IT'S JUST A JOKE!
YOU SEEMED REALLY ENTHUSIASTIC ABOUT IT.
I'M HAPPY, AND YET I'M ACTING THE OPPOSITE. DIDN'T I SHOW HOW CUTE THAT CAN BE?
THAT'S NOT TRUE.
I'M STAYING HERE...
...THIS YEAR.
THERE'S SOMETHING THAT'S BOTHERING ME.
?
WHAT IS IT?
What's bothering you?

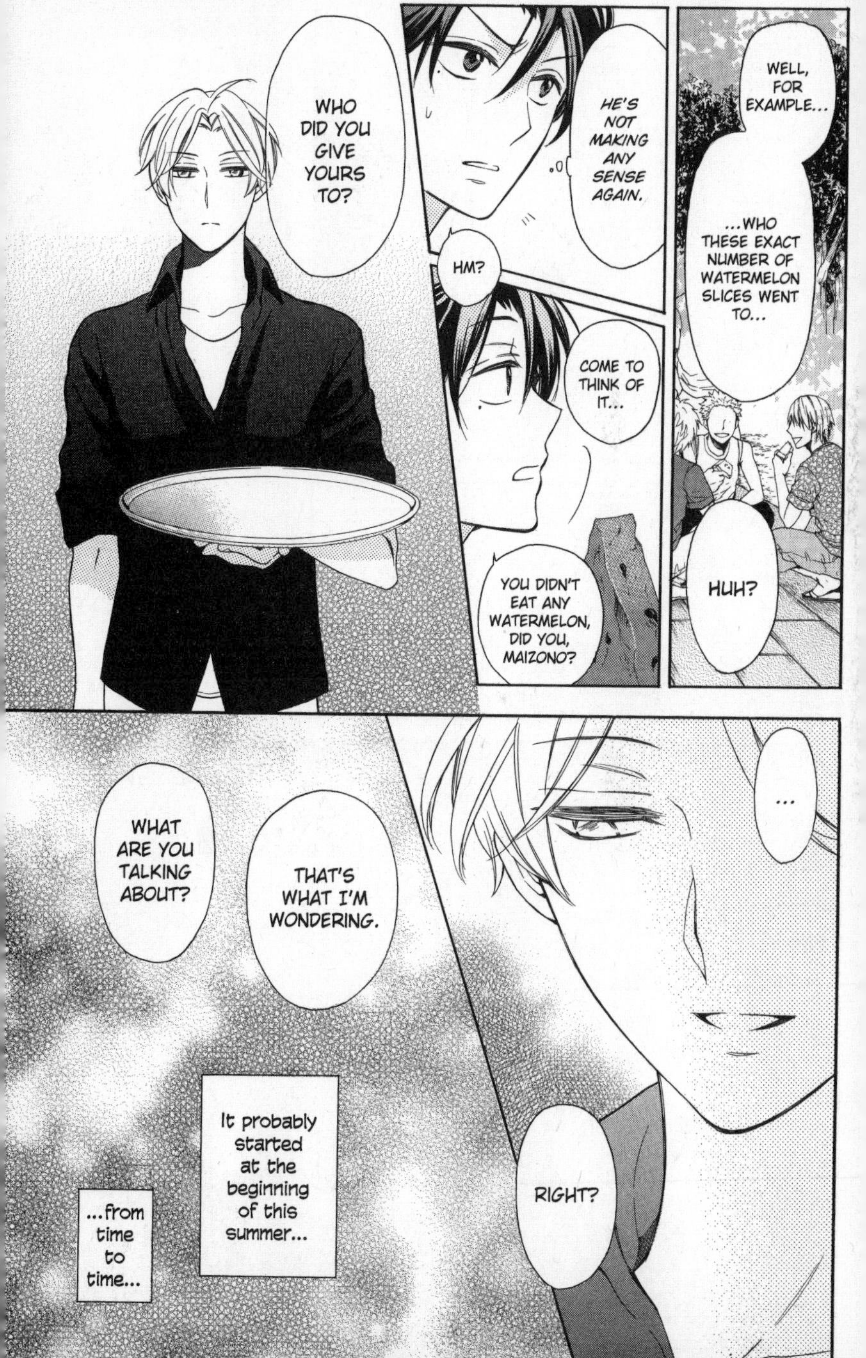
WELL, FOR EXAMPLE...
...WHO THESE EXACT NUMBER OF WATERMELON SLICES WENT TO...
HUH?
HE'S NOT MAKING ANY SENSE AGAIN.
HM?
COME TO THINK OF IT...
YOU DIDN'T EAT ANY WATERMELON, DID YOU, MAIZONO?
WHO DID YOU GIVE YOURS TO?
...
RIGHT?
THAT'S WHAT I'M WONDERING.
WHAT ARE YOU TALKING ABOUT?
It probably started at the beginning of this summer...
...from time to time...

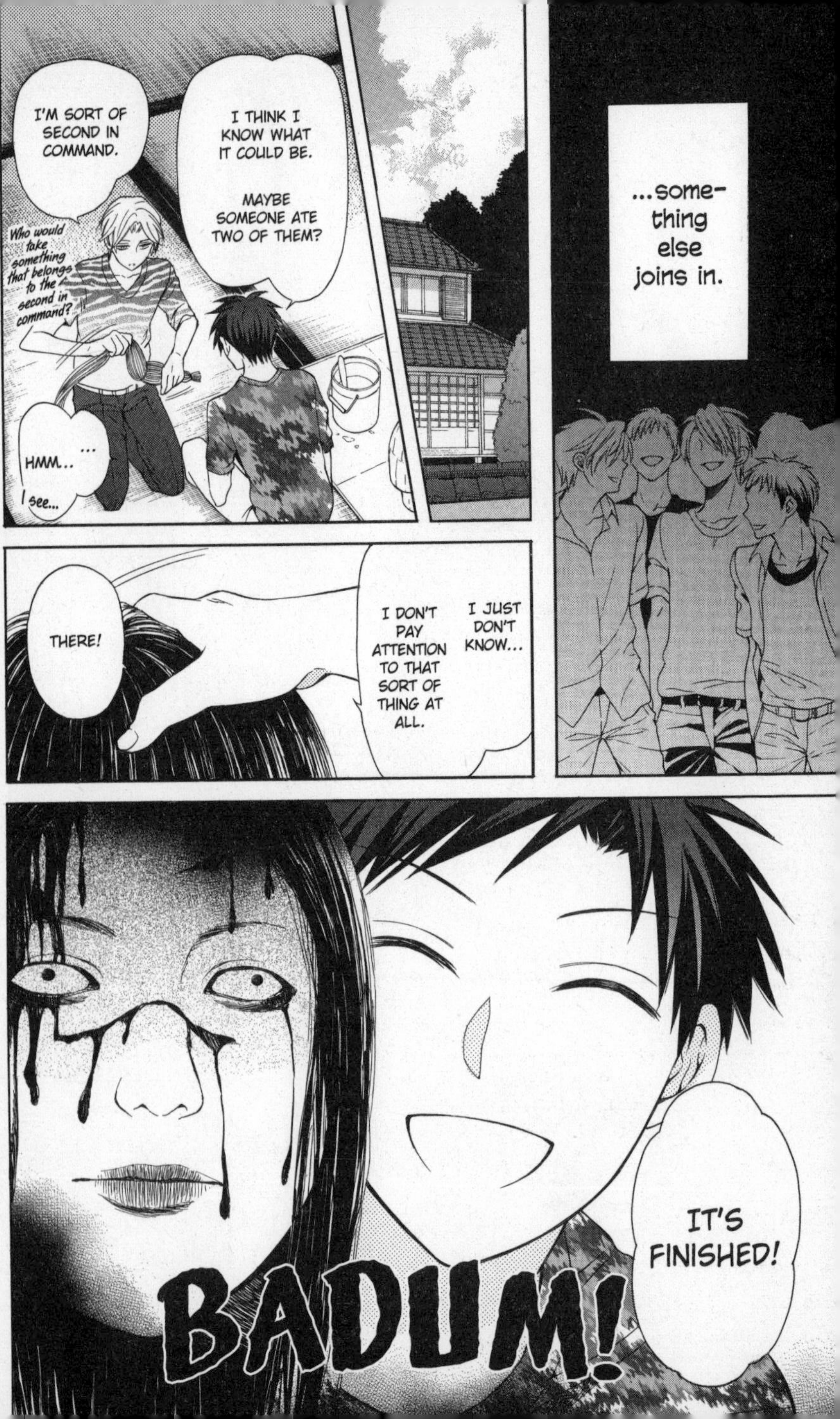
...something else joins in.
I THINK I KNOW WHAT IT COULD BE.
MAYBE SOMEONE ATE TWO OF THEM?
I'M SORT OF SECOND IN COMMAND.
Who would take something that belongs to the second in command?
...
HMM...
I see...
I JUST DON'T KNOW...
I DON'T PAY ATTENTION TO THAT SORT OF THING AT ALL.
THERE!
IT'S FINISHED!
BADUM!

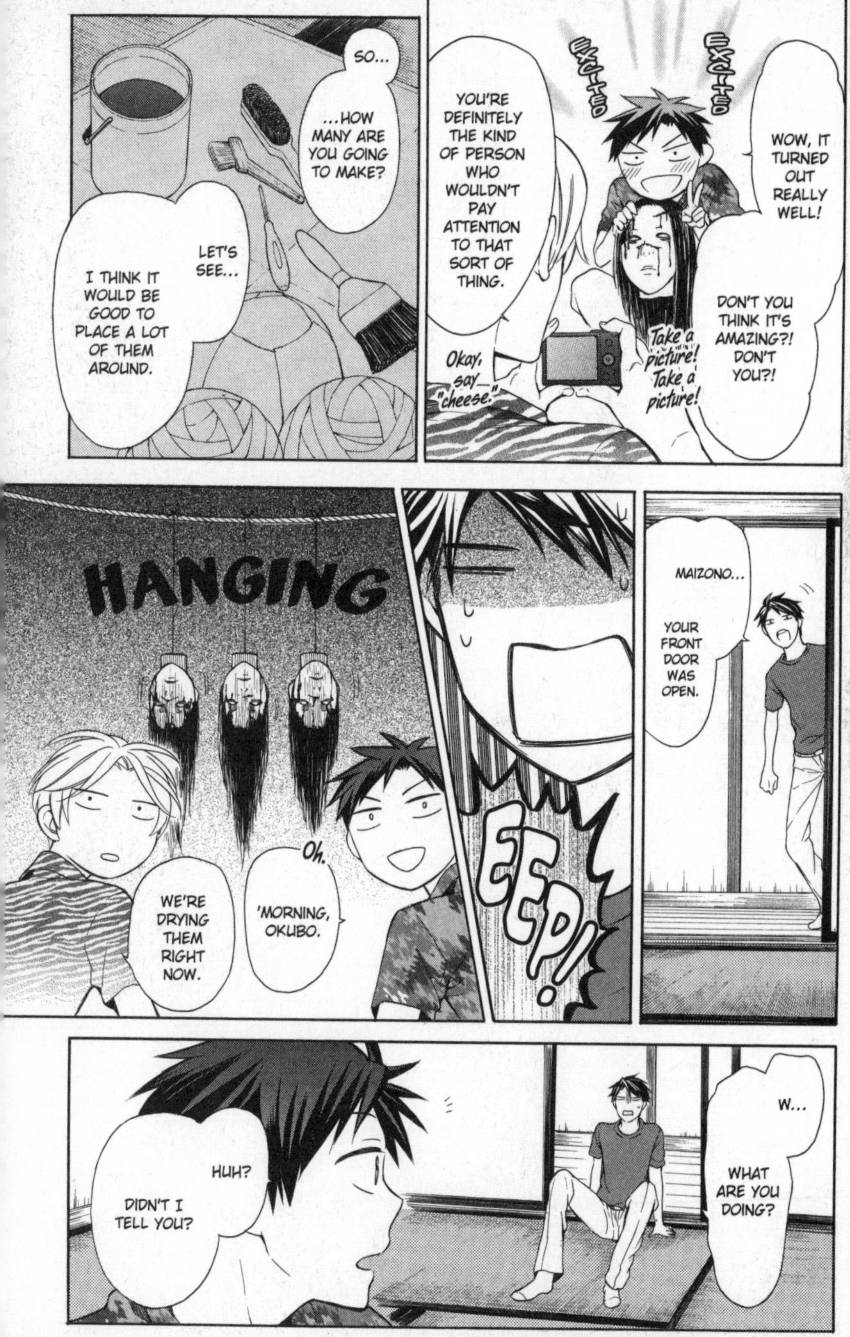
WOW, IT TURNED OUT REALLY WELL!
EXCITE
EXCITE
DON'T YOU THINK IT'S AMAZING?! DON'T YOU?!
Take a picture! Take a picture!
YOU'RE DEFINITELY THE KIND OF PERSON WHO WOULDN'T PAY ATTENTION TO THAT SORT OF THING.
Okay, say "cheese."
SO...
...HOW MANY ARE YOU GOING TO MAKE?
LET'S SEE...
I THINK IT WOULD BE GOOD TO PLACE A LOT OF THEM AROUND.
MAIZONO...
YOUR FRONT DOOR WAS OPEN.
EEP!!
HANGING
Oh.
'MORNING, OKUBO.
WE'RE DRYING THEM RIGHT NOW.
W...
WHAT ARE YOU DOING?
HUH?
DIDN'T I TELL YOU?

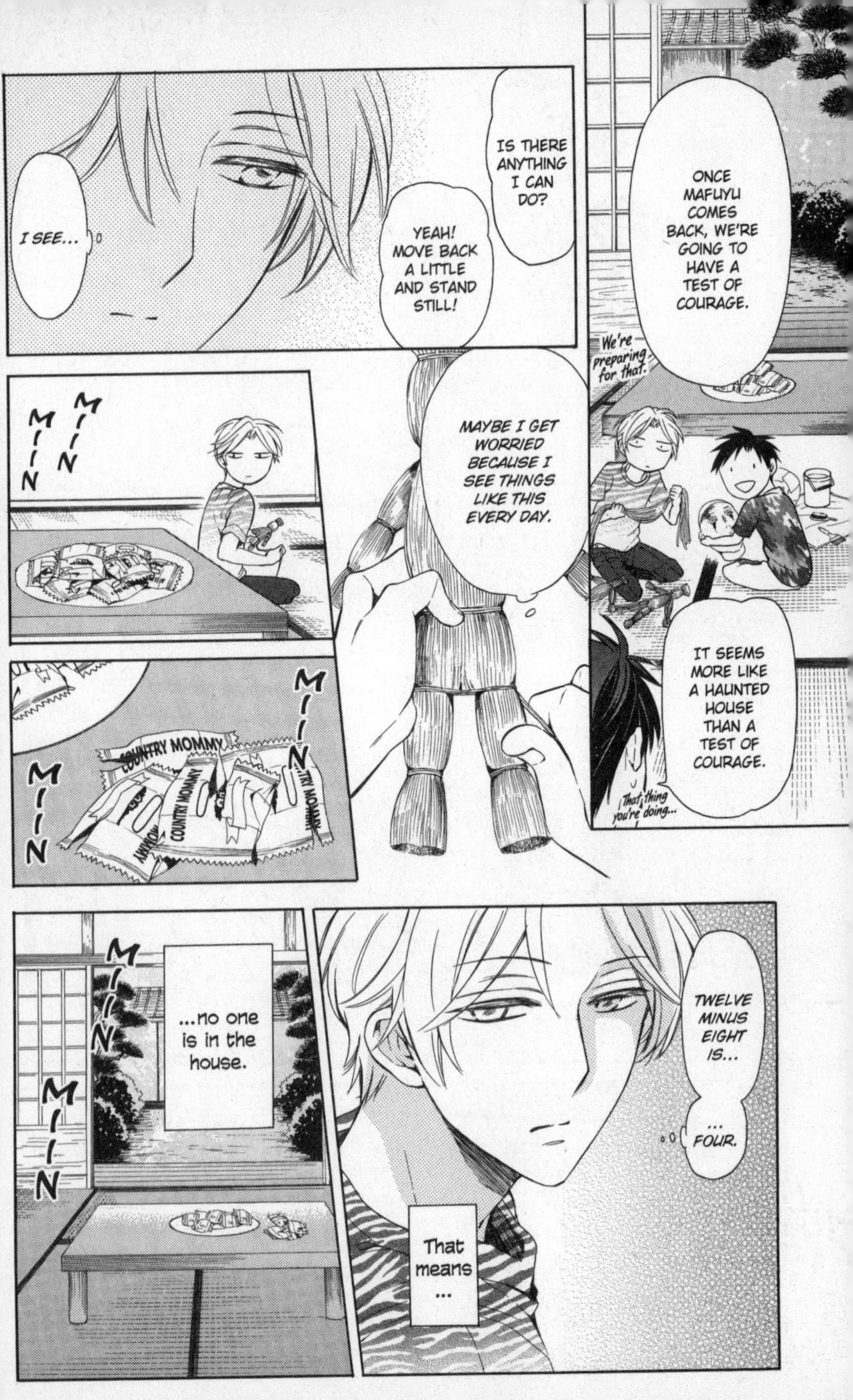
ONCE MAFUYU COMES BACK, WE'RE GOING TO HAVE A TEST OF COURAGE.
We're preparing for that.
IT SEEMS MORE LIKE A HAUNTED HOUSE THAN A TEST OF COURAGE.
That thing you're doing...
IS THERE ANYTHING I CAN DO?
YEAH! MOVE BACK A LITTLE AND STAND STILL!
I SEE...
MAYBE I GET WORRIED BECAUSE I SEE THINGS LIKE THIS EVERY DAY.
MIIN MIIN
MIIN MIIN
COUNTRY MOMMY
TWELVE MINUS EIGHT IS...
... FOUR.
That means ...
MIIN MIIN
...no one is in the house.

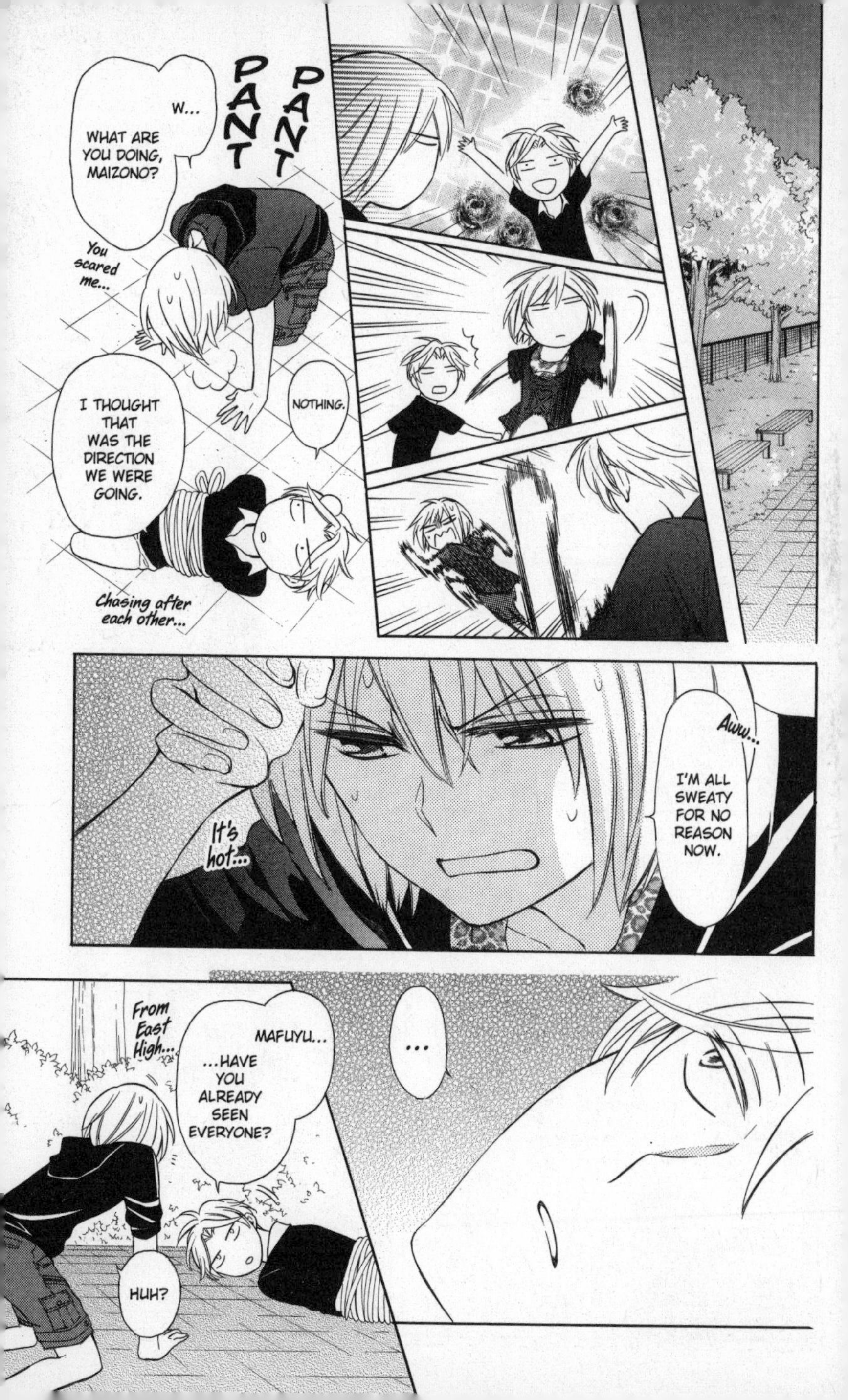
PANT PANT
W...
WHAT ARE YOU DOING, MAIZONO?
You scared me...
NOTHING.
I THOUGHT THAT WAS THE DIRECTION WE WERE GOING.
Chasing after each other...
Aww...
I'M ALL SWEATY FOR NO REASON NOW.
It's hot...
...
MAFUYU...
...HAVE YOU ALREADY SEEN EVERYONE?
From East High...
HUH?

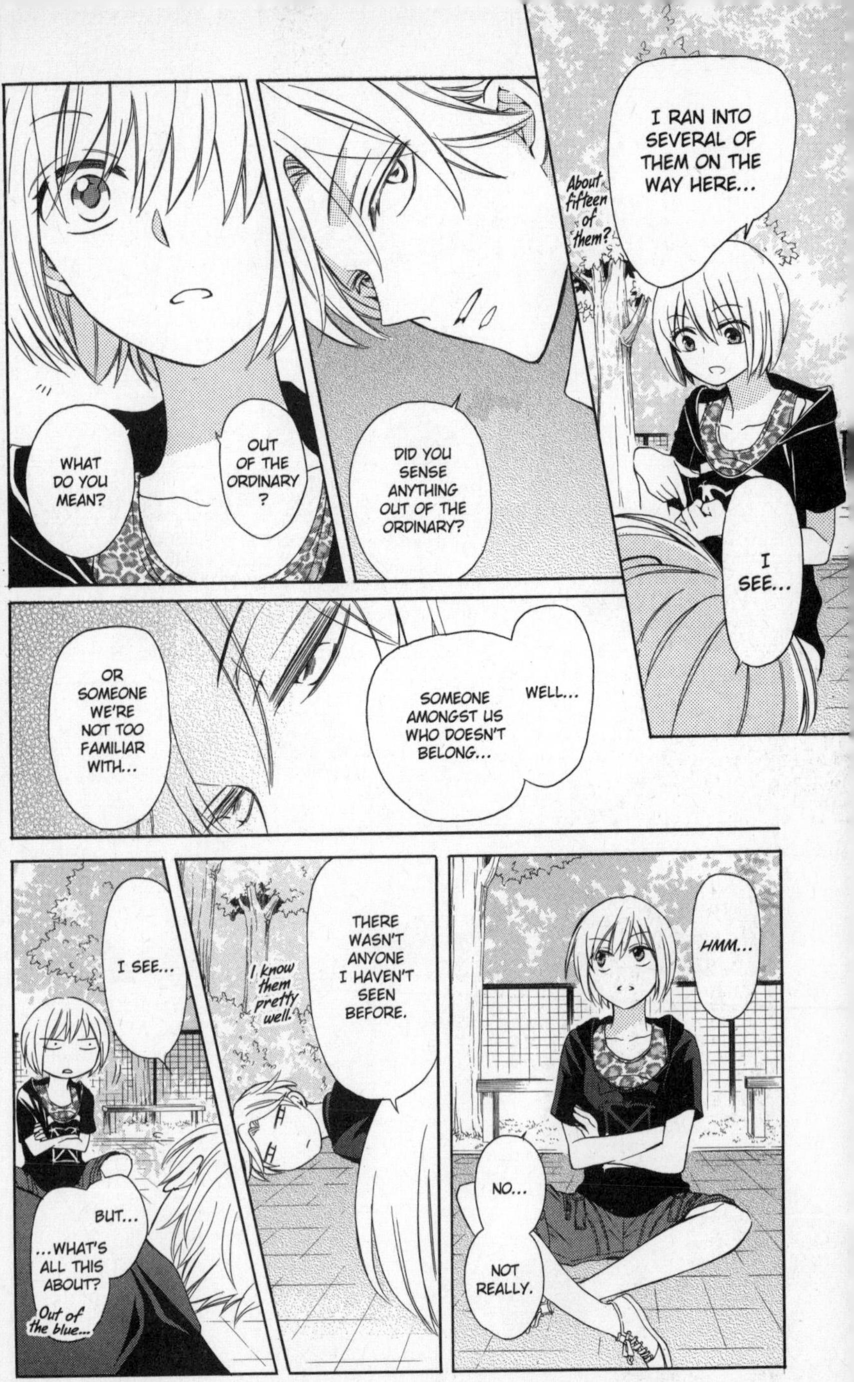
I RAN INTO SEVERAL OF THEM ON THE WAY HERE...
About fifteen of them?
I SEE...
DID YOU SENSE ANYTHING OUT OF THE ORDINARY?
OUT OF THE ORDINARY?
WHAT DO YOU MEAN?
WELL...
SOMEONE AMONGST US WHO DOESN'T BELONG...
OR SOMEONE WE'RE NOT TOO FAMILIAR WITH...
HMM...
NO...
NOT REALLY.
THERE WASN'T ANYONE I HAVEN'T SEEN BEFORE.
I know them pretty well.
I SEE...
BUT...
...WHAT'S ALL THIS ABOUT?
Out of the blue...

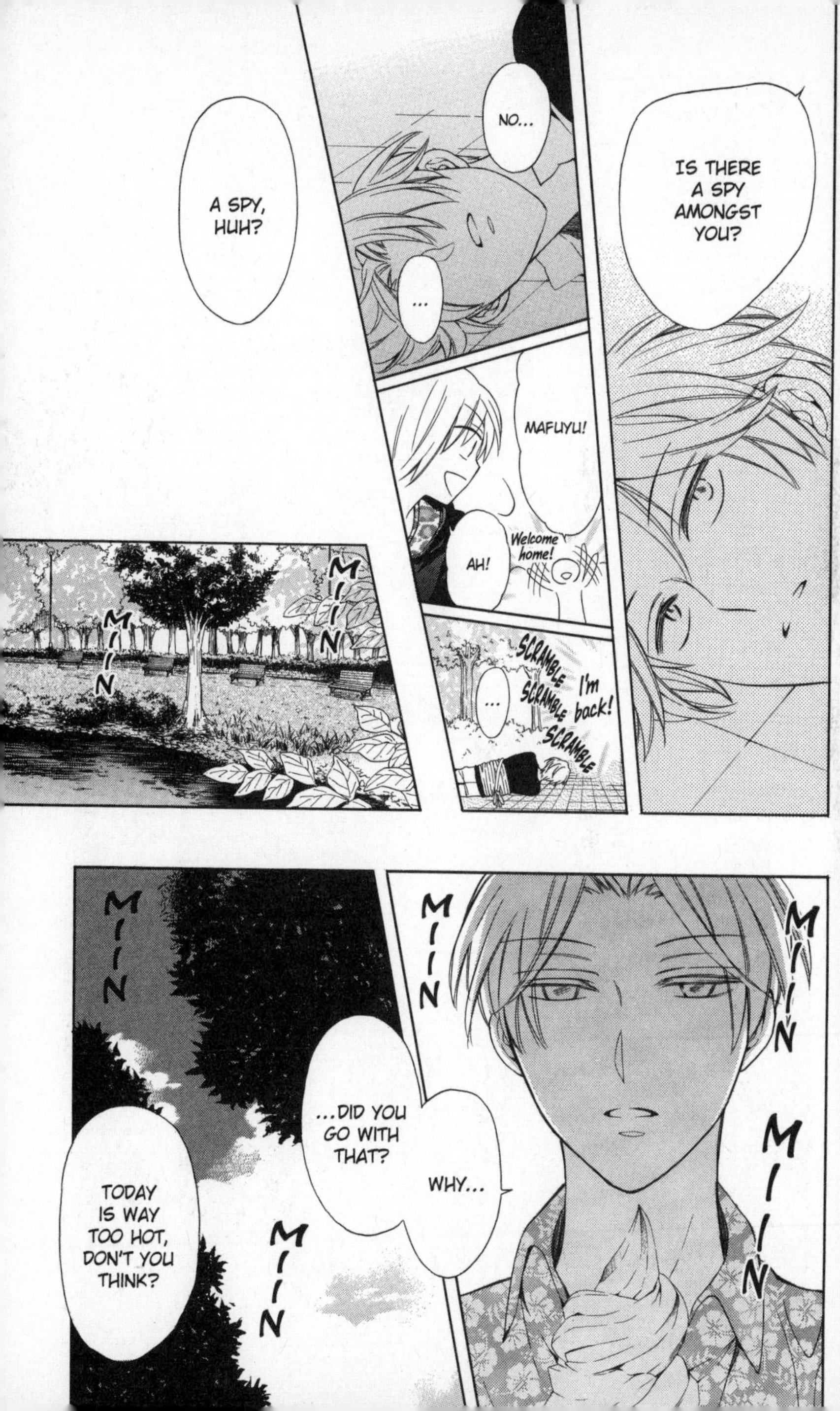
IS THERE A SPY AMONGST YOU?
NO...
...
MAFUYU!
Welcome home!
AH!
I'm back!
SCRAMBLE SCRAMBLE SCRAMBLE
...
A SPY, HUH?
MIIN
MIIN
MIIN
MIIN
WHY...
...DID YOU GO WITH THAT?
MIIN
MIIN
TODAY IS WAY TOO HOT, DON'T YOU THINK?
MIIN

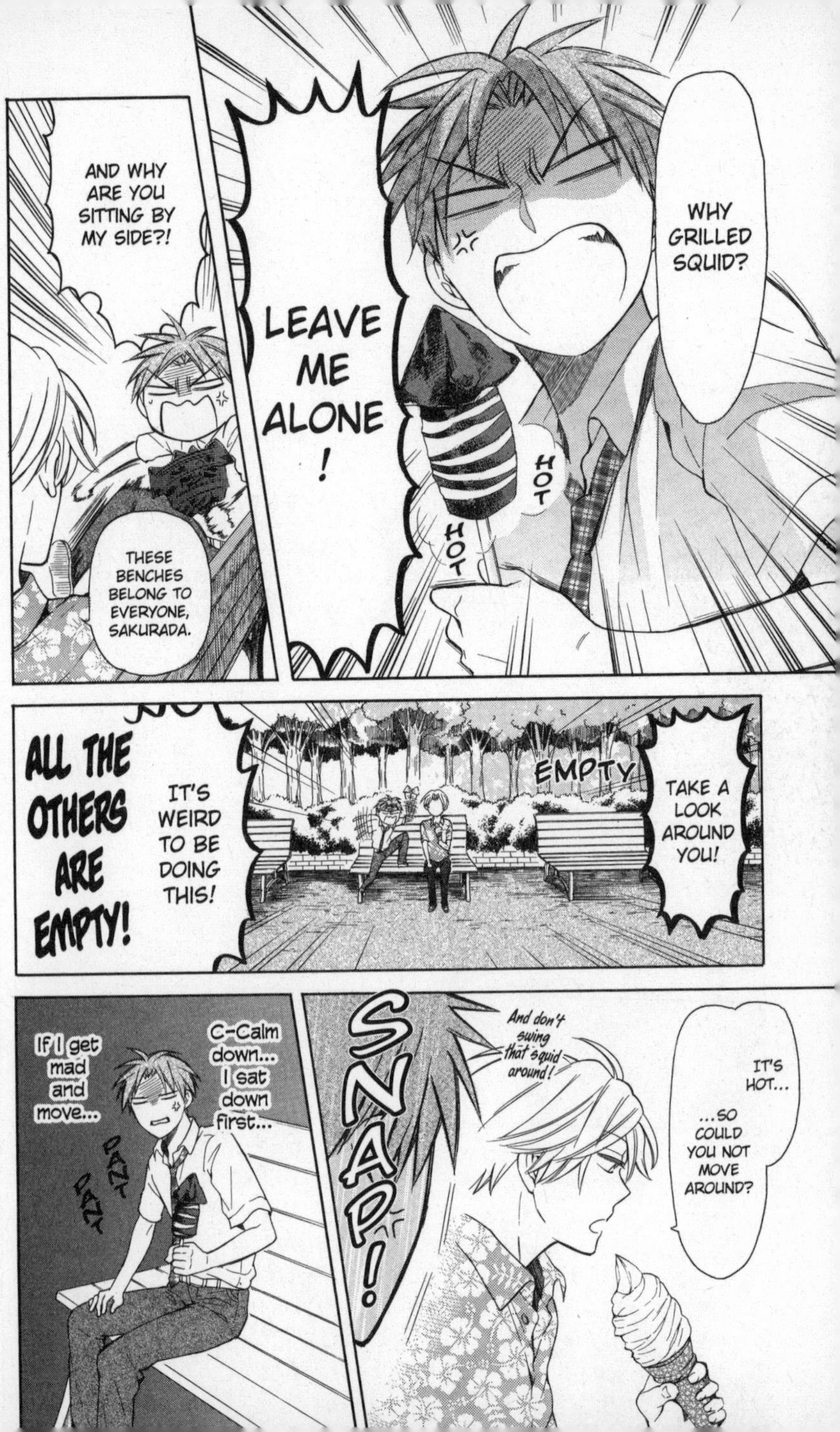
WHY GRILLED SQUID?
LEAVE ME ALONE!
HOT HOT
AND WHY ARE YOU SITTING BY MY SIDE?!
THESE BENCHES BELONG TO EVERYONE, SAKURADA.
TAKE A LOOK AROUND YOU!
EMPTY
IT'S WEIRD TO BE DOING THIS!
ALL THE OTHERS ARE EMPTY!
IT'S HOT...
...SO COULD YOU NOT MOVE AROUND?
And don't swing that squid around!
SNAP!
C-Calm down... I sat down first...
If I get mad and move...
PANT PANT

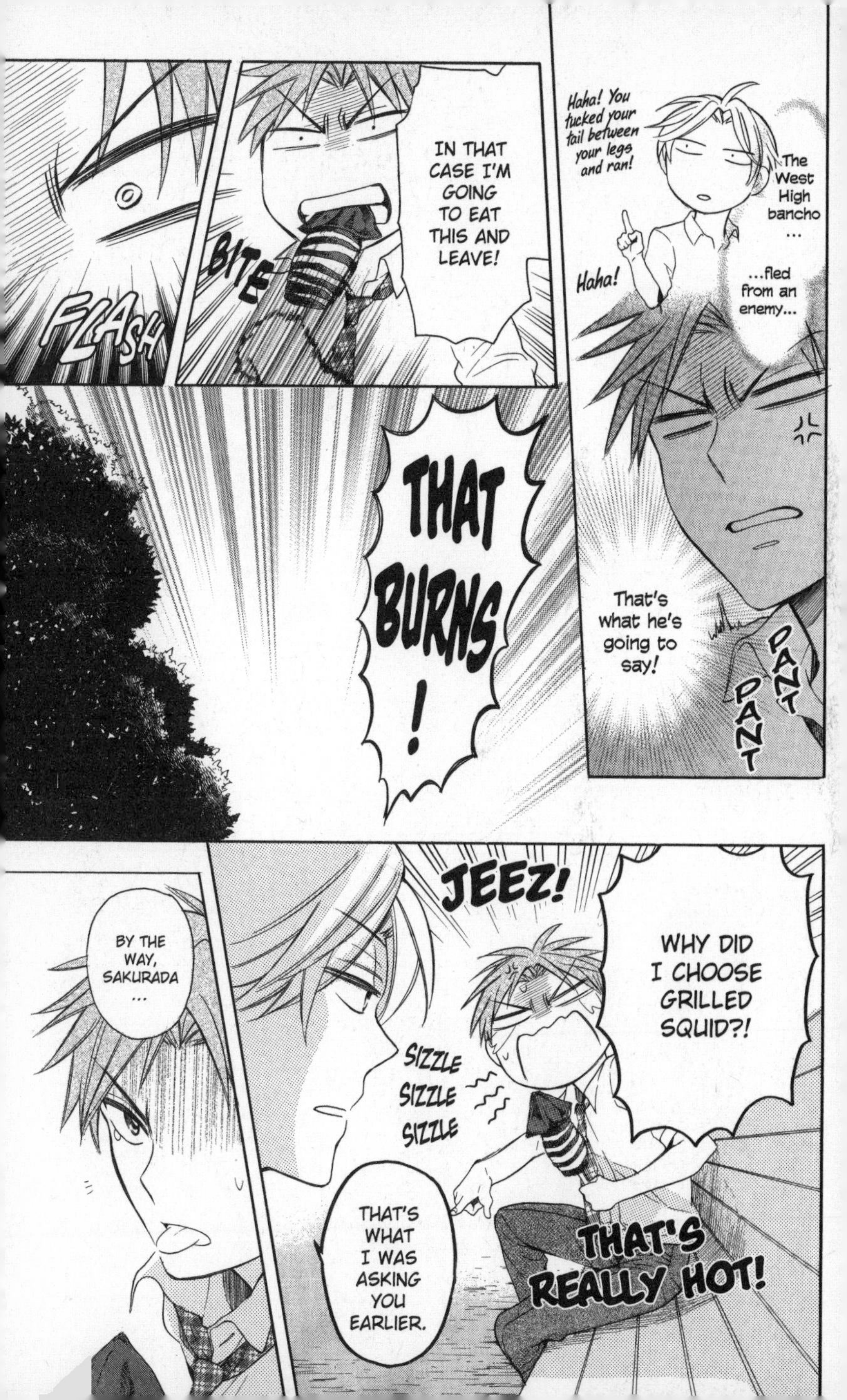
The West High bancho ...
Haha! You tucked your tail between your legs and ran!
...fled from an enemy...
Haha!
That's what he's going to say!
PANT PANT PANT
IN THAT CASE I'M GOING TO EAT THIS AND LEAVE!
BITE
FLASH
THAT BURNS!
JEEZ!
WHY DID I CHOOSE GRILLED SQUID?!
SIZZLE SIZZLE SIZZLE
THAT'S REALLY HOT!
THAT'S WHAT I WAS ASKING YOU EARLIER.
BY THE WAY, SAKURADA ...

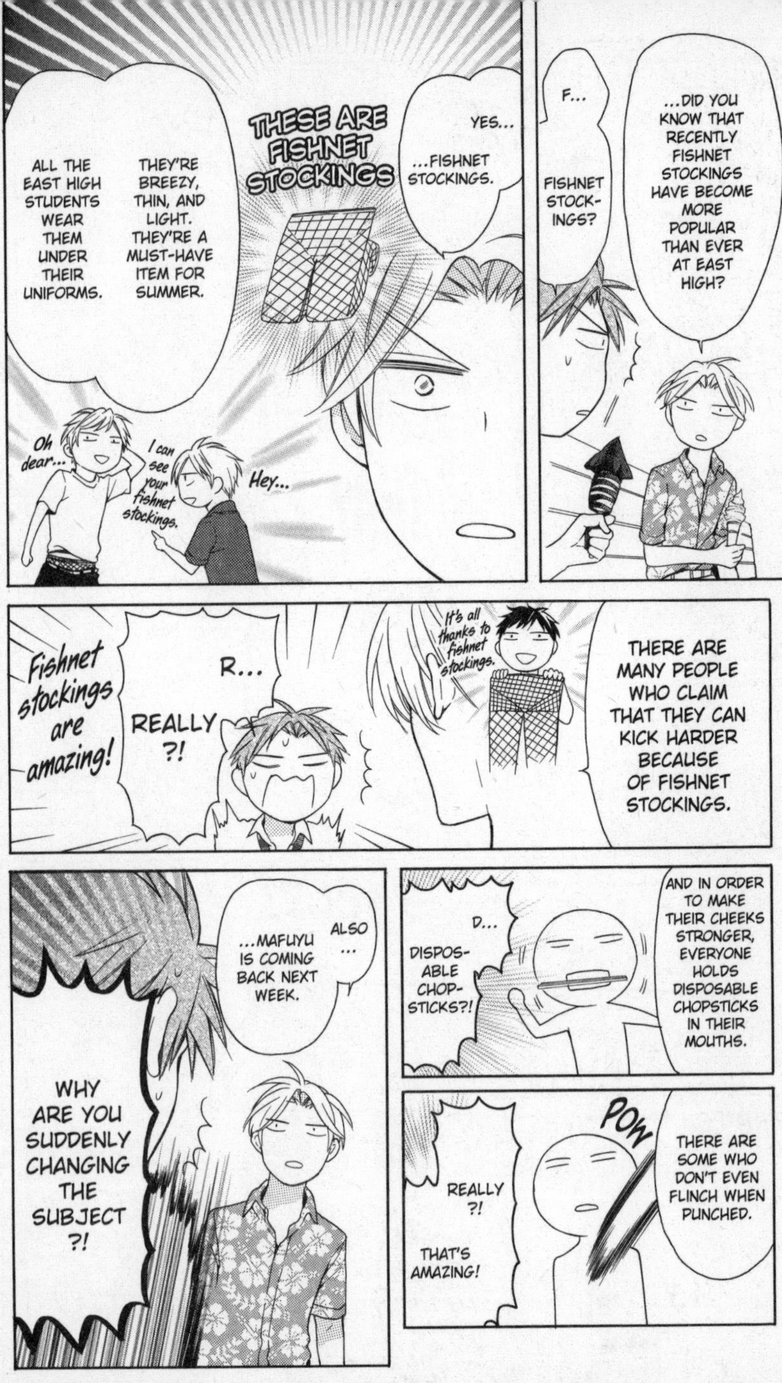
...DID YOU KNOW THAT RECENTLY FISHNET STOCKINGS HAVE BECOME MORE POPULAR THAN EVER AT EAST HIGH?
F...
FISHNET STOCK-INGS?
YES...
...FISHNET STOCKINGS.
THESE ARE FISHNET STOCKINGS
THEY'RE BREEZY, THIN, AND LIGHT. THEY'RE A MUST-HAVE ITEM FOR SUMMER.
ALL THE EAST HIGH STUDENTS WEAR THEM UNDER THEIR UNIFORMS.
Hey...
I can see your fishnet stockings.
Oh dear...
THERE ARE MANY PEOPLE WHO CLAIM THAT THEY CAN KICK HARDER BECAUSE OF FISHNET STOCKINGS.
It's all thanks to fishnet stockings.
R...
REALLY?!
Fishnet stockings are amazing!
AND IN ORDER TO MAKE THEIR CHEEKS STRONGER, EVERYONE HOLDS DISPOSABLE CHOPSTICKS IN THEIR MOUTHS.
D...
DISPOS-ABLE CHOP-STICKS?!
POW
THERE ARE SOME WHO DON'T EVEN FLINCH WHEN PUNCHED.
REALLY?!
THAT'S AMAZING!
ALSO...
...MAFUYU IS COMING BACK NEXT WEEK.
WHY ARE YOU SUDDENLY CHANGING THE SUBJECT?!

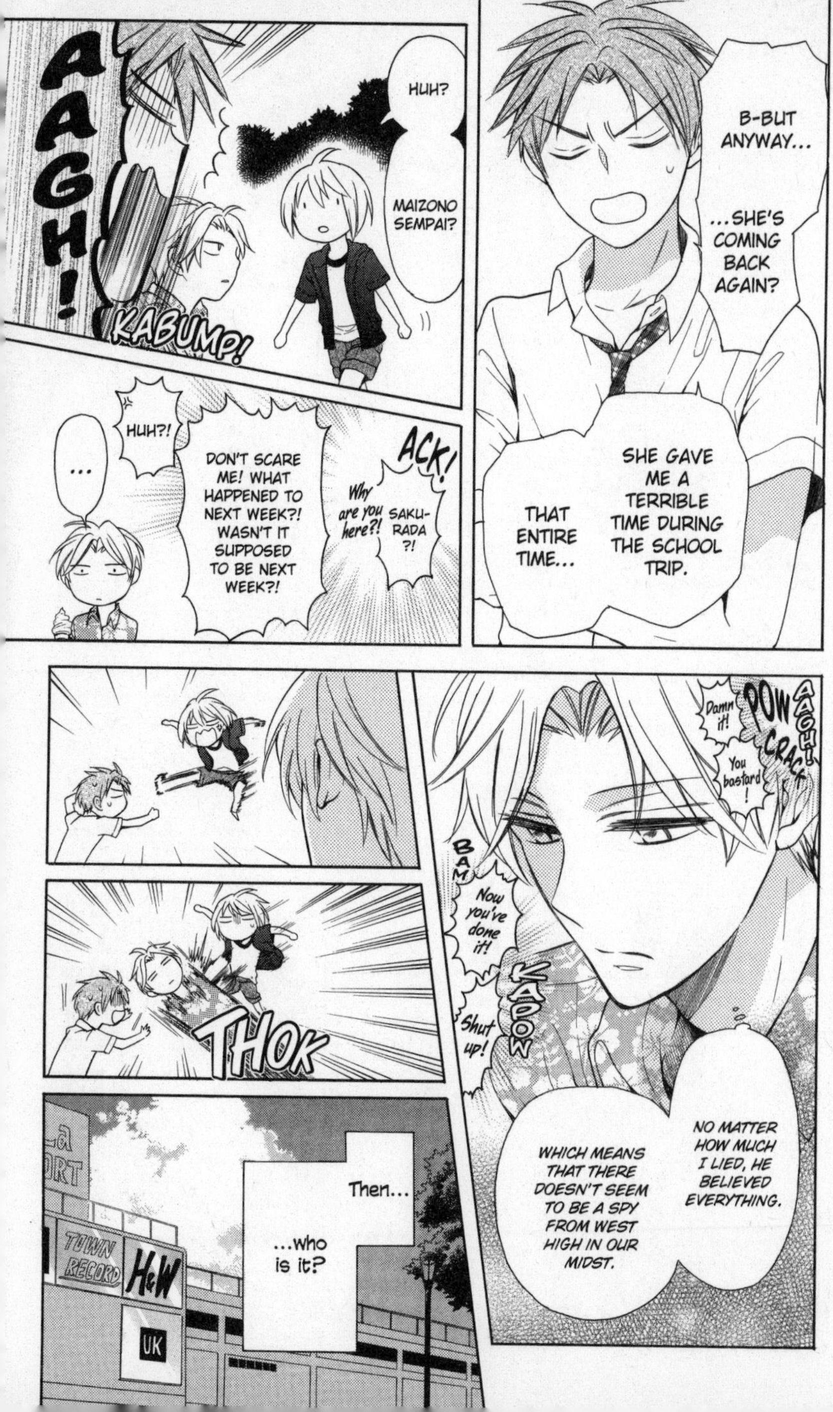
B-BUT ANYWAY...
...SHE'S COMING BACK AGAIN?
SHE GAVE ME A TERRIBLE TIME DURING THE SCHOOL TRIP.
THAT ENTIRE TIME...
HUH?
MAIZONO SEMPAI?
AAGH!
KABUMP!
ACK!
SAKURADA?!
Why are you here?!
DON'T SCARE ME! WHAT HAPPENED TO NEXT WEEK?! WASN'T IT SUPPOSED TO BE NEXT WEEK?!
HUH?!
...
AAGH!
POW
CRACK
Damn it!
You bastard!
BAM
Now you've done it!
KAPOW
Shut up!
NO MATTER HOW MUCH I LIED, HE BELIEVED EVERYTHING.
WHICH MEANS THAT THERE DOESN'T SEEM TO BE A SPY FROM WEST HIGH IN OUR MIDST.
THOK
Then...
...who is it?
TOWN RECORD
H&W
UK

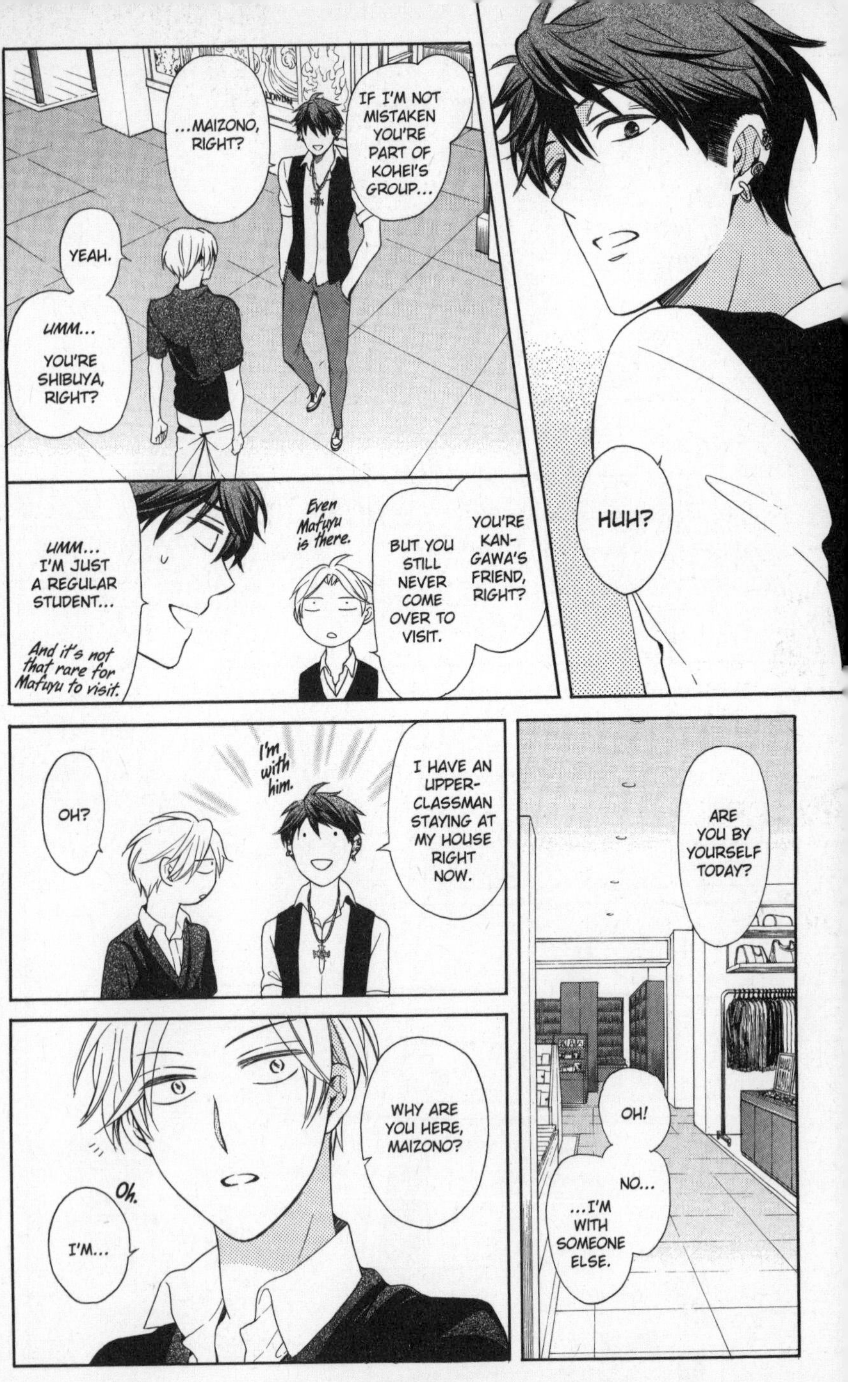
HUH?
IF I'M NOT MISTAKEN YOU'RE PART OF KOHEI'S GROUP...
...MAIZONO, RIGHT?
YEAH.
UMM... YOU'RE SHIBUYA, RIGHT?
YOU'RE KAN-GAWA'S FRIEND, RIGHT?
BUT YOU STILL NEVER COME OVER TO VISIT.
Even Mafuyu is there.
UMM... I'M JUST A REGULAR STUDENT...
And it's not that rare for Mafuyu to visit.
ARE YOU BY YOURSELF TODAY?
OH!
NO... ...I'M WITH SOMEONE ELSE.
I HAVE AN UPPER-CLASSMAN STAYING AT MY HOUSE RIGHT NOW.
I'm with him.
OH?
WHY ARE YOU HERE, MAIZONO?
Oh.
I'M...

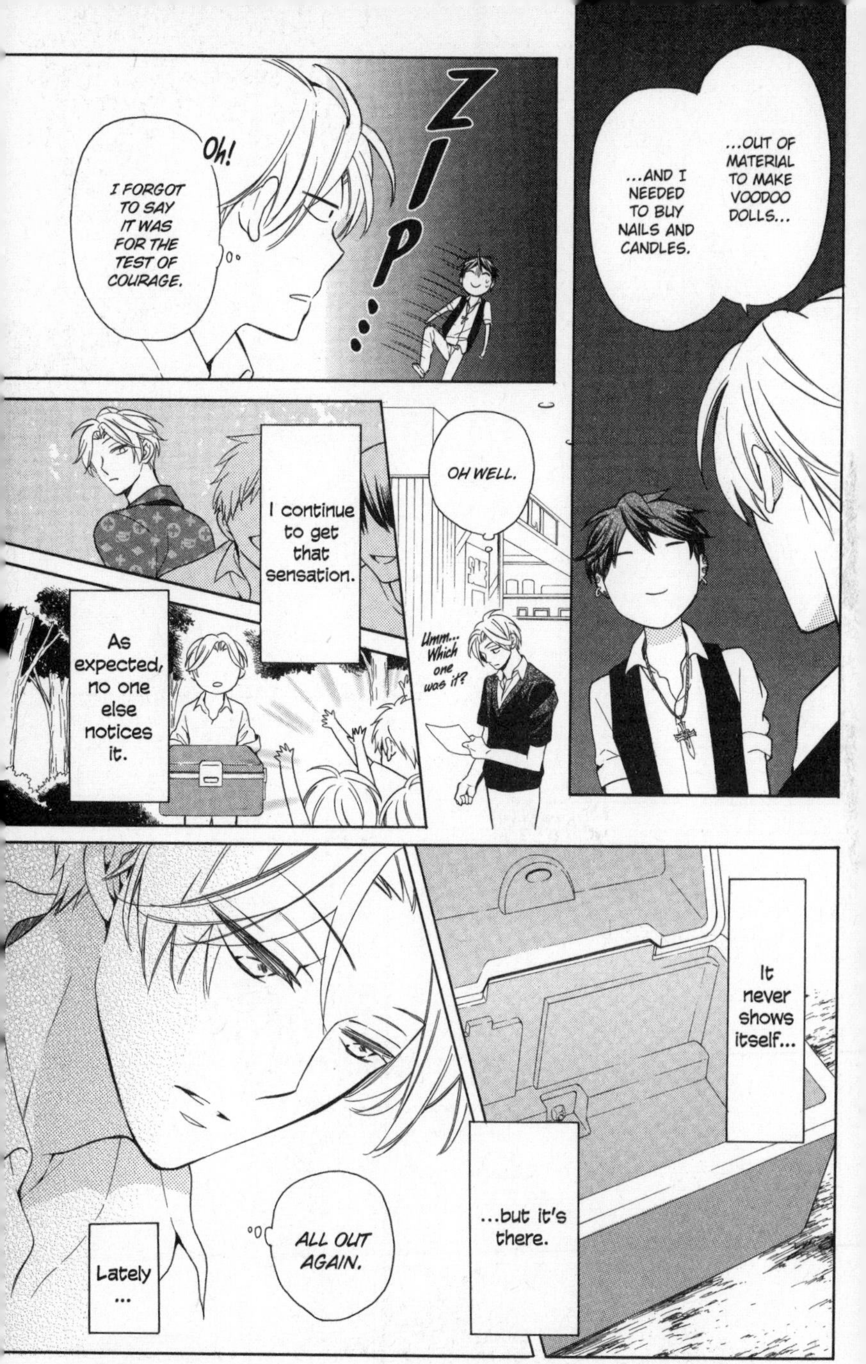
...OUT OF MATERIAL TO MAKE VOODOO DOLLS...
...AND I NEEDED TO BUY NAILS AND CANDLES.
ZIP...
Oh!
I FORGOT TO SAY IT WAS FOR THE TEST OF COURAGE.
OH WELL.
Umm... Which one was it?
I continue to get that sensation.
As expected, no one else notices it.
It never shows itself...
...but it's there.
ALL OUT AGAIN.
Lately...

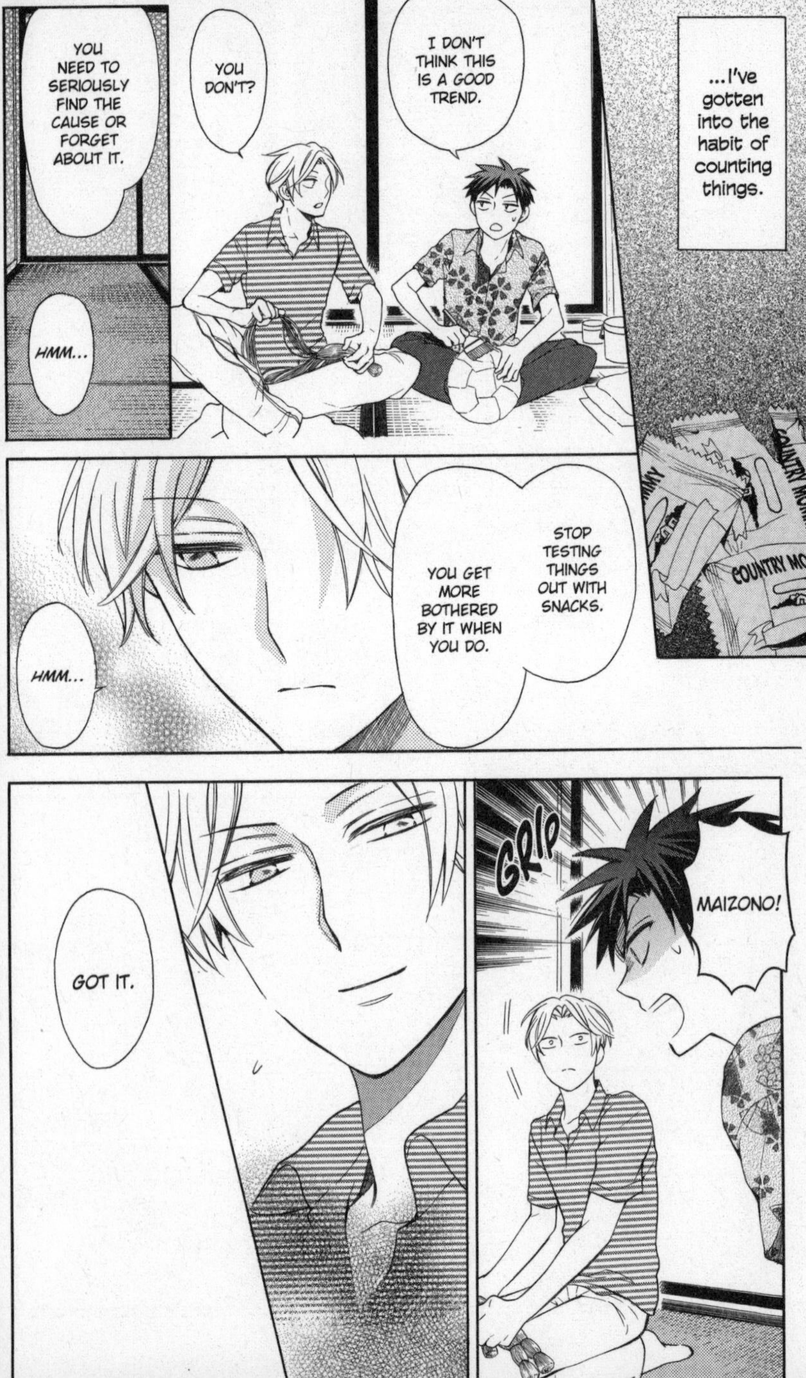
...I've gotten into the habit of counting things.
COUNTRY MOMMY
COUNTRY MOMMY
I DON'T THINK THIS IS A GOOD TREND.
YOU DON'T?
YOU NEED TO SERIOUSLY FIND THE CAUSE OR FORGET ABOUT IT.
HMM...
STOP TESTING THINGS OUT WITH SNACKS.
YOU GET MORE BOTHERED BY IT WHEN YOU DO.
HMM...
GRIP
MAIZONO!
GOT IT.

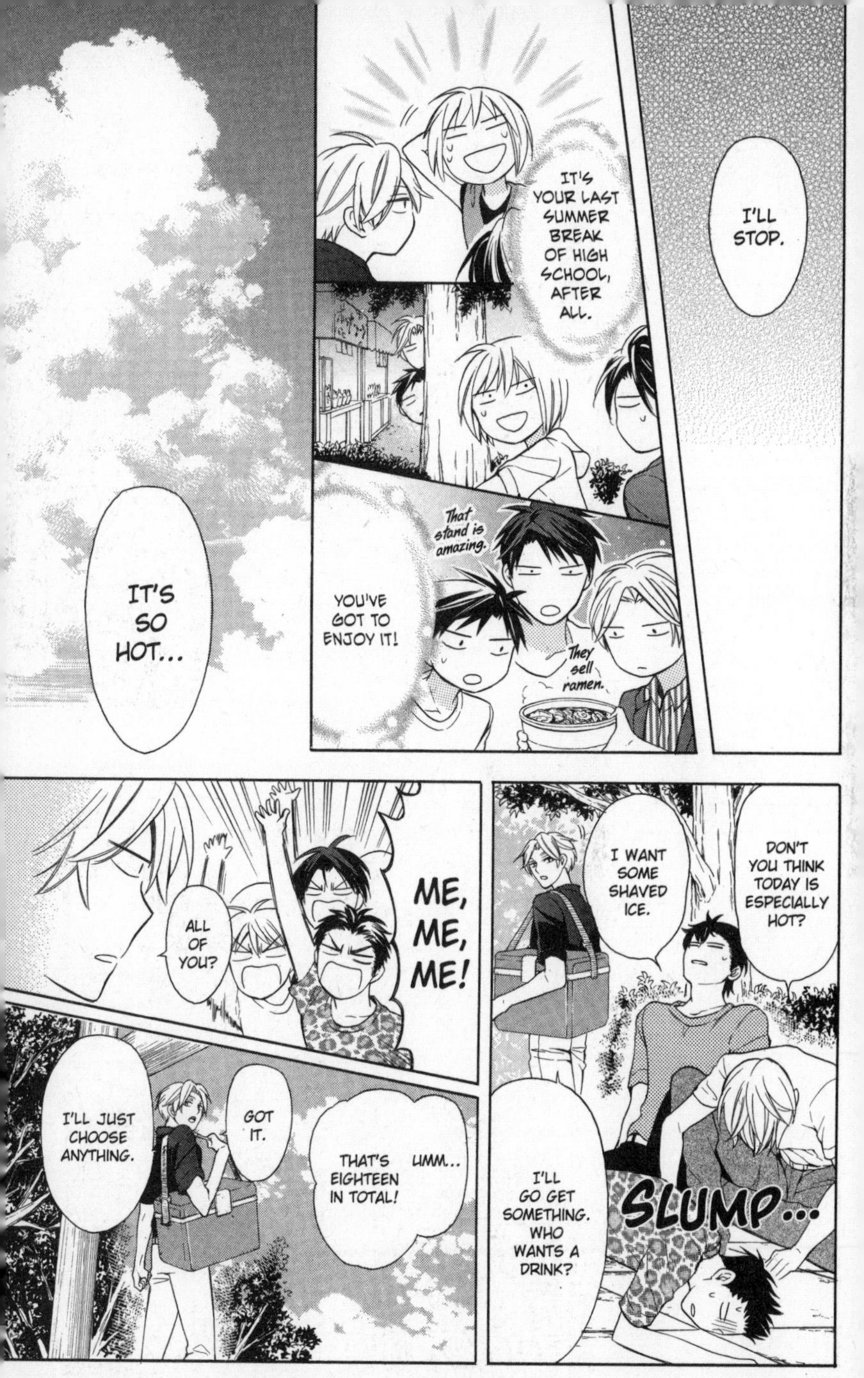
I'LL STOP.
IT'S YOUR LAST SUMMER BREAK OF HIGH SCHOOL, AFTER ALL.
That stand is amazing.
YOU'VE GOT TO ENJOY IT!
They sell ramen.
IT'S SO HOT...
DON'T YOU THINK TODAY IS ESPECIALLY HOT?
I WANT SOME SHAVED ICE.
SLUMP...
I'LL GO GET SOMETHING. WHO WANTS A DRINK?
ME, ME, ME!
ALL OF YOU?
UMM...
THAT'S EIGHTEEN IN TOTAL!
GOT IT.
I'LL JUST CHOOSE ANYTHING.

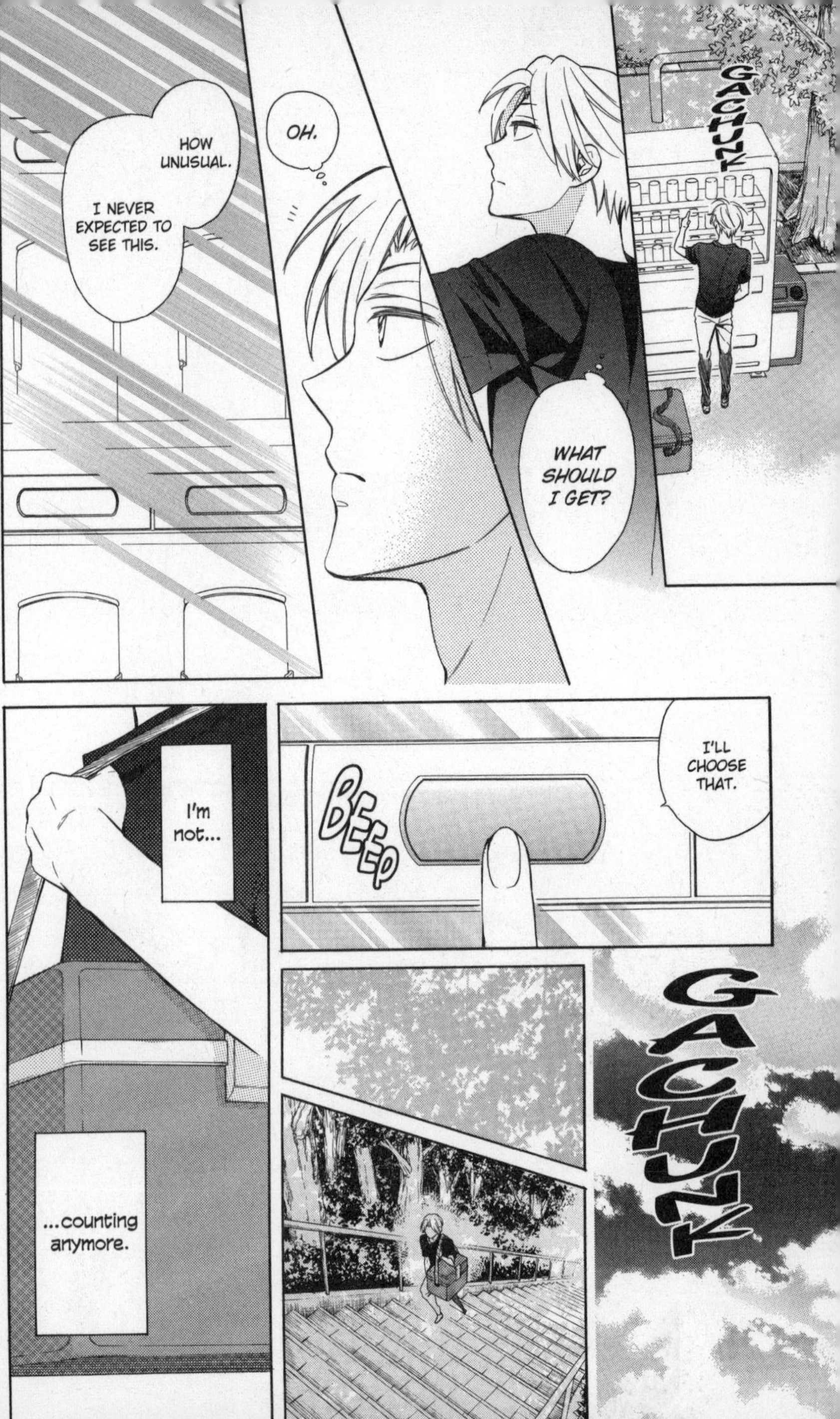
GACHUNK
WHAT SHOULD I GET?
OH.
HOW UNUSUAL.
I NEVER EXPECTED TO SEE THIS.
I'LL CHOOSE THAT.
BEEP
GACHUNK
I'm not...
...counting anymore.

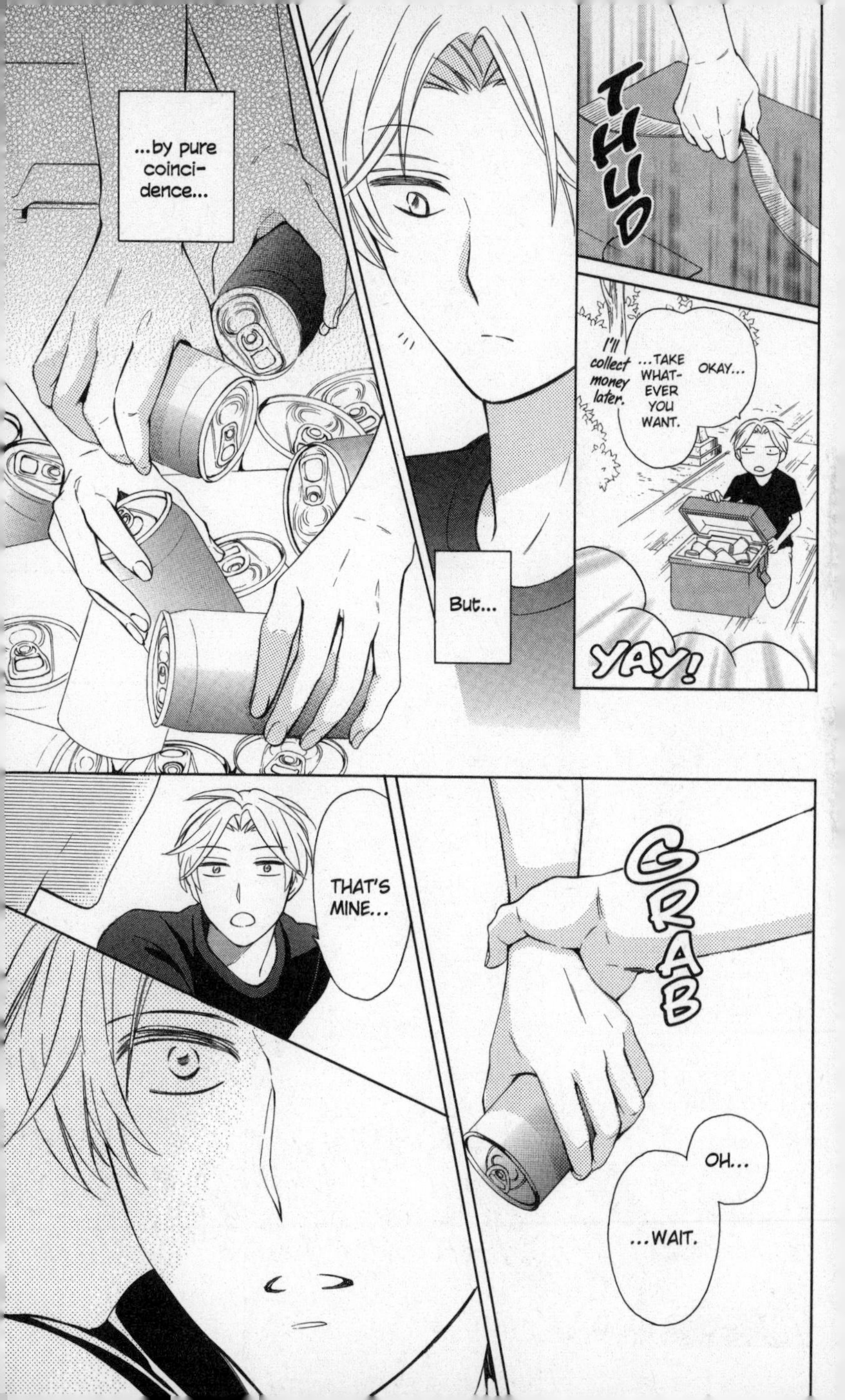
THUD
OKAY...
...TAKE WHATEVER YOU WANT.
I'll collect money later.
YAY!
But...
...by pure coincidence...
GRAB
OH...
...WAIT.
THAT'S MINE...

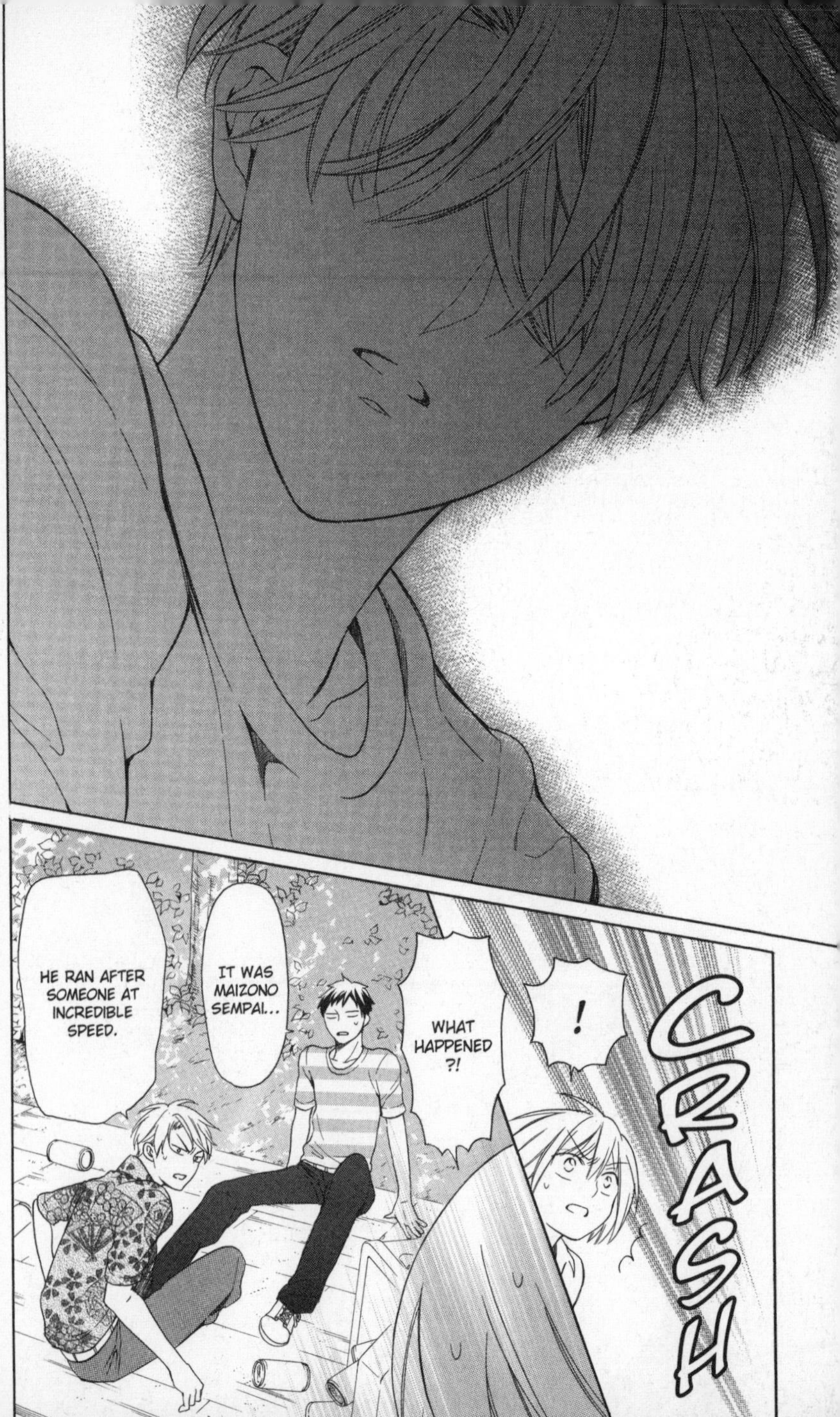
CRASH
!
WHAT HAPPENED ?!
IT WAS MAIZONO SEMPAI...
HE RAN AFTER SOMEONE AT INCREDIBLE SPEED.

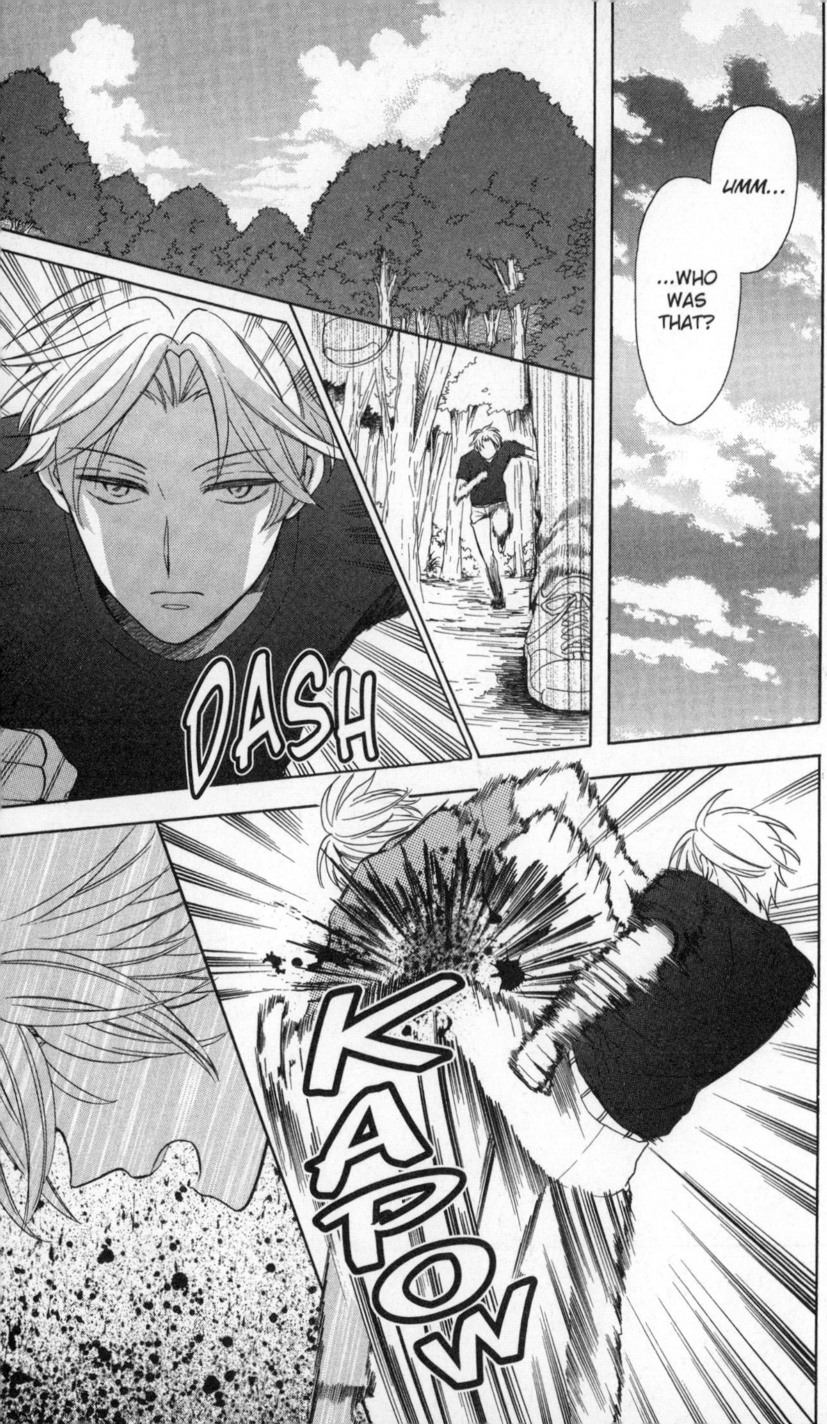
UMM...
...WHO WAS THAT?
DASH
KAPOW

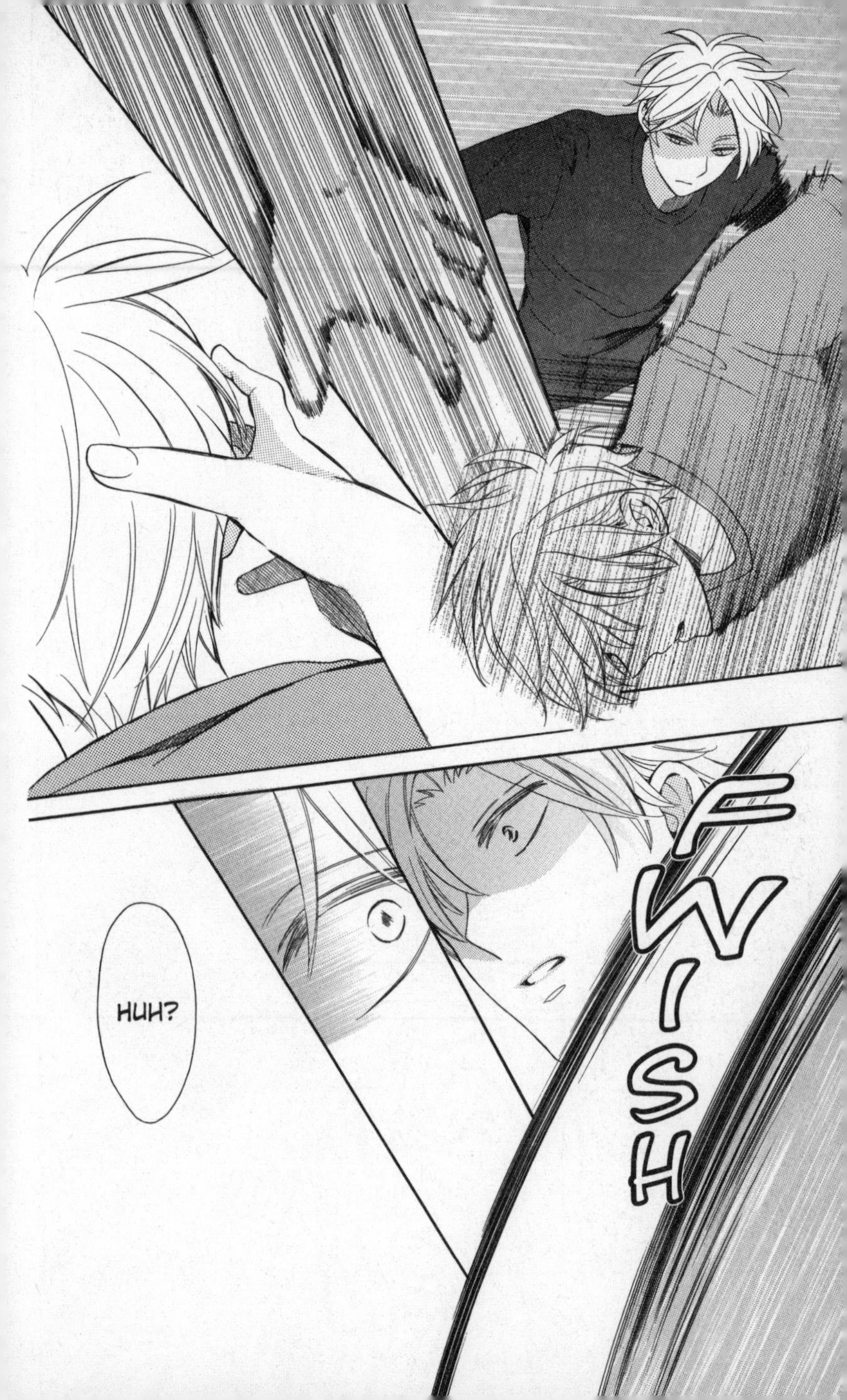
FWISH
HUH?

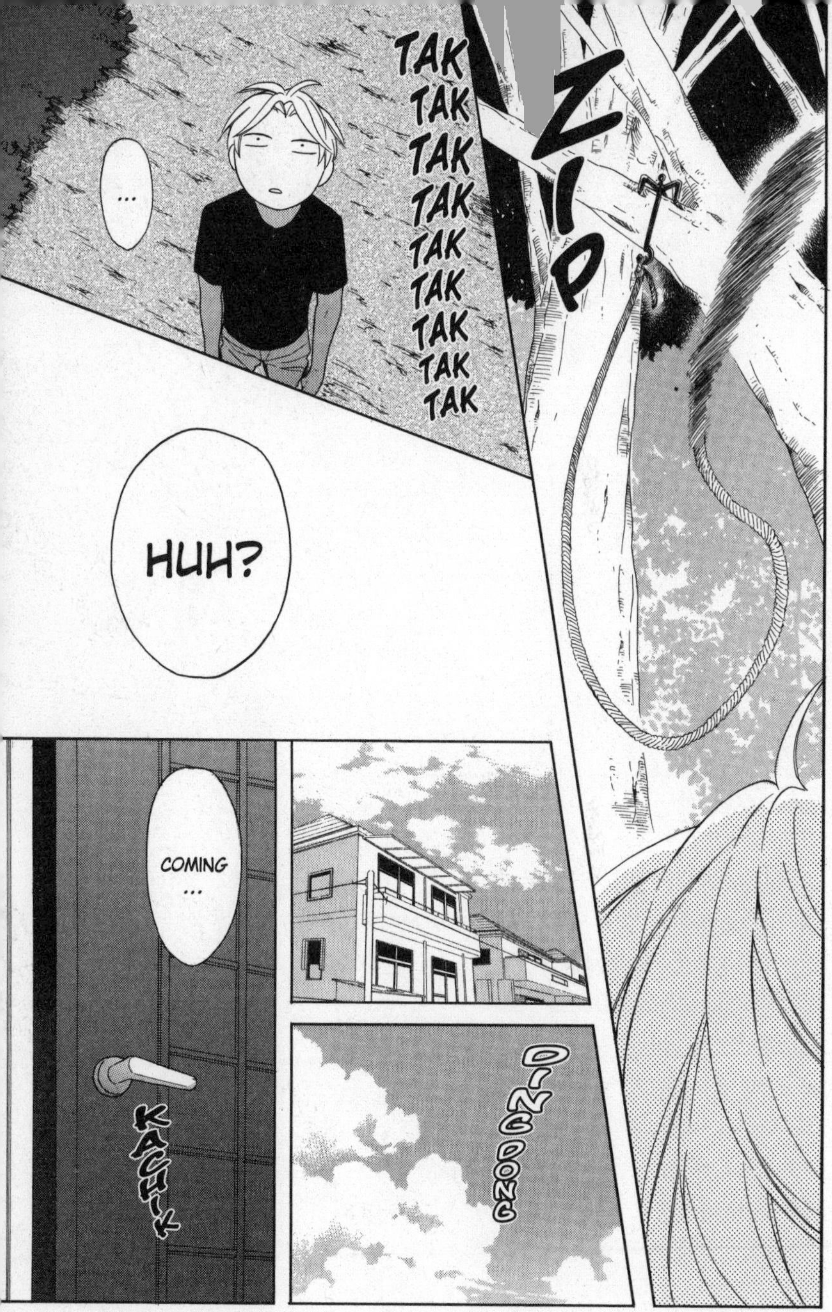
ZIP
TAK TAK TAK TAK TAK TAK TAK TAK TAK
...
HUH?
DING DONG
COMING ...
KACHIK

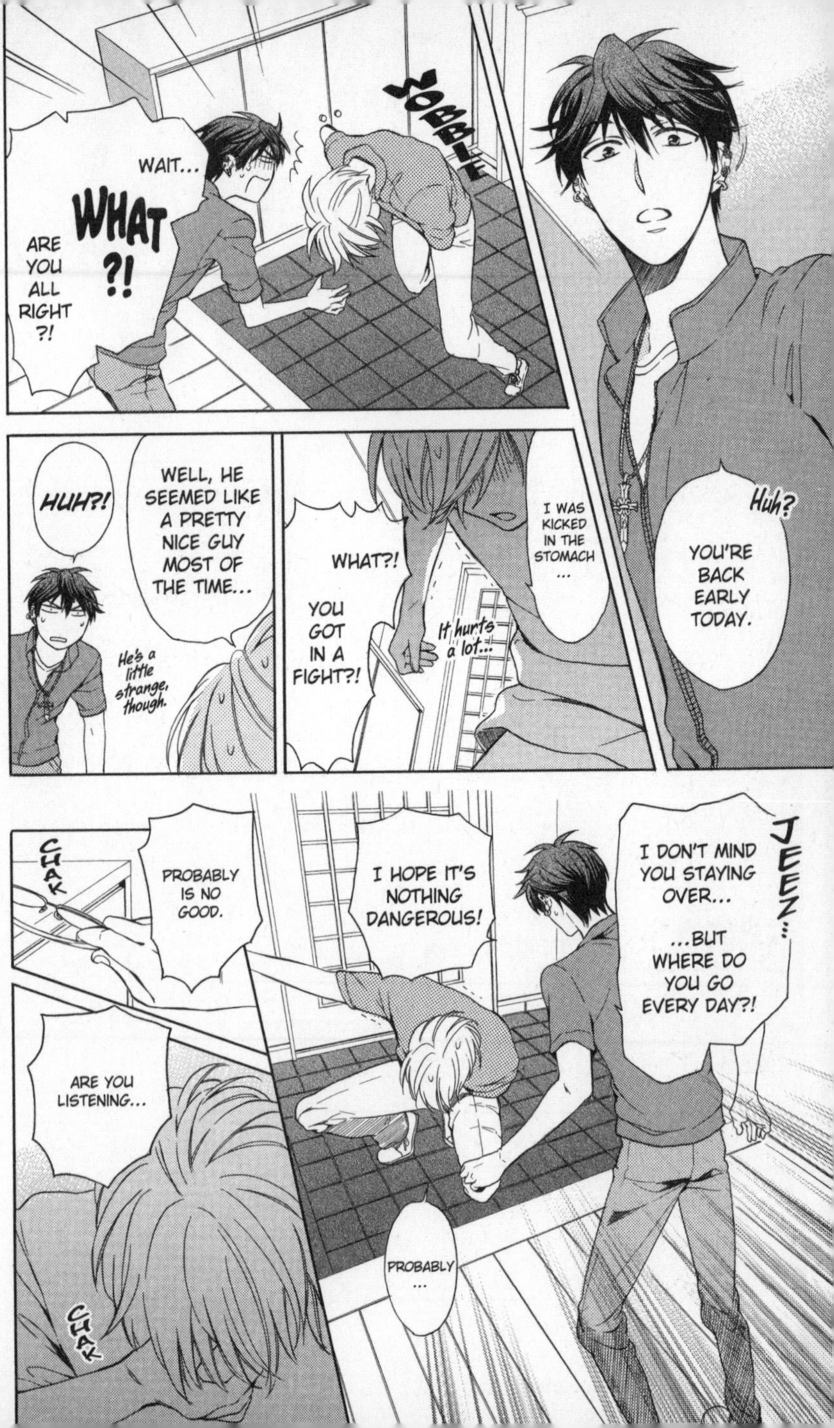
Huh?
YOU'RE BACK EARLY TODAY.
WOBBLE
WAIT...
WHAT ?!
ARE YOU ALL RIGHT ?!
I WAS KICKED IN THE STOMACH ...
WHAT?!
YOU GOT IN A FIGHT?!
It hurts a lot...
WELL, HE SEEMED LIKE A PRETTY NICE GUY MOST OF THE TIME...
HUH?!
He's a little strange, though.
JEEZ..
I DON'T MIND YOU STAYING OVER...
...BUT WHERE DO YOU GO EVERY DAY?!
I HOPE IT'S NOTHING DANGEROUS!
PROBABLY ...
PROBABLY IS NO GOOD.
CHAK
ARE YOU LISTENING...
CHAK

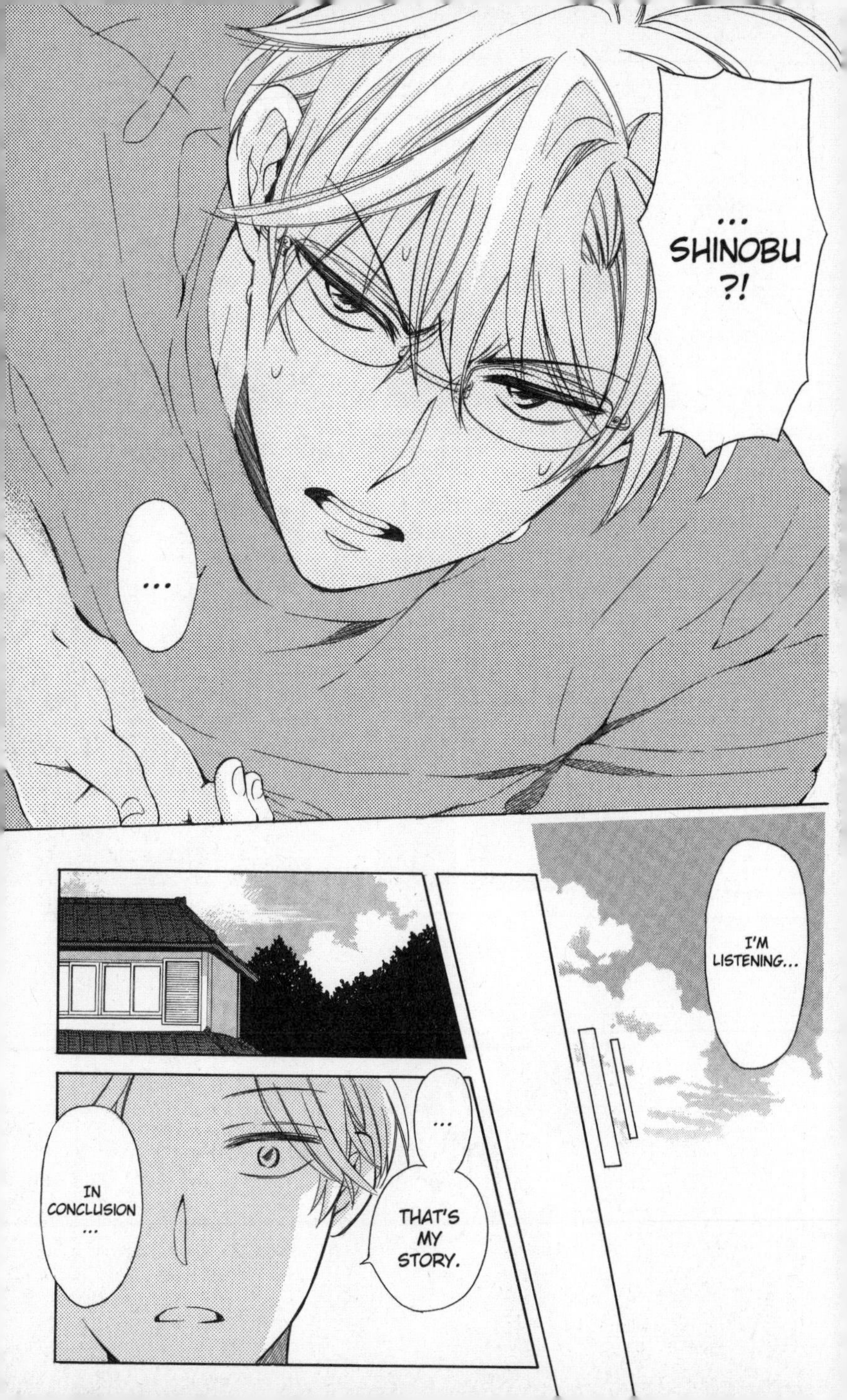
... SHINOBU ?!
...
I'M LISTENING...
...
THAT'S MY STORY.
IN CONCLUSION ...

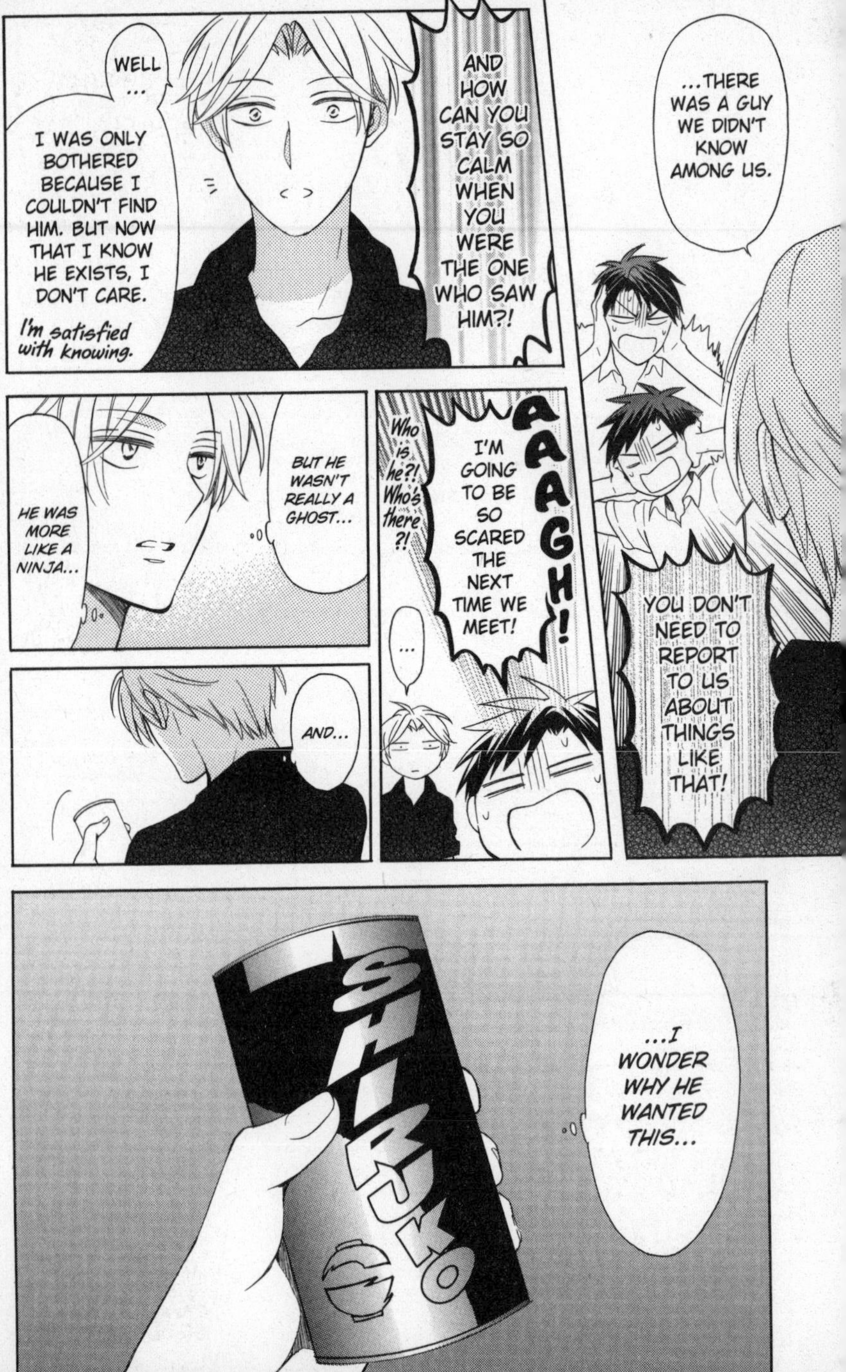
...THERE WAS A GUY WE DIDN'T KNOW AMONG US.
YOU DON'T NEED TO REPORT TO US ABOUT THINGS LIKE THAT!
AND HOW CAN YOU STAY SO CALM WHEN YOU WERE THE ONE WHO SAW HIM?!
WELL...
I WAS ONLY BOTHERED BECAUSE I COULDN'T FIND HIM. BUT NOW THAT I KNOW HE EXISTS, I DON'T CARE.
I'm satisfied with knowing.
AAAGH!
I'M GOING TO BE SO SCARED THE NEXT TIME WE MEET!
Who is he?! Who's there?!
...
BUT HE WASN'T REALLY A GHOST...
HE WAS MORE LIKE A NINJA...
AND...
SHIRUKO
...I WONDER WHY HE WANTED THIS...

Data

BIRTHDAY / AUGUST 12

BLOOD TYPE / TYPE B

HEIGHT / 6'3"

OCCUPATION / MATH TEACHER • SECOND YEAR, CLASS 1 HOMEROOM TEACHER • PUBLIC MORALS CLUB ADVISOR

FAMILY STRUCTURE / GRANDFATHER, STEPFATHER, MOTHER

Q) WHAT DO YOU DO ABOUT FOOD?

Hey, you bastard! You need to get me beer.
I can't buy that. I'll be stopped by the police.

The supermarkets are closed by the time Takaomi gets home, so he has Mafuyu do his shopping for him. In return, he gives her food (packed lunches, etc.).

MAFUYU'S CHILDHOOD FRIEND, AND THE PERSON WHO TAUGHT HER HOW TO FIGHT. DURING HIS DAYS AS A STUDENT, HE DID WHATEVER HE WANTED, BUT AFTER AN INCIDENT WITH HIS GRANDFATHER, HE PURSUED THE PATH OF A TEACHER. WHETHER HE'S SUITED FOR THE JOB IS DUBIOUS, AND EVEN HE THINKS IT'S WEIRD. HE'S THE ONLY ADULT OF THE MAIN CAST, BUT HE ACTS LIKE A CHILD.

Takaomi Saeki

Person

FAVORITE FOOD / ALL JAPANESE FOOD

PERSONALITY PREFERENCE / INTERESTING PEOPLE. ROMANTICALLY, HE LIKES PEOPLE WHO DON'T FALL FOR HIM. THERE IS A CHILDISH SIDE TO HIM THAT IS VERY SOFT ON PEOPLE WHO HAVE GOTTEN TO KNOW HIS INNER SELF, AND DISLIKES BEING AWAY FROM THEM. BUT THERE ARE ONLY VERY FEW PEOPLE WHO HAVE DONE THAT.

FAVORITE ALCOHOL BRANDS / KUBOTA MANJU (SAKE) AND YEBISU (BEER)

INTERESTS / VIDEO GAMES

WEAKNESS / DETAILED WORK • PEOPLE IMPORTANT TO HIM

CURRENT WORRIES / HIS NEIGHBOR BRINGS HER HOMEWORK OVER. IT'S A REAL BOTHER.

DAYS OFF SPENT / VISITING HIS GRANDFATHER. FORMING PERSONAL CONNECTIONS.

Data

BIRTHDAY / APRIL 16

BLOOD TYPE / TYPE A

HEIGHT / 5'9"

CLASS / SECOND YEAR, CLASS 1

FAMILY STRUCTURE / ????

Q) WHAT DO YOU DO FOR LUNCH WHEN MAFUYU ISN'T AROUND?

I just do whatever. I go to the cafeteria with Yui...
And I sometimes eat with Okegawa and Shibuya.

HIS FIRST NAME AND FAMILY STRUCTURE ARE UNKNOWN. MANY PEOPLE HAVE CALLED HIM SERIOUS AND DENSE, BUT WHAT IS THE TRUTH?

Hayasaka

Person

FAVORITE FOOD / HOTPOTS

PERSONALITY PREFERENCE /SUPER BUN

INTERESTS / JIGSAW PUZZLES, DOMINOS (HE LIKES DETAILED WORK)

DISLIKES / FALLING TECHNIQUES

CURRENT WORRIES / KUROSAKI STILL HASN'T COME TO ANY ASSEMBLIES. EVEN OKEGAWA, WHO USED TO SKIP OUT ON THEM WITH HER, HAS STARTED GOING TO THEM. WHEN I TRIED TO DRAG HER TO ONE, SHE SAID THAT SHE CAN'T GO BECAUSE SHE GETS TOO EXCITED. SOMETIMES I STILL DON'T UNDERSTAND HER.

CLOSE RELATIONSHIPS / "I GUESS KUROSAKI AND YUI?"

DAYS OFF SPENT / DISTURBANCES HAPPEN REGULARLY IN THE BOY'S DORM, SO HE STOPS THEM OR JOINS THEM. (LAST WEEK WAS AN ARM WRESTLING EVENT.) HE OCCASIONALLY GOES TO THE ARCADE TO PLAY THE ROCK-PAPER-SCISSORS GAME.

Data

BIRTHDAY / DECEMBER 24

BLOOD TYPE / TYPE AB

HEIGHT / 5'9"

CLASS / SECOND YEAR, CLASS 2

FAMILY STRUCTURE / FATHER, MOTHER

Q) DO YOU PERM YOUR HAIR?

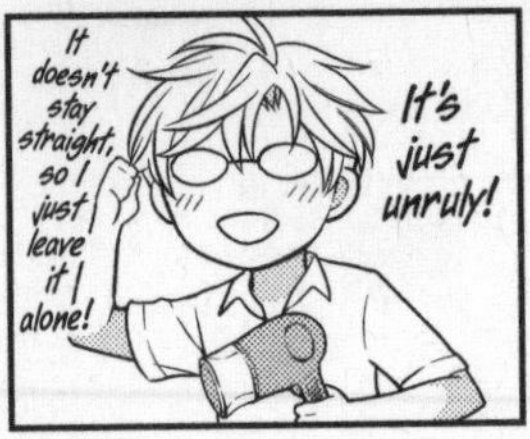
It doesn't stay straight, so I just leave it alone!
It's just unruly!

AN ONLY CHILD. HE IS A MAN OF ACTION, BUT HE LACKS DECISIVENESS. HE HAS GIVEN UP THINKING FOR HIMSELF AND WANTS SOMEONE ELSE TO MAKE DECISIONS FOR HIM. HE IS BLIND TO THE FEELINGS OF OTHERS AND HIS OWN.

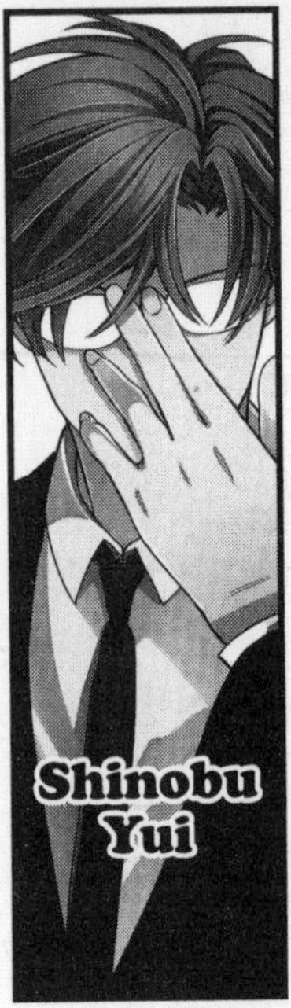
Shinobu Yui

Person

FAVORITE FOOD / NATTO ON RICE

PERSONALITY PREFERENCE / SOMEONE WHO WILL ALWAYS STAY BY HIS SIDE AND PAY ATTENTION TO HIM

INTERESTS / ASIDE FROM NINJAS, NOTHING HOLDS HIS INTEREST FOR VERY LONG

DISLIKES / HORROR RELATED THINGS • THRILL RIDES • THE INTERNET • STAYING IN ONE SPOT BY HIMSELF

CURRENT WORRIES / "THE FACT THAT HAYASAKA AND KUROSAKI HAVE PACKED LUNCHES OR BREAD FOR LUNCH, SO THEY DON'T GO TO THE CAFETERIA VERY OFTEN. BUT I HATE BREAD! I THINK THEY SHOULD BUY SCHOOL LUNCH. BUT SOMETIMES, HAYASAKA EATS SCHOOL LUNCH IN THE CAFETERIA! IT'S ON THE DAYS THAT KUROSAKI EATS PACKED LUNCHES WITH AYABE!"

CLOSE RELATIONSHIPS / "THAT WOULD BE HAYASAKA! AT FIRST, I THOUGHT HE WAS SCARY, BUT HE'S A GOOD GUY! AT SCHOOL, HE'S USUALLY WITH KUROSAKI, BUT AT THE DORMS, HE'S WITH ME! BASED ON OUR TOTAL TIME TOGETHER, I'M HIS BEST FRIEND!"

YUI SEEMS LIKE HE ACTS WITHOUT HESITATION, BUT HE DOESN'T THINK FOR HIMSELF AT ALL. USING MIYABI'S ORDER AS A REASON TO USE THE ART OF THE ECHO, HIS RESOLVE NEVER WAVERS, BUT UPON BEING ALONE, HE REALIZES HIS TRUE FEELINGS FOR THE FIRST TIME.

Data

BIRTHDAY / MAY 15

BLOOD TYPE / TYPE A

HEIGHT / 6'1"

CLASS / THIRD YEAR, CLASS 4

FAMILY STRUCTURE / FATHER, MOTHER, TWO OLDER BROTHERS (ADULTS)

Q) WHAT HAPPENED RECENTLY TO NEKOMATA?

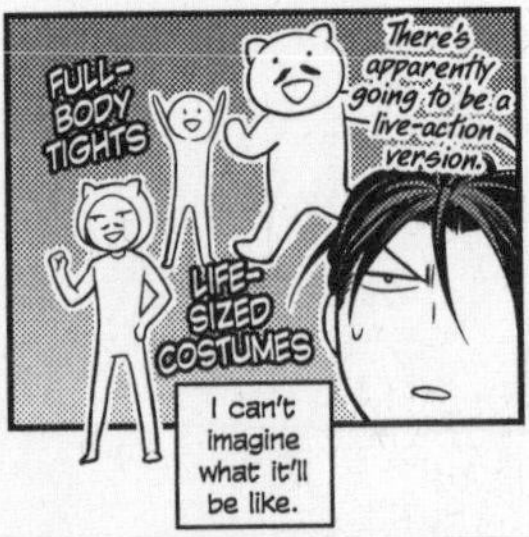
There's apparently going to be a live-action version.
FULL-BODY TIGHTS
LIFE-SIZED COSTUMES
I can't imagine what it'll be like.

HIS TWO OLDER BROTHERS WERE EXCELLENT STUDENTS EVER SINCE HE WAS LITTLE. THIS MADE HIM SULKY AND TURNED HIM INTO THE PERSON HE IS TODAY. HE USUALLY USES BRUTE STRENGTH, BUT HIS SAVAGE INTUITION ALLOWS HIM TO HOLD UP IN BATTLES OF WITS AS WELL.

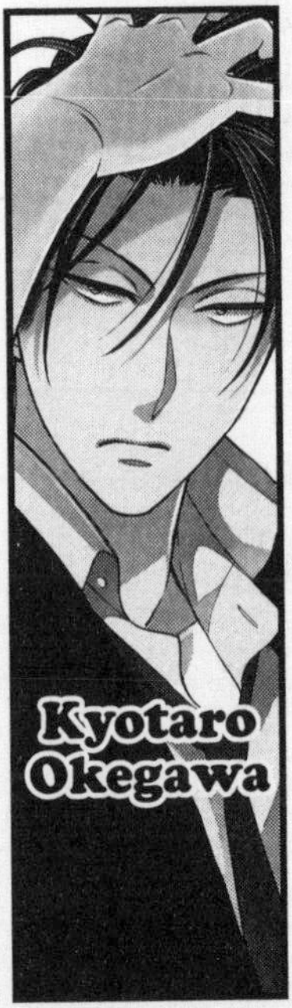
Kyotaro Okegawa

Person

FAVORITE FOOD / CREAM PUFFS

PERSONALITY PREFERENCE / A COOL PERSON WITH DETERMINATION

INTERESTS / MOTORCYCLES, MAKING MINIATURE MODELS

DISLIKES / TESTS, WAKING UP EARLY

CURRENT WORRIES / "CAN I GRADUATE THIS YEAR? RECENTLY, SNOW'S DAILY LIFE HAS BECOME MORE DRAMATIC, AND I CAN'T LOSE TO HER."

CLOSE RELATIONSHIPS / "CLOSE RELATIONSHIPS... THERE ISN'T ANYONE WHO'S MY EQUAL... I GUESS IT WOULD HAVE TO BE MORSE. THERE AREN'T MANY PEOPLE WHO CAN UNDERSTAND HOW COOL NEKOMATA-SAN IS. COME TO THINK OF IT, WHERE CAN WE WATCH A DVD? I CAN'T ASK HER TO COME TO MY ROOM, SO IT WOULD HAVE TO BE MORSE'S... I-IT'S NOT AS IF I WANT TO GO TO HER ROOM!"

THERE'S NOTHING DARK ABOUT OKEGAWA. DESPITE HIS BEING BANCHO, HE'S A PEACEFUL PERSON. AT THE BEGINNING, HE WAS THE FINAL BOSS, BUT NOW, HE'S A HIGH SCHOOL SUPER SENIOR WHO PLAYS WITH CATS AND PIGEONS. HE'S A HEARTWARMING CHARACTER.

Data

BIRTHDAY / JULY 2

BLOOD TYPE / TYPE O

HEIGHT / 5'11"

CLASS / FIRST YEAR, CLASS 2

FAMILY STRUCTURE / GRANDMOTHER, FATHER, MOTHER, THREE OLDER SISTERS

Q) WHY DO YOU HAVE MAKEUP TOOLS?

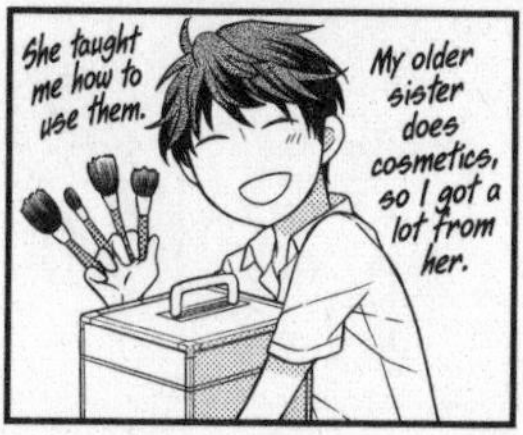
My older sister does cosmetics, so I got a lot from her.
She taught me how to use them.

HE GREW UP SURROUNDED BY GIRLS. BECAUSE OF THAT, HE UNDERSTANDS GIRLS AND IS KIND TO THEM, BUT IT PREVENTS HIM FROM HAVING ROMANTIC RELATIONSHIPS.

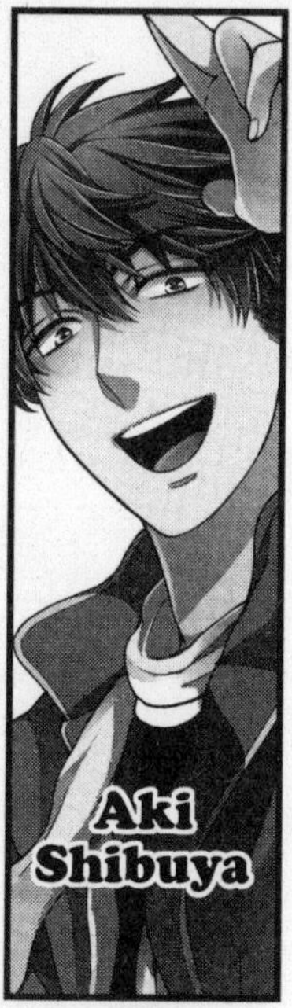
Aki Shibuya

Person

FAVORITE FOOD / NEW SNACKS ON SALE. LIMITED-RUN SNACKS ARE EVEN BETTER

PERSONALITY PREFERENCE / SOMEONE HE IS UNSURE OF WHAT THEY'RE THINKING

INTERESTS / FISHING

DISLIKES / CHANGE OF HEARTS

CURRENT WORRIES / HE WANTS TO PUT ON A LITTLE MORE MUSCLE AND WEIGHT

CLOSE RELATIONSHIPS / "I SUPPOSE KOHEI. HE PROTECTED ME A LOT IN MIDDLE SCHOOL! RIGHT NOW, THE R.A. LOOKS AFTER ME. APPARENTLY, HE MAKES A LUNCH FOR MAFUYU EVERY DAY. I WONDER IF HE'LL MAKE ONE FOR ME TOO IF I ASK."

I MADE SHIBUYA AT THE SAME TIME AS THE STUDENT COUNCIL MEMBERS, SO TO ME, HE'S AN ODD CHARACTER WHO, DESPITE BEING A MEMBER OF THE PUBLIC MORALS CLUB, IS MORE LIKE A MEMBER OF THE STUDENT COUNCIL. HE SEEMS LIKE HE'D BE MORE DISPOSED TO ROMANCE THAN ANYONE ELSE, BUT HE'S ACTUALLY A DELICATE GUY MORE CYNICAL THAT ANYONE ELSE.

Data

BIRTHDAY / SEPTEMBER 24

BLOOD TYPE / TYPE O

HEIGHT / 5'4"

CLASS / SECOND YEAR, CLASS 4

FAMILY STRUCTURE / FATHER, MOTHER, THREE YOUNGER BROTHERS, TWO YOUNGER SISTERS

Q) WHERE DO YOU GET YOUR CLEANING SUPPLIES?

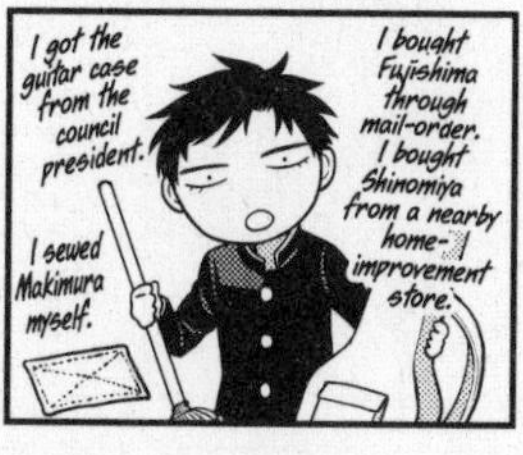
I bought Fujishima through mail-order. I bought Shinomiya from a nearby home-improvement store.
I got the guitar case from the council president.
I sewed Makimura myself.

HE'S INVINCIBLE ONLY IN DIRTY PLACES. A MASTER OF HOUSEHOLD CHORES.

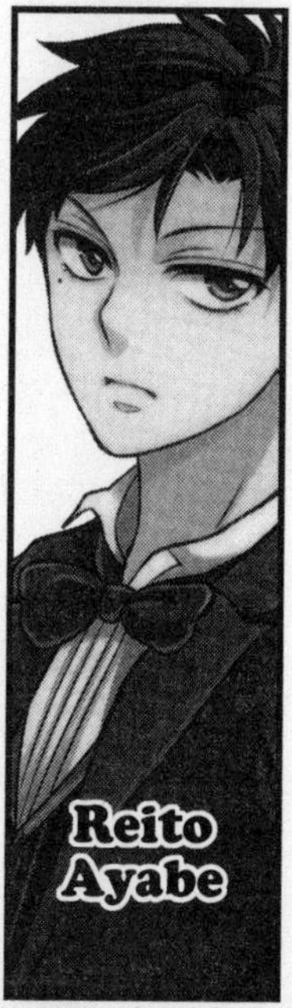
Reito Ayabe

Person

FAVORITE FOOD / CROQUETTES. HIS SPECIALTY IS FRIED EGGS.

PERSONALITY PREFERENCE / SOMEONE RELIABLE. SOMEONE WHO ISN'T GOOD AT CLEANING.

INTERESTS / TAKING PICTURES. (BUT HE'S NOT PICKY ABOUT THE KIND OF CAMERA.)

DISLIKES / ADULTS

CURRENT WORRIES / "I WANT TO BUY A GOOD DUSTPAN, BUT I'VE BECOME ATTACHED TO SUGITA, SO I CAN'T. ALSO, SHINOMIYA IS AT HER LIMIT. (HER HANDLE CAME OFF.)"

CLOSE RELATIONSHIPS / KUROSAKI AND SHIBUYA.

AYABE USED TO SUPPRESS ALL KINDS OF THINGS AND WAS OVERFLOWING WITH CONTRADICTIONS. BUT HE MADE PEACE WITH HIS FAMILY AND BECAME THE DOTING OLDER BROTHER HE USED TO BE. HE STILL HAS HIS SUPER CLEANING TIME AND IS ABLE TO CONTROL IT SOMEWHAT. BUT IF HE'S TOSSED INTO A DIRTY PLACE, HE'LL EXPLODE.

Data

BIRTHDAY / OCTOBER 25

BLOOD TYPE / TYPE A

HEIGHT / 6'6"

CLASS / SECOND YEAR, CLASS 4

FAMILY STRUCTURE / FATHER, MOTHER, YOUNGER BROTHER

Q) WHAT'S THE DEAL WITH THE STUDENT COUNCIL'S BLUE UNIFORMS?

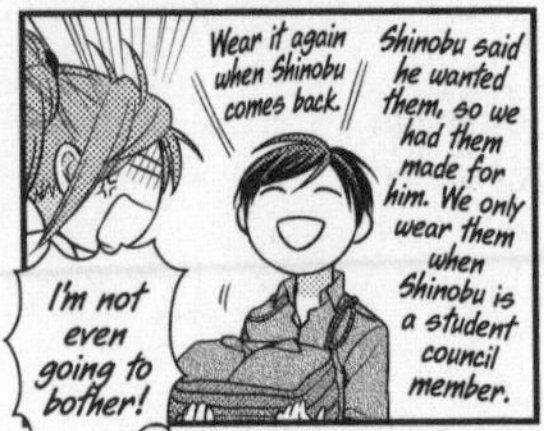
Shinobu said he wanted them, so we had them made for him. We only wear them when Shinobu is a student council member.
Wear it again when Shinobu comes back.
I'm not even going to bother!

THE SENSIBLE MEMBER OF THE STUDENT COUNCIL. SHE WATCHES OVER MIYABI.

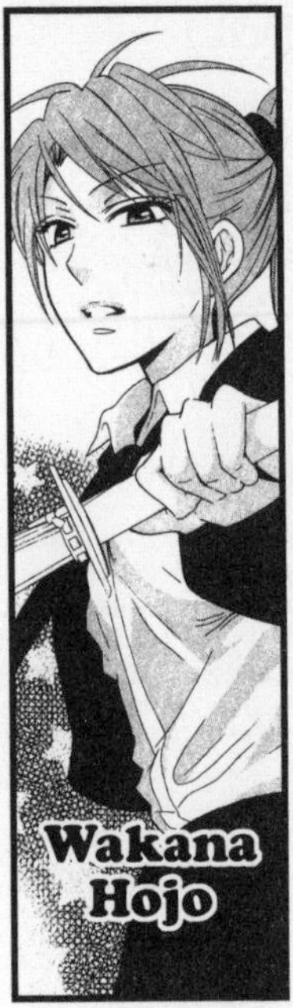
Wakana Hojo

Person

FAVORITE FOOD / SHIRUKO

PERSONALITY PREFERENCE / A CALM, MATURE PERSON

INTERESTS / COLLECTING LIMITED-EDITION STARBUCKS CUPS

DISLIKES / REPTILES • LARGE DOGS

CURRENT WORRIES / I GAINED SOME WEIGHT RECENTLY. I'M THINKING OF EXERCISING.

CLOSE RELATIONSHIPS / HANABUSA AND YUI.

HAVING SPENT MIDDLE SCHOOL WITH MIYABI AND YUI, WAKANA BELIEVED THAT THE RELATIONSHIP BETWEEN THOSE TWO WOULD NEVER CHANGE, EVEN MORE THAN THEY DID. SO WHEN YUI WAS QUICK TO BETRAY MIYABI AND GO AWAY, SHE WAS MORE ANGRY AND SHOCKED THAN ANYONE ELSE. MEANWHILE, YUI HAS MATURED DURING HIS TIME AWAY, BUT WAKANA STILL HASN'T NOTICED.

Data

BIRTHDAY / AUGUST 18

BLOOD TYPE / TYPE A

HEIGHT / 5'9"

CLASS / SECOND YEAR, CLASS 3

FAMILY STRUCTURE / FATHER, MOTHER, TWO YOUNGER SISTERS

Q) WHAT ARE YOU LIKE IN CLASS?

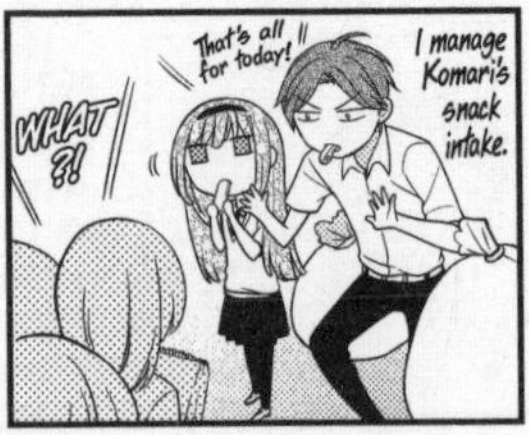
I manage Komari's snack intake.
That's all for today!
WHAT ?!

THE INTELLECTUAL OF THE STUDENT COUNCIL. HE ALWAYS GOES BY THE BOOK AND IS UNSURE OF HOW TO HANDLE UNEXPECTED CIRCUMSTANCES.

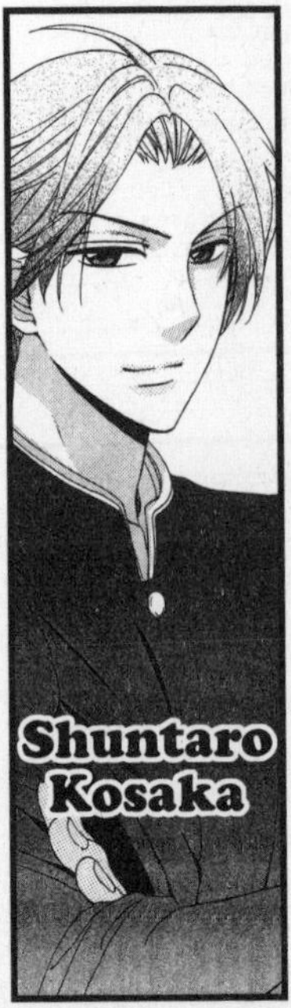
Shuntaro Kosaka

Person

FAVORITE FOOD / VEGETABLE CURRY

PERSONALITY PREFERENCE / SOMEONE CALMING TO BE WITH

INTERESTS / OBTAINING QUALIFICATIONS

DISLIKES / UNEXPECTED CIRCUMSTANCES. BUGS AND ANIMALS (SMALL OR LARGE) THAT SUDDENLY ATTACK.

CURRENT WORRIES / A GIRL IN CLASS INVITED ME TO SEE A MOVIE WITH HER, BUT SHE GOT MAD WHEN I EXPLAINED THE MOVIE TO HER. SO WHY DID SHE INVITE ME?! I PREPARED FOR IT BEFORE GOING!

KOSAKA DOESN'T KNOW HOW TO COPE WITH THINGS. RECENTLY, HE'S BEEN TRYING TO EXPAND HIS WORLD BY TAKING UP HOBBIES. BUT HE ENDS UP RELYING ON HOW-TO BOOKS TO ENJOY THEM, I GUESS PEOPLE DON'T CHANGE THAT EASILY.

Data

BIRTHDAY / FEBRUARY 22

BLOOD TYPE / TYPE A

HEIGHT / 5'1"

CLASS / SECOND YEAR, CLASS 5

FAMILY STRUCTURE / GRANDFATHER, FATHER, MOTHER

Q) HOW IS YOUR GRANDFATHER DOING?

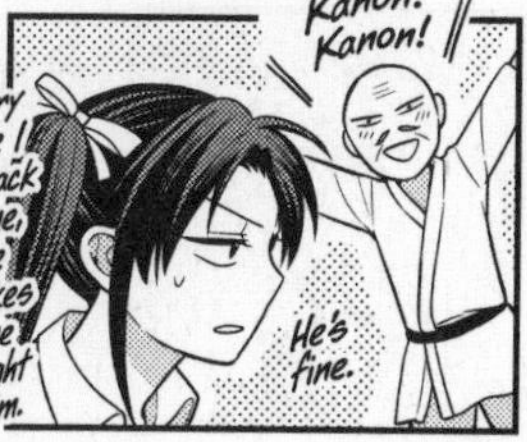

Kanon! Kanon!
He's fine.
Every time I go back home, he makes me fight him.

THE MAN-HATING LEADER OF THE GIRLS' CLASS.

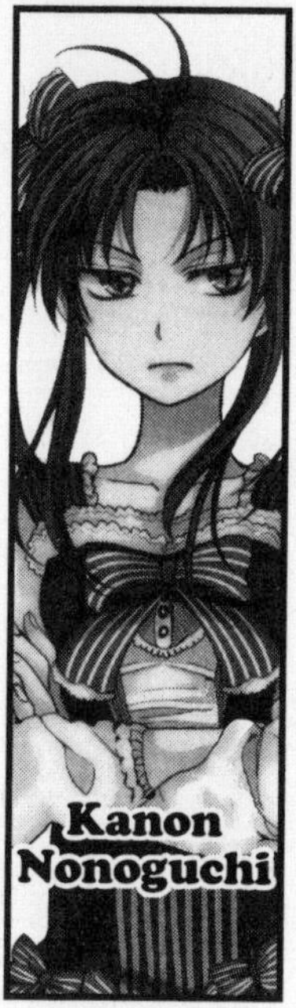

Kanon Nonoguchi

Person

FAVORITE FOOD / NAGOYA-STYLE GRILLED EEL ON RICE

PERSONALITY PREFERENCE / A KIND PRINCE

INTERESTS / RUNNING, PIANO

DISLIKES / SPEAKING POLITELY, READING INSTRUCTION MANUALS

CURRENT WORRIES / I CAN'T SEE NATSUO. I SHOULD HAVE ASKED HIM FOR HIS CONTACT INFORMATION.

CLOSE RELATIONSHIPS / HOJO.

KANON REJECTS THE IDEA OF A PRINCE YET WISHES FOR A PRINCE MORE THAN ANYTHING ELSE. NATSUO'S APPEARANCE FREES HER FROM MANY YEARS OF FIERCE BATTLES AND HAS PUT HER MIND AT PEACE. I THINK THAT ATTACKING MEN WAS HER WAY OF EXPRESSING HER WEAKNESS, AND I THINK SHE'S BECOME STRONGER.

Data

BIRTHDAY / MAY 5

BLOOD TYPE / TYPE B

HEIGHT / 4'7"

CLASS / SECOND YEAR, CLASS 3

FAMILY STRUCTURE / FATHER, MOTHER

Q) HOW HAS SHIBUYA BEEN LATELY?

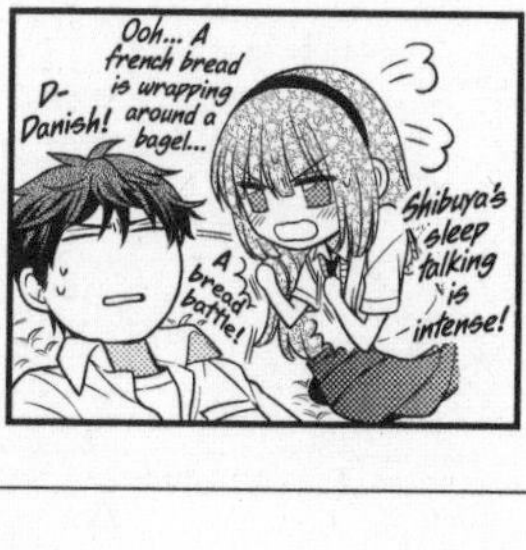

Ooh... A french bread is wrapping around a bagel...
D-Danish!
A bread battle!
Shibuya's sleep talking is intense!

THE LAZY GIRL WHOSE HOBBY IS WATCHING HOT GUYS.

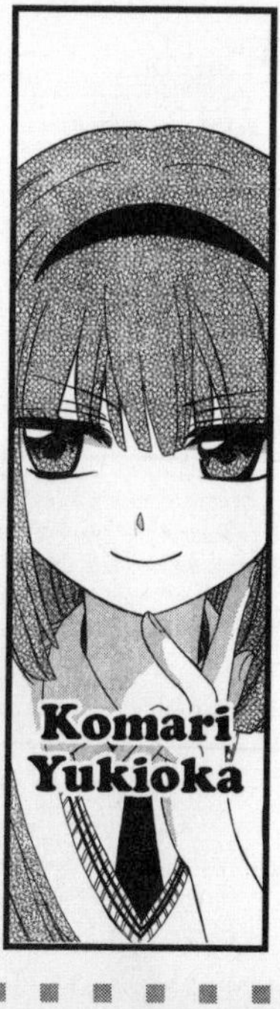

Komari Yukioka

Person

FAVORITE FOOD / POTSTICKERS

PERSONALITY PREFERENCE / SHIBUYA

INTERESTS / NAPPING AFTER A MEAL

DISLIKES / DANCING, BEAUTIFUL MOVEMENTS (UNABLE TO DO THEM)

CURRENT WORRIES / I ADORE JEANS AND TRIED TO WEAR THEM, BUT THEY DON'T LOOK GOOD ON ME AT ALL.

CLOSE RELATIONSHIPS / MIYABI AND KOSAKA.

SHE WAS SOMEONE WHO DIDN'T GET ALONG WITH SHIBUYA AT FIRST AND VICE VERSA, BUT SHE IS FINALLY ABLE TO INTERACT WITH HIM LIKE A NORMAL PERSON. SHE DOESN'T UNDERSTAND OTHERS, DOESN'T KNOW HOW TO EXPRESS HERSELF, AND FINDS CONVERSATION BOTHERSOME, BUT I THINK SHE'LL LEARN HOW TO ENJOY TALKING TO OTHERS.

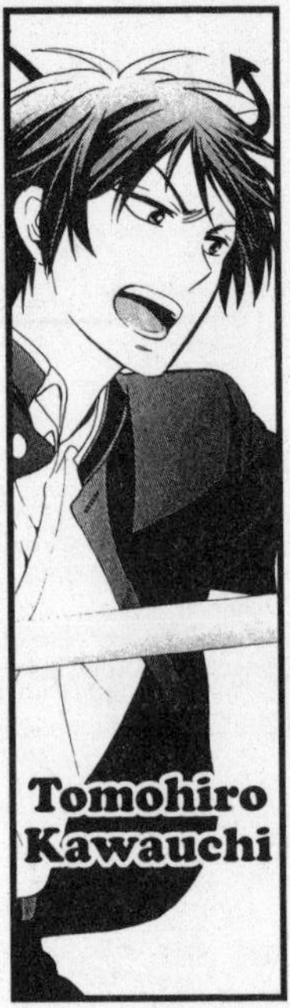
Tomohiro Kawauchi

MIDORIGAOKA ACADEMY'S INFORMANT AND SECOND-IN-COMMAND.

Data

BIRTHDAY / JUNE 2

BLOOD TYPE / TYPE AB

HEIGHT / 5'8"

CLASS / THIRD YEAR, CLASS 4

FAMILY STRUCTURE / FATHER, MOTHER, YOUNGER SISTER

Q) WHAT'S SOMETHING THAT HAS HAPPENED RECENTLY THAT DOESN'T SIT WELL WITH YOU?

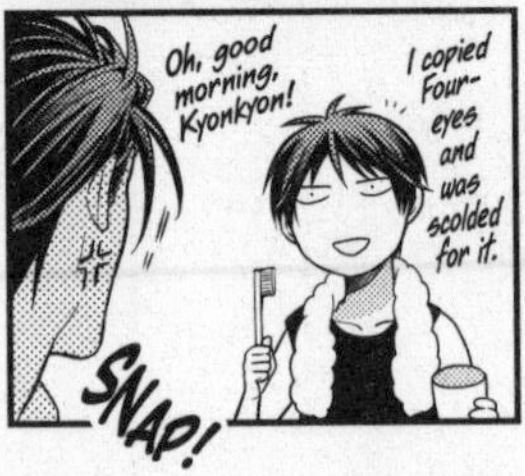
I copied Four-eyes and was scolded for it.
Oh, good morning, Kyonkyon!
SNAP!

Person

FAVORITE FOOD / OMELETTE RICE

PERSONALITY PREFERENCE / A DAINTY GIRL WHO WANTS HIM TO PROTECT HER

INTERESTS / CHESS, WATCHING ROMANTIC MOVIES (HE MAKES FUN OF THEM BUT LOVES WATCHING THEM)

DISLIKES / GIRLS' FAKE NAILS. (THEY'RE A DANGEROUS WEAPON.)

CURRENT WORRIES / I WANT TO KNOW WHAT OKEGAWA'S PLANS ARE AFTER HE GRADUATES, BUT HE DOESN'T WANT TO TELL ME.

CLOSE RELATIONSHIPS / OKEGAWA AND GOTOH.

HE HAS VERY STRONG OPINIONS. HE FORCES HIS IDEAS ONTO OTHERS AND TRIES TO GLORIFY THEM. HE SEEMS SMART, BUT HE TENDS TO OVERLOOK THE NATURE OF THINGS. HE NEEDS TO BROADEN HIS POINT OF VIEW A LITTLE!

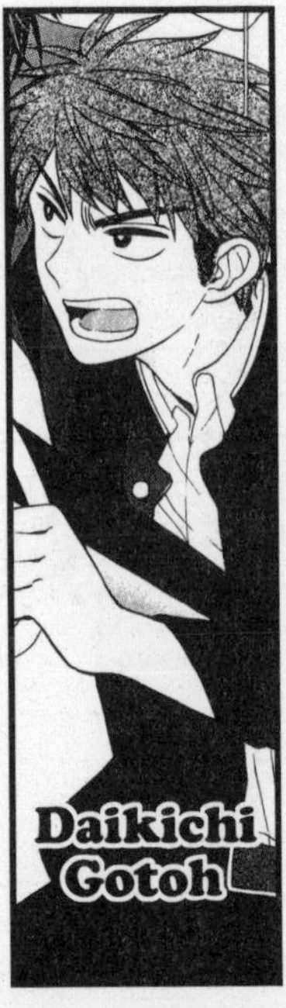
Daikichi Gotoh

INCREDIBLY LUCKY AND THIRD-IN-COMMAND.

Data

BIRTHDAY / FEBRUARY 9

BLOOD TYPE / TYPE O

HEIGHT / 5'7"

CLASS / THIRD YEAR, CLASS 3

FAMILY STRUCTURE / FATHER, MOTHER, YOUNGER BROTHER, YOUNGER SISTER

Q) WHAT WOULD HAPPEN IF HE WAS WITH OKUBO?

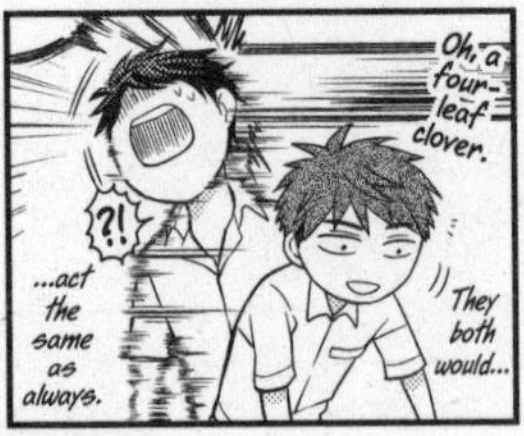
Oh, a four-leaf clover.
?!
They both would...
...act the same as always.

Person

FAVORITE FOOD / KINPIRA GOBO

PERSONALITY PREFERENCE / A BUSTY GIRL WHO CAN EAT FISH NEATLY

INTERESTS / MAGIC TRICKS (BUT HE'S NOT VERY GOOD AT THEM)

DISLIKES / THE NUBRA (THAT'S MISLEADING...)

CURRENT WORRIES / WHEN WE CHANGED SEATS, I ENDED UP NEXT TO KAWAUCHI AND OKEGAWA. I DON'T LIKE HOW THE CLASS BECOMES TENSE WHEN KAWAUCHI SAYS ANYTHING.

CLOSE RELATIONSHIPS / KAWAUCHI AND OKEGAWA.

THE CONSCIENCE OF MIDORIGAOKA IS PEACEFUL AND CAREFREE NO MATTER WHERE HE IS. DESPITE BEING LOVED BY THE GODDESS OF LUCK, HE IS BLAND BECAUSE HIS DREAMS ARE ALWAYS APPROPRIATE FOR SOMEONE OF HIS STATURE.

A MAN'S REQUEST

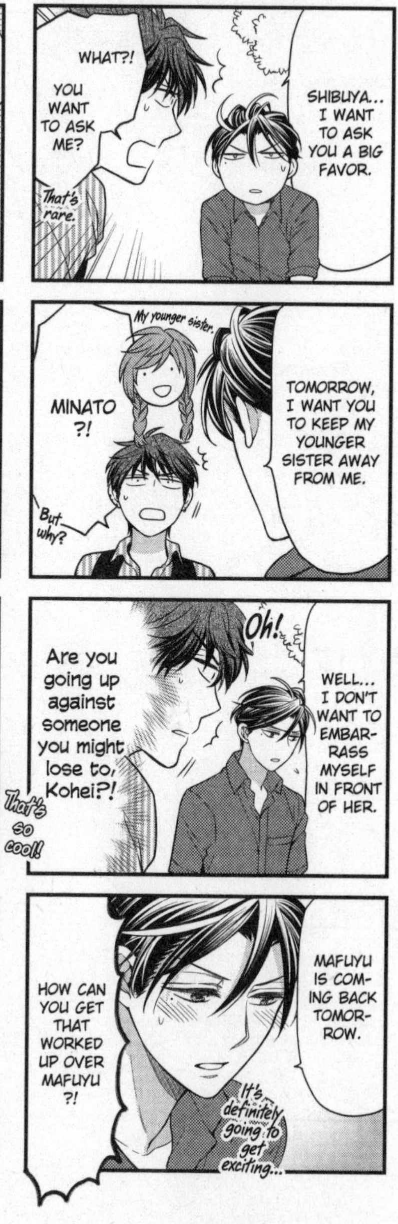
SHIBUYA... I WANT TO ASK YOU A BIG FAVOR.
WHAT?! YOU WANT TO ASK ME?
That's rare.
TOMORROW, I WANT YOU TO KEEP MY YOUNGER SISTER AWAY FROM ME.
My younger sister.
MINATO?!
But why?
WELL... I DON'T WANT TO EMBARRASS MYSELF IN FRONT OF HER.
Oh!
Are you going up against someone you might lose to, Kohei?!
That's so cool!
MAFUYU IS COMING BACK TOMORROW.
HOW CAN YOU GET THAT WORKED UP OVER MAFUYU?!
It's definitely going to get exciting...

THE FACE IN HER MEMORIES

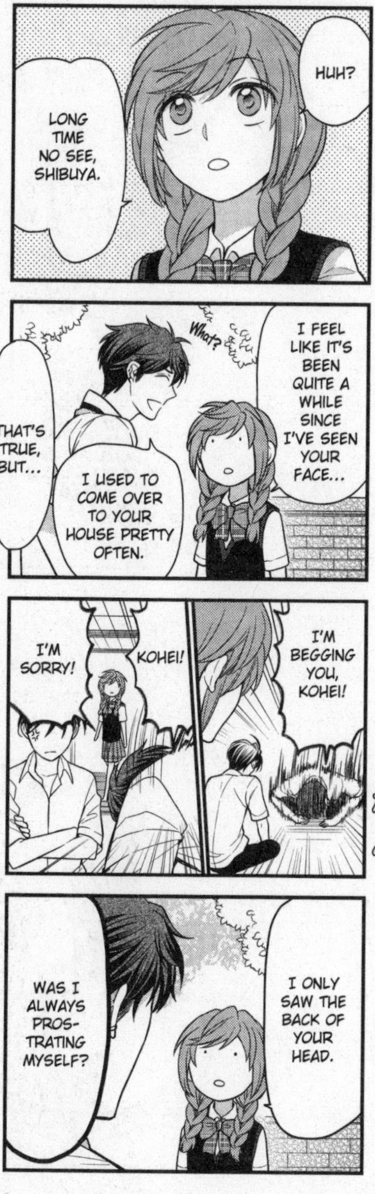
HUH?
LONG TIME NO SEE, SHIBUYA.
I FEEL LIKE IT'S BEEN QUITE A WHILE SINCE I'VE SEEN YOUR FACE...
What?
THAT'S TRUE, BUT...
I USED TO COME OVER TO YOUR HOUSE PRETTY OFTEN.
I'M BEGGING YOU, KOHEI!
KOHEI!
I'M SORRY!
I ONLY SAW THE BACK OF YOUR HEAD.
WAS I ALWAYS PROS-TRATING MYSELF?

APPEAL TO SAFETY

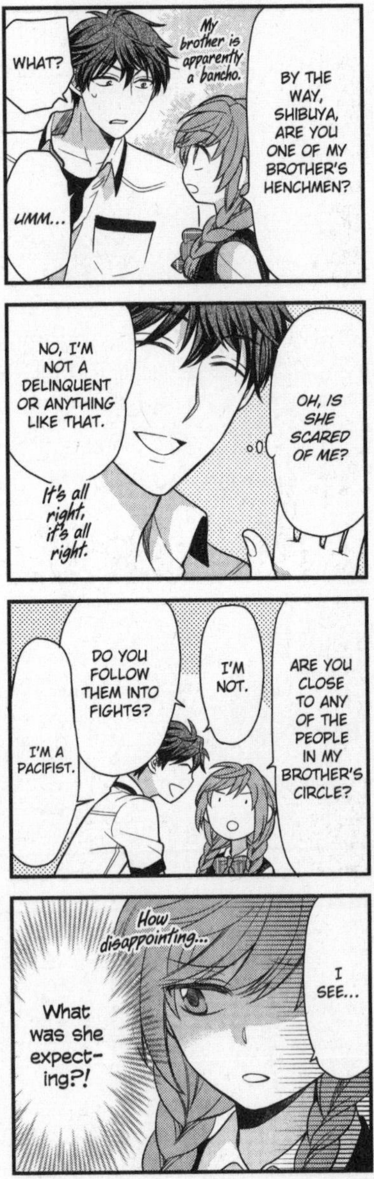

BY THE WAY, SHIBUYA, ARE YOU ONE OF MY BROTHER'S HENCHMEN?
My brother is apparently a bancho.
WHAT?
UMM...
OH, IS SHE SCARED OF ME?
NO, I'M NOT A DELINQUENT OR ANYTHING LIKE THAT.
It's all right, it's all right.
ARE YOU CLOSE TO ANY OF THE PEOPLE IN MY BROTHER'S CIRCLE?
I'M NOT.
DO YOU FOLLOW THEM INTO FIGHTS?
I'M A PACIFIST.
I SEE...
How disappointing...
What was she expecting?!

DIFFERENCE IN AGE

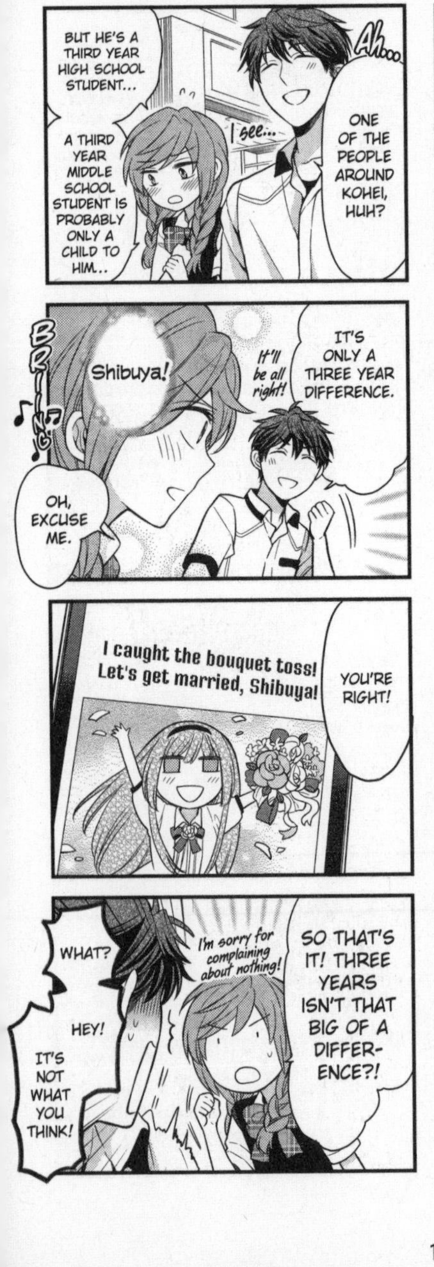

ONE OF THE PEOPLE AROUND KOHEI, HUH?
Ah...
I see...
BUT HE'S A THIRD YEAR HIGH SCHOOL STUDENT...
A THIRD YEAR MIDDLE SCHOOL STUDENT IS PROBABLY ONLY A CHILD TO HIM..
IT'S ONLY A THREE YEAR DIFFERENCE.
It'll be all right!
Shibuya!
OH, EXCUSE ME.
YOU'RE RIGHT!
I caught the bouquet toss! Let's get married, Shibuya!
SO THAT'S IT! THREE YEARS ISN'T THAT BIG OF A DIFFER-ENCE?!
I'm sorry for complaining about nothing!
WHAT?
HEY!
IT'S NOT WHAT YOU THINK!

SOMETHING AGE APPROPRIATE

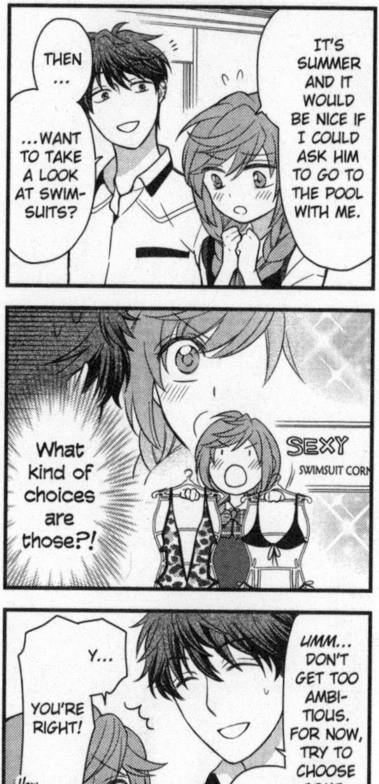
IT'S SUMMER AND IT WOULD BE NICE IF I COULD ASK HIM TO GO TO THE POOL WITH ME.
THEN ...
...WANT TO TAKE A LOOK AT SWIM-SUITS?
SEXY
SWIMSUIT CORN
What kind of choices are those?!
UMM... DON'T GET TOO AMBI-TIOUS. FOR NOW, TRY TO CHOOSE SOME-THING...
...THAT SUITS YOU BEST.
Y...
YOU'RE RIGHT!
Oh!
How careless of me!
Oh!
DO YOU THINK THIS WOULD LOOK NICE ON YOUR GIRL-FRIEND?
KID'S CORNER
Is it a little big?
UH...
Yukioka!

EXTREME SIZE CHANGE

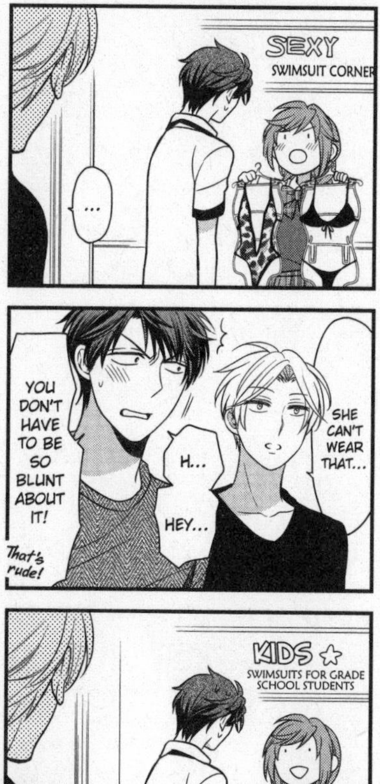
SEXY
SWIMSUIT CORNER
...
SHE CAN'T WEAR THAT...
H...
HEY...
YOU DON'T HAVE TO BE SO BLUNT ABOUT IT!
That's rude!
KIDS
SWIMSUITS FOR GRADE SCHOOL STUDENTS
SHE CAN'T WEAR THAT...
YEAH...

CHOOSING MINATO'S SWIMSUIT

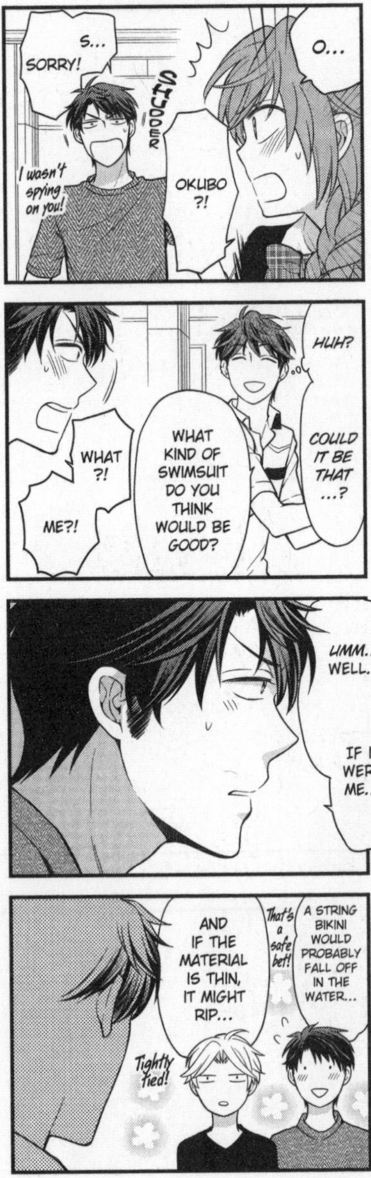
O...
OKUBO ?!
S... SORRY!
SHUDDER
I wasn't spying on you!
HUH?
COULD IT BE THAT ...?
WHAT KIND OF SWIMSUIT DO YOU THINK WOULD BE GOOD?
WHAT ?!
ME?!
UMM... WELL...
IF IT WERE ME...
A STRING BIKINI WOULD PROBABLY FALL OFF IN THE WATER...
That's a safe bet!
AND IF THE MATERIAL IS THIN, IT MIGHT RIP...
Tightly tied!

SWIMSUIT FOR THE POOL

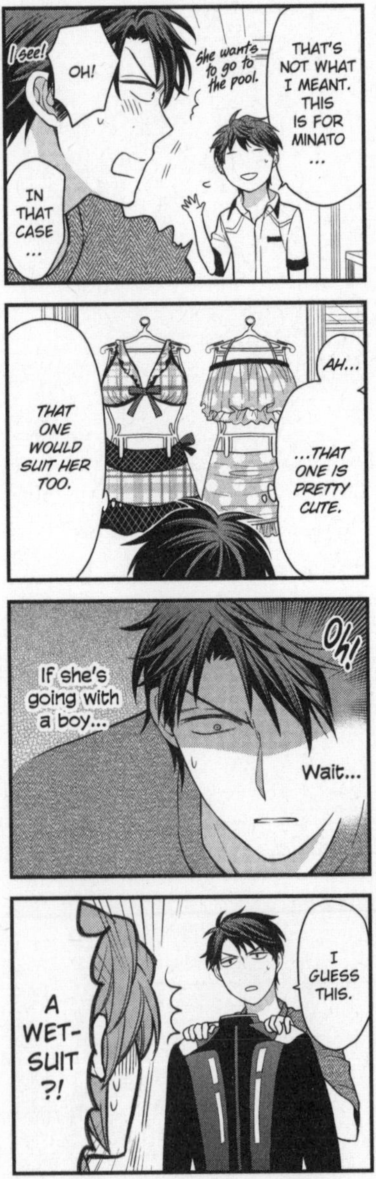
THAT'S NOT WHAT I MEANT. THIS IS FOR MINATO ...
She wants to go to the pool.
OH!
I see!
IN THAT CASE ...
AH...
...THAT ONE IS PRETTY CUTE.
THAT ONE WOULD SUIT HER TOO.
Oh!
Wait...
If she's going with a boy...
I GUESS THIS.
A WET-SUIT ?!

DEPENDING ON THEIR DEFENSES

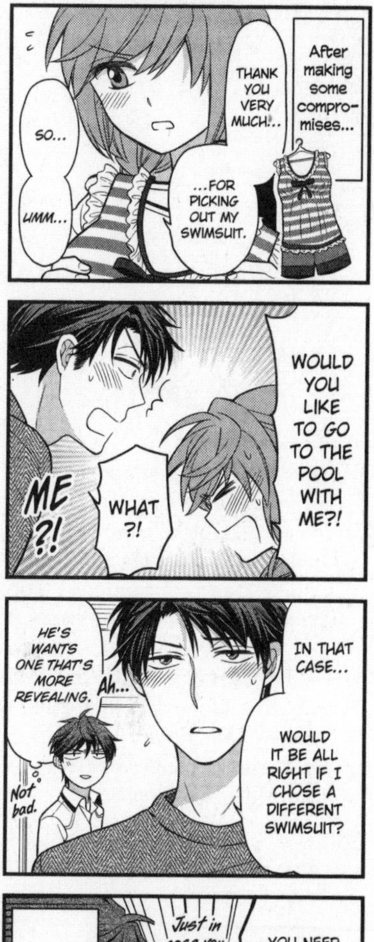
After making some compromises...
THANK YOU VERY MUCH!...
...FOR PICKING OUT MY SWIMSUIT.
SO...
UMM...
WOULD YOU LIKE TO GO TO THE POOL WITH ME?!
WHAT ?!
ME ?!
IN THAT CASE...
WOULD IT BE ALL RIGHT IF I CHOSE A DIFFERENT SWIMSUIT?
Ah...
HE'S WANTS ONE THAT'S MORE REVEALING.
Not bad.
YOU NEED ONE THAT'S STURDY AND WON'T RIP!
Just in case you get hit by whatever happens to me!
He got even more protective.

ARRIVING AT THE STATION

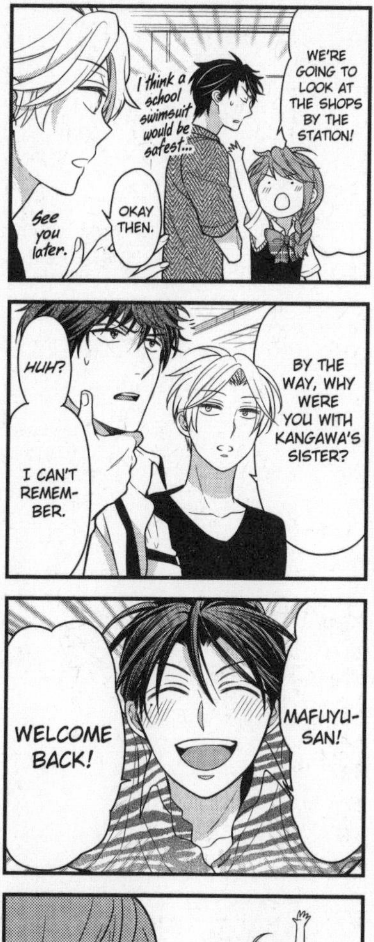
WE'RE GOING TO LOOK AT THE SHOPS BY THE STATION!
I think a school swimsuit would be safest...
OKAY THEN.
See you later.
BY THE WAY, WHY WERE YOU WITH KANGAWA'S SISTER?
HUH?
I CAN'T REMEMBER.
MAFUYU-SAN!
WELCOME BACK!

Izumi Tsubaki began drawing manga in her first year of high school. She was soon selected to be in the top ten of *Hana to Yume's* HMC (*Hana to Yume* Mangaka Course), and subsequently won *Hana to Yume's* Big Challenge contest. Her debut title, *Chijimete Distance* (Shrink the Distance), ran in 2002 in *Hana to Yume* magazine, issue 17. Her other works include *The Magic Touch* (*Oyayubi kara Romance*) and *Oresama Teacher*, which she is currently working on.

ORESAMA TEACHER
Vol. 17
Shojo Beat Edition

STORY AND ART BY
Izumi Tsubaki

English Translation & Adaptation/JN Productions
Touch-up Art & Lettering/Eric Erbes
Design/Yukiko Whitley
Editor/Pancha Diaz

ORESAMA TEACHER by Izumi Tsubaki © Izumi Tsubaki 2013
All rights reserved. First published in Japan in 2013 by HAKUSENSHA, Inc., Tokyo.
English language translation rights arranged with HAKUSENSHA, Inc., Tokyo.

The stories, characters and incidents mentioned in this publication are
entirely fictional.

No portion of this book may be reproduced or transmitted in any form or
by any means without written permission from the copyright holders.

Printed in the U.S.A.

Published by VIZ Media, LLC
P.O. Box 77010
San Francisco, CA 94107

10 9 8 7 6 5 4 3 2 1
First printing, October 2014

www.viz.com

www.shojobeat.com

PARENTAL ADVISORY
ORESAMA TEACHER is rated T for Teen and
is recommended for ages 13 and up. This
volume contains violence.
ratings.viz.com

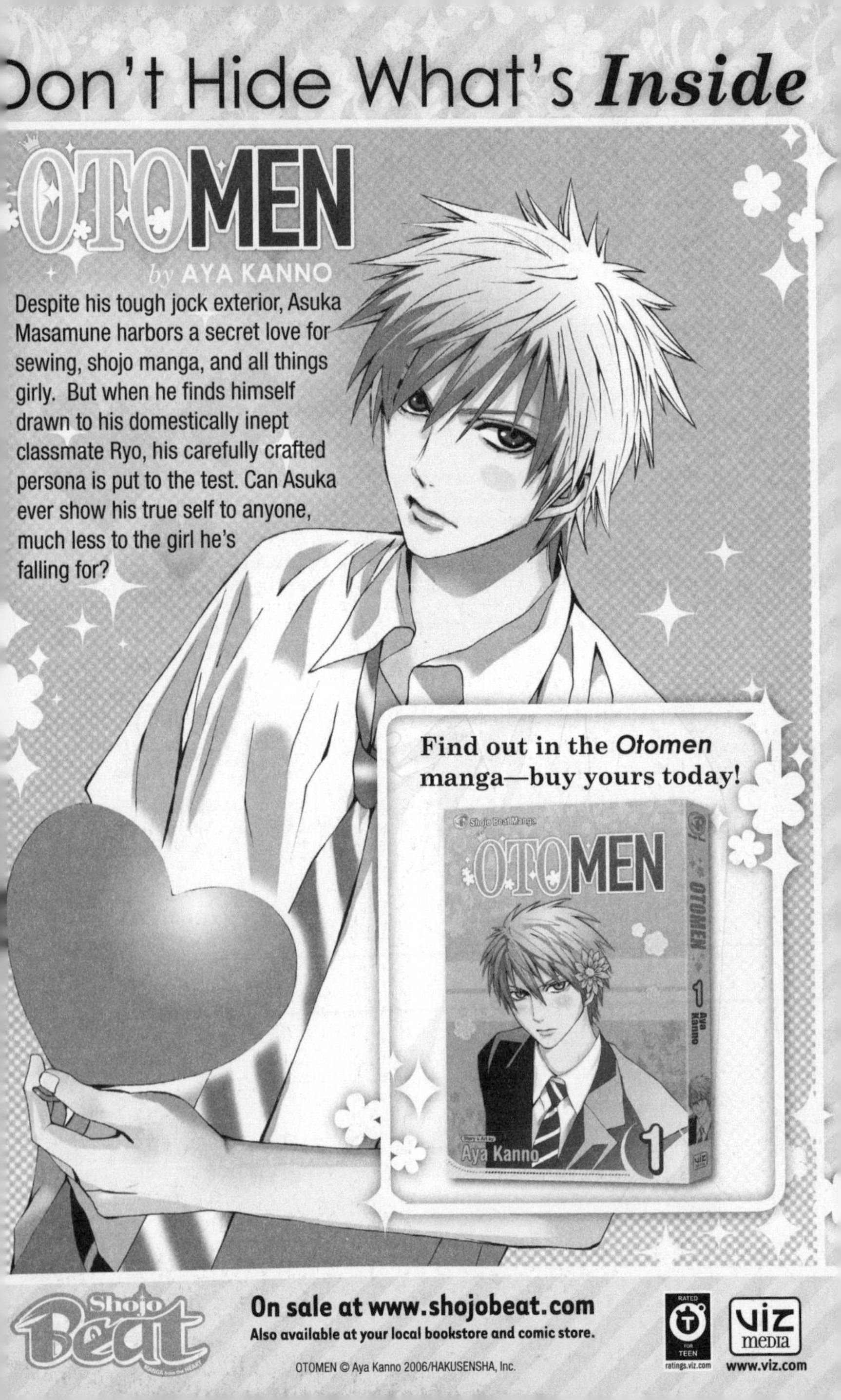
Don't Hide What's *Inside*
OTOMEN
by AYA KANNO
Despite his tough jock exterior, Asuka Masamune harbors a secret love for sewing, shojo manga, and all things girly. But when he finds himself drawn to his domestically inept classmate Ryo, his carefully crafted persona is put to the test. Can Asuka ever show his true self to anyone, much less to the girl he's falling for?
Find out in the *Otomen* manga—buy yours today!
Shojo Beat Manga
OTOMEN
Aya Kanno
1
Shojo Beat
On sale at www.shojobeat.com
Also available at your local bookstore and comic store.
OTOMEN © Aya Kanno 2006/HAKUSENSHA, Inc.
RATED T FOR TEEN
ratings.viz.com
VIZ media
www.viz.com

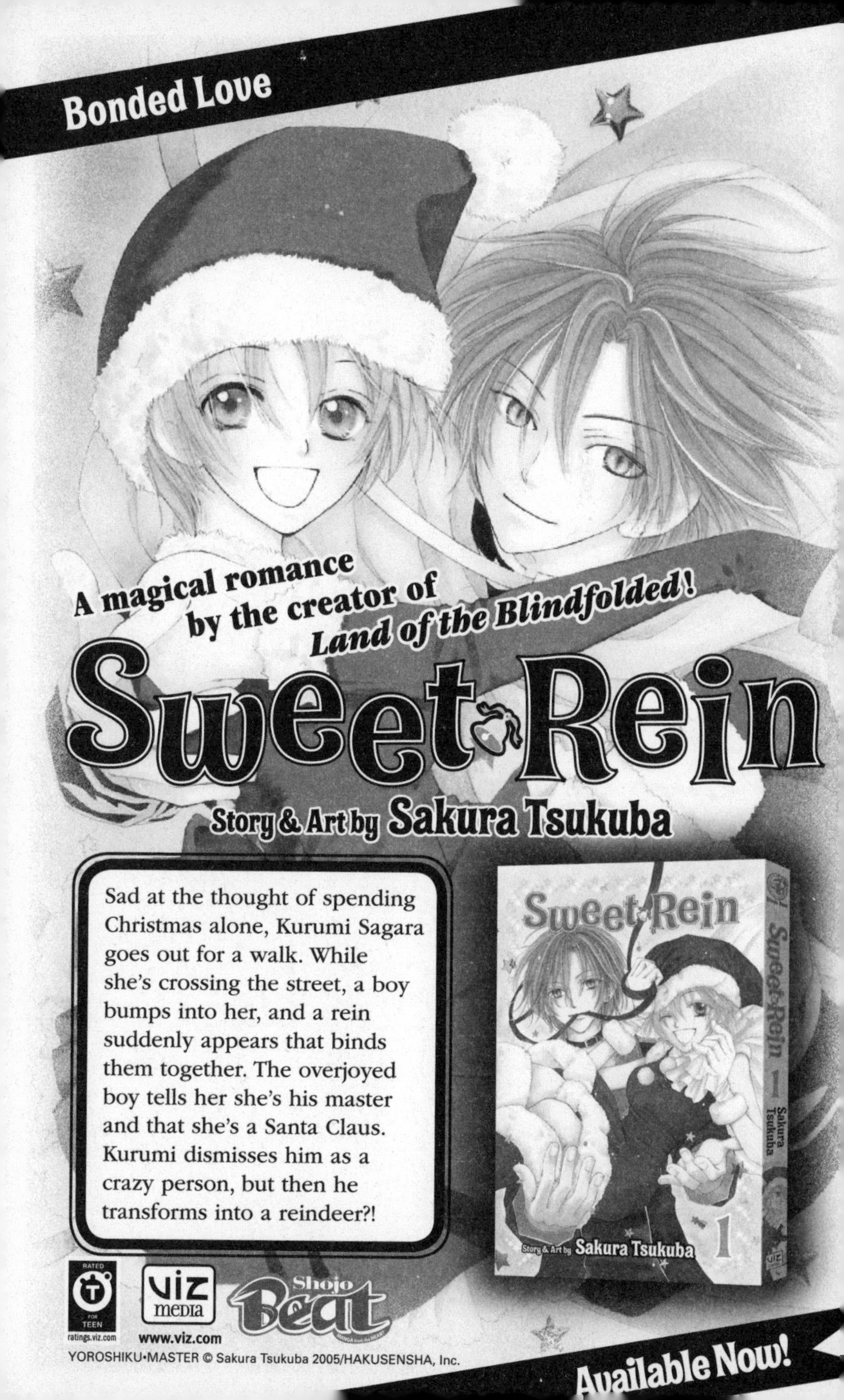
Bonded Love
A magical romance by the creator of Land of the Blindfolded!
Sweet Rein
Story & Art by Sakura Tsukuba
Sad at the thought of spending Christmas alone, Kurumi Sagara goes out for a walk. While she's crossing the street, a boy bumps into her, and a rein suddenly appears that binds them together. The overjoyed boy tells her she's his master and that she's a Santa Claus. Kurumi dismisses him as a crazy person, but then he transforms into a reindeer?!
Sweet Rein
Story & Art by Sakura Tsukuba
1
RATED T FOR TEEN
ratings.viz.com
VIZ media
www.viz.com
Shojo Beat
YOROSHIKU•MASTER © Sakura Tsukuba 2005/HAKUSENSHA, Inc.
Available Now!

A **Publisher's Weekly** bestseller!

What happens when the hottest boy in school
...is a girl?

Find out in these **3-in-1** collections of the hit shojo series

Story & Art by **HISAYA NAKAJO**

Mizuki Ashiya has such a crush on a track star named Izumi Sano that she moves from the U.S. to Japan to enroll in the all-male high school he goes to! Pretending to be a boy, Mizuki becomes Sano's roommate...

...but how can she keep such a big secret when she's so close to the guy she wants?

IN STORES NOW!

3-in-1 Vol. 1 ISBN: 978-1-4215-4224-9
3-in-1 Vol. 2 ISBN: 978-1-4215-4225-6
3-in-1 Vol. 3 ISBN: 978-1-4215-4229-4

Only **$14.99 US / $16.99 CAN** each!

Hanazakari no Kimitachi he
© Hisaya Nakajo 1996/HAKUSENSHA, Inc.

library wars
Love & War

STORY & ART BY **Kiiro Yumi**   ORIGINAL CONCEPT BY **Hiro Arikawa**

Winning the war on information, one book at a time

When the federal government tries to rid society of "unsuitable" books, an underground group of librarians and bibliophiles vows to fight back.

They are the Library Forces. And this is their story.

$9.99 USA / $12.99 CAN *
ISBN: 978-1-4215-3488-6

Manga on sale at **store.viz.com**
Also available at your local bookstore or comic store

www.shojobeat.com

Toshokan Sensou LOVE&WAR
© Kiiro Yumi and Hiro Arikawa 2008/HAKUSENSHA, Inc.
* Prices subject to change

RATED
T
FOR OLDER
TEEN
ratings.viz.com

www.viz.com

∪IZM∧NG∧

Read manga anytime, anywhere!

From our newest hit series to the classics you know and love, the best manga in the world is now available digitally. Buy a volume* of digital manga for your:

- iOS device (**iPad®**, **iPhone®**, **iPod®** touch) through the **VIZ Manga** app

- Android-powered device (**phone or tablet**) with a browser by visiting **VIZManga.com**

- **Mac or PC computer** by visiting **VIZManga.com**

VIZ Digital has loads to offer:

- 500+ ready-to-read volumes
- New volumes each week
- FREE previews
- Access on multiple devices! Create a log-in through the app so you buy a book once, and read it on your device of choice!*

To learn more, visit www.viz.com/apps

* Some series may not be available for multiple devices.
  Check the app on your device to find out what's available.

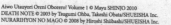

Aiwo Utauyori Oreni Oborero! Volume 1 © Mayu SHINJO 2010
DEATH NOTE © 2003 by Tsugumi Ohba, Takeshi Obata/SHUEISHA Inc.
NURARIHYON NO MAGO © 2008 by Hiroshi Shiibashi/SHUEISHA Inc.

Surprise!

You may be reading the wrong way!

It's true: In keeping with the original Japanese comic format, this book reads from right to left—so action, sound effects, and word balloons are completely reversed. This preserves the orientation of the original artwork—plus, it's fun! Check out the diagram shown here to get the hang of things, and then turn to the other side of the book to get started!

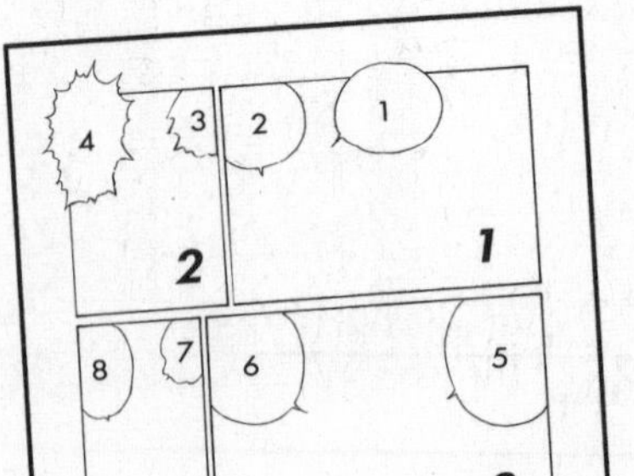
1
2
1
3
4
2
5
6
3
7
8
4
9
5
142

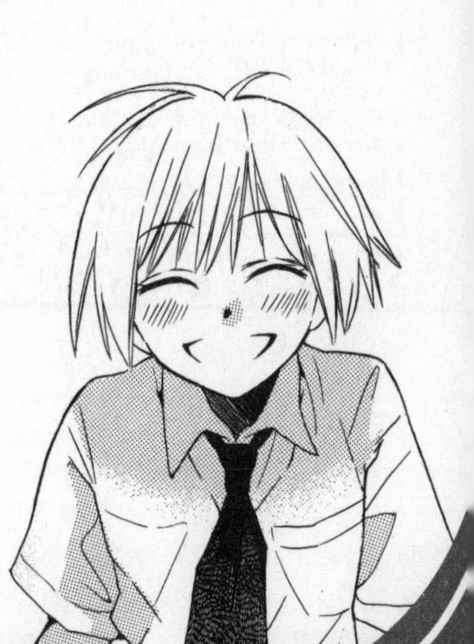